Rabbinic Drinking

Rabbinic Drinking

What Beverages Teach Us about Rabbinic Literature

Jordan D. Rosenblum

UNIVERSITY OF CALIFORNIA PRESS

University of California Press
Oakland, California

© 2020 by Jordan D. Rosenblum

Library of Congress Cataloging-in-Publication Data

Names: Rosenblum, Jordan, author.
Title: Rabbinic drinking : what beverages teach us about
   rabbinic iterature / Jordan D. Rosenblum.
Identifiers: LCCN 2019029992 (print) | LCCN 2019029993
   (ebook) | ISBN 9780520300422 (cloth) |
   ISBN 9780520300439 (paperback) |
   ISBN 9780520971837 (ebook)
Subjects: LCSH: Drinking in rabbinical literature |
   Drinking vessels—Religious aspects—Judaism.
Classification: LCC BM496.9.D75 R67 2020 (print) |
   LCC BM496.9.D75 ebook) | DDC 296.1/20839412—dc23
LC record available at https://lccn.loc.gov/2019029992
LC ebook record available at https://lccn.loc.gov
   /2019029993

Manufactured in the United States of America

27 26 25 24 23 22 21 20
10 9 8 7 6 5 4 3 2 1

Dedicated to the Members of the SBL Suite

Debra Scoggins Ballentine, Nathaniel DesRosiers, Gregg Gardner, Steven Larson, Kevin McGinnis, Daniel Ullucci, Arthur Urbano, and Lily Vuong

In vino veritas!

CONTENTS

Acknowledgments ix

Introduction
1

1. The Literature and History of the Rabbinic Movement
9

2. Biblical Interpretation
36

3. Social Boundaries
66

4. Gender and Sexuality
96

5. Magic, Idolatry, and Illicit Religious Practice
130

6. Sabbath, Festivals, and Holidays
161

7. Prayer and Ritual
192

8. Ritual Purity
216

9. Health and Hygiene
244

Conclusion
273

Glossary 277
Subject Index 283
Citation Index 303

ACKNOWLEDGMENTS

Scholarship is often a lonely enterprise. Much of this book was written while alone in my office, pouring over ancient and modern texts, mumbling to myself, and then typing—and quickly erasing—words on my computer. But, like drinking, scholarship is most enjoyable in the company of others. It is my pleasure to acknowledge those who helped me improve my work, both by listening to my arguments and by pointing out that, while my mind might dwell in antiquity, I live in modernity.

I begin by thanking a group of scholars and friends to whom I dedicate this book. Every year at the annual conference of the American Academy of Religion and the Society of Biblical Literature, a group of friends from graduate school crams into a hotel suite. Some are regulars and others come only occasionally. Together, we joke, we discuss scholarship, and we drink. I wish to acknowledge the intellectual, professional, and personal debt that I owe to Debra Scoggins Ballentine, Nathaniel DesRosiers, Gregg Gardner, Steven Larson, Kevin McGinnis, Daniel Ullucci, Arthur Urbano, and Lily Vuong.

Over the course of writing this book, I benefited from the feedback of several colleagues. For references, suggestions, information, and pep talks I thank Febe Armanios, Michal Bar-Asher Siegal, Beth Berkowitz, Sarah Bond, Catherine Bonesho, Jonathan Brumberg-Kraus, Boğaç

Ergene, David Freidenreich, Gregg Gardner, Jane Kanarek, Drew Kaplan, Susan Marks, Chance McMahon, Michael Naparstek, Saul Olyan, Vadim Putzu, Rachel Neis, Eric Orlin, Michael Satlow, Brian Sowers, Daniel Ullucci, Moulie Vidas, and Luke Whitmore. Technical questions related to beer were provided by Taylor Beck, an award-winning brewer.

I also benefitted from presenting my work in public. For inviting me to present my inchoate ideas, I thank Brooklyn College; Central Washington University; Indiana University; Middlebury College; Universität Erfurt; University of British Columbia; University of Minnesota; University of Puget Sound; University of Wisconsin-Madison; and Yale University.

Support for this research was provided by the Office of the Vice Chancellor for Research and Graduate Education at the University of Wisconsin-Madison with funding from the Wisconsin Alumni Research Foundation. I also gratefully acknowledge Burt Belzer (z"l), who endowed the professorship that I hold. This is the first book of mine that he will read not on earth, but in the Heavenly Academy.

For assistance with photography, I thank Dov Berger (a *sofer*, or scribe, available for hire!); Catherine Bonesho and Taylor Beck; and Ralph Grunewald.

This book represents the distillation of ideas presented in numerous classes taught over more than a decade at the University of Wisconsin-Madison. My students pushed me towards greater clarity, asking both simple and nuanced questions that continually required me to refine my argument. In particular, I thank the students in my Spring 2019 "Classical Rabbinic Literature in Translation" course, who allowed me to test-drive the manuscript of this book. I also thank David Freidenreich and his students at Colby College, who read and commented on a draft of this book in Spring 2019.

Numerous colleagues at the University of Wisconsin-Madison deserve acknowledgement. For sharing meals, gossip, and making work meetings more enjoyable than I otherwise could expect, I thank Lonnie Berger, Michael Bernard-Donals, Thomas DuBois, Ernesto Livorni, Tony Michels, Steve Nadler, Corrie Norman, Dan Quint, Susan Ridgely, and Judith Sone.

Eric Schmidt, Andrea Torres, Gabriela Ramirez-Chavez, and the team at University of California Press have been amazing. From our first phone conversation, Eric has provided humorous and helpful guidance.

As the saying goes, "it takes a village." I owe an enormous debt of gratitude to my village. Tovah and Elias Walsh make playdates with our kids something that I look forward to as well. I thank Daniel Kapust and Eunsook Jung for great conversations (and great food). Jennifer Pruitt and Mark Hammond are amazing neighbors and friends. Rob Peyton, Michael Napartsek, and Mitch the Drummer allow me to keep my garage band dreams alive. Stanley Zipper and Ross Wolfson continue to tell inside jokes that are now three decades old. To any colleague or friend that I have forgotten to acknowledge, I owe you a drink.

For support and encouragement, I thank my family: my mother and stepfather Harold (Fess); Ian; Uncle Rom, Aunt Debby, and Avi; Dad, Rose, and Mike; Aunt Elaine; Ron and Eugenie; and Sarah, Scott, and the newest member, Maceo.

Finally, the members of my household deserve my greatest debt of gratitude. My son Josiah reminds me that, no matter how busy my day, there is always time to stop and play with LEGO. My wife, Valerie, challenges me to be a better person. I have learned so much from her, both in matters practical and academic. Indeed, the idea for this book came during a walk with Valerie while we pushed our newborn son around in a stroller. Trying to articulate what I was thinking of working on, Val asked perceptive questions. By the end of that walk, Val had pointed me in the right direction. As in all things, she is my compass.

Introduction

My first serious encounter with rabbinic literature came during my freshman year in college. This experience was reminiscent of another college activity: drinking a little too much. In both, I experienced a feeling of euphoria and pleasant disorientation, followed by a splitting headache. When reading rabbinic texts, I became intoxicated by drinking in the twists and turns in rabbinic logic; the hypothetical world in which the ancient Rabbis lived—much like Charlie in the Chocolate Factory—was a place of wonder and unlimited imagination. But it also made my head hurt, because coming to grips with it required a tremendous amount of concentration and prior knowledge. It forced me to keep so much information straight (wait, which Rabbi said what? And in what order?) that I found myself reaching for an aspirin.

After a while, I got my sea legs. The twists and turns in rabbinic literature no longer left me nauseated. That does not mean that I could take them for granted. Just when I thought that I could navigate what is often called "the sea of Talmud," a wave would come crashing down and capsize me. These texts are hard work. Nonetheless, I kept coming back to them. Eventually, studying rabbinic literature became my profession. But I have never forgotten how I felt when I first encountered these texts. This book is my attempt to help others sail the beautiful, and stormy, sea of Talmud.

WHAT IS THIS BOOK?

Rabbinic literature presents many obstacles for entry both to those who wish to study and to those who aim to teach these texts. Given the amount of background knowledge they presume, where does one start? For example, here are the opening lines of a few famous passages from the first major rabbinic document, the Mishnah:

> From what time may one recite the *Shema'* in the evening? (*m. Berakhot* 1:1)
> A woman is acquired in the three ways ... (*m. Qiddushin* 1:1)
> Two people are holding a cloak ... (*m. Bava Metzi'a* 1:1)

What is the *Shema'* and why does it matter when one recites it? What does saying women are "acquired" mean? And is the cloak (Hebrew *tallit*) a specific or general example? Is the ruling that follows limited to this one specific garment or does it refer to a general category? Does it apply just to cloaks or also to pants? Only to clothing or to all chattels corporeal? And how the heck am I supposed to know?!

By focusing on drinking—including the beverages themselves and the laws associated with producing and imbibing them—this book introduces key themes in rabbinic literature. For example, we learn about the *Shema'*, a central rabbinic prayer, from a discussion among Rabban Gamaliel's sons, who come home late from a drinking party and want to know if they can still recite the *Shema'* (chapter 7). We learn about issues of gender asymmetry, both in general and in regard to marriage, by looking at rabbinic attitudes to gender and alcohol consumption (chapter 4). And the question of whether a law is specific or general is addressed throughout this book (see, e.g., the discussion of meat and milk in chapter 3).

Though this may seem like an odd comparison, in many ways writing about the ancient Rabbis is similar to the problem that Susan McHugh articulates at the beginning of her book *Dog*:

> The problem facing everyone who writes about dogs is that there are thousands, if not millions, of people who have already done so. Like dogs themselves, dog literature abounds and, in part because of this wealth of materials, dog books tend to lose in coherence what they gain in comprehensiveness. In attempting to reconcile too much information, such texts take on a randomness that even those of us who call ourselves "dog people" find tedious. Predictably, these documents of dogs frustrate even the most comprehensive attempts at categorization, and threaten to rub our noses in the mess we make of understanding dogs. But in their chaos they also remain faithful to our confusing (sometimes confused) experiences with canine companions. The difficulty of representing dogs—let alone accounting for how they have become a central part of the human experience—reflects the ongoing struggle of defining what a dog is. (2004, 7)

As with dogs, there are thousands of volumes devoted to the study of the ancient Rabbis—and even one devoted to the Rabbis *and* dogs (Ackerman-Lieberman and Zalashik 2013)! In writing about them, one is obliged to sacrifice either cohesion or comprehensiveness. In this book, I have opted for cohesion, to present general overviews of rabbinic themes by focusing on selected, fairly representative, texts about drinking and drinkables. My goal is neither to cover everything ever written about a given beverage (e.g., beer or wine) or a given rabbinic theme, nor to cover every theme in rabbinic literature; rather, it is to use some texts about some beverages in order to survey a variety of key themes in rabbinic literature.

Yet as we learn throughout this book, rabbinic texts presume a tremendous amount of background knowledge. We often enter a conversation midstream and not from the beginning. It is like never having watched a baseball game and then being asked to work as the home plate umpire. Absent the type of guided learning offered by rabbinic study academies (both ancient and modern), this book seeks to give access to rabbinic literature to anyone who wishes to study it, regardless of prior learning.

Why should such an introduction focus on texts about drinking? Quite aside from the obvious fact that two beverages, water and (for an infant) breast milk, are essential for our survival, regulation of drinking communicates rabbinic values of moderation and self-restraint; ritual celebration; financial support of a husband for his wife while she is breastfeeding; and interactions with non-Jews, to name but a few. Key rabbinic views on matters ranging from interactions with non-Jews to actions permitted on holidays are conveyed via rabbinic conversations about beer, for example. And, finally, the fascinating texts on the subject of drinking bequeathed to us by ancient Rabbis, in which the mundane and even the comical mingles with the profound, make for engaging reading.

HOW TO READ THIS BOOK

If you are reading these words, you likely have begun reading this book as most readers approach any volume: starting from the beginning. I have designed it to be read in the usual manner. However, it can also be read in a variety of combinations.

Readers following the Table of Contents will find that this book proceeds in a logical linear fashion. After the Introduction, we proceed to a chapter that surveys the history and literature of the rabbinic movement. After this background information has been digested, eight thematic chapters follow. The first thematic chapter, chapter 2, focuses on biblical interpretation, which is essential to the underlying claim of authority that permeates rabbinic literature. From there, we move on to a discussion of social boundaries (chapter 3), in which we learn the fundamental schema the Rabbis developed for separating Us from Them. Building on this information, the next two chapters explore how the themes of gender and sexuality (chapter 4) and magic, idolatry, and illicit practices (chapter 5) offer concrete examples of how some of these social boundaries are embodied (both figuratively and literally). After discussing illicit practices, we turn to practices that are not only licit but indeed often commanded: chapter 6 deals with the Sabbath, festivals, and holidays; chapter 7, with prayer and ritual. Finally, we have two chapters on themes relevant to both physical and spiritual bodies: ritual purity (chapter 8) and health and hygiene (chapter 9).

For readers who wish to chart their own paths through this volume, however, each chapter can stand alone. Although I try not to repeat myself, I briefly reintroduce key concepts when they appear. Each chapter focuses on individual rabbinic texts, but there are numerous references to other texts for you to explore on your own and a list of suggested readings, with full citation of each entry, even if it has already appeared earlier in the book.

However you read this volume, its goal is to introduce key themes in rabbinic literature; more than that, I hope to show why after I began reading the Rabbis, I simply could not stop.

A BRIEF NOTE ON TRANSLATION STYLE

All translations of biblical and rabbinic documents in this book are my own. They range in length from a sentence to a page, since adequate introduction of the various rabbinic themes explored requires interacting closely with the rabbinic sources. Over the course of writing the book, I developed a series of principles to guide my translation, which are worth briefly spelling out here.

My primary intention is to convey the feel, flow, and language of each text. Therefore, my translations sometimes employ language that sounds wooden. Though it might not be the most felicitous English prose, such translations reflect what the Hebrew or Aramaic words say and how the various texts are saying it. However, as any translator knows, to translate is to make choices and, implicitly or explicitly, to comment on what a given text "means." (This is something the Rabbis themselves do, for example, when they decide whether a text should be read literally or is open for symbolic interpretation; see Yadin 2004, 48–79.) In a related point, I sometimes deviate from a more wooden and/or literal reading when I feel that a particular idiom better conveys the meaning. In sum, I stick to a more wooden style, except when I do not. In all cases, I have done my best to explain why I made certain linguistic (and hence interpretive) choices.

In Hebrew and Aramaic, as in many languages, nouns and their associated verbs are assigned gender. Hebrew and Aramaic gender is binary: masculine or feminine. This gendering of language may reflect an explicit or implicit assumption about a given term or concept (e.g., the Hebrew word *betulah*, "virgin," always appears only in the feminine form). Where possible, I have translated gendered Hebrew and/or Aramaic text neutrally (e.g., whereas Hebrew and Aramaic have separate forms for masculine and feminine third person plural pronouns, English "they" is not explicitly gendered). However, when it was clear that the gendered language is based on gendered assumptions (i.e., the subject or agent of a given action can only refer to one gender, usually male), my translation reflects that.

Though it is important not to import our own presumptions or values into ancient documents, I feel it is necessary also to include here a principle employed throughout this book with regard to gendered pronoun. In translating rabbinic texts, I have endeavored to convey ancient rabbinic assumptions: sometimes they meant male or female, but often they simply meant male. I render those texts accordingly, and explain their logic in my commentary. But writing about their texts, I favor gender-neutral pronouns, especially the "singular they." Though it violates standard English grammar, many argue for revising this grammatical rule, because many people do not identify with either pole of the gender binary. For those who are non-gender-binary, therefore, changing "he" to "he/she" continues to exclude them. I embraced the "singular they" after teaching several non-gender-binary students. Hearing their stories and reflecting on how a simple change to my language could make a big difference in conveying acceptance and inclusion led me to adopt this principle. In the words of Rabbi Hanina: "I have learned much from my teachers, and from my colleagues more than from my teachers, but from my students more than from them all" (*b. Ta'anit* 7a). Having learned from my own students, I do my best to avoid pronouns; but sometimes circumlocutions are too clunky. In such cases, unless a very specific gender is the subject of discussion, I use the "singular they."

Another principle governs my transliteration of Hebrew and Aramaic words. In general, I employ a standardized transliteration style: Hebrew or Aramaic words appear in italics; transliterations reflect vocalized sound; and the letters *'aleph, 'ayin,* and *ḥet* are represented by ', ', and *ḥ,* respectively. I depart from this slightly when rendering the names of rabbinic figures. Rabbis' names do not appear in italics or more technical transliteration. However, I do not anglicize rabbinic names (e.g., I write Yehoshua not Joshua). This decision results from my own idiosyncratic opinion that prefers to refer to a person by their own name while at the same time not bogging the name down in too technical a transliteration.

The very fact that I include as many Hebrew and Aramaic words as I do relates to yet another principle. For those readers already familiar with the texts in their original languages, certain key words might be well known or simply of interest. For readers who are new to reading rabbinic texts, including some words in the original language allows them to get a sense of what the text sounds like. I try not to use too many of these words; and to ensure that it does not become too confusing for the novice, I include a glossary of Hebrew and Aramaic words at the end. There is one additional reason why I include these terms in the original. When rabbinic texts are studied in traditional settings, the conversation that ensues is often a mixture of Hebrew, Aramaic, and whatever other languages the students speak (Yiddish, English, etc.). Therefore, including some Hebrew and Aramaic terms throughout this book draws the reader into the rabbinic study academy (Hebrew *beyt ha-midrash*), where they can enjoy the experience of working through a rabbinic passage (Aramaic *sugya'*).

CONCLUSION

We are now almost ready to take a plunge into the sea of Talmud. But before we do, we should learn a little bit about the history and literature of the Rabbis. So pour yourself a drink and turn the page as our adventure begins.

SUGGESTED READINGS

Ackerman-Lieberman, Phillip, and Rakefet Zalashik, eds. 2013. *A Jew's Best Friend? The Image of the Dog throughout Jewish History*. Portland, OR: Sussex Academic Press.

McHugh, Susan. 2004. *Dog*. London: Reaktion Books.

Yadin, Azzan. 2004. *Scripture as Logos: Rabbi Ishmael and the Origins of Midrash*. Philadelphia: University of Pennsylvania Press.

ONE

The Literature and History of the Rabbinic Movement

The religion of the Hebrew Bible is one of sacrifice. Priests offer animals, grain, and wine on physical altars to a deity (see, e.g., Numbers 28:1–8). So when the Romans destroyed the central cultic location—the Temple in Jerusalem—in 70 C.E., it created a dire, chaotic situation with far-reaching religious, economic, social, and political consequences. At first, there was an expectation of return, since the Jerusalem Temple had been destroyed before, six centuries earlier in 586 B.C.E., but rebuilt about seventy years afterward, in 515 B.C.E. Once it became clear, however, that the expectation of rebuilding the Temple would remain unfulfilled, many Jewish communities struggled. One such community is the subject of this entire book: the early rabbinic movement.

A BRIEF HISTORY OF ANCIENT JUDAISM

Before we turn to the Rabbis, we need to understand what came before them. For that, we begin with the Hebrew Bible. There is no room here to unpack the entirety of this collection of various mythic and historical texts edited over a span of about a thousand years, but there are a few structural and thematic elements of the biblical corpus that are necessary background knowledge (especially in regard to beverage-related matters).

First, a word on nomenclature. Throughout this book, I use the term "Hebrew Bible." There is actually no one "*the* Bible" for everyone. Some bibles are based on a mainly Hebrew text and some are based on Greek texts. Still others are based on Latin texts. These texts are ordered differently, both in terms of the overall structure (e.g., does 2 Chronicles appear as the final book or more towards the middle of the canon?) and the division of individual verses. Some bibles "count" the Ten Commandments differently (cf. Exodus 21:1–17 and Deuteronomy 5:4–21 in various bibles). Further, the different underlying languages sometimes lead to major theological differences. To offer a famous example: read the Hebrew of Isaiah 7:14, "Behold, the young woman [Hebrew *ha-'almah*] is pregnant and about to give birth to a son," and you see nothing worthy of note. But read the Greek of Isaiah 7:14, which refers to a pregnant *parthenos* – a Greek word that can mean "young woman," but also can mean "virgin"—and you might puzzle over this birth. Thus, when Christians turn to Isaiah 7:14 and offer it as proof for the virgin birth, they can certainly claim that those words are found in their Bible. And when Jews look at the Hebrew text and see nothing that serves as proof for the virgin birth, they can certainly claim that those words are not found in their Bible. These words are neither present nor absent from *the* Bible; but they are present or absent from certain bibles.

Since the Rabbis rely on the Hebrew text, I refer to the Hebrew Bible throughout this book. But even this term is not perfect. Though the Hebrew Bible is almost completely written in Hebrew, there are sections that are written in Aramaic, a related Semitic language. To get a sense of the overlap between these two languages, compare Italian to Spanish. For our purposes, though, "Hebrew Bible" is a better term than "Old Testament," which presupposes the New Testament, with its Christian perspective. Finally, the Rabbis do not, of course, refer to the Hebrew Bible as the Old Testament. A common designation employed by many modern Jews (but, in fact, dating from the post-rabbinic period) is *Tanakh*, an acronym for the Hebrew words of the three major sections into which they divided the entire corpus: *Torah* (Genesis,

Exodus, Leviticus, Numbers, and Deuteronomy, often called "the Five Books of Moses"); *Nevi'im* (or "Prophets," which refers mainly to the three major and twelve minor prophets, but also to certain historical books such as 1 and 2 Kings); and *Ketuvim* (or "Writings," which encompasses a variety of works, including Psalms, Proverbs, Song of Songs, and 1 and 2 Chronicles). "Hebrew Bible" is a scholarly designation, intended to combine specificity (it refers to a particular text in a particular order) and avoid the potentially polemical language of either Old Testament or *Tanakh*.

Furthermore, since the Rabbis consider the Hebrew Bible to be an accurate recounting of actual events, I do not devote significant attention to various historical problems represented in many biblical accounts. The purpose of this brief survey is not to introduce scholarly criticism of biblical literature and history, but rather to orient the reader to the biblical text as perceived by rabbinic authors. Mythic and fictive accounts are therefore summarized, rather than problematized.

The Hebrew Bible begins at the very beginning, with the Creation story. Actually, there are two different Creation stories (cf. Genesis 1:1–2:4a and Genesis 2:4b–25). For a text that portrays itself as authoritatively recounting the very beginning of the world, it seems to display no awareness of the repetition of this narrative and no concern for the fact that certain details contradict one another (e.g., animals are created on different days, and the creation of humans occurs in dramatically different manners). Communities that inherit these biblical texts will have to grapple with these, and other, textual "problems"—or as "opportunities" for additional interpretation, which is how the Rabbis view them.

Following the Creation narrative, the mythic history of the Hebrew Bible unfolds at first as a dysfunctional family drama: from Adam and Eve's family post-exile from the Garden of Eden; to Noah surviving a flood while aboard an ark full of animals, and then becoming the first person to plant a vineyard, become intoxicated on wine, and drunkenly disrobe (Genesis 9:20–22); to God promising Abraham that he will father a great nation (Genesis 12:1–3; 17:1–22), which begins in earnest when Abraham and his wife Sarah finally, in their nineties, conceive a son, Isaac; to the many adventures of Isaac and his family, including his twin sons Esau and Jacob, the latter of whom wrestles an angelic being and, in doing so, is renamed Israel, after which the Israelites are named (Genesis 32:23–33); to one of Jacob's sons, Joseph, being sold by his jealous brothers into slavery and ending up in Egypt (Genesis 37), where he interprets the dreams of the Pharaoh's cupbearer (Genesis 40), becomes successful, and eventually reunites with his brothers (whom he forgives, but not without teaching them a lesson, which involves his silver drinking goblet; see Genesis 44:1–17). And all of that is only in Genesis.

Exodus introduces us to Moses. We first learn that Moses was born at a bad time to be an Israelite boy: the Egyptian Pharaoh has decreed that all Israelite boys must be killed (Exodus 1:15–16). This is an important element of the plot, since it explains why Moses is placed in a basket and floated down the Nile, where he is discovered by Pharaoh's daughter and adopted into the royal family (Exodus 1:22–2:10). Despite this upbringing, Moses kills a man whom he saw attacking "an Israelite man, one of his brethren" (Exodus 2:11–12). He flees, rightfully fearing retaliation. This all sets the biblical chain of events in motion: God speaking to Moses from a burning bush (Exodus 3–4); Moses petitioning Pharaoh, on behalf of God, to "Let My people go!" (e.g., Exodus 5:1); to the ten plagues with which God afflicts the Egyptians (Exodus 7–12); to the Exodus from Egypt, including the drowning of the Pharaoh (Exodus 14:26–29); to the Revelation at Mount Sinai (Exodus 19–31); to the forty years spent wandering in the desert.

The Revelation at Mount Sinai will play a vital role in the development of subsequent rabbinic theology, but the biblical narrative proceeds to detail various other laws related to priestly practice and Festival celebration. All of this presumes a religion based on cultic offering of animals, grain, and wine by a professional, hereditary, male priesthood. It also presumes a continued connection to a promised land, which Moses is not allowed to enter, due to a water-related dispute

(Exodus 20:1–13), though he sets up a succession plan and a successor, named Joshua (Deuteronomy 31–34).

With the death of Moses, we enter the second section of the Hebrew Bible: *Nevi'im*, or "Prophets." As Moses' successor, we should not be surprised that the first book is named after Joshua and that it details the military conquest and division of the Promised Land. This theme continues in Judges, a book that includes several fascinating stories. For example, we learn of Yael, a woman who tricks a rival general named Sisera by welcoming him into her tent, serving him milk, giving him a blanket and telling him to sleep while she stands guard, whereafter taking a tent pin and mallet, she "drove the pin through his temple until it went down into the ground. Thus, he fell into the sleep of death and died" (Judges 4:18–21; cf. 5:24–27). In subsequent books, we learn of the transition of the government from rule by judges to the rise of the united monarchy. Kings Saul, David, and Solomon rule over a kingdom uniting the northern part of the country, named Israel, and the southern part, named Judah. The years of the united monarchy are filled with fascinating stories of intrigue (and often questionable morals), but things come apart after the death of Solomon. A civil war ensues, and the northern and southern parts of the country split up. The northern kingdom of Israel lasts until 722 B.C.E., when it falls to the Assyrians. The southern kingdom of Judah lasts longer, but when it is conquered by the Babylonians in 586 B.C.E., a major theological crisis ensues, because it includes Jerusalem, where the Temple, the central cultic shrine built by Solomon, is located. We learn about much of this from both the historical books in this section and the various prophetic books, which spell out the numerous moral and ritual failings of the Israelites blamed for these disastrous events.

The third, and final, section of the Hebrew Bible is called *Ketuvim*, or "Writings," and contains a variety of different genres. It opens with Psalms, a collection of 150 liturgical poems. Psalm 137, a lament for the loss of Jerusalem in 586 B.C.E., for example, processes the raw, vivid emotion aroused by this enormous calamity. Psalm 137 begins with a group of refugee Israelites weeping "by the rivers of Babylon" (137:1), as they ponder, "How shall we sing the Lord's song on foreign soil?" (137:4). Mourning turns to rage, with a call for the destruction of Babylon and the chilling final line: "Happy shall be the one who seizes your babies and dashes them against the rocks!" (137:9). On a happier note, it also features a line that will appear multiple times in this book: "wine gladdens the heart of man" (Psalm 104:15).

Next is Proverbs, which, as the name suggests, is a collection of various proverbs. As we shall learn in subsequent chapters of this book, many of these proverbs address the folly of intoxication. Afterwards, we encounter the complex theology of Job, which is followed by the subsection often called "The Five Scrolls." According to rabbinic practice, these scrolls (Hebrew *megillot*) are each read as part of the liturgy of a particular Jewish holiday: Song of Songs is read on Passover; Ruth on Shavuot; Lamentations on the Ninth of Av; Ecclesiastes on Sukkot; and Esther on Purim (see chapter 6). Finally, there are a few books that represent themselves as historical narratives of various kinds. For example, the books of Ezra and Nehemiah describe King Cyrus—the Persian ruler who conquered the Babylonians in 539 B.C.E.—allowing the Israelites to return to the Promised Land and rebuild the Temple. And last, but not least, 1 and 2 Chronicles are a sort-of CliffsNotes version of Israelite history from Saul to Cyrus.

While that summary of the Hebrew Bible is by no means sufficient to understand fully the richness of the literature and history contained therein, it will suffice to set up the Second Temple period, an era bookended by two defining events: the dedication of the Second Temple in 515 B.C.E. and its destruction in 70 C.E. I devote less attention to the events in this time period, since only a few basic facts are necessary to contextualize the Rabbis. However, this is a fascinating era, deserving of much more attention than space constraints allow.

First, it is important to know that debates about the Temple play a central role throughout this time period. Groups argue about whether those in charge of the Temple were the legitimate priests and/or were following proper ritual procedure. The authors of the books of the

Maccabees and the sectarian Dead Sea Scrolls, for example, raise both of these concerns. Another prominent Jewish critic of the goings-on in the Second Temple was Jesus. Since the Temple was the sole means of assuring proper cultic practice, it really mattered who did what, and how, in that particular sacred space.

Second, when Alexander the Great arrived on the scene after conquering the Persians in 332 B.C.E., he brought along Hellenism—that is, Greek language, culture, and institutions—which proved transformative. Hellenism impacted various communities in different ways, and it eventually divided Jewish communities along a spectrum of those who were more or less willing to embrace and incorporate Hellenism. Even those who claimed to completely reject Hellenism internalized and deployed elements of it. For example, when the Maccabees led a revolt from 168–162 B.C.E. (later commemorated in the holiday of Hanukkah), they claimed to be fighting back against Hellenized Jews and the Seleucid rulers (descendants of one of Alexander's generals) who enabled them. Ironically (or, for those who have studied postcolonial theory, perhaps not ironically), after winning a brutal guerilla war, the Maccabees established the Hasmonean dynasty, which among other things based itself on a Greek style of government.

Third, the Hasmonean dynasty never lived up to its self-proclaimed promises. In 63 B.C.E., two Hasmonean brothers got into an argument about who was in charge and did what no one in antiquity should ever have done: appeal to Rome to settle the debate. The Romans came in and resolved the dispute, took charge, and did not leave. Jewish rulers now served at the whim of Rome, which imposed new taxes and policies, many of which angered local Jews. In 66 C.E., this anger boiled over into outright revolt. Though they put up a good fight, the Jewish community of Jerusalem was no match for the rightfully renowned Roman army, which brought the revolt to a fiery conclusion at the mountain retreat/fortress of Masada in 73 C.E. In the middle of the revolt, the unthinkable happened: the Romans destroyed the Second Temple.

While there was a precedent both for how to handle the destruction of the Temple and for the expectation that it would be rebuilt, this act burned a hole in the center of both the literal and figurative map of Jewish identity. What would happen now?

A BRIEF INTRODUCTION TO THE RABBINIC MOVEMENT

If this historical moment were a movie trailer, the screen would depict the Temple in smoldering ruins and, over dramatic music, a somber voice would intone: "In a world without the Temple, where many ancient Jews struggle to make sense, one small group rises from the ashes: the Rabbis."

Like a phoenix rising from the ashes (a myth known to the Rabbis, since it is found in a rabbinic commentary on the book of Genesis; see *Genesis Rabbah* 19:5), the Rabbis consider themselves to be reconstituting the body of Israel, in order to lead the Jewish people into the future. This notion is present in the founding myth of the rabbinic movement (see *b. Gittin* 56a–b; cf. *Avot d'Rabbi Natan* A4:40–77). According to this legend, Jerusalem is under siege. Realizing what is about to happen and desiring to turn theological lemons into rabbinic lemonade, Rabban Yohanan ben Zakkai sneaks out of Jerusalem disguised as a corpse, approaches the commander of the besieging Roman army, Vespasian, and predicts that he is about to be proclaimed Roman emperor. When this indeed happens, Vespasian offers: "Ask something of me and I shall give it to you." Rabban Yohanan ben Zakkai replies:

> Give me Yavneh and its sages and the line of Rabban Gamaliel and doctors to heal Rabbi Zadoq. (*b. Gittin* 56b)

Allowed to ask anything, Rabban Yohanan ben Zakkai limits his request to a small group of Jews: rabbinic sages. Now, it might be that, as the text goes on to note, Rabban Yohanan ben Zakkai "thought that perhaps [Vespasian] would not do so much, and he would not [even] save a little" (*b. Gittin* 56b). Therefore, rather than make an unreasonable request that he knew would be denied, he made the utilitarian decision to save as many as he could. But this narrative also serves to highlight the role that the Rabbis imagine for themselves: as the remnant that allows the body of Israel to rise phoenix-like from the Temple ashes.

Note what four things Rabban Yohanan ben Zakkai includes in his request. First, he asks for Yavneh, a town located in central Israel, near the west coast of Israel and the eastern end of the Mediterranean Sea (according to Google Maps, the fastest route from the Temple Mount to Yavneh takes an hour and six minutes by car and a little over twelve hours on foot). Second, he asks for sages, so that there will be rabbinic scholars to populate this new study center. Third, he asks for "the line of Rabban Gamaliel." According to rabbinic tradition, Rabban Gamaliel was the Patriarch (Hebrew *Nasi*), meaning that he was the official representative of the Jewish community to the Roman government. The office of the Patriarch came with cultural, political, and financial privileges. It was also a hereditary position, so asking for the genealogical line of Rabban Gamaliel was asking for on-going control over this important governmental position. Fourth, he asks for physicians to heal Rabbi Zadoq. Earlier on in this text, we learn that Rabbi Zadoq had observed a forty-year fast in an attempt to prevent the destruction of Jerusalem, surviving only on the occasional swig of fig juice (*b. Gittin* 56a). We subsequently learn that his medical treatment consists of slowly expanding his shriveled stomach by, over the course of three days, offering him three increasingly more substantive water-based beverages (*b. Gittin* 56a). In sum, Rabban Yohanan ben Zakkai asks for a town in which to (re)build a community; students and colleagues to help grow this community; the political, cultural, and financial capital that accompanies the office of the Patriarch; and medical attention for his friend.

Summarizing scholarly views on how this origin myth is best read, Michael Satlow writes:

> The true value of this story is as myth rather than history. It reflects a later rabbinic self-perception as peaceful inhabitants of a non-Jewish empire, perpetuators of a hoary tradition, experts in interpretation of Torah and,

implicitly, as Israel's new spiritual leaders.... Historically, though, this picture does not add up.... Rather than continuing a grand tradition, complete with its own source of temporal authority in the person of the patriarch (Rabban Gamaliel), these few early scholars—with few followers—would have been cautiously feeling their way toward a new conception of their tradition. (2006, 118)

The Yavneh Legend, as it is often called, is therefore a later recollection of an earlier time. However, at the time in which the story is set, the nascent rabbinic movement was structured around small disciple circles, in which students would sit at the feet of their rabbinic sages and "drink their words with thirst" (*m. Avot* 1:4). In fact, there likely were no "Rabbis" when the Second Temple stood. Though some Jews used the term "rabbi," meaning "my teacher" in Hebrew, as an honorific (e.g., in Mark 9:5, 11:21, and 14:45, Jesus is referred to by this title), "it did not become a formal title until after the Temple's destruction" (Satlow 2006, 118). The Rabbis themselves reflect an awareness of this, since "Rabbinic literature itself never applies the title 'rabbi' even to pre-70 figures who clearly played an important role in rabbinic prehistory, such as Hillel" (Schwartz 2014, 107).

To assign this text to a later period is not to dismiss it. Rather, it teaches us how the rabbinic movement came to view itself (see Boyarin 2004, 151–201). There is also another element to this story: the Yavneh Legend imagines the rabbinic movement as active and robust already at the time of the Temple's destruction. Rather than as a response to catastrophe, the Rabbis envision themselves as already in place—as anticipatory, not reactive. There is evidence that can support this assertion. Though not clear and linear, it seems likely that there is some connection between the rabbinic movement and the pre-70 C.E. Jewish sect called the Pharisees (see Schwartz 2014, 107–11). "The Rabbis may not have been the carriers of a continuous historical tradition, but neither did they rise out of a vacuum" (Satlow 2006, 119). Therefore, despite the well-acknowledged catastrophe of the Temple's destruction, the Rabbis imagine their prehistory to position their movement as one of continuity, not disruption. Like a street vendor who sells sunglasses until a downpour begins, and then switches to selling umbrellas, the rabbinic movement envisions itself as uniquely prepared to cope with, and ultimately transcend, this historical moment.

In the next two centuries, two events unfold that profoundly affected the rabbinic movement in two very different ways. The first event was the Bar Kohkba revolt (132–35 C.E.). At the center of this revolt is a messianic figure named Shimon ben Kosiba, whom his fans called Bar Kokhba (Aramaic for "Son of a Star") and his enemies called Bar Koziba (Aramaic for "Son of a Lie"). Though our evidence is sketchy, this revolt proved disastrous. Rome responded with its full military might and, if rabbinic martyr accounts contain even the slightest kernel of fact, gruesome violence and persecution accompanied both the war and its aftermath (see Satlow 2006, 119–20; Schwartz 2014, 92–97), dashing rabbinic hopes of a speedy rebuilding of the Temple and encouraging abstract eschatological discourse. Instead of specifics, the Rabbis envisioned divine justice being meted out, not in present, lived reality, which they call "This World" (Hebrew *'olam ha-zeh*), but in a future time, which they refer to as "The World to Come" (Hebrew *'olam ha-ba'*). They thus await The World to Come, in which the scales of justice will be rebalanced, the righteous will receive their reward, and the wicked will reap what they have sown.

The second event was the rise of the patriarchate (see Satlow 2006, 120), in respect to which the Yavneh Legend retrojects later events. Though scholars debate when precisely the patriarchate began, there is general agreement that it was after the destruction of the Second Temple (see Schwartz 2014, 118–23). Whereas the Yavneh Legend backdates this institution to "the line of Rabban Gamaliel," the first definitive Patriarch was Rabbi Yehudah ha-Nasi [= Rabbi Judah the Patriarch], who lived from the latter half of the second century until the early third century C.E. All of the statements made above apply here, since having a rabbinic figure in this official governmental position ensured that the rabbinic movement benefited from this patronage. The beginning of the third century was also the time when the first complete rabbinic documents were officially compiled; the Mishnah is dated to this time period and, according to tradition, was edited by none other than Rabbi Yehudah ha-Nasi himself. The importance of his governmental and editorial roles were so highly esteemed that when subsequent rabbinic literature refers to "Rabbi," it is understood to mean Rabbi Yehudah ha-Nasi.

As the rabbinic movement developed, two distinct centers of learning emerged: one in Roman Palestine (Syria Palaestina being the name of the Roman province), and another in Sasanian Babylonia (roughly modern-day Iraq). These communities interacted but developed their own, sometimes quite disparate, viewpoints, shaped by a variety of influences. In addition to different personalities and different geography, the different dominant cultures were an important factor: Roman/Christian in Palestine and Sasanian/Zoroastrian in Babylonia. Surrounding cultures influence the production of texts in matters large and small. For example, why should the Babylonian community concern itself with rabbinic traditions governing agricultural policy for the Land of Israel? Or, in an example more to the point for this book (and to which we shall return in future chapters), Palestinian texts discuss the beverage most commonly consumed in their larger culture (wine), while Babylonian texts ask questions about their own broader culture's preferred beverage (beer).

Within these two centers, two rabbinic groups emerge. The first group encompasses those rabbinic figures who put the pieces back together after the destruction of the Temple until around the middle of the third century C.E. Referred to as the Tannaim ("Repeaters" or "Teachers" in Aramaic; the singular is *tanna*), this group coalesces around the time of Rabbi Yehudah ha-Nasi. The opinions and debates of the Tannaim form the core of the first rabbinic documents and are treated with great respect and authority. Indeed, this is one area in which we see the division between the Tannaim and the next group of Rabbis. Whereas the Tannaim argued with one another, we begin to see rabbinic figures treat their predecessors with a slightly higher level of deference around the middle of the third century, signaling the start of the next generation. Referred to as the Amoraim ("Speakers" or "Explainers" in Aramaic; the singular is *amora*), the second group encompasses rabbinic figures active from the mid-third until roughly the early sixth centuries C.E. The Amoraim sought to expand, clarify, and interpret the opinions and arguments of the Tannaim. In doing so, they create a rich body of literature including, most famously, the Talmud (or, more accurately, the Talmuds).

From the ashes of the Temple, to the office of the Patriarch, to the halls of the Babylonian rabbinic study academies (on which see Rubenstein 2003), the rabbinic movement grew over time. To better understand this group, we need to understand a few of their major concepts.

MAJOR RABBINIC CONCEPTS

As an undergraduate in the late 1990s, when I first began writing about the rabbinic movement, I would save my papers on my computer's internal one-gigabyte hard drive. Just to be safe, I would also save each paper on a colorful 3.5-inch floppy disk. Nowadays, my computer's hard drive is massively bigger, and, like most people, I back up everything to the cloud. But what does this have to do with the Rabbis?

The Rabbis too had a system by which they backed everything up to The Cloud. How did this work? A foundational rabbinic principle is that God revealed two Torahs to Moses on Mount Sinai: the Written Torah and the Oral Torah (e.g., *b. Shabbat* 31a). For the Rabbis, the Written Torah (Hebrew *torah sh-bikhtav*) is an established canonical text: the Hebrew Bible. It is a bound text. It is *the* Torah. Oral Torah (Hebrew *torah sh-be'al peh*) is a much more wide-ranging text. It is Torah, without the definite article. It is not a bound text, but a continuous unfolding of Revelation. This dual conception allows for tradition and innovation to exist side by side. For example, whereas the Written Torah might command in Exodus 35:3 that one cannot kindle a fire on the Sabbath, it does not say whether one can fire up an Amazon Kindle in order to read a book on the Sabbath. Oral Torah allows for a process of updating.

In revealing Oral Torah to Moses at Mount Sinai, God backed up the entirety of Revelation to The Cloud. It is now available for download by authorized users—that is, the Rabbis—in order to (re-)reveal and retrieve stored divine knowledge and law. Moses downloaded the file first, and then backed it up. And this metaphor is not even anachronistic: since everything was revealed at Mount Sinai, cloud computing was revealed then as well! One can therefore think of "Oral Torah" as the official name of the rabbinic cloud server.

Oral Torah expands the boundaries of rabbinic law, to become an all-encompassing legal system. This is implied in the Hebrew term for rabbinic law, *halakhah*, meaning "path," or "way." Like the similar term in Arabic, *shari'a*, this implies walking on the proper, divinely ordained path. And everything is found on that path. Rabbinic texts investigate the *halakhah* of a variety of activities, both the elevated, like liturgy (e.g., tractate *Berakhot*, whose title means "Blessings" in Hebrew), and the mundane, like how to put on your shoes (*b. Shabbat* 61a). Often, the high and the low combine, as in discussions about what prayers to recite when using the bathroom (*y. Berakhot* 9:4, 14b; *b. Berakhot* 60a–b) or what ritual objects may be brought into the bathroom (*b. Berakhot* 23a–b).

Another manner in which Oral Torah expands the boundaries of rabbinic law is encountered in the interplay between *halakhah* and *aggadah*:

> While *halakhah* refers to the normative actions or rules by which Jews should conduct their lives and is often translated "law," *aggadah* (from the verb "to tell") refers to material of widely varying genre: sage stories, parables and legends, folktales, ethical teachings, and more. Some rabbinic works are primarily, but not wholly, halakhic, and others are largely aggadic in character; yet many halakhic works also contain aggadic elements and much *aggadah* is implicitly normative. *Halakhah* and *aggadah* are thus the warp and woof of the fabric of rabbinic learning and normativity. (Hayes 2017, 95)

Stories are not *just* stories; they are often literary vehicles through which to deliver a legal lesson. And legal narratives are often just that: narratives (see Simon-Shoshan 2012). As we shall see throughout this book, the interplay between *halakhic* and *aggadic* elements serves to shape rabbinic texts. For example, a story about children coming home late from a drinking party can quickly turn into a conversation about liturgical law (see the discussion of *m. Berakhot* 1:1 in chapter 7). Like the fable of "the boy who cried wolf," rabbinic stories can teach moral and legal lessons. But unlike a modern tax code, rabbinic legal narratives can almost seamlessly switch between complex legal detail and analysis and an interesting (even humorous) story.

In establishing the principle of dual Revelation—the Written and Oral Torah—the Rabbis transform the biblical figure of Moses into the rabbinic figure that they refer to as "Moses our Rabbi" (Hebrew *Moshe Rabbeinu*). He becomes the first Rabbi, ordained by none other than God. The Rabbis now understand themselves not only to have existed while the Temple still stood, but to have existed even *before* the Temple stood! In doing so, they create memories of controlling the Temple, which they use to stake claim on the legitimate rabbinic authority to reimagine the post-Temple world (see Cohn 2013). For example, a main tenet of the rabbinic movement is that, in addition to rabbinic prayer, textual study replaces Temple sacrifice as a primary ritual practice. Therefore, instead of killing animals or pouring wine on an altar, one reads rabbinic texts *about* killing animals or pouring wine on an altar. Of course, reading and writing *about* sacrifice are very different practices than actually performing physical sacrifice (see Ullucci 2012, 33), but not in the rabbinic conception in which the Temple (Hebrew *beyt ha-miqdash*) is seamlessly replaced by the rabbinic study-house (*beyt ha-midrash*).

This divinely preordained transition from the biblical Temple to the rabbinic study-house is exemplified in the rabbinic enterprise known as *midrash*. From a Hebrew root meaning "to investigate," *midrash* is an interpretative practice based on rabbinic assumptions about the biblical text and governed by rules of how this investigation can occur. The process of *midrash* allows for biblical texts and practices to morph into rabbinic texts and practices in a manner that, viewed through the retrospective rabbinic lens, is both natural and inevitable. *Midrash* is the bridge across which the Rabbis proceed from Moses to Moses our Rabbi. This is why the rabbinic study-house is called a *beyt ha-midrash*, literally, "The House of *Midrash*."

MOVING FROM "YES"/"NO" TO "IT DEPENDS": RABBINIC CATEGORIES AND CATEGORIZATION

Since everything is encompassed within Torah, the Rabbis devote a tremendous amount of time and energy to detailing how this all works. Following the complicated twists and turns of these narratives is quite the task, because rabbinic texts move quickly between a series of sometimes only vaguely connected topics. Hypothetical scenarios are often preferred to practical ones, making the Rabbis more theoretical physicists than experimental ones (see Cohen 2007, 134–38). Conversations often begin with the hypothetical question of "What if . . . ?" and slowly develop, branching in myriad directions, with answers that often begin, "It depends. . . ." Tangents are discussed in great detail while the supposed main topic of a text is rarely addressed. Therefore, though many texts claim to be arranged topically, you often cannot find the laws relevant to a topic only—or even mostly—within the section that supposedly addresses that topic. For example, to find the *halakhic* discussion relevant to Hanukkah, a holiday whose celebration usually occurs in December, you need to open the Talmudic tractate *Shabbat*, which, as its name implies, focuses on the Sabbath (e.g., *b. Shabbat* 21a–24b).

All legal systems have their versions of "it depends." From filing taxes to deciding whether to charge someone with murder or homicide, legal systems require the classification of actions into categories; this, in turn necessitates the weighing of various factors before reaching a decision. Binary yes/no answers are rare. One person walks up to another and punches them in the face—is that assault? It depends. Were they in a boxing ring? And even if they were, I would need to ask a few more questions before reaching a conclusion. Or, to use an illustration from rabbinic tort law: what if a thief steals something and then the value of that product changes? The answer is that it depends on the product and why its value changed. Further questions are required before an answer can be provided. For example, what if a thief steals wine and then the wine turns into vinegar? In the ancient world, wine was a prized commodity that easily turned sour into vinegar, a much less valuable commodity. Does the thief compensate the owner for the higher cost of the original product or the lower cost of the product in its present condition? (See *m. Bava Qamma* 9:2, where we learn that the thief must repay the original value for the wine.)

Along the way, the Rabbis explore, expand, and erect categories in which to slot data. Is action *x* allowable? It depends. Did it occur on the Sabbath? If so, we need to discuss all of the variables that Sabbath introduces. The category of Sabbath, for example, has numerous subcategories, all of which must play into our analysis. And what about Festival Days, which share some—but not all—of the Sabbath rules? We return to these issues in chapter 6, where among other topics we consider whether one can strain wine and beer on Sabbath and Festival Days. As we shall see, in order to answer that question, a variety of categories need to be explored and defined.

Although the same can be said of any legal system, because of the expansive nature of *halakhah*, rabbinic literature is especially given to responding to any question with "It depends...." If everything is governed by *halakhah*, and all of this was divinely revealed on Mount Sinai to Moses our Rabbi, then parsing every variable takes on an added importance. Furthermore, the very act of puzzling over these details is the rabbinic practice par excellence. Indeed, according to one text, if you add up all of the eternal good that comes from honoring one's mother and father (one of the Ten Commandments), engaging in acts of kindness, and making peace between friends, "the study of Torah is equal to them all" (*m. Pe'ah* 1:1). Finally, in a point that should not be underestimated, members of the rabbinic movement clearly enjoy this process. This is fun for them. Thus, even when a yes or no answer is easily achievable, they often prefer to ponder all of the variables before turning to the ready solution. For the Rabbis, it is about the journey as much as it is about the destination, so they often detour from the direct path in order to take the scenic route.

MAJOR RABBINIC DOCUMENTS

In this book, we look through the lens of the rabbinic drinking glass. Focusing on particular passages across various rabbinic documents, we learn how to read rabbinic texts and how specific smaller textual units (Aramaic *sugyot*; singular *sugya'*) work together in order to sketch out a map allowing us to explore key themes in rabbinic literature. We are almost ready to turn to the texts, but before we do, we need to ask a very important question: What texts?

The first major rabbinic document is the Mishnah, which, according to tradition, was redacted (the fancy scholarly word for edited) at the beginning of the third century C.E. by Rabbi Yehudah ha-Nasi. The Mishnah is divided into six large sections, referred to as Orders (Hebrew *Sedarim*; singular *Seder*), which roughly correspond to their general content:

Zera'im	"Seeds"	Agriculture, etc.
Mo'ed	"Appointed Times"	Festivals, etc.
Nashim	"Women"	Marriage Law, etc.
Neziqin	"Damages"	Torts, Civil Procedure, etc.
Qodashim	"Holy Things"	Temple Policies, Animal Slaughter, etc.
Tohorot	"Purity"	Purity Law, etc.

Each Order consists of between seven and twelve individual tractates, for a total of sixty-three tractates. Tellingly, the Hebrew word for "tractate" is *masekhet* (plural *masekhtot*), a word that literally means "web," because they capture your attention and are spun from a rich, complex silk.

Though the name of each Order roughly corresponds to its general content, each Order has both individual tractates and sections of tractates that depart from this topical arrangement. For example, *Zera'im* focuses on agriculture, but its first tractate is *Berakhot*, which, as its name implies, is about "Blessings." For this reason, I added "etc." to the list above—because there is always material beyond the main topic. Furthermore, the names of the Orders tell us something about both rabbinic priorities and their perspective. The fact that "Women" is the subject of an entire Order, for example, suggests that the Rabbis presume "Men" to be normative, and thus wish to interrogate the variables introduced in their construction of Other gendered bodies and practices (see chapter 4).

To clarify a potential confusion, Mishnah—with a capital *M*—refers to the entire corpus or to an individual tractate (e.g., "The Mishnah...," or "In Mishnah *Berakhot*..."), but mishnah—with a lowercase *m*—refers to an individual unit within the Mishnah (e.g., "In the second mishnah of the first chapter of Mishnah *Berakhot*..."). In citation, the title of a tractate of the Mishnah is preceded by an italicized lowercase *m*, punctuated by a period (*m.*), and followed by chapter and verse numbers, separated by a colon (e.g., *m. Berakhot* 1:2).

The next major rabbinic document is Tosefta. According to tradition, Tosefta was redacted shortly after the Mishnah and provides a commentary on it. This relationship is signaled in its name, since Tosefta literally means "The Addition" or "The Supplement" in Aramaic. Recent scholarship has troubled this model, because there is strong evidence that some passages in the Mishnah in fact respond to Toseftan passages, and if Mishnah predates Tosefta, how could that be? It therefore seems likely that earlier drafts of each document were in circulation, and certain passages in each were reworked in light of the other. The precise details of this process need not trouble us here. However, it is important to understand that just because Tosefta has been viewed as a supplement to Mishnah, does not mean that all Mishnaic traditions are prior to their Toseftan cousins.

On the macro level, Tosefta is structured like the Mishnah. It uses the same six Orders in the same sequence. On the micro level, however, variance is often significant. While, for the most part, the topics of each tractate unfold in a somewhat similar fashion, and sometimes even in the same phrasing, it is more common that passages in Tosefta introduce varied wording, different rulings, and entirely new content and concepts. For example, the story about Rabban Gamaliel's sons coming home late from drinking found in *m. Berakhot* 1:1 (discussed in chapter 7) is completely absent from *t. Berakhot* 1:1 (texts from Tosefta are prefaced with *t.*).

The final major grouping of rabbinic documents by the Tannaim is a collection of texts known as the Tannaitic Midrashim. As their title implies, these documents are collections of *midrash* attributed to the Tannaim. Like Mishnah and Tosefta, they also seem to have been edited in Palestine in the third century, though probably in the mid to late 200s. The Tannaitic Midrashim are exegetical commentaries on the books of Exodus (*Mekhilta d'Rabbi Ishmael* and *Mekhilta d'Rabbi Shimon bar Yohai*), Leviticus (*Sifra*), Numbers (*Sifre Numbers*), and Deuteronomy (*Sifre Deuteronomy*). A rabbinic bias is present here, because there is no commentary on Genesis, a biblical book viewed by them as more about stories than about law. This bias also explains the Aramaic title for the Midrash on Leviticus—*Sifra,* meaning "The Book." This title refers to the fact that Leviticus is chock full of laws and, as such, "in the old Jewish school system this was the first book, with which instruction began" (Strack and Stemberger 1996, 260). Yet, though the Tannaitic Midrashim focus on law (which is why they are often referred to as "The Halakhic Midrashim"), they too contain a mixture of *halakhah* and *aggada*.

The Tannaim, however, were not the only ancient Rabbis who wrote and redacted Midrash collections. Throughout the Amoraic period (and, in some cases, continuing on well into the medieval period—at least in terms of editing and perhaps in terms of more significant additions), a series of Homiletic Midrashim appear. Some of these documents bear the title "*Rabbah*," meaning "Great." For example, there is a *Rabbah* for each of the five books of the Torah (with *Genesis Rabbah*, the book of Genesis finally gets its due). There is also a *Rabbah* for each of the "Five Scrolls." The five books of the Torah are read weekly in the rabbinic synagogue and the Five Scrolls, as discussed above, each serve a liturgical role on a particular Jewish holiday. Though they likely do not contain an accurate transcript of synagogue homiletic preaching, commentaries on the biblical books that form the basis of many Sabbath and holiday prayer services offer us windows into the kinds of ideas that might have circulated in these settings. This window expands when we include other Homiletic Midrash collections, such as *Pesiqta d'Rav Kahana* and *Pesiqta Rabbati*, which are collections of *midrashic* sermons for holidays and special Sabbaths; and *Tanhuma*, a Homiletic Midrash collection that focuses on all five books of the Torah.

The document that has come to define the literary production of the Amoraim is the Talmud. *The* Talmud, however, is a misnomer, as there are actually two Talmuds (Hebrew plural *Talmudim*; meaning "study" or "curriculum"). The first Talmud is the *Yerushalmi*, otherwise known as either the Jerusalem Talmud or the Palestinian Talmud. All of these names indicate the general location of its redaction: the Land of Israel. Like Tosefta, the *Yerushalmi* follows the general structure and organization of the Mishnah. It comments on Mishnah. But it does much more than that. First, it expands beyond the Mishnah, answering questions asked therein and posing new ones. It also addresses how *halakhah* applies to new scenarios. Second, this interest is selective on both the macro and the micro level. On the macro level, not all tractates receive a *gemara'*. From an Aramaic root meaning both "to complete" and "to learn," *gemara'* is the amoraic commentary on Mishnah. The term "Talmud" actually refers to the combination of Mishnah and its relevant *gemara'*. The bias towards some tractates makes sense: of course the *Yerushalmi* includes *gemara'* on tractates associated with agricultural policies and procedures relevant to the Land of Israel. But the absence of commentary on other tractates seems curious (e.g., there is no commentary on tractate *Hullin*, which focuses on non-Temple animal slaughter and includes important discussion of the prohibition against cooking meat with milk; see chapter 3). On the micro level, the *Yerushalmi* reflects its broader cultural environment. For example, tractate *Avodah Zarah* ("Idolatry") can be read in ways to suggest the influence of the time and place of its composition and redaction (see Hayes 1997).

A product of its place and time, the *Yerushalmi* seems to have been edited in the late fourth century C.E., about a hundred years prior to the other Talmud, the *Bavli*. As a result, the *Yerushalmi* sometimes reads as less polished, as more of a rough draft than a final version. Of course, this view does not do justice to the rich and complex text of the *Yerushalmi*. However, because of this bias, and some later historical factors that led to the rise in prominence of the Babylonian rabbinic community—who preferred their Talmud, the *Bavli*—the *Yerushalmi* is often relatively neglected. When people refer to *The* Talmud, they usually mean the *Bavli*. In the past few decades, scholarship on the *Yerushalmi* has grown voluminously, especially in regard to how comparison between the *Yerushalmi* and the *Bavli* informs different experiences and perspectives of the Palestinian and Babylonian rabbinic communities respectively.

Citations of the *Yerushalmi*, based on the 1991–2001 edition of Peter Schäfer and Hans-Jürgen Becker, are prefaced with an italicized lowercase *y*, punctuated by a period (*y.*); the title is followed by both the chapter and verse numbers, separated by a colon, and the MS page number and column letter (e.g., *y. Avodah Zarah* 2:3, 41a, a text discussed in chapter 5).

The second Talmud, as we have already learned, is the *Bavli*. Edited in approximately 500 C.E., the *Bavli* has become the central text of rabbinic study. Commentaries on it abound: from the famous medieval

Rabbi and reputed wine-maker Rashi to modern-day blogs, a tremendous amount of both literal and electronic ink has been spilled in an effort to make sense of this fascinating corpus of rabbinic literary productivity. Julia Watts Belser excellently summarizes what one encounters in approaching the *Bavli*:

> The text is structured around the exposition of short units of Mishnah, and each of these units leads the Bavli into complex, open-ended legal argumentation. The discussion that follows rarely includes a definitive statement of the law itself; the Bavli often assumes its reader already knows the actual legal ruling. A student approaching a topic for the first time often looks in vain for an entry-point into the subject at hand. The text provides few handholds for the beginner and never offers an explicit description of its foundational terms or working assumptions. It eschews an explanation of basic concepts and introductory material. Instead, conversations pick up in the middle of the subject and proceed through a rigorous, detail-oriented dissection of the particulars. The Bavli's voice assumes the reader's familiarity with the entire text, moving back and forth between complex topics, trusting the reader to search out its references and unfold its meanings. (2015, 31)

One might say the same of the *Yerushalmi*, but the *Bavli* takes this process to another level. In doing so, it reflects a similar selectivity on both the macro and the micro levels. On the macro level, the *Bavli* is not interested, for example, in the agricultural policies and procedures of the Land of Israel. It is, after all, a product of Babylonia, where such matters are largely irrelevant. On the micro level, the *Bavli* reflects its broader cultural environment. Much work has been done on the interaction between the authorities cited in the *Bavli* and the broader Iranian context in recent years (e.g., Mokhtarian 2015; Secunda 2013). This is a growing area in scholarship, with all of the attendant growing pains.

Though examples from all genres of the rabbinic literary production noted above appear in this book, there is a disproportionate representation of *sugyot* from the *Bavli*. Although I introduce readers to every major rabbinic genre, the *Bavli* often contains the most extended and rich conversation from which to mine information about rabbinic themes. This does not mean that we shall only learn about the Babylonian rabbinic community. We shall also, for example, discuss how concepts are presented in earlier texts, such as the Mishnah and Tosefta, and how biblical texts are interpreted in *Numbers Rabbah* (see chapter 2). This decision also reflects my own bias, as while writing this book I regularly found myself drawn to the *Bavli*, which often offers more "stuff" with which to work. That being said, I include references to other rabbinic texts in each chapter and to other secondary sources in the Suggested Readings section that offer insight into how other rabbinic documents handle similar thematic concerns. After all, though the *Bavli* is often the most developed exposition of a topic, it is not the only text that sheds light on the width and depth of various rabbinic themes.

One final note on the citation of the *Bavli*: references to this text are prefaced with an italicized lowercase *b*, punctuated by a period (*b.*), and the relevant page number and letter (indicating the side of the folio on which the passage appears, "a" for front and "b" for back) follow the title (e.g., *b. Pesahim* 107a, a text discussed in chapter 6).

CONCLUSION

The goal of this chapter has been to provide a brief—but hopefully sufficient—introduction to the history and literature of the rabbinic movement. Additional information can be gathered from the sources cited below. But for now, please turn to chapter 2 and enter the world of the ancient Rabbis.

SUGGESTED READINGS

Alexander, Elizabeth Shanks. 2006. *Transmitting Mishnah: The Shaping Influence of Oral Tradition*. New York: Cambridge University Press.

Alexander, Elizabeth Shanks, and Beth A. Berkowitz, eds. 2018. *Religious Studies and Rabbinics: A Conversation.* New York: Routledge.

Belser, Julia Watts. 2015. *Power, Ethics, and Ecology in Jewish Late Antiquity: Rabbinic Responses to Drought and Disaster.* New York: Cambridge University Press.

Ben-Eliyahu, Eyal, Yehudah Cohn, and Fergus Millar. 2012. *Handbook of Jewish Literature from Late Antiquity.* New York: Oxford University Press.

Boyarin, Daniel. 2004. *Border Lines: The Partition of Judaeo-Christianity.* Philadelphia: University of Pennsylvania Press.

Cohen, Shaye J. D. 1999. *The Beginnings of Jewishness: Boundaries, Varieties, Uncertainties.* Berkeley: University of California Press.

———. 2007. "The Judean Legal Tradition and the *Halakhah* of the Mishnah." In *The Cambridge Companion to the Talmud and Rabbinic Literature,* ed. Charlotte Elisheva Fonrobert and Martin S. Jaffee. New York: Cambridge University Press. Pages 121–43.

Cohn, Naftali S. 2013. *The Memory of the Temple and the Making of the Rabbis.* Philadelphia: University of Pennsylvania Press.

Fonrobert, Charlotte Elisheva, and Martin S. Jaffee, eds. 2007. *The Cambridge Companion to the Talmud and Rabbinic Literature.* New York: Cambridge University Press.

Goodman, Martin. 2007. *Rome and Jerusalem: The Clash of Ancient Civilizations.* New York: Knopf.

Halivni, David Weiss. 2013. *The Formation of the Babylonian Talmud.* Trans. Jeffrey L. Rubenstein. New York: Oxford University Press.

Hayes, Christine. 1997. *Between the Babylonian and Palestinian Talmuds: Accounting for Halakhic Difference in Selected Sugyot from Tractate Avodah Zarah.* New York: Oxford University Press.

———. 2011. *The Emergence of Judaism: Classical Traditions in Contemporary Perspective.* Minneapolis: Fortress Press.

———. 2015. *What's Divine about Divine Law? Early Perspectives.* Princeton, NJ: Princeton University Press.

———. 2017. "Law in Classical Rabbinic Judaism." In *The Cambridge Companion to Judaism and Law,* ed. Christine Hayes, 76–127. New York: Cambridge University Press.

Hidary, Richard. 2010. *Dispute for the Sake of Heaven: Legal Pluralism in the Talmud.* Providence, RI: Brown Judaic Studies.

Jaffee, Martin S. 2006 [1997]. *Early Judaism: Religious Worlds of the First Judaic Millennium.* 2nd ed. Bethesda: University Press of Maryland.

Kanarek, Jane L., and Majorie Lehman, eds. 2017 [2016]. *Learning to Read Talmud: What It Looks Like and How It Happens.* Boston: Academic Studies Press.

Lapin, Hayim. 2012. *Rabbis as Romans: The Rabbinic Movement in Palestine, 100–400 c.e.* New York: Oxford University Press.

Mokhtarian, Jason Sion. 2015. *Rabbis, Sorcerers, Kings, and Priests: The Culture of the Talmud in Ancient Iran.* Oakland: University of California Press.

Rosenblum, Jordan D. 2013. "Home Is Where the Hearth Is? A Consideration of Jewish Household Sacrifice in Antiquity." In *"The One Who Sows Bountifully": Essays in Honor of Stanley K. Stowers,* ed. Caroline Johnson Hodge, Saul M. Olyan, Daniel Ullucci, and Emma Wasserman, 153–63. Providence, RI: Brown Judaic Studies.

Rubenstein, Jeffrey L. 1999. *Talmudic Stories: Narrative Art, Composition, and Culture.* Baltimore: Johns Hopkins University Press.

———. 2002. *Rabbinic Stories.* New York: Paulist Press.

———. 2003. *The Culture of the Babylonian Talmud.* Baltimore: Johns Hopkins University Press.

Satlow, Michael L. 2006. *Creating Judaism: History, Tradition, Practice.* New York: Columbia University Press.

———. 2014. *How the Bible Became Holy.* New Haven, CT: Yale University Press.

Schäfer, Peter, and Hans-Jürgen Becker, eds. 1991–2001. *Synopse zum Talmud Yerushalmi.* 7 vols. Tübingen: Mohr Siebeck.

Schwartz, Seth. 2001. *Imperialism and Jewish Society, 200 B.C.E. to 640 C.E.* Princeton, NJ: Princeton University Press.

———. 2014. *The Ancient Jews from Alexander to Muhammad.* New York: Cambridge University Press.

Secunda, Shai. 2013. *The Iranian Talmud: Reading the Bavli in Its Sasanian Context.* Philadelphia: University of Pennsylvania Press.

Simon-Shoshan, Moshe. 2012. *Stories of the Law: Narrative Discourse and the Construction of Authority in the Mishnah.* New York: Oxford University Press.

Steinsaltz, Adin. 1989. *The Talmud: The Steinsaltz Edition: A Reference Guide.* New York: Random House.

Strack, H.L., and Günter Stemberger. 1996. *Introduction to the Talmud and Midrash.* Translated and edited by Markus Bockmuehl. Minneapolis: Fortress Press.

Ullucci, Daniel C. 2012. *The Christian Rejection of Animal Sacrifice.* New York: Oxford University Press.

Vidas, Moulie. 2014. *Tradition and the Formation of the Talmud.* Princeton, NJ: Princeton University Press.
Wimpfheimer, Barry Scott. 2011. *Narrating the Law: A Poetics of Talmudic Legal Stories.* Philadelphia: University of Pennsylvania Press.
———. 2018. *The Talmud: A Biography.* Princeton, NJ: Princeton University Press.
Yadin, Azzan. 2004. *Scripture as Logos: Rabbi Ishmael and the Origins of Midrash.* Philadelphia: University of Pennsylvania Press.

TWO

Biblical Interpretation

> Moses received Torah from Sinai and transmitted it to Joshua, and Joshua [transmitted it] to the Elders, and the Elders [transmitted it] to the Prophets, and the Prophets transmitted it to the Men of the Great Assembly. (*m. Avot* 1:1)

In this famous text, Moses' biblical ascent of Mount Sinai in Exodus 19 forms the first link in an unbroken chain of transmission: the divine wisdom imparted to Moses is transmitted to Joshua; who passes it on to the Elders (see Joshua 24:31); who in turn pass it on to the Prophets; who pass it on to the Men of the Great Assembly. This latter group is understood to be a collective of wise men who lived during the Second Temple period and preserved traditions in order to transmit them to the final link in the chain: the Rabbis.

What rabbinic literature claims to represent, then, is an authentic tradition that dates back to God's Revelation on Mount Sinai. For the Rabbis, that moment of Revelation revealed not one but two Torahs: the Written Torah and the Oral Torah. The Written Torah (Hebrew *torah sh-bikhtav*) consists of the Hebrew Bible: a bound text composed and edited by God, an inerrant and intentional author. The Oral Torah (Hebrew *torah sh-be'al peh*), on the other hand, is a process: it is a series of continuously revealed texts that interpret, expand, augment, and update the Written Torah. To use modern technological terms: all of Torah was revealed at Mount Sinai, but the Written Torah was downloaded and exists in hard copy, while the Oral Torah was backed up to

The Cloud (literally and figuratively), to be downloaded via the rabbinic process of debate whenever certain files are needed.

Torah encompasses all aspects of life—from civil and criminal law, to ritual and ethical practices; from how to pray, to how to go to the bathroom. To quote another famous rabbinic dictum from the same tractate:

> Ben Bag Bag said: Turn it and turn it [again], for everything is in it. (*m. Avot* 5:22)

If you search and cannot find what you are looking for, you can always download it from The Cloud with Oral Torah.

One common enterprise in which Oral Torah engages is the explication of Written Torah. Reading through the Hebrew Bible, one encounters many instances that complicate and challenge the claim that the Written Torah was composed by a divine author. One passage contradicts another. A word is misspelled. Sometimes words or phrases seem to be either omitted or added in the wrong place. The organization can appear haphazard. And sometimes, the meaning of a given text is simply opaque. In order to address these matters, the Rabbis developed *midrash* (from a Hebrew root meaning "to investigate"), a hermeneutical practice based on certain assumptions and governed by certain rules (see Bakhos 2006; 2009). For example, if a word is misspelled in the Hebrew Bible, that is because God *meant* to misspell it, and not because a human author did not use spell check. And if God used a specific word in Leviticus and then that same word appears again in Deuteronomy, God meant to do so in order to authorize a Rabbi to derive via *midrash* a principle from that wording.

In this chapter, we explore what texts about beverages can teach us about the presumptions and principles that govern rabbinic biblical interpretation. Though I am unable to cover every aspect of *midrash* herein, the fascinating passages that follow—including tales of human combustion and Freudian slips—provide a survey of the main contours of rabbinic exegesis. And, as we shall soon learn, this enterprise will put a smile on your face.

"WORDS OF TORAH ARE SYMBOLIZED BY WATER": DRINKING DIVINE WISDOM

Without water, there is no life. Summarizing the science behind the human biological need for water, Andrew Smith notes:

> In its purest form, water has no calories, proteins, fats, carbohydrates, vitamins, or minerals, yet it is the most important nutrient for humans. It is the universal solvent, and many substances, such as minerals (calcium, sodium), gases (oxygen, carbon dioxide), and nutrients (B vitamins and vitamin C), are easily dissolved in it; water is an essential part of the human metabolic process. Water performs a variety of functions in the body. It helps carry nutrients to cells, removes waste, and is vital to maintaining the body's temperature. Without regular infusions of water—which for humans should not exceed three days—life ends. (Smith 2013, 1)

Though the Rabbis do not speak in the same scientific terms, they display awareness of the necessity for access to drinking water. This vital need appears in a variety of contexts. For example, in regard to civil law, the Rabbis note that, while pits dug in various locations may belong to the general public or to private individuals, "Streams and flowing springs, behold, they belong to everyone" (*t. Bava Qamma* 6:15). If water is life, then every life needs access to water.

The vital need for water marks this liquid as a prime candidate for symbolic interpretation. Water is often compared to something else that the Rabbis deem essential for existence: Torah. Water ensures physical survival in This World (Hebrew *'olam ha-zeh*), the present, lived reality; and Torah ensures spiritual survival both in This World and in The World to Come (Hebrew *'olam ha-ba'*), a future time when the righteous receive their reward and the wicked get what they deserve. For example:

> Why is man compared to "fish of the sea" [Habakkuk 1:14]? To teach you that just as fish of the sea die as soon as they are lifted onto dry land, so too men die as soon as they separate themselves from words of Torah and from the commandments. (*b. Avodah Zarah* 3b)

A man without Torah is like a fish without water. For this reason, the Rabbis often draw on water metaphors (as do early Christian monastics; see Bar-Asher Siegal 2013, 101–3).

To offer another example, this time from dry land: Exodus 15:22–26 recounts an incident where the Israelites, having fled slavery in Egypt, "went three days in the desert, and they did not find water" (Exodus 15:22). Three days without water is life-threatening. One commentary on this biblical text asserts:

> "and they did not find water" [Exodus 15:22]: "Words of Torah are symbolized by water." (*Mekhilta d'Rabbi Ishmael Beshalah Vayassa* 1; on this passage, see Boyarin 1994, 58–70)

Wandering in the desert, the Israelites are dying of thirst. This explains what follows in the biblical account, wherein the severely parched Israelites rebel against Moses. Though disapproved of, their actions are understandable, given their mortal need both for water and for spiritual "water."

In particular, the Rabbis focus on the ability of water to be imbibed and to become embodied knowledge. They imagine water as embodied Wisdom that the body absorbs and incorporates in the simultaneous act of physical and spiritual digestion. To find an excellent example of this assertion, we return to the desert. Post-Exodus, why did God not lead the Israelites straight from Egypt into the Land of Israel? Why did they need to wander for forty years in the desert? It turns out there was a good reason for God making the Israelites roam around the desert:

> The Holy One Blessed be He says: If I should bring the Israelites into the Land right now, each person would immediately take possession of a field or a vineyard, and they would neglect Torah. Rather, I will take them into the wilderness for forty years, that they might eat manna and drink well-water, so that Torah will be absorbed into their bodies. (*Mekhilta d'Rabbi Ishmael Beshalah Vayehi* 1; on this text, see Rosenblum 2010, 61–63)

Taking the direct route would have resulted in the Israelites settling too quickly into the Land of Israel. Instead, God had them take the (very!) scenic route. Along the way, they ate manna and drank well-water, both of which symbolize knowledge. After forty years of these constant acts of eating and drinking, the individual Israelite bodies and the corporate body of Israel had both literally and figuratively absorbed Torah. They were now ready to enter God's promised land.

Thus far, we have learned that: (a) water and Torah are essential for survival; (b) there is "a widespread rabbinic tendency to describe Torah and its transmission through metaphors of nourishing sustaining liquids" (Belser 2015, 36), especially water; and (c) water and Torah are absorbed into the body, ontologically changing the drinker and imparting physical and spiritual vitamins and nutriment. While these assumptions are important, they still do not fully explain why I would begin a chapter on rabbinic biblical interpretation with a discussion of water. For this, we must turn to another text:

> Another interpretation: "May my discourse come down as rain" [Deuteronomy 32:2]. Just as rains falls on trees and imparts its distinctive flavor into each and every one of them—the grapevine with its flavor, the olive tree with its flavor, the fig tree with its flavor—so too words of Torah are all one, but they comprise Written Torah and Oral Torah, [the latter of which includes] *midrash*, laws, and narratives. (*Sifre Deuteronomy* 306; my translation is influenced by Fraade 2012, 41–42; and 1991, 96–97)

In Deuteronomy 32, Moses delivers his final speech to the Israelites, including his hope that:

> May my discourse come down as rain, my speech distill as the dew, like storm-showers on the grass, and rain-showers on the herb. (Deuteronomy 32:2)

As rain penetrates the ground and nourishes vegetation, Moses fervently desires that his words will penetrate the Israelites and nourish the seed he planted, so that it grows into a mighty (family) tree. In short, Moses hopes that his words are embodied and embodying water.

As the opening line of our text indicates ("Another interpretation"), this speech proved irresistible to the Rabbis, who offered numerous interpretations of this verse (e.g., *Sifre Deuteronomy* 306; *b. Ta'anit* 7a). In our present text, the words of Moses are "understood to contain already the diverse forms of rabbinic Oral Torah, which despite their distinctive 'tastes' 'are all one,' that is, derive from a single divine source and revelatory event" (Fraade 2012, 42). Rain falls on the ground and imparts various flavors to various plants. The grape does not taste like the olive; and neither taste like the fig. But rain—whether a heavy downpour, a gentle mist, or the morning dew—all comes from a single source.

Torah is like rain. It comes from a single, divine source. God's "rain" is divided into two types: Written Torah and Oral Torah (or, in the language used in this text, Scripture and Mishnah; Hebrew *miqra'* and *mishnah*, respectively). Oral Torah is further subdivided into three distinct flavors: *midrash*, *halakhot* ("laws"), and *haggadot* ("narratives"). Like grapes, olives, and figs (clearly, the three-part example is not accidental), *midrash*, laws, and narratives are all different flavors nourished from a single source. The Torah-as-water metaphor therefore supports the entire rabbinic system: God gave Moses Torah—both Written and Oral. Like rain, Moses' Torah nourished many types of plants/texts. But the key ingredient of all of these is God's rain.

Water, the beverage that supports all animal and vegetal life, becomes the defining metaphor for rabbinic authority to interpret Scripture. For this reasons, students can say to their Rabbi:

> We are all your students, and from your water we drink! (*y. Sotah* 3:4, 18d; *y. Hagigah* 1:1, 75d; *b. Hagigah* 3a; cf. *b. Bava Metzi'a* 84b)

Once (unilaterally) granted this authority, the Rabbis begin to develop a set of interpretative practices and presumptions. It is to some of these hermeneutical principles that we now turn.

"EVE MIXED WINE FOR ADAM": WINE AND DIVINE EDITORSHIP OF THE HEBREW BIBLE

According to the Rabbis, God composed, edited, and dictated to Moses the entire Torah—including the various dots and crowns adorning the

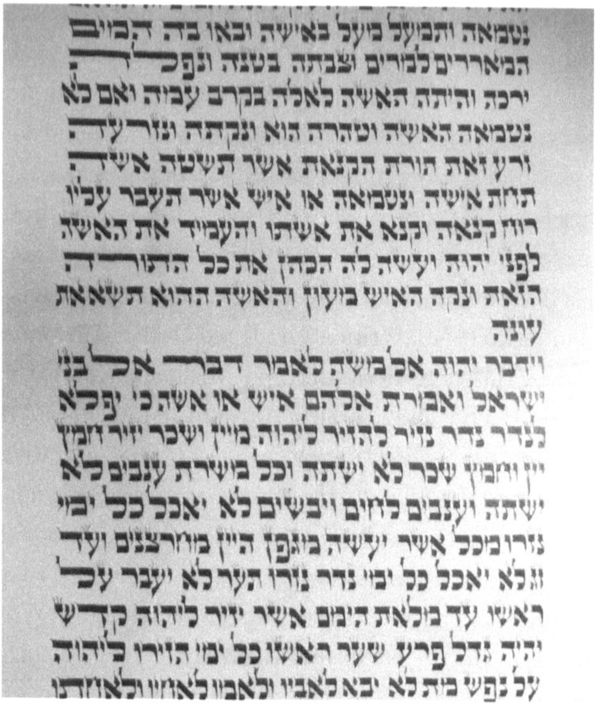

נטמאה והבעיל בועל באישה ובאו בה המים
הבאררים לבדים וצבתה בטנה ונפל
ירכה והיתה האשה לאלה בקרב עמיה ואם לא
נטמאה האשה וטהרה הוא ונקתה ונזרעה
זרע זאת תורת הקנאת אשר תשטה אשה
תחת אישה ונטמאה או איש אשר תעבר עליו
רוח קנאה וקנא את אשתו והעמיד את האשה
לפני יהוה ועשה לה הכהן את כל התורה
הזאת ונקה האיש מעון והאשה ההוא תשא את
עונה
וידבר יהוה אל משה לאמר דבר אל בני
ישראל ואמרת אלהם איש או אשה כי יפלא
לנדר נדר נזיר להזיר ליהוה מיין ושכר יזיר חמץ
יין וחמץ שכר לא ישתה וכל משרת ענבים לא
ישתה וענבים לחים ויבשים לא יאכל כל ימי
נזרו מכל אשר יעשה מגפן היין מחרצנים ועד
זג לא יאכל כל ימי נדרו נזרו תער לא יעבר על
ראשו עד מלאת הימם אשר יזיר ליהוה קדש
יהיה גדל פרע שער ראשו כל ימי הזירו ליהוה
על נפש מת לא יבא לאביו ולאמו לאחיו ולאחתו

Figure 1. Modern Torah scroll. The end of Numbers 5 and the beginning of Numbers 6. Photo: Dov Berger.

normative rabbinic Torah scroll (see the famous conversation on this topic between Moses and God on *b. Menahot* 29b; and fig. 1). Modern scholars attribute these marks to later rabbinic scribal communities, but the Rabbis understand this entire project to be concurrent with Revelation: the text was delivered as is.

If that is the case, how then does one explain instances in which words seem to be misspelled? Or repeated? Or contradictory? On several occasions throughout this book, we discuss instances in which the Rabbis attempt to find meaning in various biblical texts. But here we grapple with an important issue: if God intended every letter to be written in the exact sequence in which it appears in the Torah scroll, that means that there is a reason why one text follows another. Each letter, word, verse, paragraph, chapter, and book is organized with a divine intentionality, which must be uncovered. And the process for that recovery is via *midrash* (see Sommer 2012, 64–69).

An excellent example of this interpretative process relates to rabbinic exposition of the relationship between Numbers 5 and 6. Numbers 5 spells out the biblical ritual by which a jealous husband accuses his wife of adultery (the *sotah*, Hebrew for "suspected adulteress"; discussed in detail in chapter 4), despite his lack of evidence that any transgression occurred. Immediately following this narrative, Numbers 6 examines the *nazir*, a layperson who voluntarily vows to abstain from certain practices, one of which is drinking any intoxicant, especially wine. (The most famous *nazir* in the Hebrew Bible is Samson, whose story can be found in Judges 13–16.) Why do these two texts appear side by side? Keeping in mind the rabbinic principle that God is an intentional and infallible editor, there must be something that can be learned from this organization. So what is that lesson? Over the course of several pages, *Numbers Rabbah* 10:1–4 answers this question. While I cannot cover the entirety of this text (which, in typical rabbinic style, includes several asides and additional, semi-related conversation), I focus here on four instances in which Numbers 5 and 6 are connected via one beverage: wine.

Throughout the various attempts to connect these two passages, a theme emerges: wine leads to transgressions; transgressions are particularly sexual in nature; the *nazir* abstains from wine; and therefore, these texts should be read together as suggesting that too much wine leads to sexual sin. To offer a concise and concrete example of this logic:

> Another interpretation: Just as the *nazir* is separated from wine, so too I separate the *sotah* from the rest of women on account of wickedness. (*Numbers Rabbah* 10:1)

The first two words of this text—"Another interpretation" (literally, "another word/matter"; Hebrew *davar aher*)—is a common rabbinic phrase in *midrashic* literature that signals an important technique:

the Rabbis report various interpretations, some of which might even contradict one another. As is discussed in chapter 1, the Rabbis are interested in spirited, multifaceted dialogue rather than humdrum, monolithic monologue. Therefore, they regularly offer a variety of viewpoints on a single topic, one after another, rarely with any commentary indicating a preference for any particular opinion. Often, a new interpretation is prefaced simply with the terse introduction: "Another interpretation."

In this interpretation, Numbers 5 and 6 combine to teach a singular lesson. Just as the *nazir* takes a vow to separate from wine, so too does God (= "I") separate the *sotah* from the rest of women. Just as wine intoxicates the sober mind, so too the (suspected) adulteress leads faithful wives astray. Separation from wickedness is the overarching lesson. And wine, it would seem, is the beverage drunk while sliding down the slippery slope towards sin. For this reason, God placed Numbers 5 and 6 beside one another.

This lesson gets reiterated several times throughout *Numbers Rabbah* 10:2–4. For example, after connecting wine to adultery, the following conclusion is reached:

> Thus we learn that wine leads to whoring. And therefore, The Holy One Blessed be He wrote in the Torah the section about the *nazir* after the section about the *sotah*, so that a man should not act like an adulterer and adulteress act, who drink wine and disgrace themselves; but rather, the one who is afraid of sin should separate himself from wine. Therefore, it is said: "When either a man or a woman clearly [utter a vow, the vow of the *nazir*, to set themself apart for the Lord ...]" [Numbers 6:2]. (*Numbers Rabbah* 10:2)

Too much wine can lead to sexual impropriety (on the gendering of "whoring," see chapter 4). To caution Jews, God (referred to by the common rabbinic title of "The Holy One Blessed be He") placed the biblical section (Hebrew *parshah*) concerning the *sotah* prior to that of the *nazir*. This act of divine editorship serves as a moral lesson, instructing those who fear sin to "separate" (Hebrew *yazir*, from the same root as *nazir*) themselves from wine. After all, "wine leads to whoring."

Lest this point was unclear, the very next section of *Numbers Rabbah* concludes similarly:

> Thus we learn that wherever there is wine, there is *'ervah*. And therefore, The Holy One Blessed be He wrote the section about the *nazir* after the section about the *sotah*, because wine leads to *'ervah*. And therefore, a man should separate himself from [wine], so that it should not lead him into error. And therefore, it is said: "When either a man or a woman clearly [utter a vow, the vow of the *nazir*, to set themself apart for the Lord ...]" etc. [Numbers 6:2]. (*Numbers Rabbah* 10:3)

Rabbinic texts can get repetitive: a good point is often worth making twice. While this passage repeats the previous pericope almost word for word, the concern here is that wine leads to *'ervah*: that is, to nakedness (particularly "genital nakedness"; see Neis 2013, 93) and, relatedly, to sexual transgression. The naked body imagined is almost always female; and the sexual transgressions are often biblically forbidden sexual relations, such as incest or prohibited sexual partners (e.g., Leviticus 18:18 prohibits having intercourse with a woman and then "uncovering the nakedness" [Hebrew *'ervatah*] of her sister). Divine editorship therefore instructs that wine leads to nudity and sexual transgression.

If a good point is worth making twice, then it is worth making three times. In the next section of *Numbers Rabbah*, we encounter the same basic argument, albeit woven into a much richer interpretive fabric:

> "And I have not the understanding of a man [Hebrew *'adam*]" [Proverbs 30:2]. This [refers] to the first man [Hebrew *'adam*], because through the wine that he drank, the world was cursed on his account. For Rabbi Avin said: Eve mixed wine for Adam [Hebrew *'adam*] and he drank; as it is said: "And when the woman saw [Hebrew *va-tere'*] that the tree was good for eating" [Genesis 3:6], and it is written: "Do not look [Hebrew *'al tere'*] at wine when it glows red, etc." [Proverbs 23:31]. "And I have not learned wisdom..." [Proverbs 30:3]—from the wisdom of the Torah, because in every place that wine is written in the Torah, it makes a mark. "... or have knowledge of the Holy One" [Proverbs 30:3]: If one wants to sanctify himself so that he does not stumble into sin by whoring, he should separate himself from wine, but

I disgraced myself by whoring. "... or have knowledge of the Holy One" [Proverbs 30:3]: therefore, it is said: [The Holy One Blessed be He wrote] the section about the *nazir* after [the section about the] *sotah*. (*Numbers Rabbah* 10:4)

We begin with a citation from the book of Proverbs, which is read in two ways. First, this passage (and the other citations of Proverbs below) highlights the limits of human knowledge. Second, the word for "man" (Hebrew *'adam*, which can also mean more broadly "humanity") is read as referring to the primordial man, Adam (Hebrew *'adam*). At the very beginning of history, wine led to the entire world being cursed. And how do we know this? After all, there is no mention of wine in the biblical account of Garden of Eden! According to Rabbi Avin, however, not only was there wine there, but Eve mixed Adam's wine! (On mixing wine, see chapter 9.)

What proof does Rabbi Avin have for this assertion? Rabbi Avin links two biblical verses based on a shared word. Once linked, the context or content of one verse is understood to shed light on the other verse. The analogy (Hebrew *gezerah shavah*; see Lieberman 1994, 58–68; Yadin 2004, 82–83) is one of the basic rabbinic hermeneutic principles (in general, see Strack and Stemberger 1996, 15–30). Remember that the biblical author is presumed to be divine, and therefore chose each word for specific reasons (note the plural here, as much can be learned from each word). So when God says in Genesis 3:6 that, "the woman saw [Hebrew *va-tere'*] that the tree was good for eating," the verb for Eve's gaze was intentional (on the rabbinic gaze, see Neis 2013). One can then skip ahead to Proverbs 23:21 and see that the same verb for sight is used: "Do not look [Hebrew *'al tere'*] at wine when it glows red, etc." (translations of Proverbs throughout this chapter are informed by Fox 2009). In Proverbs 23:21, wine is the subject of the gaze; and therefore, via the rabbinic hermeneutic principle of analogy, Eve in Genesis 3:6 "saw" wine. Now that we know that Eve gazes upon wine, all of the concerns associated with wine can be read into our text—especially those associated with an unquenchable appetite for sex. Therefore, when

Eve mixes wine for Adam, it can be read in the sense of Eve using sexuality to seduce Adam, thereby leading him down a dissolute path. Hence, "through the wine that he drank, the world was cursed on his account."

Read in light of this analogy, the lesson about wine and sexual transgression should have been obvious to the reader. But it clearly was not. Therefore, the Torah had to keep repeating this lesson. And how do we know this? According to Proverbs 30:3: "And I have not learned wisdom." No matter how many times this lesson was told, it was never learned. The wisdom of the Torah kept reminding its readers by making sure that in every instance in which wine appears in the Torah, it left an indelible mark—like a scarlet *A*—to demonstrate the evils that befall one who drinks too much wine.

The second half of Proverbs 30:3, "or have knowledge of the Holy One," further reminds its readers that they have continually failed to grasp this lesson. They should have known to separate themselves from wine in order not to stumble into sin (the Hebrew verb here, *yikashel*, can mean either stumble or lead to sin, so I have tried to convey both meanings simultaneously). But they did not learn their lesson. Instead, they disgraced themselves by whoring. They needed yet another reminder. To impart this lesson one more time, the divine editor placed Numbers 6 immediately following Numbers 5.

CONTRADICTING TEXTS: INSULTS, WINE, AND SPONTANEOUS HUMAN COMBUSTION

If God composed the Torah in an intentional manner, then when texts contradict one another, there must be a way to resolve that tension. And/or such contradictions must offer a riddle that, once solved, will unlock deeper meanings and additional lessons. Otherwise, the entire house of cards would collapse and nothing would mean anything.

A fascinating example of this general principle in action is encountered in a text that begins with the development of the biblical canon—

that is, the normative and authoritative edition of the Hebrew Bible—
and ends with two instances of spontaneous human combustion.

> And also the Book of Proverbs [the sages] wanted to suppress, for its statements contradict one another. And why did they not suppress it? They said: Did we not study the book of Ecclesiastes and find resolutions [to its contradictory statements]? Here too, let us study.
>
> And which of its statements contradict one another? It is written: "Do not answer a fool according to his folly" [Proverbs 26:4]; but [in the next verse] it is written: "Answer a fool according to his folly" [Proverbs 26:5].
>
> There is no difficulty. This concerns words of Torah, and that concerns general matters.
>
> It is like when a certain man came before Rabbi and said to him: Your wife is my wife, and your children are my children. [Rabbi] said to him: Would you like to drink a cup of wine? He drank and burst [i.e., explodes, or spontaneously combusts].
>
> [Similarly,] a certain man came before Rabbi Hiyya and said to him: Your mother is my wife, and you are my son. [Rabbi Hiyya] said to him: Would you like to drink a cup of wine? He drank and burst. (*b. Shabbat* 30b)

As the opening indicates, this text appears in the middle of a larger rabbinic passage (Aramaic *sugya'*) that debates whether to suppress—that is, to declare noncanonical—certain biblical books. The reason for potentially suppressing such works is that they feature contradictory statements. However, the Rabbis were able to resolve these contradictions to their own satisfaction; and hence, both Ecclesiastes and Proverbs become canonical.

The question of whether to canonize these books points to an interesting concern (on this process in general, see Satlow 2014). The Torah is understood to be divinely authored and edited. The rest of the Hebrew Bible (the sections known as the Prophets and the Writings) gains its authority by means of being declared canonical by the Rabbis. Once a book acquires this status, it can be used to interpret other texts and to offer support as a proof text. For example, Genesis is canonical because God declared it so; Proverbs is canonical because the Rabbis declared it so. But notice that earlier in this chapter, Genesis 3:6 and

Proverbs 23:31 were analogically connected via the same Hebrew verb for sight. As canonical books, they can be interpreted together. And, in that case, God was presumed to know that Proverbs would be canonized using that precise verb in that precise context, which is why that same verb appears in Genesis and allows for the rabbinic interpretation via analogy.

But the first step to canonization in the case of Proverbs was to show that its contradictions were not really contradictions. Rather, they were riddles to be solved and whose solutions offered new knowledge. Such is the case with Proverbs 26:4–5, which reads in full:

> Do not answer a fool according to his folly, lest you become just like him.
> Answer a fool according to his folly, lest he be wise in his own eyes.

Should I answer the fool or not? The answer, as we are learning to expect, is: it depends. Our first clue to this answer is the common rabbinic phrase "There is no difficulty" (Aramaic *la' qashya'*), which indicates that two texts/opinions do not contradict each other. Sometimes this is because they refer to different situations; in other cases, this is because one text follows the ruling of one authority, and the other follows the ruling of another authority. Either way, it signals that an apparent contradiction can be resolved.

In the present case, the resolution offered is that: "This concerns words of Torah, and that concerns general matters." This wording is potentially confusing. But rather than resolve that confusion in my translation, I wanted to convey the complexities the text presents. A more lucid translation would have been: "This [latter verse, that is Proverbs 26:5] concerns words of Torah, and that [former verse, that is Proverbs 26:4] concerns general matters." Therefore, if the fool is pontificating on words of Torah, you should answer him, "lest he be wise in his own eyes." But if the fool is pontificating on general, not-anywhere-near-as-important-as-Torah matters, then you should not answer him, "lest you become just like him." The verses do not contradict because they each refer to a different situation. In fact, not only do they not contradict, but they complement one another in order to provide complete guidelines for dealing with a fool.

Next, two examples of dealing with a non-Torah-talking fool are provided (*b. Shabbat* 30b also goes on to offer examples of interacting with a Torah-talking fool, but I omit discussion of those examples because no wine is involved). In each case, a non-Torah-talking fool walks up to a Rabbi and insults his lineage: in the first case, he claims to have had an affair with Rabbi's wife, so that his wife committed adultery and his children are not his own; in the second case, he claims to have had an affair with Rabbi Hiyya's mother and that he is actually Rabbi Hiyya's father. By claiming to have had an affair with the wife/mother of a Rabbi, the non-Torah-talking fool alleges, not only that he has committed adultery, but that he has fathered the wife/mother's children. Any child that results from such an encounter is considered a *mamzer* (Hebrew plural *mamzerim*). Note that this is not a child born out of wedlock (sometimes pejoratively called a "bastard"), but the product of an adulterous or incestuous sexual encounter. "A full Jew in every other way, a *mamzer* (male or female) was forbidden from marrying another Jew who was not a *mamzer*" (Satlow 2006, 183). Therefore, Rabbi's children and Rabbi Hiyya himself would be forever stigmatized in regard to rabbinic marriage.

Imagine how you might react in this case. A fool waltzes up to you, insults your mother or partner, and then claims that you or your children are *mamzerim*. I pity the fool who does so. With that mental image in mind, contrast how Rabbi and Rabbi Hiyya react: they offer the fool a glass of wine. Of all the responses you might have expected, I would wager that that was not even in the top 100. But remember Proverbs 26:4: "Do not answer a fool according to his folly, lest you become just like him." And remember that this is understood to refer to the non-Torah-talking fool, which is the exact type of fool standing before us. Any verbal response would have been to answer a fool according to his folly, so instead they offer him a glass of wine. He accepts the drink and takes a sip. He then explodes. What goes without saying is that these two instances of spontaneous human combustion are divine retribution. In not responding to their respective non-Torah-talking fools, Rabbi and Rabbi Hiyya leave it to God to deal with the fool. Rabbi and Rabbi Hiyya act in accordance with normative rabbinic law (Hebrew *halakhah*). The non-Torah-talking fools do not. Their combined actions lead to the explosive conclusion in which biblical contradictions are resolved and justice is served.

"IT GOES DOWN SMOOTHLY": WINE AND TEMPTATION

Although the Hebrew Bible cannot contradict itself, a single verse can still teach multiple lessons. Of course, that does not stop Rabbis from debating which is *the* "correct" interpretation of a given verse—even while, at the same time, there is an often tacit acknowledgment that there can be multiple, nonexclusionary, "correct" interpretations (and, hence, potentially divergent rulings based upon these multiple interpretations). Scholars often summarize this trend towards legal pluralism by citing the famous rabbinic phrase: "These and these are the words of the living God" (*y. Yevamot* 1:6, 3b; *b. Eruvin* 13b; *b. Gittin* 6b; and, on legal pluralism, see Hidary 2010).

We encounter an interesting example of this phenomenon in a text that opens by quoting a verse already familiar to us:

> "[Do not look at wine when it glows red,] when it gives its gleam in the cup, when it goes down smoothly" [Proverbs 23:31].
> Rabbi Ami and Rabbi Assi [debated the interpretation of this verse].
> One said: Whoever sets his eye in his cup, all *'arayot* appear to him like a plain.
> And one said: Whoever sets his eye in his cup, the entire world appears to him like a plain. (*b. Yoma* 74b–75a)

I translate Proverbs 23:31 initially based on its biblical context, so as to throw into relief the rabbinic interpretative activity that follows. Though the biblical context of the "folly of drunkenness" (Fox 2009,

740) pervades the rabbinic exposition of this verse, the two Rabbis cited derive additional information from its wording.

After quoting Proverbs 23:31, we learn that two Rabbis debated the meaning of this biblical drinking proverb. Accomplished scholars and friends, Rabbi Ami and Rabbi Assi were referred to by honorifics such as "the distinguished priests of the Land of Israel" (*b. Gittin* 59b) and "the judges of the Land of Israel" (*b. Sanhedrin* 17b). Yet, while we learn that these two august amiable authorities debated the meaning of this verse (along with several other scriptural passages; see *b. Yoma* 74b–75a), we are not told explicitly who gave which interpretation. Rather, the text simply notes, "one said" one interpretation, and "one said" the other.

According to the first interpretation, Proverbs 23:31 teaches that, "Whoever sets his eye in his cup, all *'arayot* appear to him like a plain." How is this meaning derived? In Proverbs 23:31, the phrase, "when it gives its gleam in the cup" could also be translated as: "when he sets his eye in his cup" (see Fox 2009, 741). Reading the text the latter way explains the opening clause of the Rabbi's interpretation ("Whoever sets his eye in his cup …"). Next, the author relies on the common *midrashic* practice of the pun. First, in the phrase "like a plain," the words "plain" (Hebrew *mishor*) and "smoothly" (Hebrew *meysharim*) are punned; and second, the word for "smoothly" (Hebrew *meysharim*) commonly refers to "rectitude" or "upright path" in Proverbs (see Fox 2009, 741). The first pun introduces the notion of the drunk man seeing certain things as a smooth plain. The second pun turns this level plain into a slippery slope, sliding from the upright path down into the depths of depravity. This is where *'arayot* comes into focus. *'Arayot*, the plural of *'ervah*, refers to forbidden sexual relations, especially adultery (see Satlow 1995, 140). Therefore, the intoxicated man who focuses on the wine in his cup, rather than on walking on the upright path of moral rectitude, encounters no obstacle as he stumbles down a path descending to sexual transgression.

The second interpretation draws on many of the same readings. In fact, the first interpretation could be included in the second, since the intoxicated man now sees the entire world as a smooth plain, upon which he can stumble unobstructed towards whatever illicit desire he fancies. Rashi, a medieval commentator and reputed winemaker, understands this second interpretation to refer to the fact that "other people's money appears permitted to him" (Rashi on *b. Yoma* 75a)—meaning that the drunk man has no moral compunction against theft. There is, however, no reason to narrow this second interpretation just to the realm of theft or sexual transgression; rather, it seems more general than broad: the intoxicated man who focuses on the wine in his cup, rather than on walking on the upright path of moral rectitude, encounters no obstacle in his path as he stumbles down a spiral of sordid transgression.

In the end, these two readings represent a difference of degree more than of kind. Though there are many instances in which a greater interpretive variance is found, the same general principle holds: multiple correct opinions can be offered, and there is not necessarily a need to resolve them into a single, correct opinion. Furthermore, these two readings show another *midrashic* trend, wherein debate about interpretation leads to a larger commentary on the slippery slope from tippling to temptation to transgression.

CUP OR POCKET? DIRTY MISSPELLINGS AND CLEAN LANGUAGE

We have learned that the Rabbis believe that: (a) the Hebrew Bible is divinely authored and edited, so every word, phrase, and paragraph is intentional, meaningful, and informative; and (b) multiple precise interpretations can be derived from any word, phrase, or paragraph. A fascinating intersection of these two concepts relates to instances where the Rabbis acknowledge a grammatical or spelling error in the written text of the Torah, and then develop a tradition to account for it.

Once the biblical text is understood to be a divine text, a problem arises: how does one deal with instances in which a word is misspelled or grammatical rules are violated? If a text is written by a person of flesh and blood (a common rabbinic term for a human), then the answer is simple: human error. But when the author is God, it is not so simple. In order to deal with such instances, a practice developed known as *qere* and *ketiv*, which is well summarized by the two Aramaic words that form its title, *qere* ("that which is read") and *ketiv* ("that which is written"). This practice therefore results in the biblical text written (*ketiv*) on a Torah scroll remaining in its present form, while a separate tradition records how a given word is read (*qere*) when a given Torah portion is read aloud.

This approach has two interrelated advantages. First, it preserves the text "as is," while still correcting apparent errors. Second, the written and read texts are placed side by side, allowing for interpretation based on both the "correct" and "incorrect" text. Taken together, they reinforce the basic presumption of divine authorship and editorship. God *intentionally* misspells words, makes grammar mistakes, and so on. In doing so, God creates both the *qere* and *ketiv*. Therefore, additional interpretations are divinely authorized based on both the "mistake" *and* the "correction." Every "mistake" is really an opportunity.

A great example of *qere* and *ketiv* involves a variant of the interpretative tradition of Proverbs 23:31, discussed throughout this chapter. We learn:

> "[Do not look at wine when it glows red,] when it gives its gleam *ba-kis*, [when it goes down smoothly]" [Proverbs 23:31].
> "*Ba-kis*" is written (Aramaic *ketiv*), [which teaches that] through the cup (Hebrew *ba-kos*) he sets his eye in the "pocket" (Hebrew *ba-kis*). Torah spoke in a euphemism in order to teach that [the intoxicated man] will engage in *'ervah*. (*Numbers Rabbah* 10:2; cf. *Leviticus Rabbah* 12:1)

The *ketiv* of Proverbs 23:31 is *ba-kis*, meaning "in the pocket." However, based on context, clearly the "correct" version should be *ba-kos*, meaning "in the cup." These two words differ only in their third letter. In the Hebrew alphabet script, the third letter of the word *ba-kis* is a *yud* (י), which if drawn just a little longer vertically becomes a *vav* (ו), the third letter of the word *ba-kos*. In English, you could compare this to the difference between a lowercase *i* and a lowercase *j*. This is a common scribal error and the "fix" is obvious. For this reason, *ba-kos* becomes the *qere* and is reflected in standard printings of the Masoretic text.

Although modern scholars may refer to this as "a common scribal error" (as I just did), for the Rabbis, the *qere* and *ketiv* tradition allows for additional, divinely authorized interpretation. God actively chose to misspell this word, so it must offer deeper insight. The intoxicated man "sets his eye in the pocket"—and "pocket" is a euphemism for female genitalia. Note that the phrase used here for "euphemism" literally means "clean language" (Hebrew *lashon naqiy*). "Torah [i.e., God] spoke" in clean language in order to teach a dirty lesson: once again, we learn that wine leads to *'ervah*, that is, to nakedness (particularly "genital nakedness"; see Neis 2013, 93) and, relatedly, to sexual transgression.

Elsewhere, the Rabbis spell out traditions of employing euphemism for the reading of certain texts that are perceived as obscene (see *b. Megillah* 25b), suggesting that this is not an isolated case. Furthermore, the notion that this particular *qere* and *ketiv* tradition offers a clean euphemism for a dirty word is supported by the discussion in the previous section, above. Remember that, in regard to *b. Yoma* 74b–75a, two puns led to the level plain becoming catawampus; as a result, the moral high ground tilted downward into a slippery slope toward depravity. And what was at the bottom of this slope? *'Arayot*, the plural of *'ervah*. The connection between *'arayot* and *'ervah* resulted from the following statement: "Whoever sets his eye in his cup, all *'arayot* appear to him like a plain." Now, read that same line, substituting the *qere* for the *ketiv*: "Whoever sets his eye in his 'pocket,' all *'arayot* appear to him like a plain." Therefore, this euphemism might lurk tacitly in the background. Additionally, "in his pocket" might explain Rashi's reading of the second interpretation that, "other people's money appears permitted to him" (Rashi on *b. Yoma* 75a). The pocket is a common place to deposit money, so the *ketiv* of *ba-kis* might have primed Rashi to think about money. Sometimes a pocket is a just a pocket.

The tradition of *qere* and *ketiv* provides yet another interpretive practice in which the Rabbis square the circle of the biblical text. In doing so, they show how the Hebrew Bible is perfectly imperfect.

"BLESSINGS OF THE BREASTS": BREASTFEEDING AS DIVINE MIRACLE

Genesis 49:25 speaks of the blessings bestowed by *Shaddai*, a common name for God. These blessings include "blessings of the breasts" (Hebrew *birkat shadai'im*). This clever pun in biblical Hebrew between God (Hebrew *shaddai*) and breasts (Hebrew *shadai'im*) points to an association that appears elsewhere in rabbinic texts: namely, the fact that the elixir of life for all infants (breast milk) and the source of *all* life have the same origin, God. And given this association, the miraculous appearance of breast milk is occasionally used by the Rabbis to address potential issues or ambiguities in the biblical text. Therefore, these conversations can serve as case studies of many of the hermeneutical principles discussed throughout this chapter.

The first example relates to the biblical Matriarch Sarah. As the wife of the Patriarch Abraham, Sarah led an adventurous and complicated life, including twice being passed off as Abraham's sister instead of his spouse (see Genesis 20 and 26). One adventure eluded her, however: namely, motherhood. But then, ten years short of her hundredth birthday, God decided to fulfill a divine promise made to Abraham (see Genesis 17:15–22, in which God promises that Sarah will have a son named Isaac). The Rabbis realize that the idea of a ninety-year-old first-time mother strains credulity, which informs the following *midrash*:

> "And [Sarah] said: Who would have said to Abraham that Sarah would nurse children?!" [Genesis 21:7].
>
> How many "children" did Sarah nurse? Rabbi Levi said: On the day that Abraham weaned Isaac, his son, he made a grand feast [see Genesis 21:8]. All the people of the world gossiped amongst themselves, saying: Have you

seen that old man and old woman who brought a foundling from the market and say, "He is our son!" And not only that, but they make a grand party in order to bolster their claim!

What did Abraham our Patriarch do? He went and invited all of the great men of the generation, and Sarah our Matriarch invited their wives. And every wife brought her child with her, but did not bring her wet nurse. And a miracle occurred with regard to Sarah our Matriarch, and her breasts opened up like two fountains and she nursed all of them. (*b. Bava Metzi'a* 87a; for parallels and discussion, see Haskell 2012, 17–27; Rosenblum 2016, 176–77)

The generative question that this *midrash* seeks to answer is: why does Sarah talk of nursing "children" (Hebrew *banim*)—in the plural—when she, in fact, has only borne Isaac, that is *a single child?*. Grammatically, the answer is actually fairly straightforward: in biblical Hebrew, plurals often simply indicate species (Sarna 1989, 146). The Rabbis, however, believe that the Hebrew Bible was composed by God and that every word—even if seemingly enigmatic, unclear, or misspelled—is intentionally written as such, and therefore encodes potentially profound meaning. A plural noun where a singular noun is expected marks this text for interpretation (see Yadin 2004, 48–79), and to explain it, the Rabbis turn to the verse that immediately follows, which records Abraham organizing a grand feast (Hebrew *mishteh gadol*, literally, "big drinking party") to celebrate Isaac's weaning (Genesis 21:8). They report what they believe to have occurred on that day. As the festivities began, everyone was incredulous that old Abraham and old Sarah could actually be Isaac's biological parents, and people presumed that Abraham and Sarah had found an abandoned baby in the market and are passing it off as their own child. In order to prove the doubters wrong, Abraham and Sarah invite them all to the weaning party.

At the weaning party, two miracles occur. The first miracle is that although all the mothers rely on wet nurses, they forget to bring them to the *mishteh gadol*. I consider this a miracle because, had the mothers either breastfed their own children or thought to bring along their wet nurses to do so, the second miracle could not have occurred. The second miracle is that just when Sarah is preparing to wean baby Isaac—that is, to stop producing breast milk—her body suddenly gushes it, enabling her to feed everyone's offspring. This embodies Sarah's motherhood. After all, if she can nurse everyone's babies, could she not conceive, give birth to, and feed her own son? For the Rabbis, then, the plural "children" in Genesis 21:7 contains this entire story. "Child" would not tell the whole story, which is why God wrote "children."

Another instance in which the Rabbis use the miraculous appearance of breast milk in order to address a potential issue or ambiguity in the biblical text is in regard to a male character in the Hebrew Bible, Mordecai, the cousin of Esther, hero of the book of Esther and the story of Purim (on beverages in the celebration of this holiday, see chapter 6). In Esther 2:7, we learn that Mordecai raised Esther after she was orphaned. This will be an important detail, but it is not this verse that generates the *midrash* of Mordecai breastfeeding. Rather, it is because, in Esther 2:5, Mordecai is referred to using the past tense of the "to be" verb (Hebrew *hayah*): "A Jewish man *was* (Hebrew *hayah*) in the capital city Shushan, whose name was Mordecai..." In its context, this grammatical detail does not seem important. A Jewish man *was* a resident of Shushan, that is, Susa, the capital of the Persian Empire. So what? We turn to *Genesis Rabbah* 30:8 to find out:

> Rabbis said: Whoever it is said in regard to him "he was" (Hebrew *hayah*) fed and sustained.
>
> Noah fed and sustained [the inhabitants of the ark] all twelve months, as it is said: "And you, take for yourself from all food [that is eaten and store it away, and it will be food for you and for them]" [Genesis 6:21].
>
> Joseph fed and sustained, [as it is said]: "Joseph sustained [his father, and his brothers, and all his father's household ...]" [Genesis. 47:7]
>
> Moses fed and sustained [the Israelites while they wandered] all forty years in the desert.
>
> Job fed and sustained, [as it is said]: "Or have I eaten my morsel myself alone, [and the orphan ate none of it]" [Job 31:17]—did not the orphan eat from it?!
>
> But indeed did Mordecai feed and sustain? Rabbi Yudan said: One time, he made the rounds of all the wet nurses, but could not find a wet nurse for

Esther, so he nursed her himself. Rabbi Berekiah and Rabbi Abbahu in the name of Rabbi Eliezer [said]: Milk came to him and he nursed her.

When Rabbi Abbahu expounded upon this, his audience laughed. He said to them: But is there not a mishnah [see *m. Makhshirin* 6:7]: "Rabbi Shimon ben Eliezer says: The milk of a male is pure."

According to rabbinic tradition, if a man "was" (Hebrew *hayah*) in the Hebrew Bible, then he "fed and sustained" others. To support this claim, several examples are provided (references to the appropriate "was" verse for each character were provided earlier in *Genesis Rabbah* 30:8). Noah and Joseph have explicit verses. However, notice what is omitted: the important part of the verse, that is, the section that directly indicates that they fed and sustained other people. This is a common feature of rabbinic literature, wherein the citation of a biblical proof text includes only a partial quotation of the verse and often not the relevant part of the verse. This is why I include the rest of the biblical verse in square brackets above. The Rabbis expect their audience to have memorized the Hebrew Bible and therefore presume that hearing the first half of a verse will jog their audiences' memory, allowing them to fill in the textual gap. This same presumed knowledge allows them to not quote a verse in regard to Moses. After all, anyone who has read Exodus knows that Moses spent significant time in the desert making sure that the Israelites were fed. The verse from Job is a little more complicated, but it is read to prove their general point: Job, like Noah, Joseph, and Moses, fed other people and hence all are referred to using "was" in the Hebrew Bible.

We are left now with Mordecai. We know that he is a "was" man, but how do we know that he "fed and sustained"? A rabbinic legend is told in which Mordecai went in search of a wet nurse for the infant Esther. Unable to locate one, Mordecai nurses her himself. (The grammar of this passage makes a subtle point, as "he nursed her himself" is literally, "he was [Hebrew *hayah*] her nurse.") Though Mordecai's lactation is reported in a matter-of-fact manner, there needs to be further discussion for obvious reasons. After all, it is not every day that a man lactates and nurses an infant. Hence, a rabbinic tradition adds that Mordecai's milk suddenly came in and he nursed her. However, that comment might serve to clarify that this was not a "one-time" event, as Rabbi Yudan's comments seem to indicate ("One time, he ..."); rather, Mordecai continuously "fed and sustained" Esther, and he never hired a wet nurse. Therefore, another clarification is required. Rabbi Abbahu reports that people used to laugh when he taught this tradition, but he would remind them that there is indeed a mishnah that unambiguously states that male breast milk is pure (see Bregman 2017; Rosenblum 2016, 154–55). In fact, in the Mishnah tractate that reports this information, we only learn about female breast milk *after* we learn about the significantly less common male breast milk (see *m. Makhshirin* 6:7–8). Since it is plausible, Rabbi Abbahu argues, the story is not laughable.

Taken together, these two texts illustrate how the Rabbis use accounts of miraculous breastfeeding as a means of biblical interpretation (cf. Rosenblum 2016, 175–78). Needless to say, however, rabbinic literature also uses other stories and creative interpretations to address ambiguities in the biblical text—see, for example, the famous story about Abraham smashing the idols in his father's idol shop in *Genesis Rabbah* 38:13.

TORAH BRIGHTENS THE FACE

Midrash is the process through which the complex details of God's commandments are analyzed and comprehended, assuring compliance with *halakhah*. But that does not mean that it has to be drudgery. In fact, for the Rabbis, this interpretive activity is more hobby than homework. While interpreting Torah is serious business, it is also serious fun.

Lest the reader depart from this chapter thinking that this labor of love is more labor than love, let us examine a text in which this issue comes to the forefront:

> Rabbi Yudah bey Rabbi Ilai drank the four cups of Passover night, and bandaged his head until the Festival [of Shavuot].

A certain matron saw him with his face lit up. She said to him: Old man, old man. You are one of three things: either you are a wine drinker; or you are a lender on interest; or you are a pig breeder.

He said to her: May that woman's breath expire! I am none of these three things! Rather, my learning is within me; for it is written: "The wisdom of a person brightens his face" [Ecclesiastes 8:1]. (*y. Pesahim* 10:1, 37c)

Our *sugya'* opens with an instance of excessive drinking. We learn that Rabbi Yudah bey Rabbi Ilai drank the four cups of wine required for the celebration of Passover (on this practice, see chapter 6). Perhaps unaccustomed to drinking this much wine, he ends up with a headache (which is why he bandaged his head), a symptom likely caused by dehydration. But this is not just any headache (on headaches in rabbinic literature, see Preuss 2004, 304–5); this post-Passover headache persists for fifty days—that is, the length of time between Passover and Shavuot. Quite a hangover!

The detail of Rabbi Yudah bey Rabbi Ilai drinking wine partly cues the tale that follows. The other association that generates this story is the reference to Shavuot ("Weeks" in Hebrew; also known as Pentecost ["Fiftieth Day" in Greek]), a biblical festival later associated with the divine revelation of the Torah at Mount Sinai (e.g., *b. Shabbat* 86b; *b. Pesahim* 68b). Therefore, the Festival of Shavuot necessarily gestures towards the importance of Torah and Torah knowledge.

The tale that follows proved quite popular in rabbinic literature, with versions appearing twice more in the Jerusalem Talmud (*y. Shabbat* 8:1, 11a; *y. Sheqalim* 3:2, 47c) and once in the Babylonian Talmud (*b. Nedarim* 49b), as well as in other rabbinic collections. In our present version, a certain matron (Aramaic *matronah*), that is to say, a high-status non-Jewish woman, encounters Rabbi Yudah bey Rabbi Ilai with his face aglow. She greets him by referring to him as "old man" (Aramaic *saba'*), a term that can also mean "Tanna." Not coincidentally, Rabbi Yudah bey Rabbi Ilai is indeed a card-carrying member of the earliest group of rabbis, the Tannaim.

Upon gazing at this old man/Tanna, the matron concludes that his face can only be lit up for one of three reasons, and none of them are good. First, because he is a wine drinker. By this, the matron implies that he is a drunkard, a condition of unrestrained alcohol addiction of which the Rabbis disapprove (see chapter 9). Second, because he lends at interest. Acts of usury are strongly condemned in both biblical (e.g., Exodus 22:25; Leviticus 25:36) and rabbinic literature. For example, elsewhere we learn that:

> [Usurers] declare the Torah a fraud and Moses a fool, and they say: "If Moses would have known how profitable we would be, he never would have written [the prohibitions against usury]!" (*t. Bava Metzi'a* 6:17)

Or, third, because he is a pig breeder. Not on only is eating pork biblically forbidden (Leviticus 11:7; Deuteronomy 14:8), but the Rabbis extend this taboo even to pig-breeding:

> [Jews] may not raise pigs anywhere. (*m. Bava Qamma* 7:7)

Whether outside the Land of Israel or in it, pigs can neither be eaten nor raised by Jews (on the context of this passage, see Berkowitz 2018, 132–38; and on how this affects modern law in the state of Israel, see Barak-Erez 2007). Regardless of which scenario applies—whether drunk on wine or excited by the high profit margins and fast cash made by engaging in biblically and rabbinically forbidden business—the matron believes that his lit-up face is a sign of his bad life choices.

While Rabbi Yudah bey Rabbi Ilai does not disagree that his face positively glows, for him it is a sign of his good life choices. After conjuring an end to the matron's breathing (an allusion to Ezekiel 37:9, according to Bokser 1994, 59n40), he denies being any "of these three things." Why, then, is his face aglow? Because "my learning is within me"—meaning that his frequent study of Torah has led to a deep knowledge of rabbinic traditions (on this translation, see Sokoloff 2002, 550). The biblical proof text reinforces this assertion. How do we know that, besides wine drinking, usury, and pig-breeding, Torah learning can light up one's face? Because it is written in Ecclesiastes 8:1: "The wisdom of a person brightens his face." For Rabbi Yudah bey Rabbi Ilai, it is Torah—and not wine—that brightens his face.

In the continuation of this *sugya'*, which I do not quote in full because of its lack of reference to beverages, Rabbi Yohanan's students remark on the bright face of Rabbi Abbahu. They believe his visible joy is because he "has found a treasure." Rabbi Yohanan replies, "Perhaps he has heard a new biblical interpretation?" and then inquires of Rabbi Abbahu, "What new biblical interpretation have you heard?" Rabbi Abbahu answers that he has heard "An old supplementary teaching" (Aramaic *tosefta' 'atiqta'*). It is not a "new" lesson that he has learned, but an "old" one, which is indeed a "treasure." For this reason Rabbi Abbahu's face lights up and the *sugya'* concludes: "And [Rabbi Yohanan] applied the scriptural verse to [Rabbi Abbahu]: 'The wisdom of a person brightens his face' [Ecclesiastes 8:1]."

Learning Torah is a joy. In the process of this joyous practice, Torah knowledge becomes embodied in those who learn it. The light of Torah then shines through them, illuminating their faces.

CONCLUSION

Viewed through the drinking glass, the main presumptions and principles that govern rabbinic biblical interpretation become visible. If—as the Rabbis presume—God is the author and editor of the Torah, then seeming contradictions, misspellings, ambiguities, and even the organizational logic of the texts themselves are really intentional opportunities to learn more. Torah is perfectly imperfect.

There is much more to *midrash* than can be discussed in this chapter, but these beverage-related texts have certainly imparted enough wisdom to brighten our faces, though likely not enough Torah water to quench our thirst.

SUGGESTED READINGS

Bakhos, Carol, ed. 2006. *Current Trends in the Study of Midrash.* New York: Brill.
———. 2009. "Recent Trends in the Study of Midrash and Rabbinic Narrative." *Currents in Biblical Research* 7/2: 272–93.
Bar-Asher Siegal, Michal. 2013. *Early Christian Monastic Literature and the Babylonian Talmud.* New York: Cambridge University Press.
Barak-Erez, Daphne. 2007. *Outlawed Pigs: Law, Religion, and Culture in Israel.* Madison: University of Wisconsin Press.
Belser, Julia Watts. 2015. *Power, Ethics, and Ecology in Jewish Late Antiquity: Rabbinic Responses to Drought and Disaster.* New York: Cambridge University Press.
Berkowitz, Beth A. 2018. *Animals and Animality in the Babylonian Talmud.* New York: Cambridge University Press.
Bokser, Baruch M., trans. 1994. *Yerushalmi Pesahim: The Talmud of the Land of Israel: A Preliminary Translation and Explanation.* Completed and edited by Lawrence H. Schiffman. Chicago: University of Chicago Press.
Boyarin, Daniel. 1994 [1990]. *Intertextuality and the Reading of Midrash.* Bloomington: Indiana University Press.
Bregman, Marc. 2017. "Mordecai Breastfed Esther: Male Lactation in Midrash, Medicine, and Myth." In *The Faces of Torah: Studies in the Texts and Contexts of Ancient Judaism in Honor of Steven Fraade,* ed. Michal Bar-Asher Siegal, Tzvi Novick, and Christine Hayes, 257–74. Göttingen: Vandenhoeck & Ruprecht.
Brumberg-Kraus, Jonathan. 2018. *Gastronomic Judaism as Culinary Midrash.* New York: Lexington Books.
Fox, Michael V. 2009. *Proverbs 10–31: A New Translation with Introduction and Commentary.* New Haven, CT: Yale University Press.
Fraade, Steven D. 1991. *From Tradition to Commentary: Torah and Its Interpretation in the Midrash Sifre to Deuteronomy.* Albany: State University of New York Press.
———. 2012. "Concepts of Scripture in Rabbinic Judaism: Oral Torah and Written Torah." In *Jewish Concepts of Scripture: A Comparative Introduction,* ed. Benjamin D. Sommer, 31–46. New York: New York University Press.
Haskell, Ellen Davina. 2012. *Suckling at My Mother's Breasts: The Image of a Nursing God in Jewish Mysticism.* Albany: State University of New York Press.
Hidary, Richard. 2010. *Dispute for the Sake of Heaven: Legal Pluralism in the Talmud.* Providence, RI: Brown Judaic Studies.

Kanarek, Jane L. 2014. *Biblical Narrative and the Formation of Rabbinic Law*. New York: Cambridge University Press.
Kugel, James L. 1990. *In Potiphar's House: The Interpretive Life of Biblical Texts*. New York: Harper Collins.
Lieberman, Saul. 1994 [1950]. *Hellenism in Jewish Palestine*. 2nd ed. Reprint. New York: Jewish Theological Seminary of America.
Neis, Rachel. 2013. *The Sense of Sight in Rabbinic Culture: Jewish Ways of Seeing in Late Antiquity*. New York: Cambridge University Press.
Preuss, Julius. 2004 [1978]. *Biblical and Talmudic Medicine*. Translated and edited by Fred Rosner. New York: Rowman & Littlefield.
Rosenblum, Jordan D. 2010. *Food and Identity in Early Rabbinic Judaism*. New York: Cambridge University Press.
———. 2016. "'Blessings of the Breasts': Breastfeeding in Rabbinic Literature." *Hebrew Union College Annual* 87: 147–79.
Sarna, Nahum M. 1989. *The JPS Torah Commentary: Genesis*. Philadelphia: Jewish Publication Society.
Satlow, Michael L. 1995. *Tasting the Dish: Rabbinic Rhetorics of Sexuality*. Atlanta, GA: Society of Biblical Literature.
———. 2006. *Creating Judaism: History, Tradition, Practice*. New York: Columbia University Press.
———. 2014. *How the Bible Became Holy*. New Haven, CT: Yale University Press.
Smith, Andrew F. 2013. *Drinking History: Fifteen Turning Points in the Making of American Beverages*. New York: Columbia University Press.
Sokoloff, Michael. 2002 [1990]. *A Dictionary of Jewish Palestinian Aramaic of the Byzantine Period*. 2nd ed. Baltimore: Johns Hopkins University Press.
Sommer, Benjamin D. 2012. "Concepts of Scriptural Language in Midrash." In *Jewish Concepts of Scripture: A Comparative Introduction*, 64–79. New York: New York University Press.
Strack, H. L., and Günter Stemberger. 1996. *Introduction to the Talmud and Midrash*. Translated and edited by Markus Bockmuehl. Minneapolis: Fortress Press.
Yadin, Azzan. 2004. *Scripture as Logos: Rabbi Ishmael and the Origins of Midrash*. Philadelphia: University of Pennsylvania Press.

THREE

Social Boundaries

Humans drink for a variety of reasons. We drink to survive. We drink to rejoice. We drink to remember. And we drink to forget. During all of these moments of drinking, we communicate a wide range of cultural assumptions when, for example, a modern hipster chooses to ironically drink a "low-brow" beer like Pabst Blue Ribbon, or a working-class East Coast American orders a black coffee from Dunkin' Donuts rather than a latte from Starbucks. These assumptions inform the lyrics of popular songs, from Willie Nelson singing about "whiskey for my men, and beer for my horses," to Snoop Dogg rapping about "sippin' on gin and juice." Cultures assign to drinks everything from gender (e.g., scotch is masculine and appletinis—and those who drink them—are feminine) to proper times of year (e.g., eggnog for Christmas, champagne for New Year's Eve). By looking into the contents of a glass, therefore, we can learn much about the person holding it and what their larger culture presumed about them.

In this chapter, we focus on what beverages teach about the concept of Self and Other in rabbinic literature. Intoxicants (especially wine and beer) are the beverages most often relevant to this, a trend that has continued well beyond antiquity (see Dynner 2013; Davis 2012; though, as Liberles 2012 notes, similar comments apply to coffee for Jews in early modern Germany). The ancient Rabbis used drinks to map the contours of their social boundaries: between rabbinic Jews and their external and internal Others (i.e., respectively, non-Jews and non-rabbinic Jews).

THE IDOL IN HER BRA: WINE AS SOCIAL BOUNDARY

In the ancient Mediterranean, wine was the beverage of choice, consumed by both rich and poor, albeit in different qualities and quantities—distinctions conveying social and economic status. Though widely imbibed, those who drank their wine undiluted with water—that is, "unmixed" (Greek *akratos*)—were seen as uncultured, as were those from other regions who drank other intoxicants, such as beer. Wine served a key function in the Greek *symposion* and Latin *convivium*, where social, economic, and gender status dictated one's roles in the events (in general, see Beer 2010, 84–100).

In regard to wine, the Rabbis who live in Roman Palestine were very much a product of their environment. Though, as we shall see, they used wine to establish a social boundary between Jew and non-Jew, they notably chose neither to reject drinking wine nor to reject drinking it with non-Jews completely. Instead, they regulated every aspect of the production and consumption of wine. Thus, while rabbinic Jews could still drink wine, at every moment they were reminded in doing so of the difference between Us and Them.

To say that the Rabbis embrace drinking wine is thus to state the obvious. Inheriting a biblical tradition that "wine gladdens the heart of man" (Psalm 104:15), they use this scriptural verse to justify various wine-related behaviors. For example:

> It is a commandment (Hebrew *mitzvah*) incumbent upon man to bring joy to his children and the members of his household on the Festival [of Passover].
>
> How does one bring them joy? With wine, as it is written: "wine gladdens the heart of man" [Psalm 104:15]. (*t. Pisha* 10:4)

Festivals require joyous celebration and it is a man's duty to bring that joy to his children and his household (likely a synecdoche for his wife). And how does he bring this joy? By serving wine.

Wine, one of the three members of the so-called Mediterranean Triad, receives its own rabbinic blessing ("... who creates the fruit of the vine"; *m. Berakhot* 6:1; see, in general, Kraemer 2009, 73–86; and chapter 7), a distinction also awarded to another member of the Triad, bread, but not to meat—though it is a foodstuff also associated with rejoicing in rabbinic literature. Wine becomes a central ritual component of rabbinic festival practice, from the blessing of wine on the Sabbath to the four cups consumed at the Passover *Seder* (see *m. Pesahim* 10; chapter 7). Wine is also featured at other times of rabbinic rejoicing, such as the wedding feast—which is often simply referred to as "the drinking party" or "the house of drinking" (as it is in the very first few words of the Mishnah; see *m. Berakhot* 1:1, discussed in chapter 7).

Of course, wine is also prominent in rabbinic ritual rejoicing because biblical texts detail the practice of libation, or the ritual pouring out of wine, as sacrifice in the Jerusalem Temple (e.g., Numbers 28:7; discussed *b. Sukkah* 49b). And while libation to God by a Jewish priest in the Jerusalem Temple is viewed as a positive commandment, the Rabbis devote most of their attention to the inversion of this practice: libation to a pagan god or gods by an idolater (on ritual inversion, see chapter 5). In fact, the tractate of the Mishnah that centers on the topic of idolatry (Hebrew *Avodah Zarah*; literally, "Foreign Worship") closes with an extended discussion of social relations with idolaters during the production, storage, and consumption of wine (*m. Avodah Zarah* 4:8–5:11; also see 2:4). Again, we must note that wine is neither completely banned, nor is drinking wine with a non-Jew. However, the entire process—from the beginning of production to the transport, storage, and eventual consumption of wine—is heavily regulated. At every step of the way, these regulations serve to erect a social boundary, reminding all parties involved that there is a difference between Us and Them.

At the core of these regulations is a central belief: namely, that non-Jews are, in the words of Sacha Stern (2013), "compulsive libationers," who cannot resist the urge to pour wine to their deity/deities. And since, as we shall see further in chapter 5, once wine is libated it is classified as "libated wine" (Hebrew *yayn nesekh*), with an associated series of complicated prohibitions, then this means that any interaction between Us and Them that involves wine—even if it is Our wine—must be heavily monitored.

A representative example of this social surveillance is encountered in *m. Avodah Zarah* 5:4–5, which states:

> (5:4) ... [If a Jew] left a non-Jew [alone and unsupervised] in his store, even though he goes in and out—[the wine in the Jew's store] is permitted; but if [the Jew] informed [the non-Jew] that he was departing—[then the wine is prohibited] if there was enough time to bore a hole [in the wine barrel], and to stop it up, and for the clay to dry. Rabban Shimon ben Gamaliel says: if there was enough time to open it up, and to close it up, and for it to dry.
>
> (5:5) [If a Jew] was eating with [a non-Jew] at the [same] table, and [the Jew] left a bottle [of wine] on the table and a bottle on the side-table, and left [the non-Jew alone and unsupervised] and went out—what is on the table is prohibited, and what is on the side-table is permitted. But if he said to [the non-Jew]: "Mix [wine with water] for yourself and drink!"—then even that which is on the side-table is prohibited. [Wine in] open jugs is prohibited; sealed [wine jugs are prohibited] if there was enough time to open it, and to close it up, and for it to dry.

In this scenario, which "resembles a cops-and-robbers game" (Schäfer 2002, 338), Jews must remain eternally vigilant when leaving non-Jews alone with wine, because non-Jews are imagined as unable to resist the urge to libate wine—even going to the comical extreme of boring holes in wine barrels and then resealing them to hide their idolatrous actions. Jews and non-Jews may drink wine together, but non-Jews are not to be trusted around Jewish wine without supervision (for further discussion, see Freidenreich 2011, 57–60, 69–72; Rosenblum 2010a, 81–83; Stern 2013, 21–22). To offer a modern parallel: how would you feel about someone if you were willing to share a drink with them, but would not leave them alone in your apartment while you ran a quick errand, for fear that they would mess with your stuff? Thus, while Jews and non-Jews may share wine, the asymmetric regulations make it much easier to share a glass of wine with a fellow Jew. After all, if the one left unsupervised with wine is a Jew, then none of these fears arise (and no rabbinic prohibitions apply).

But can a non-Jew ever be left alone, unsupervised with wine? While we return to the subject of leaving a non-Jew alone with a Jewish beverage later in this chapter, the Rabbis create an interesting loophole wherein this is possible, based on the rabbinic belief that idolaters "do not libate [cooked wine]" (*b. Avodah Zarah* 29b). Therefore:

> Cooked wine (Hebrew *yayin mevushal*) is not subject to the libation [prohibition]. (*b. Avodah Zarah* 30a)

Oddly, for such a strong statement, no ancient non-Jewish evidence supports this claim. There is, however, a rabbinic tradition that cooked wine is invalid for use in the Jerusalem Temple (*m. Menahot* 8:6). It appears then that the rabbinic belief that cooking wine invalidates it for Jewish ritual use is imported into a pagan sacrificial context. Therefore, even if left alone with Jewish cooked wine, a non-Jew would have no desire to libate it, since the Rabbis assume that it is not suitable for idolatrous libation. In doing so, rabbinic wine legislation accords with other rabbinic laws that seek to accommodate the world full of gods they inhabit via a conscious misinterpretation—what Pierre Bourdieu would call a misrecognition—of certain practices (in general, see Schwartz 2001, 162–76). Jews and non-Jews could drink together, so long as the wine was produced, stored, and consumed under constant Jewish supervision, though the rules could be relaxed provided that the production method was altered and the wine was cooked (on how this impacts the modern kosher wine industry, see Horowitz 2016, 127–61; Fishkoff 2010, 109–30).

The concern of interacting with non-Jews when wine is involved is not just that a Jew could drink libated wine itself, but that wine is a slippery slope that leads towards social intimacy; and social intimacy leads to sexual intimacy; and inviting a non-Jew into your bed might lead to your inviting their idolatrous gods into your heart. This fear is directly addressed in *Sifre Numbers* 131, a fascinating text that comments on Numbers 25:1–3. Before we turn to *Sifre Numbers* 131, it is worth reviewing the biblical text itself:

> While Israel dwelled in Shittim, the people profaned themselves by whoring with the daughters of Moab. And they invited the people to the sacrifices for their gods. And the people ate [the sacrificial meat], and bowed down to their gods. Thus Israel religiously devoted itself to Ba'al Pe'or, and the anger of the Lord was kindled against Israel. (Numbers 25:1–3)

Dwelling among the Moabites while wasting time until they cross into Canaan, Israelite men profane themselves by whoring with Moabite women. As is discussed further in chapter 4, "whoring" is a transgressive practice, in both the literal carnal act and the metaphorical theological act. "Whoring" violates gendered bodies: the women who are depicted as literally prostituting themselves and the female collective body of Israel, which violates its covenant to be monogamous (that is, monotheistic) with its husband, God. Ignoring earlier warnings about this sort of practice (see Exodus 34:15–16), the Israelite men's sexual appetite leads them to satiate their other appetite and partake of sacrificial meat. In doing so, this text claims, the Israelites devote themselves to the false god Ba'al Pe'or and incense the one, true God.

Picking up on many of the elements of this biblical account, the Rabbis imagine the encounter between Israelite men and Moabite women as a broader warning against Jewish men drinking wine with non-Jewish women. To do so, they first minimize the concern for "libated wine" by noting that: "And the wine of Gentiles had not yet been forbidden to Israel" (*Sifre Numbers* 131). Since Israel (i.e., Jews) had not yet received a prohibition against drinking Gentile wine, then what follows is less about the wine itself than about the situation in which it is imbibed. Next, we learn:

> [A non-Jewish woman] would say to a [Jewish man]: "Would you like to drink wine?" He would drink and the wine would burn within him and he would say to her: "Listen to me!" She would take out an image of Pe'or from under her bra and say to him: "Rabbi, is it your desire that I listen to you? Then bow to this!" (*Sifre Numbers* 131)

In rabbinic Hebrew, "listen to me" is an idiom meaning "have sex with me." This is one of those instances when scholars do not have to work hard: when I claim that this text imagines a scenario in which sharing a glass of wine with a non-Jewish woman is a slippery slope that leads to intoxication, sexual desire, and ultimately idolatry, I need only quote the very words themselves. This obvious observation is furthered by the ancient author's comical touch—in which the non-Jewish woman is described as conveniently stashing an idol in her bra just for such an occasion. (On the idol Pe'or whom she pulls from her bra, and this text in general, see Rosenblum 2010b, 24–25.) After all, if a non-Jew is willing to stuff her bra with idols, should a nice Jewish boy really share a glass of wine with her?!

"BECAUSE OF INTERMARRIAGE": BEER AS SOCIAL BOUNDARY

While the wine of—or the wine left alone with—a non-Jew is suspect because of concern about libation, what about non-wine intoxicants? Since the Rabbis are aware that wine is the only beverage libated by idolaters, do the same stigmas attach to other beverages that, while still alcohol, are not subject to idolatrous libation? This question is especially important for the rabbinic community that resides in Babylonia, where beer (and not wine) is the beverage of choice. (This is why, for example, the Babylonian Rabbis debate whether Jewish ritual blessings associated with the Sabbath could be recited over beer instead of wine; see *b. Pesahim* 107a, discussed in chapter 6). As we shall see, the social concerns expressed in the previous section come even more to the forefront in rabbinic discussions of non-wine intoxicants and social boundaries with non-Jews.

An excellent starting place for our exploration is a rabbinic text that raises an important, and practical, legal question: what do rabbinic Jews do if they are invited to their non-Jewish neighbor's wedding? The answer is:

> Even if [the Jews in attendance] eat and drink [only] from their own [food and beverages] and their own servant stands and serves them, they are idolaters, as it is said: "And he will invite you and you will eat from his sacrifice" [Exodus 34:15]. (*t. Avodah Zarah* 4:6; cf. *b. Avodah Zarah* 8a–b)

In this scenario, despite the fact that Jews bring their own food and beverages, and have their own (presumably Jewish) servants attend to them, and serve them their own food and drink, it is the very social situation that is itself not kosher (see Rosenblum 2010b, 21–23). Indeed, this is the precise kind of social invitation prohibited by Exodus 34:15. Therefore, even when the fear of actual idolatrous libation is removed, the social fear of celebrating at an idolater's wedding (referred to herein as a "drinking party" [Hebrew *mishteh*]) generates a social boundary. And this barrier is justified on the basis of a biblical passage, which is parsed to indicate that the one invited to such an event will end up consuming—and hence participating in—an idolatrous sacrifice.

Note that the language of *t. Avodah Zarah* 4:6 does not specify the type of beverage consumed. Though it is a text written in a Palestinian context, it refers to "Jews [who reside] outside the Land [of Israel]"—meaning that it is written in a wine-drinking culture about Jews living in other cultures, especially in beer-drinking Babylonia. As one might expect, when this tradition is interpreted in the Babylonian Talmud, the context shifts. And so does the beverage in one's hand. For example, when discussing how long before a non-Jew's wedding a Jew should deem commensality with them to be a non-kosher practice, one answer provided is: once the preparation for the wedding itself has begun.

And how do you know that idolaters have begun to prepare for a wedding?

> From when they [begin to] brew barley in the vat [in order to make special beer for the wedding]. (*b. Avodah Zarah* 8a–b; see Freidenreich 2011, 74–76)

From that moment until the end of the festive period, sharing a beer with a non-Jew is tantamount to engaging in idolatry. In Babylonia, beer is the beverage of joyous celebration.

But beer is also the beverage of everyday consumption in Babylonia. So what about drinking beer with a non-Jew on an ordinary, non-festive occasion? Such beverages are kosher to drink, provided that a Jew leaves a non-Jew's tavern first. Thus, we learn:

> It was stated: Why did they prohibit the beer of idolaters? Rami bar Hama said [in the name of] Rabbi Yitzhak: Because of intermarriage....
>
> For Rav Pappa, they would bring [the beer] out of the door [of the non-Jew's tavern], and he would drink it [there]. For Rav Ahai, they would bring it to his house, and he would drink it [there]. Both of them [agreed that the prohibition existed in order to prevent] intermarriage, [but] Rav Ahai made a greater buffer. (*b. Avodah Zarah* 31b)

Non-wine intoxicants prepared by idolaters are not libated. Beer can never be "libated wine." Why, then, do the Rabbis express concern about "the beer of idolaters"? Because, once again, the Rabbis are aware that drinking together can lead to romance—that social intercourse is the first step down a slippery slope that leads to sexual intercourse.

And the romance need not be between the two drinkers themselves. For example, imagine the scenario described in another rabbinic text:

> Two men were drinking wine under the willows in Babylonia. One took a wine cup, handed it to his friend, [and] said: Betroth for me your daughter to my son! (*b. Qiddushin* 45a)

Drinking buddies might want their children to be to married, so be wary with whom you drink.

The non-wine alcohol of an idolater is not subject to the libation prohibition and therefore it cannot be banned in and of itself. Instead, we once again encounter an instance in which it is the social situation and not the beverage that is deemed non-kosher (fear of intermarriage is also cited among rabbinic prohibitions of non-Jewish wine in *b. Avodah Zarah* 36b; on both texts, see Freidenreich 2011, 72–73.) Thus, two Rabbis are described as ordering Gentile beer, but drinking it off premises. In the case of Rav Pappa—himself a renowned brewer whose craft beers made him rich (see *b. Pesahim* 113a; *b. Bava Metzi'a* 65a)—he would drink non-Jewish beer as soon as he had walked outside of the non-Jewish bar. Rav Ahai, on the other hand, was stricter and would not drink non-Jewish beer until he was safely within the confines of his own home. The two Rabbis agreed that the beer was kosher, but the social situation was not; they simply disagreed about how much physical distance one must place between oneself and the non-Jewish tavern. Or, to offer a simple mnemonic: Sit on Their stool? Against the rule. Take it away? You are OK.

THE VENOMOUS OTHER: UNCOVERED DRINKS AND DANGER TO LIFE

Furthering this need to establish a physical distance and social barrier in regard to the non-Jew is the rabbinic fear of leaving a beverage uncovered. Originally, this concern is couched simply in terms of a snake sneaking a sip from an uncovered beverage and, as a result, excreting its venom and threatening the life of the one who imbibes the drink (see *m. Terumot* 8:4–5). In the Talmud, this fear becomes attached to non-Jews (see Freidenreich 2011, 73–74, 247n27; Wasserman 2017, 139–49). As David Kraemer (2009, 69–72) persuasively argues, this association transforms the non-Jew into the venomous Other. Avoiding social—and sexual—encounters with non-Jewish "snakes," especially when beverages are involved, is therefore a means to preserving a Jew's physical and spiritual well-being.

David Kraemer's argument is furthered by the fact that the Rabbis debate whether the prohibition of drinking uncovered liquids extends to both cooked wine and beer (see *y. Avodah Zarah* 2:3, 41a; *b. Avodah Zarah* 30a, 31b)—two categories of beverages that we have just seen are much less problematic for Jewish ingestion. For example:

> Rabbi Immi had guests. He said to them: If my cooked wine had not been left uncovered, then would I have not given it to you to drink?
>
> Rav Bibi said to him: Bring it and we will drink.
>
> [Rabbi Immi] said: He who wants to die should go and die in his own house! (*y. Avodah Zarah* 2:3, 41a)

Rabbi Immi apologizes to his guests for not serving them wine. He had intended to offer them cooked wine, but he accidentally left the wine uncovered. Rav Bibi dismisses this concern, and asks to drink the wine regardless of the fact that it was left uncovered.

Cooked wine might avoid the prohibition of "libated wine," but the fear of snakes—or "snakes"—remains. "Weaving a network of associations between non-Jews and the creeping threat of strange, sneaky beasts" (Wasserman 2017, 149), the literal venom of the snake that threatens a Jew's physical well-being is connected with the metonymic and metaphoric "venom" of the "snake" that threatens a Jew's spiritual well-being. Even when the associated beverage—cooked wine or beer—is not subject to libation, the venomous Other remains coiled, ever ready to attack. For this reason, snakes and "snakes" are still the subject of rabbinic suspicion. And why would you drink with someone so suspicious and serpentine?

MILK FROM AN OTHER MOTHER: BREAST MILK AS SOCIAL BOUNDARY

Like a wide variety of foodstuffs in rabbinic literature, the kosher status of animal milk depends not only on the status of the animal itself, but on the status of the one who prepared it (in general, see Rosenblum

2010a, 75–91). Thus, if a kosher female animal is milked by a Jew, the resulting milk is kosher; if that animal is milked by a non-Jew, its milk is not kosher. As always, there is an exception: if a non-Jew milked the animal under Jewish supervision, the milk is kosher (see *m. Avodah Zarah* 2:6; on the interpretation of this mishnah in the Babylonian Talmud, see Hayes 1997, 230n38). Even then, as we should expect, based on the previous section, there is concern about leaving milk milked by a non-Jew uncovered (see *y. Shabbat* 1:7, 3d). But when we discuss animal milk, we too often neglect one very important category of animal milk: namely, human breast milk.

The Rabbis devote significant attention to human breast milk, which they distinguish from milk produced by non-human animals (in general, see Rosenblum 2016b). Like modern parenting blogs, the Rabbis have definite opinions about breastfeeding. In other chapters, we see how breast milk relates to rabbinic issues ranging from ritual purity, gender, health, and biblical interpretation. Breast milk also plays an interesting role in discussions of social boundaries; *m. Avodah Zarah* 2:1, which I quote here in its entirety, best contextualizes the relevant issues:

> [Jews] do not leave [their] cattle in the inns of non-Jews, because [non-Jews] are suspected of bestiality. And a [Jewish] woman may not be alone with them, because they are suspected of sexual transgressions. And a [Jewish] man may not be alone with them, because they are suspected of bloodshed. A Jewish woman may not serve as a midwife for a non-Jewish woman, because she delivers a child for idolatry; but a non-Jewish woman may serve as a midwife for a Jewish woman. A Jewish woman may not nurse the child of a non-Jewish woman; but a non-Jewish woman may nurse the child of a Jewish woman in her own premises. (cf. *t. Avodah Zarah* 3:1–3)

In this mishnah, a variety of interactions with non-Jews are deemed problematic on the basis of their being suspected of numerous nefarious acts, including bestiality, rape, and murder. Attention is then turned towards childbearing and childrearing. We learn that a Jew may hire a non-Jewish midwife, but not vice versa, since a non-Jew may deliver a

Jew into the world, but a Jew may not assist in the birth of an idolater. I include all of this background material because it helps to explain the final statement: that a Jewish woman may not serve as a wet nurse for a non-Jew, but a non-Jewish woman may serve as a wet nurse for a Jew, provided that she nurses the child in the Jew's own home. We need the earlier statements to help us fully comprehend this remark. First, we must understand that the concern for a Jewish woman nursing a non-Jewish baby is the same as her serving as a midwife: in both instances, the Jewish woman would be assisting in the rearing of a future idolater. When a non-Jewish woman serves as a midwife or a wet nurse for a Jewish baby, however, she is helping to birth and raise a Jew, of which the Rabbis heartily approve. Hence, the asymmetric legislation. Second, we learn that non-Jews are considered suspicious and unable to control their animalistic instincts, so we also fear for the safety of a Jewish child (and cattle!) in their care. Commenting on this passage (see *b. Avodah Zarah* 26a), one Rabbi goes so far as to fear that a non-Jewish wet nurse would smear poison on her breasts before nursing a Jewish baby! Thus, even though a non-Jew may nurse a Jewish child, the Gentile woman must do so at the Jew's home. This need for supervision also echoes rabbinic regulations involving non-human animal milk, wherein a non-Jew may milk cattle and produce kosher milk, provided that there is Jewish supervision.

Once again, we encounter a beverage whose rabbinic regulation allows for social interaction with non-Jews. However, the associated rabbinic rules lead to very controlled interactions, in which the non-Jew is viewed as not only suspicious, but a dangerous Other.

ITS MOTHER'S MILK: BOUNDARIES BETWEEN INTERNAL OTHERS

If sharing beverages with non-Jews is fraught with peril, drinking with Jews is not without its own potential pitfalls. The Rabbis recognize that there are both external Others and internal Others. External Others are non-Jews who "often appear in rabbinic literature as mirror opposites of Israelites, and so sharpen the rabbis' definition of Israel"; whereas internal Others are non-rabbinic Jews, that is, Jews who are either unaware of or uninterested in complying with rabbinic law, who "often appear in rabbinic literature as *mirror opposites of the rabbis* and so sharpen the rabbis' definition of their own class" (Hayes 2007, 243, original emphasis; also see Porton 1988; Stern 1994).

The Hebrew Bible's best-known beverage-related prohibition appears verbatim in three separate instances:

> Do not cook a kid in its mother's milk. (Exodus 23:19, 34:26; Deuteronomy 14:21)

This is what the Rabbis refer to as a "negative commandment," and what I call a "Thou Shalt Not" commandment, adopting the archaic English of the King James Bible, which renders this verse as "Thou shalt not seethe a kid in its mother's milk." According to *b. Makkot* 23b–24a, the Hebrew Bible contains 365 negative commandments and 248 positive commandments ("Thou Shalt ..."), a total of 613 commandments.

What exactly does it mean when the Israelites are commanded not to cook a kid in its mother's milk? It turns out that this negative commandment is deceptively simple, leading to a complex and fascinating history of interpretation (in general, see Rosenblum 2016a, 24–25, 54–56, 95–97, 112–16). For some ancient Jews, like Philo of Alexandria (ca. 20 B.C.E.–50 C.E.), this was a literal commandment: do not cook a baby animal in the actual milk of its actual mother, because doing so would be cruel (*On the Virtues*, 142–44). After all, that literal milk nurtured and sustained that literal baby animal, so cooking them together brutally confuses life and death.

When the Rabbis turn their gaze to this biblical legislation, however, they read the text very differently. It is not a particular law, but a general one; it is not about a specific animal and specific milk, but rather is about *all* meat and *all* milk.

All meat is forbidden to be cooked with milk, except for the meat of fish and locusts.

And it is forbidden to serve it with cheese on the table, except for the meat of fish and locusts.

One who vows [to abstain] from meat is permitted [to eat] the meat of fish and locusts. (*m. Hullin* 8:1)

The first line clearly refers to the negative commandment of the Hebrew Bible. However, as is typical for the Mishnah, the biblical text looms in the background, but is rarely directly cited. We learn that, according to the Rabbis, this biblical injunction was against cooking *all* meat with *all* milk. We also learn that "meat" does not include fish and locusts, so one can cook locusts in milk and not violate the biblical prohibition (Fun Fact: locusts are kosher; see Leviticus 11:21–22). This is explicit in the final formulation, as rabbinic literature often uses the vow to explore whether something is included in a given category. "If I vow to abstain from x, may I partake of y?" is a common rabbinic method for inquiring whether y belongs in the category of x. For example, if a person vows not to eat, but they drink, have they violated their vow? This question explores whether "drinking" is included with the category of "eating" (see *b. Shevu'ot* 22b–23b, which concludes that indeed it is). Furthermore, one way to vow to avoid something is to proclaim that "This is for me like libated wine" (e.g., *y. Nedarim* 2:4, 37b; and 6:6, 39c). By comparing whatever one vows to avoid to the forbidden category of "libated wine," the Rabbis can consider the effects of proclaiming that something that would otherwise be permitted is now, for the vower, deemed to be completely forbidden.

The switch from milk to cheese further highlights the move from a particular law to a general law. The Hebrew Bible bans cooking a kid in its mother's *milk,* and cheese is not milk. (Though, returning for a moment to the subject of the vow, it is debated whether one who vows to abstain from milk is permitted to eat cheese curds; but all agree that one who vows to abstain from cheese curds is permitted to drink milk; see *y. Nedarim* 6:8, 39d.) In the first statement, the Rabbis echo the biblical wording of milk, and then immediately pivot to cheese. Coupled with the definition of "meat" already discussed, this move furthers the idea that anything in the category of meat cannot be cooked with anything in the category of milk, and in a hot climate, prior to refrigeration, milk quickly soured, so in biblical times it was more commonly consumed as cheese rather than in liquid form (see MacDonald 2008, 35–36).

Now that we have clarified this from a particular to a general law, how does it help us understand rabbinic social boundaries? Remember that the biblical injunction does not necessitate the rabbinic interpretation. Furthermore, we have clear evidence that some pre-rabbinic Jews, such as Philo of Alexandria, interpreted the biblical prohibition as a particular rather than as a general law. David Kraemer offers a persuasive argument for the profound effects of this novel rabbinic interpretation:

> On a purely pragmatic level, if the milk-meat prohibition is an innovation, promulgated by the rabbis and accepted only by those who followed them, then this enactment will effectively have separated rabbinic from non-rabbinic Jews on significant occasions [when meat is eaten]. Presumably, non-rabbinic Jews continued to eat like pre-rabbinic Jews. That is, if they respected Jewish custom at all (and the evidence suggests that many did), they will have avoided the animals proscribed by the Torah. But [they] needed have no concern for the mixing of meat and dairy. The small rabbinized population, by contrast, will have distinguished themselves from the general Jewish population by creating separation between meat and dairy. The new rabbinic prohibition, in other words, separated Jew from Jew (at least on certain occasions) and set off rabbinic Jews as the keepers of what was then a more esoteric law. (2009, 50)

In promulgating a new reading of the text, the Rabbis are not merely engaging in biblical exegesis; they are developing a completely new dietary practice. In doing so, they distinguish between how rabbinic and non-rabbinic Jews interact with meat and milk. Both groups believe that they are following the biblical commandment to the letter of the law. And indeed they are, only they have differing interpretations of how that affects their recipe planning. As a result, when meat and milk are served, a non-rabbinic Jew can eat at the table of a rabbinic Jew, since the latter's general interpretation necessarily encompasses the former's particular ruling—if *all* meat and *all* milk products are not cooked together, then there is no way that the meat of a kid can be cooked with the milk of its actual mother. The same does not apply in the reverse, meaning that a rabbinic Jew can no longer eat at the table of the non-rabbinic Jew. Both groups of Jews believe themselves to be adhering to biblical food laws, but their differing interpretations erect a social boundary down the middle of their table.

THERE'S NO COMMUNICATION LIKE EXCOMMUNICATION: FOWL AND SOCIAL FRACTURES

Differing interpretations of the negative commandment "Do not cook a kid in its mother's milk" lead to further social fractures. We have just seen that the reading of this prohibition as a general law distinguishes rabbinic Jews via exegetical and dietary practice from non-rabbinic Jews. Probing deeper, we discover that differing interpretations of the limits of this law further distinguish among rabbinic Jews themselves.

We begin our exploration of this topic by returning to a text discussed in the previous section. Picking up where we left off above, we learn:

> Fowl may go up with cheese on the table, but it may not be eaten; the words of the House of Shammai.
> But the House of Hillel says: It may neither go up, nor may it be eaten. (*m. Hullin* 8:1)

Famous for their disagreements, the Houses of Shammai and Hillel debate whether fowl and cheese may be served on the same table. But they both agree that fowl and cheese may not be eaten together.

This minor quibble points to a broader debate (in general, see Rosenblum 2018). Fowl are not mammals, a taxonomic classification defined by their inability to produce milk (on the gendered history behind this taxonomy, see Schiebinger 2004, 40–74). Fowl do not lactate and would not be included in a literal reading of "Do not cook a kid in its *mother's milk*." But remember that the Rabbis have read this negative commandment as a general, not a particular, law. Fowl complicates matters.

Trying to work this out, the Mishnah quickly returns to this issue:

> One who brings up fowl with cheese on the table does not transgress a negative commandment. (*m. Hullin* 8:3)

Once again, the question of whether cooking fowl and milk together would violate biblical law is not addressed. Rather, we learn that simply bringing both fowl and dairy food to the table does not transgress a negative commandment. This terminology is important, because it merely states that doing so does not violate biblical law; but it leaves open the possibility that it violates subsequent rabbinic law.

The conflict between the biblical wording and the biological fact that fowl do not lactate is met head-on in the next mishnah:

> Rabbi Aqiva says: Undomesticated animals and fowl are not prohibited by the Torah, as it is said: "Do not cook a kid in its mother's milk," three times, to exclude undomesticated animals, fowl, and impure domesticated animals.
>
> Rabbi Yosi the Galilean says: It is said, "Do not eat any carrion" [Deuteronomy 14:21], and it is said, "Do not cook a kid in its mother's milk" [Deuteronomy 14:21]: that which is forbidden on account of "carrion," it is forbidden to cook in milk.
>
> Fowl, which is forbidden on account of carrion, might one conclude that it is forbidden to cook in milk?
>
> Scripture says, "in its mother's milk," to exclude fowl, which has no mother's milk. (*m. Hullin* 8:4)

Before we turn to the content of their remarks, the reader is expected to know that the two contemporaneous rabbinic figures are not your average Rabbi Joe. Rabbi Aqiva is a legendary figure who has been the focus of numerous scholarly studies and biographies (for two recent examples, see Holtz 2017; Yadin-Israel 2015); and, though less famous, Rabbi Yosi the Galilean is no pip-squeak. So their words carry weight.

Turning to the content of their remarks, we find Rabbi Aqiva arguing that the three repetitions of this negative commandment in the Hebrew Bible are intended to exclude three types of animal, one of which was fowl. His statement can be read in two ways: (1) as arguing that fowl can be cooked in milk without violating biblical law; or (2) as arguing that fowl cannot be cooked in milk, but not on the basis of biblical law (thus, "fowl are not prohibited by the Torah," but are prohibited by subsequent rabbinic law; on this interpretation, see Yadin-Israel 2015, 107). Either way one reads the text, cooking fowl in milk is not biblically prohibited.

Rabbi Yosi the Galilean's statement can be read similarly, though it works in a slightly different manner. First, one must know that Deuteronomy 14:21 reads in full:

> Do not eat any carrion; to the resident outsider (Hebrew *ger*) who is within your gates you shall give it, and he will eat it; or sell it to the nonresident alien (Hebrew *nokhri*); for a holy people are you to the Lord your God. Do not cook a kid in its mother's milk.

This verse begins by discussing carrion (Hebrew *nevelah*; discussed further in chapter 5). In the Hebrew Bible, carrion is an animal that dies a natural death; it is slaughtered neither by a human nor a non-human animal. Though Israelites are not permitted to consume carrion, they may derive benefit from it by offering it to a resident outsider or a nonresident alien (on these terms, see Olyan 2000, 63–102). Doing so apparently marks the Israelites as a holy people. And, somewhat awkwardly attached to this verse, is the prohibition: "Do not cook a kid in its mother's milk."

Rabbi Yosi the Galilean connects the beginning and the end of Deuteronomy 14:21. He argues that what is forbidden based on the carrion prohibition is also forbidden in regard to the meat/milk prohibition. Then he asks a follow-up question: fowl that is carrion is certainly prohibited, but does that mean—based on his previous logic—that it is also subject to the meat/milk prohibition? This is when the precise wording of the biblical text is important: Scripture (i.e., God; see chapter 2) intentionally worded the prohibition in regard to "its mother's milk" to teach that fowl are not included. After all, fowl "has no mother's milk."

Although *m. Hullin* 8:4 may either speak to an allowance for cooking fowl in milk or merely be an acknowledgement that such a prohibition is extrabiblical but nonetheless in force, there is evidence that some subsequent rabbinic communities interpreted the text as the former, and thereby allowed the cooking of fowl in milk:

> Levi visited the house of Yosef the Fowler. They served him a peacock's head [cooked] in milk. He did not say anything to them.
>
> When [Levi] came before Rabbi [and reported these events, Rabbi] said to him: Why did you not excommunicate them?!
>
> [Levi] said to him: It was the locale of Rabbi Yehudah ben Beterah, and I thought, perhaps he expounded for them in accordance with Rabbi Yosi the Galilean, who said: "to exclude fowl, which has no mother's milk." (*b. Hullin* 116a; cp. *b. Shabbat* 130a)

As might be expected of one who hunts wild birds for a living, Yosef (Joseph) the Fowler offers fowl for dinner, and not just fowl but a fowl's *head* (Aramaic *resha'*), which is cooked in milk. The name of this fowler (Aramaic *rishba'*) seems no coincidence! Levi does not say anything (but, according to some manuscript traditions, does not eat the dish; see Rosenblum 2018, 185–86n33).

Later, when Levi reports these events, Rabbi asks: "Why did you not excommunicate them?!" Excommunication is a serious threat. One who is excommunicated is expelled from the community and ostracized. They no longer have access to their social, familial, economic, and theological networks. But Levi has a strong basis for his (in)action: perhaps Yosef the Fowler's cooking is based on Rabbi Yosi the Galilean's ruling in *m. Hullin* 8:4. If so, then how could Levi excommunicate someone for following the ruling of an earlier sage? As Richard Hidary notes:

Rabbi wants to excommunicate Yosef for violating the law. This itself is notable for the way Rabbi would deal with halakhic deviation. Levi's response, however, diffuses the attack. Assuming that Rabbi accepted this response, it seems that even Rabbi would consent to pluralism if the practice was done in a city that accepts a different opinion as law. (2010, 152)

Hidary correctly states that one could read this text as accepting the notion of legal pluralism, that is, that multiple normative views can coexist within a legal system. However, we are not told Rabbi's response to Levi. Perhaps he agreed. Perhaps he did not. Either way, the normative weight of Rabbi—Rabbi Yehudah ha-Nasi, who edited the Mishnah in which Rabbi Yosi the Galilean's opinion are recorded—suggests that there is a growing concern, if not yet a dominant consensus, against this legal position. And social pressure is brought to bear on those who adopt this licit, but not necessarily preferable, perspective. They might not be excommunicated, but Levi certainly will not return for another meal.

FOWL IN PAJAMAS: MILK, MENSTRUATION, AND MARITAL SEPARATION

Having earlier discussed the roles of gender and sexuality in distinguishing among external Others, we now turn our attention to these factors in the case of internal Others (see also chapter 4): the debate about whether fowl can be cooked in milk also illuminates another social dichotomy, that between Jewish men and Jewish women.

It might seem surprising that conversation about cooking fowl in milk would speak to this topic, but the rabbinic mind makes fascinating connections. Here we encounter a text proposing that certain mixtures in certain contexts and at certain moments may be cause for concern:

> They inquired: May a *niddah* [a menstruating woman] sleep with her husband [in the same bed], she in her garment and he in his garment?
>
> Rav Yosef said: Come and learn: "Fowl may go up with cheese on the table, but it may not be eaten; the words of the House of Shammai. But the

House of Hillel says: It may neither go up, nor may it be eaten" [*m. Hullin* 8:1].

It is different there, because there are no minds.

It is indeed reasonable that where there are [separate] minds it is different, because the latter part [of *m. Hullin* 8:2] teaches: "Rabban Shimon ben Gamaliel says: Two guests may eat on one table, this one eats meat and that one eats cheese, without concern."

But was it not stated concerning it: Rav Hanin bar Ammi said in the name of Shmuel: This was taught only when they do not know one another. But when they know one another, it is forbidden.

And these [that is, the *niddah* and her husband] too know one another.

Now, is this [analogy correct]?

There, there are [separate] minds, [but] no change [from usual practices]; but here, there are [separate] minds and there is a change [from usual practices]. (*b. Shabbat* 13a)

A *niddah*, often rendered in English as "menstruant," is more correctly a woman who is deemed to be menstruating. I say *deemed* because the status can be applied retroactively (i.e., if a woman discovers that she is menstruating, that status applies retroactively to the last time that she checked whether she was menstruating) and beyond the actual period of menstruation (in general, see Fonrobert 2000). As discussed in chapter 8, menstrual blood is the most tabooed bodily liquid. Therefore, during the time that a woman is in the status of *niddah*, numerous ritual purity rules apply. For example, she may not mix her husband's cup of wine (see *b. Ketubbot* 4b; 61a). Despite these rules, Fonrobert argues that rabbinic "literature does not reflect or even allude to a practice of excluding menstruating women from social life" (2000, 19). While I agree with Fonrobert's general conclusion, the fact remains that *niddah* is a category that only applies to women, is heavily tabooed, and predominantly imagines itself in relation to the ritual purity status of men. For these reasons, I believe it worth our attention to think about how *niddah* constructs a social boundary between male and female Jews.

While there are several *niddah*-related prohibitions found in the Hebrew Bible, one particular regulation influences the first line of our text:

> Do not approach a woman to uncover her nakedness while she has the impurity of a *niddah*. (Leviticus 18:19; cf. Leviticus 20:18)

The implied normative subject of this sentence is a man. He is the active agent doing the approaching, while the non-normative woman is passive—she is the one approached. Normally, given certain other parameters, a man may approach a woman (i.e., his wife) to uncover her nakedness. But when a woman "has the impurity of a *niddah*," he may not do so. It is this latter case that piques our text's interest. That is why we wonder whether a woman who is in the status of *niddah* may sleep in the same bed as her husband, provided that they are both wearing nightclothes. After all, neither of them is naked, so have they actually violated this biblical prohibition?

Rav Yosef answers this question by referencing *m. Hullin* 8:1 about serving fowl and cheese on the same table. Separately, fowl and cheese (or milk) are kosher and can be consumed. Concern only arises when they are served and/or consumed together. Similarly, certain mixtures of human beings are kosher or not. In this example, *niddah* is a temporary status remedied with the completion of a biological process, the passage of a specified length of time, and immersion in a ritual bath (Hebrew *miqveh*). While a woman is in this status, a man may not mix with her in a "kosher" manner. Therefore, they must be kept separate.

But does this analogy work? The anonymous editorial voice of the Talmud raises a potential problem: "It is different there, because there are no minds." This brief sentence requires further explanation. "It is different there" means that the case of fowl and cheese in *m. Hullin* 8:1 is not the same as that of the married couple in nightdress. In regard to fowl and cheese, there is only one diner at the table, which means that there is only one "mind" thinking through the issues. But in the marital bed, there are two "minds"—that is, the *niddah* and her husband—who can think through the issues. In the latter case, two people can ensure that no violation of biblical law occurs.

The notion that, in the parlance of our time, two minds are better than one "is indeed reasonable." Further, it is supported by *m. Hullin* 8:2, a text in which two guests may share a table and eat separate meals—one meat-based and one milk-based—and not raise concern. However, the wording of *m. Hullin* 8:2 is important—the two people sharing different meals at the same table are "guests" (Hebrew *'akhsena'in*) and not "friends" (Hebrew *ḥaverim*). This distinction is made explicit by a tradition reported in the name of Shmuel by Rav Hanin bar Ammi: "This was taught only when they do not know one another. But when they know one another, it is forbidden." If two strangers share a table, they are not likely to share food with one another. The same cannot be said, however, when two friends share a table. And if friends know each other, all the more so a husband and wife! Therefore, just as friends cannot share a table when one eats fowl and the other eats cheese, a married couple—regardless of whether they wear nightdress—cannot share a bed while the wife is in the status of *niddah*.

Like a good proof, the text now checks its logic: "Now, is this [analogy correct]?" "There," where guests share a table, there are two people (= "minds"), but they are eating in accordance with their normal practice. So even if they do not know one another, they might strike up a conversation and then exchange food, thus leading to the forbidden mixing of fowl and cheese. Nothing marks the meal as particularly different. But "here," where a wife and husband share a bed, there are two people (= "minds"), *and* they have deviated from their usual bedtime routine. Here, the presumption is that married couples sleep together in the nude (both Palestine and Babylonia are hot climates, after all). So the very presence of nightclothes would remind both "minds" that they cannot engage in a forbidden mixture. Thus, this does not offer proof that a *niddah* and her husband cannot sleep in the same bed so long as they wear nightclothes (though the *gemara'* continues on *b. Shabbat* 13a and proves that they cannot do so, using another line of reasoning).

The analogy between a clothed *niddah* and her husband sharing a bed and serving fowl and milk on the same table does not work.

Checking our work, we realize that we are comparing apples to oranges. Despite the breakdown in this logic, conversation about fowl and cheese/milk elucidates how *niddah* regulations alter the daily relationship between rabbinic husband and wife. Though the analogy is not perfect, in both cases, certain mixtures (fowl/milk and husband/wife), in certain contexts (in the pot/bed), and at particular moments (while cooking/menstruating) establish a boundary between foods/people whose association is otherwise permitted.

SAYING "AMEN" TO THE PRAYER OF SOMEONE WHO IS JEW-*ISH*

An important internal Other is the Samaritan (Hebrew *kuti*; plural *kutim*). Though the Samaritans claim a shared history with the ancient Israelites, they subsequently branched off and forged their own similar, but distinct, path. For this reason, they are an intermediate group for the Rabbis (in general, see Porton 1988, 132–40). In some regards, the Samaritans are considered Jews; and in others, they are accounted as non-Jews. For this reason, I speak of the Rabbis' viewing Samaritans as Jew-*ish*.

The Rabbis invoke the category of the Samaritan when they wish to consider how this interesting variable affects a given law. For example, is bread baked by a Samaritan classified as bread baked by a Jew or a non-Jew? (For discussion, see Rosenblum 2010a, 158–61.) Is Samaritan wine equivalent with Gentile wine, and hence prohibited? (For discussion, see *y. Avodah Zarah* 5:4, 44d.) Often, the answer to a question would be a relatively straightforward binary yes/no if the categories considered were Jew/non-Jew. Introducing the variable of the Samaritan—the Jew-*ish* internal Other—therefore allows for more complex legal exploration.

An excellent example of this rabbinic tendency to use Samaritans in this manner is encountered during a conversation about blessings over wine. Moving on from the issue of whether wine served after the meal is consumed should be blessed prior to reciting the Grace after Meals, or vice versa, the following statement appears:

> They respond "Amen" after a Jew recites a blessing, but they do not respond "Amen" after the Samaritan recites a blessing, until one hears the entire blessing. (*m. Berakhot* 8:8)

This text immediately asserts that is appropriate to respond "Amen" to any blessing recited by a Jew. It also presumes that it would be inappropriate to respond "Amen" to any blessing recited by a non-Jew. That would be the simple binary, and hence the less interesting question. Much more interesting is to inquire about the case of the Samaritan. Remember that a Samaritan is Jew-*ish*. In this case, the Samaritan is a Jew because their blessing is potentially Amen-able. But Samaritans are Jew-*ish* in that their blessings cannot be Amen-ed until heard in their entirety. Only then, once the blessing's content is deemed rabbinically suitable, may a Jew respond "Amen" (see Rosenblum 2010a, 176).

This ruling highlights the social fault line of this internal Other. A Samaritan is kind of like "Us," and kind of like "Them." Inhabiting the interstitial space between binary poles, this category functions to clarify the boundaries of the normative "Us." In sum, it uses the Jew-*ish* to define the Jewish.

This conclusion is furthered by another text. In its exposition of this mishnah, the Jerusalem Talmud ponders an issue tacit in *m Berakhot* 8:8: the fact that a Jew cannot respond "Amen" to a non-Jew's blessing. What if the non-Jew offered a very Jewish blessing? Thus, we learn:

> It was taught in a *baraita*: [If] a non-Jew recited a blessing invoking *Ha-Shem*, they respond "Amen" after it. (*y. Berakhot* 8:9, 12c)

Taking for granted that, in general, a Jew should not respond "Amen" to the blessing of a non-Jew, this text considers the case of a non-Jew invoking the name of *Ha-Shem*—a common rabbinic title for God (literally, "The Name" in Hebrew). Thus, can a Jew respond "Amen" when a non-Jew offers a blessing in the name of the Jewish God? The answer is yes.

There are two interesting features of this text that require further elaboration. First, it would seem that, so long as a Jew hears the non-Jew invoke *Ha-Shem*, the Jew can respond "Amen" to the non-Jew's blessing. It does not require that the Jew wait "until one hears the entire blessing." If that is the case, then the non-Jew is treated less stringently than the Samaritan! Before we come to this conclusion, however, we need to consider the second interesting feature that requires elaboration. The text is introduced as being a *baraita'*, that is, a tradition reputed to be of tannaitic origin that is cited in an amoraic text. I say "reputed" because sometimes these traditions may not actually be tannaitic in origin, but may be the invention (for pious and/or polemical reasons) of later amoraic authors. In this case, however, we actually have a tannaitic text that contains this same tradition, but with an important addition:

> [If] a non-Jew recited a blessing invoking *Ha-Shem*, they respond "Amen" after it.
>
> [But if] a Samaritan recites a blessing invoking *Ha-Shem*, they do not respond "Amen" after it until one hears the entire blessing. (*t. Berakhot* 5:21; emended based on textual evidence; see Lieberman 2001, 28)

The previous version presents a unique case in which the blessing of the non-Jew is Amen-able, but leaves open the question of whether this also applies to the Samaritan. (Or, perhaps, given that it cites—and perhaps condenses—an earlier source, *y. Berakhot* 8:9, 12c saw this question as already resolved.) In *t. Berakhot* 5:21, this ambiguity is resolved: once Jews hear a non-Jew invoke *Ha-Shem*, they are free to respond "Amen" without worrying what comes afterwards; but if the one reciting the blessing is a Samaritan, then the Jew must wait until the entire blessing is recited before determining whether it is worthy of an "Amen."

Why is the Samaritan treated more stringently than the non-Jew? Because the Samaritan is Jew-*ish*. Once the non-Jew has invoked *Ha-Shem*—the Jewish God—it would seem that the larger fear of idolatry, of worshipping another god, is obviated. But the Samaritan is not an idolater. Therefore, even after the Samaritan invokes *Ha-Shem*, one still needs to listen in order to make sure that other theologically problematic phrases are not uttered. If everything else in the blessing is appropriate, only then can one respond "Amen."

We learned above that sharing beverages with non-Jews is fraught. So too is sharing beverages with those who are Jew-*ish*.

CONCLUSION

Beverages appear often in rabbinic texts that navigate the boundary between external and internal Others. Notably, neither the people nor their beverages are completely forbidden. Rather, a complex negotiation occurs. For example, the rabbinic Jew must listen to the blessing recited by the Jew-*ish* or non-Jewish person before knowing whether to ignore it or respond "Amen." And the beer of non-Jews may be drunk—just not in a non-Jewish tavern. Beverages are even invoked in trash-talk put-downs, as when the degenerate son of a venerable father is pejoratively called "Vinegar, son of Wine" (*b. Bava Metzi'a* 83b). In all of these instances, beverages aid in the process of "social digestion": "breaking down and reassembling the building blocks of society" (Rosenblum 2010a, 45).

SUGGESTED READINGS

Beer, Michael. 2010. *Taste or Taboo: Dietary Choices in Antiquity*. Totnes, Devon, UK: Prospect Books.

Berkowitz, Beth A. 2014 [2012]. *Defining Jewish Difference: From Antiquity to the Present*. New York: Cambridge University Press.

———. 2018. *Animals and Animality in the Babylonian Talmud*. New York: Cambridge University Press.

Davis, Marni. 2012. *Jews and Booze: Becoming American in the Age of Prohibition*. New York: New York University Press.

Dynner, Glenn. 2013. *Yankel's Tavern: Jews, Liquor, and Life in the Kingdom of Poland*. New York: Oxford University Press.

Fishkoff, Sue. 2010. *Kosher Nation: Why More and More of America's Food Answers to a Higher Authority.* New York: Schocken Books.

Fonrobert, Charlotte Elisheva. 2000. *Menstrual Purity: Rabbinic and Christian Reconstructions of Biblical Gender.* Stanford, CA: Stanford University Press.

Freidenreich, David M. 2011. *Foreigners and Their Food: Constructing Otherness in Jewish, Christian, and Islamic Law.* Berkeley: University of California Press.

Hayes, Christine. 1997. *Between the Babylonian and Palestinian Talmuds: Accounting for Halakhic Difference in Selected Sugyot from Tractate Avodah Zarah.* New York: Oxford University Press.

———. 2007. "The 'Other' in Rabbinic Literature." In *The Cambridge Companion to the Talmud and Rabbinic Literature,* ed. Charlotte Elisheva Fonrobert and Martin S. Jaffee, 243–69. New York: Cambridge University Press.

Holtz, Barry W. 2017. *Rabbi Akiva: Sage of the Talmud.* New Haven, CT: Yale University Press.

Horowitz, Roger. 2016. *Kosher USA: How Coke Became Kosher and Other Tales of Modern Food.* New York: Columbia University Press.

Kraemer, David C. 2009 [2007]. *Jewish Eating and Identity through the Ages.* New York: Routledge.

Liberles, Robert. 2012. *Jews Welcome Coffee: Tradition and Innovation in Early Modern Germany.* Waltham, MA: Brandeis University Press.

Lieberman, Saul, ed. 2001 [1955]. *The Order of Zera'im.* In *The Tosefta: According to Codex Vienna, with Variants from Codex Erfurt, Genizah Mss. and Editio Princeps (Venice 1521), Together with References to Parallel Passages in Talmudic Literature and a Brief Commentary.* 4 vols. New York: Jewish Theological Seminary.

MacDonald, Nathan. 2008. *What Did the Ancient Israelites Eat? Diet in Biblical Times.* Grand Rapids, MI: William B. Eerdmans.

Miliard, Mike. 2007. "Thinkin' about Dunkin': How One Little Post-War Doughnut Shop Became Synonymous with Boston's Identity." *Providence Phoenix* 20, no. 10 (March 9–15): 6–9.

Olyan, Saul M. 2000. *Rites and Rank: Hierarchy in Biblical Representations of Cult.* Princeton, NJ: Princeton University Press.

Porton, Gary G. 1988. *Goyim: Gentiles and Israelites in Mishnah-Tosefta.* Atlanta, GA: Scholars Press.

Rosenblum, Jordan D. 2010a. *Food and Identity in Early Rabbinic Judaism.* New York: Cambridge University Press.

———. 2010b. "From Their Bread to Their Bed: Commensality, Intermarriage, and Idolatry in Tannaitic Literature." *Journal of Jewish Studies* 61, no. 1: 18–29.

———. 2016a. *The Jewish Dietary Laws in the Ancient World*. New York: Cambridge University Press.

———. 2016b. "'Blessings of the Breasts': Breastfeeding in Rabbinic Literature." *Hebrew Union College Annual* 87: 147–79.

———. 2018. "Thou Shalt Not Cook a Bird in Its Mother's Milk? Theorizing the Evolution of a Rabbinic Regulation." In *Religious Studies and Rabbinics: A Conversation*, ed. Elizabeth Shanks Alexander and Beth A. Berkowitz, 175–87. New York: Routledge.

Schäfer, Peter. 2002. "Jews and Gentiles in Yerushalmi Avoda Zara." In *The Talmud Yerushalmi and Graeco-Roman Culture*, ed. Schäfer, 3: 335–52. Tübingen: Mohr Siebeck.

Schiebinger, Londa. 2004 [1993]. *Nature's Body: Gender in the Making of Modern Science*. 2nd ed. New Brunswick, NJ: Rutgers University Press.

Schwartz, Seth. 2001. *Imperialism and Jewish Society, 200 B.C.E. to 640 C.E.* Princeton, NJ: Princeton University Press.

Stern, Sacha. 1994. *Jewish Identity in Early Rabbinic Writings*. New York: Brill.

———. 2013. "Compulsive Libationers: Non-Jews and Wine in Early Rabbinic Sources." *Journal of Jewish Studies* 64, no. 1: 19–44.

Wasserman, Mira Beth. 2017. *Jews, Gentiles, and Other Animals: The Talmud after the Humanities*. Philadelphia: University of Pennsylvania Press.

Yadin-Israel, Azzan. 2015. *Scripture and Tradition: Rabbi Akiva and the Triumph of Midrash*. Philadelphia: University of Pennsylvania Press.

FOUR

Gender and Sexuality

In the past few decades, scholars (e.g., Boyarin 1995; Kraemer 2011; Satlow 1995) have begun to investigate rabbinic assumptions about gender and sexuality. These topics are intertwined, since the social performance of gender informs conversations about "proper" sexual practice, and vice versa. Discussions of both topics show how cultural constructions associated with gender and sexuality create communal norms that privilege certain identities (especially those of elite men). Over time, and in line with a general trend in academia, these investigations have moved from the periphery to the center; that is, it is no longer considered cutting-edge or controversial to assert that rabbinic literature, like almost all ancient literature, was written by men, for men, and about men. In fact, when I taught about gender in an undergraduate Religious Studies theory seminar at the University of Wisconsin in the fall of 2015, one student expressed surprise that there was even a need to devote an entire class session to this topic; after all, she argued, this is so obvious that everyone knows it! What was seen as innovative when I was an undergraduate in the late 1990s is viewed by many of my students today as the trite scholarship of an older generation.

Nevertheless, it is worth taking a moment to justify the logic of this chapter. After all, much of the material contained herein could have been located in other chapters (and, indeed, some of it appears elsewhere too). Consideration of gender and sexuality deserves its own chapter for several reasons, most of all because in some instances, the pendulum has swung too far in the opposite direction: namely, in correcting for what "goes without saying" scholars sometimes treat this material as so obvious that, once again, it "goes without saying." Yet, without a firm grasp on some of the basic principles of how gender and sexuality operate within this corpus, one cannot truly understand rabbinic literature.

Just as we learned in the previous chapter that Jews and non-Jews are not fungible in rabbinic literature, we need to realize that neither are men and women; "*When a woman appears in a rabbinic story, her appearance as a woman is almost never incidental; her character is not interchangeable with a male one*" (Satlow 2002, 226, original emphasis). For example, in a famous tale, a student hides under his Rabbi's bed, in order to learn proper sexual decorum between a husband and wife. Understandably upset that his private conjugal moment has turned into office hours, the Rabbi demands that the student leave. "It is Torah, and I must learn it!" the latter exclaims (*b. Berakhot* 62a; for discussion, see Biale 1997, 53; Boyarin 1995, 122–25). The genders of the characters in this tale are not interchangeable. First, the rabbinic practice of Torah study is gendered as male (Satlow 1996). Second, while both student and Rabbi are named (Rav Kahana and Rav, respectively), the wife's name is never revealed. She is just a literary foil. One cannot imagine a scenario in which a named female student hides under the bed of her named female Rabbi while the latter has sex with her unnamed husband. This asymmetry points towards larger assumptions about gender and sexuality, many of which appear in texts that modern readers might find challenging and/or difficult to read.

Many readers will feel excluded from the heteronormative, male perspective of rabbinic literature. I cannot presume to speak for them, but I want to offer at least one suggestion for reading these texts that I personally find compelling. Discussing how feminist Jewish readers might engage with and connect to the similar rabbinic texts discussed in her own book, Elizabeth Shanks Alexander asserts:

> When feminists in our day follow the rabbinic arguments and exegesis that I have re-animated in the pages of this book, they can be seen to be participating in the ritual Torah study that is prompted by the ancient texts. Feminist readers of the text reenact the work of organizing, analyzing, ordering, and mastering tradition that, in antiquity, was central to the social and religious formation of rabbinic sages. By implicating themselves in the scholastic afterlife of rabbinic texts, feminist readers paradoxically participate in a *beit midrash* [rabbinic study academy] from which they are excluded. It is intriguing to consider the fact that feminists can *report* something they find to be very discouraging (that women cannot participate in Torah study that has the effect of reproducing the covenantal community) even while they *perform* the exact opposite.... When feminists re-animate the exercises that constituted ritual Torah study in the ancient *beit midrash*, they constitute themselves de facto as the next generation in the covenantal community forged by Torah study. (2015, 249)

This chapter asks what rabbinic conversations about beer, wine, breast milk, bitter waters, and magical potions teach us about ancient rabbinic presumptions about gender and sexuality. When modern readers—whatever their own assumptions, interpretations, and identifications—engage in the very practice of rabbinic text study, they are able to perform that practice in multiple ways that can reproduce and/or reshape ancient rabbinic practice. In doing so, they too can declare: "It is Torah, and I must learn it!"

RAV HISDA ADVISES HIS DAUGHTERS: THE ASYMMETRIC PERFORMANCE OF GENDER

One area where we can detect assumptions about gender is in regard to advice about decorum. Decorum is a performative category—it relates to social rules regulating proper action. It tells us not to pick our noses in public; not to talk with food in our mouths; and not to discuss religion, sex, or politics at the dinner table. It also tells us what it is "appropriate" for one to wear, act, or say, often along gendered lines. So examining rabbinic advice on decorum is fruitful for our present purposes.

Like a lot of advice, our example comes in the form of parental admonition: Rav Hisda instructing his daughters in social propriety. But before we get to what Rav Hisda says to his daughters, we encounter a series of statements addressed to rabbinic scholars, mostly by Rav Hisda. These young men are his students. But more than that, they are his academic children, sons not by birth but by reason of study (see Eilberg-Schwartz 1990, 229–34). He tells them how to act when poor and when rich, but mostly when poor. To give a flavor of this general advice:

> And Rav Hisda said: One who is able to eat barley bread but [instead] eats wheat bread transgresses on account of "You shall not destroy" [Deuteronomy 20:19].
> And Rav Pappa said: One who is able to drink beer but [instead] drinks wine transgresses on account of "You shall not destroy." (*b. Shabbat* 140b)

The biblical verse cited above prohibits those besieging a city to chop down fruit trees, "for you may eat from them" (Deuteronomy 20:19). The Rabbis develop this into a broader principle of not being wasteful. Rav Hisda is advising his poor students to not waste their money buying more expensive food (wheat bread) when cheaper ones (barley bread) are available. Rav Pappa chimes in and suggests that one who drinks wine when beer is available is similarly wasteful (see Geller 2004, 239). We should be a little more suspicious of this second statement. First of all, Rav Pappa is a Babylonian Rabbi, and there is a Babylonian preference for beer over wine. Second, and more important, Rav Pappa made a sizable fortune as a brewer, so he clearly has a financial interest (see *b. Pesahim* 113a; *b. Bava Metzi'a* 65a; chapter 3). Rav Pappa is so associated with beer that he is even described as owning a beer-drinking ox! (See *b. Bava Qamma* 35a; Berkowitz 2018, 57–59.) Imagine how skeptical you might be were the CEO of Anheuser-Busch or MillerCoors to make the same statement.

Now that we have the flavor of the advice that Rav Hisda (and friends) were giving their students—their male children, as it were—we are ready to analyze his other advice:

> Rav Hisda said to his daughters: You should be modest [even] in the presence of your husbands: you should not eat bread in the presence of your husbands; you should not eat a vegetable at night; and you should not eat dates at night; and you should not drink beer at night; and you should not relieve yourself where your husbands relieve themselves; and when a person knocks at the door, do not say "Who is it?" (Aramaic *manu*; the masculine pronoun), but rather "Who is it?" (Aramaic *mani*; the feminine pronoun).
>
> He holds a pearl in one hand and a furnace in his other hand. You should show them the pearl, but the furnace you should not show them until they are tormented, and then you should show them. (*b. Shabbat* 140b)

In the ancient Mediterranean (and, I would argue, in most of the modern world as well) there is much more concern expressed for the modesty of a woman than that of a man. For example, in ancient Hebrew, there is no word for "male virgin"—the Hebrew word for "virgin" (*betulah*) always appears in the feminine form. It is imagined as a concept that applies—and hence *matters*—solely in regard to women. As Michael Satlow aptly states: "Female virginity was a sine qua non, but male virginity was a case of non sequitur" (2001, 120). A "virgin" is *always* female. (On using wine to "test" for virginity, see *b. Ketubbot* 10b; Satlow 2001, 173.) Likewise, the physical appearance of women is of greater concern than that of men. For example, while numerous sources discuss the importance of female beauty for suitability for marriage, "Jewish sources from antiquity ascribe no importance to male beauty for making a match" (Satlow 2001, 119).

This knowledge about ancient asymmetrical assumptions of gender helps us understand the very first words uttered by Rav Hisda: "You should be modest [even] in the presence of your husbands." Right off the bat, he presumes that women ought to be modest *in general*. What he therefore addresses is the case when a woman is alone with her husband. In this time of private intimacy, Rav Hisda still cautions his daughters to be modest. (It is for this reason that I added "[even]" to my translation.) But what does it mean to be "modest"? Rav Hisda gives us a series of specific examples. Yet, as we shall soon see, the precise meaning of these specific examples is not always crystal clear.

The modest wife, according to Rav Hisda, does not eat bread in the presence of her husband. According to the renowned medieval commentator and reputed wine-maker Rashi, this piece of advice refers to the fact that sometimes women eat more than a piece of bread; and in overeating, they repulse their husbands. When Rav Hisda discusses men eating, his concern is for quality: that men not waste money on better food when cheaper food is available. Here, in regard to women, his concern is quantity: that women not eat too much food. This suggests a rhetoric of disgust, in that female table manners might revolt their husbands. It also suggests a rhetoric of concealment—that women not eat in front of their husbands, lest they turn them off. There is no analogous concern for husbands eating in front of—and potentially repulsing—their wives.

This regulation of the female mouth—which is not unique to ancient Judaism (see, e.g., Tompkins 2012)—continues in Rav Hisda's next morsels of advice. Why should women not eat vegetables at night? Again according to Rashi, this is because doing so will give them bad breath. And why should women not eat dates and drink beer at night? In the words of Rashi: "They cause diarrhea and lead to flatulence" (Rashi on *b. Shabbat* 140b). If Rashi's interpretations are correct, then taken together women are being cautioned to make sure to watch their diet close to bedtime, so as to assure that they have minty-fresh breath and do not befoul the bedroom's airspace with their bodily functions. Overtones suggest that this is because they would turn off their husbands sexually, especially given the fact that earlier in this same Talmud tractate it is presumed that married couples usually sleep together naked (see *b. Shabbat* 13a, discussed in chapter 3; Rosenblum 2018, 181–82).

Furthermore, the concern with diarrhea seems to be a concern with bodily elimination, since the next piece of advice cautions women against relieving themselves in the same location as their husbands. There is significant discussion of the normative rabbinic law (Hebrew *halakhah*) of the bathroom (see Schofer 2010, 53–76), and gender and the rabbinic bathroom is a topic beyond my scope here (see, e.g., the comment on *b. Gittin* 45a that women gossip in the bathroom; and on gender and gossip in rabbinic literature, see Peskowitz 1997, 131–53). Here, the concern appears rather straightforward: if seeing a woman eat too much bread is a cause for concern, how much the more so is seeing her defecate? Women must regulate their mouths and bodily functions for the benefit of their husbands.

Turning from a wife interacting with *her* husband, Rav Hisda advises his daughters to greet all who come calling at their door assuming that they are female. Hebrew and Aramaic are gendered languages, meaning that there are separate pronouns for greeting male and female visitors. In this text, women are encouraged to default to the feminine pronoun and, concomitantly, both to invite and to expect only female visitors. Expecting—and receiving—male visitors would suggest sexual impropriety. This is also part of a general trend in rabbinic literature, where women are discouraged from talking with men (e.g., *m. Avot* 1:5; *b. Eruvin* 53b). Here women's voices are both literally and metaphorically silenced.

I set Rav Hisda's final piece of advice apart from the rest, because it represents both a departure in structure and content from his previous advice. Here, Rav Hisda engages in a time-honored awkward parental tradition: talking with one's children about the birds and the bees. And Rabbis, like many parents, often turn to euphemism rather than explicitly stating what they mean—hence we call it "the bird and the bees" rather than "the sex talk." Once again, I think that Rashi offers the most plausible interpretation: "pearl" is her breasts and "furnace" is her vulva (while Rashi states the former outright, he refers to the latter using the common rabbinic euphemism of "that place"; Rashi on *b. Shabbat* 140b). Therefore, Rav Hisda tells his daughters to show their husbands their breasts in order to arouse them to the point of suffering (i.e., intense physical desire), and then to show them their vulva so as to initiate vaginal intercourse. Note that the role of the woman in this sexual act is as object: her body is a subject of gaze, touch, and penetration (see Neis 2013, 117–29). Her passive role facilitates her husband's active role, penetrating her and enabling procreation.

Rav Hisda's advice to his daughters serves as an introduction to the asymmetrical performance of gender. Women are expected to eat, drink beer, defecate, answer the doorbell, and fornicate in ways that mark those practices as "modest"—and hence appropriate for the rabbinic woman. Let us now look at a husband's economic obligation to his wife, and how that regulates—and is regulated by—her actions.

A WIFE'S WINE ALLOWANCE: A HUSBAND'S OBLIGATION TO SUPPORT HIS WIFE

When we imagine a wedding today, we often think of a joining of two souls, united in affection, standing before their families and friends and promising to love, honor, and cherish each other, followed by a party. In ancient (and modern) Judaism, however, a wedding might be all of that, but a central feature is the signing of a boilerplate marriage contract (Hebrew *ketubbah*) stipulating certain economic arrangements (on ancient Jewish marriage, see Satlow 2001, esp. 199–224). For example, in the standard modern Aramaic *ketubbah*, after the date, location, and relevant names are listed, the following wording appears:

> Be my wife according to the laws of Moses and Israel. And I shall work, honor, feed, and support you in accordance with the practice of Jewish husbands, who work, honor, feed, and support their wives faithfully.

The text continues on to enumerate the amount of money that the husband will set aside for his wife; promises her food, clothing, necessities, and her conjugal rights; and then spells out several other specific details of the marital economic arrangements. It ends: "And everything is valid and binding."

Immediately, the gender asymmetry of this text is obvious. The husband is the speaker: *he* is marrying and the wife is the one *being* married. Marriage is an arrangement that requires the exchange of money and vows—and the husband promises to do what Jewish men are expected to do: that is, to "work, honor, feed, and support their wives (literally, "their women") faithfully." Some of the support that wives are promised is spelled out—including their conjugal rights (Hebrew *'onah*; see Satlow 1995, 265–82). Other elements of this support are elaborated in other rabbinic texts, which often seek to clarify the terms covered in the *ketubbah*. In this section and the one that follows, we discuss how the economics of marriage can be understood by looking at two different gendered beverages: wine and breast milk.

As one might expect, significant portions of the tractate *Ketubbot* focus on details of the rabbinic marriage contract, or *ketubbah* (Hebrew plural *ketubbot*). This includes stipulations for standard marriages, and those that might deviate from the norm. For example, there is conversation in *m. Ketubbot* 5:8 about how economic arrangements are to be handled when husband and wife live apart, and the husband uses an intermediary in order to pay his wife her weekly allowance for food, clothing, and household needs. Included in this mishnah are some specific foodstuffs, but no mention of beverage appears. This leads later Rabbis to discuss drinks:

> Whereas wine is not taught [in *m. Ketubbot* 5:8]. This supports [a statement by] Rabbi Eliezer. For Rabbi Eliezer said: They do not provide wine for a wife. But if you say, [in Hosea 2:7 it states]: "I will go after my lovers, who give me my bread and my water, my wool and my linen, my oil and my drink," [this refers to] things that a woman desires. And what are they? Jewelry. (*b. Ketubbot* 64b–65a)

This passage (Aramaic *sugya'*) opens by noting that, in the list that appears in *m. Ketubbot* 5:8, wine is not mentioned. A saying attributed to Rabbi Eliezer is then introduced, since the present argument provides support for a statement attributed to him. According to Rabbi Eliezer, in general—and not just in the case of a wife supported by her husband through an intermediary—wives do not receive weekly wine allowances. A verse from Hosea is introduced, in which a female voice expresses expectations of support from her lovers: they will give her bread, water, wool, linen, oil, and drink.

Some background knowledge is required to understand what is happening here. First of all, Hosea, which is part of the Twelve Minor Prophets in the Hebrew Bible, prominently features the theme of a cheating, unfaithful wife (a metaphor for Israel cheating on her husband, God). Therefore, the gendered image of a verse from Hosea of a woman expecting support from her lovers already suggests the potential for sexual impropriety. Second, remember that this situation involves a couple living apart, so there seems to be concern that a wife drinking wine alone might lead her to desire sex more regularly than her husband could physically be available to offer it (as Rashi's commentary also implies). Third, the reference to "drink" in Hosea 2:7 is initially presumed to be wine (after all, water has already been mentioned, so this must be something else). Fourth, the verb "desires" is actually a pun. The roots of the Hebrew words drink (*sh-q-i*) and desire (*sh-u-q*) look similar, so it is punning that what the woman (Hebrew *'isha*; which could also be translated as "the wife") desires is not drink, but jewelry (itself a gendered assumption). At the same time, it is implying that wine leads to desire, which continues the metaphor of sexuality that pervades this passage.

These assumptions develop as the *sugya'* continues. For the sake of brevity, I summarize the next two sections of the *sugya'*, before we return to a more in-depth analysis. Next, we have further support for a wife not being provided with wine. Then, the question is raised of whether a woman who is accustomed to drinking wine prior to her marriage is allotted wine after her marriage. And then the following comments appear:

> It is taught in a *baraita'*: One cup [of wine] is beneficial for a woman; two [cups] is a disgrace; three [cups lead to her] making explicit sexual

propositions; four [cups lead to her] making sexual propositions even to a donkey in the marketplace, [since she is so drunk that] she does not care [with whom she has sex].

Rava said: This was taught only when her husband is not with her, but [if] her husband is with her, [then] we have no problem with it. (*b. Ketubbot* 65a)

While the text continues on, it is in the statement above that we get to the heart of the matter. There is a concern that drunkenness leads to expressions of sexuality. And rabbinic fear of these overt expressions of sexuality in particular suggests the presence of asymmetric gendered assumptions (a similar fear is expressed by ancient Roman authors; see Pomeroy 1995, 153–54). We begin with the fact that we are discussing wives drinking wine, not husbands. It would seem that the latter is not worthy of anywhere near equal commentary (though on rabbinic temperance, see chapter 9). Evidence for this concern is found in a *baraita'*, a rabbinic tradition reputed to be of tannaitic origin that is cited in an amoraic text, that discusses how much wine a woman—but *not* a man—should drink. One glass of wine is beneficial (for health, appearance, etc.). But any more is detrimental. If a woman pours herself a second glass of wine, she brings herself to disgrace. If she pours herself a third glass, then she will start making explicit sexual propositions. If she pours herself a fourth glass, then she will be so drunk that she will not care whether her sexual propositions are made to a human or non-human animal. (In another gendered context, *b. Avodah Zarah* 22b claims that non-Jewish men are especially desirous of having sex with non-human animals owned by Jews!)

But then notice how Rava modifies this statement. A woman alone should only drink one cup of wine at most. But if her husband is around, then she can drink as much as she wants. Rava's logic, it would seem, is that if the woman becomes drunk with her husband around, he can control her urges by offering her a rabbinically approved outlet for them: namely, himself. But without the control of her husband, a woman is not to be trusted with wine. For this reason, a potentially absent husband would not provide his wife with wine.

MOTHER'S MILK: GENDER AND THE OBLIGATION TO BREASTFEED

Another fascinating example of gender and asymmetric rabbinic regulations involves a beverage that scholars too often fail to address: breast milk. This oversight ignores the fact that it has been less than two hundred years that safe, reliable, and effective non-breast milk options have existed. In antiquity, and throughout history until very recent times, breastfeeding by either the biological mother or a wet nurse was the only way for an infant to survive.

As one might expect, rabbinic texts discussing breastfeeding contain multiple assumptions about gender (in general, see Rosenblum 2016). Primary among these presumptions is that it is a wife's obligation that "she nurses her child" (*m. Ketubbot* 5:5). However, note my wording in the previous sentence: *it is a wife's obligation.* When *m. Ketubbot* 5:5 refers to breastfeeding, it appears in a list of expected labors that a wife performs on behalf of her husband (including such other household chores as cooking and washing clothes). The Rabbis imagine breastfeeding as a wife's duty to her husband. Remember that these texts were written by men, for men, and about men. Therefore, it is not surprising that they envision breastfeeding in terms of their wives' obligation to them, rather than in terms of a mother's obligation to feed her own biological child. Modern conceptions of breastfeeding often depict it in terms of maternal attachment and benefit to the child (for a critical discussion, see Jung 2015). For the Rabbis, however, it is about the wife's obligation to her husband, and the father's obligation to his child.

This asymmetric understanding creates a potential nightmare scenario: in the event of a divorce, the biological father has an obligation to feed his not-yet-weaned child; however, his ex-wife no longer has an obligation to feed her ex-husband's child. Perhaps shockingly, the fact that the infant *is her own biological child* is not a matter of concern to the Rabbis. In a case such as this, can a father force his ex-wife to nurse their biological child? No. And yes.

> If [the biological mother] was divorced, [then her ex-husband] cannot compel her to nurse [their child]. If her child recognizes her, [then her ex-husband] can compel her to nurse and pays her a wage and she nurses [the infant], because of the danger to its life. (*t. Ketubbot 5:5*)

In general, an ex-husband cannot compel his ex-wife to feed her child. Her obligation was to her husband, not to her own biological child; and since the child's father is no longer her husband, her obligation no longer exists. However, an exception exists (there is almost always an exception in rabbinic law!): if the infant recognizes its own mother, then the ex-wife can be forced to breastfeed her own biological child, though she is paid a wage for doing so. When she was her ex-husband's wife, she did not receive a wage, but rather a household budget that covered her needs. In fact, while married, "if she is nursing, they reduce her [other] household chores and increase her food budget" (*m. Ketubbot 5:9*). This increased budget even covered wine, since the Rabbis believed that "wine increases the [production of] breast milk" (*y. Ketubbot 5:13*, 30b; cf. *b. Ketubbot 65b*). The language of "wage" here indicates that she is being treated as a wet nurse—that is, as a third party contracted for services rendered. The child may recognize her as its mother, but legally she is treated as a nonmaternal contracted laborer. Her breast milk is not mother's milk, but a purchased commodity.

Infants, however, recognize not only the sight, but also the smell of their mother. This association is present almost immediately after birth. Therefore, it would be assumed that infants would recognize their own mother. This presumption means that the latter scenario will almost certainly come to pass, and the ex-wife/ biological mother can be compelled to nurse her ex-husband's/her own biological child. While the end result will be the same, the gender asymmetry forces the Rabbis to grapple with this potentially dangerous scenario. If the relevant law were gender-symmetrical, both biological parents would have an equal obligation to feed their own biological child. Married or divorced, the obligation would remain incumbent upon them both. As that is not the case, the Rabbis must turn to concern for the child's life in order to rectify a potentially dangerous situation of their own making. Remember that in antiquity, access to breast milk was vital to an infant's ability not only to thrive, but to survive. Today we may debate whether "breast is best," but in the (not so distant) past, there were no other viable options so the potential repercussions were dire (on this debate, see Bentley 2014; Jung 2015).

While danger to life plays out in a variety of other breast milk related scenarios in rabbinic literature (see Rosenblum 2016, 165–69), another relevant asymmetrical gender law deserves attention: namely, why is male breast milk said to be pure? As is discussed further in chapter 8 on ritual purity, the Rabbis believe that breast milk is transformed menstrual blood. This association (common not only in the ancient world but in Western medicine until the eighteenth century) leads the Rabbis to debate to what extent the complex set of menstrual purity regulations should be applied to breast milk. In general, while the Rabbis debate straightforward scenarios, they display a particular proclivity towards the anomalous—and, frankly, the weird. Like the newspaper editor bored with the headline "Dog Bites Man," but ready to print "Man Bites Dog" on the front page, the Rabbis are drawn to the unusual and extraordinary. A female lactating? Commonplace. A male lactating? Interesting!

To be fair, though rare, there are many reported cases of male lactation, technically referred to as male galactorrhea. And, since it is possible (no matter how improbable), then the Rabbis are interested in understanding the relevant normative rabbinic law (Hebrew *halakhah*). They conclude that: "the milk of a male is pure" (*m. Makhshirin* 6:7; in general, see Rosenblum 2016, 154–55). This decision is based on two premises. The first premise, discussed in more detail in chapter 8, is that men do not menstruate and, since female breast milk is transformed menstrual blood and men do not menstruate, then male breast milk must be something else. Therefore, the impurity regulations regarding (female) menstrual blood do not transfer to male breast milk. The second premise is a common presumption in the ancient

Mediterranean: namely, that female bodies are porous, leaky, and uncontrolled (see Balberg 2014, 142–44, 173; Fonrobert 2000, 61–63). Male bodies are the opposite: whole, contained, and controlled (or, at least controllable, since men who do not control their bodies are deemed effeminate). Lactating women release their milk (referred to as "let down") both voluntarily and involuntarily, as their breasts respond to hormonal and environmental stimuli. For these reasons, the Rabbis express a variety of purity-related concerns regarding female breast milk (see Rosenblum 2016). This same concern does not apply to male breast milk. Why? Because the Rabbis believe the male body to be controllable; hence, a male would only let down his breast milk on command. The product of a controlled and contained body, male breast milk is therefore not subject to additional purity concerns. Beverages produced by female and male bodies are subject to asymmetric regulation. Mother's milk might have various purity concerns, but father's milk does not.

BITTER WATERS AND JEALOUS HUSBANDS

Perhaps the ultimate example of gender asymmetry is encountered in the bizarre biblical ritual commonly referred to as "the bitter waters" (Hebrew *mayim ha-marim*; in general, see Destro 1989). Though the Rabbis claim in *m. Sotah* 9:9 that this ritual—often called an "ordeal" or "test"—ceased to exist after the destruction of the Second Temple (and Rosen-Zvi 2008 argues that there is reason to be skeptical that it ever occurred), they nevertheless devote most of an entire tractate to the subject: *Sotah*, meaning "suspected adulteress" (note the gender, to which we shall return).

Before turning to the Rabbis, it is worth reading much of the biblical narrative (for the full text, see Numbers 5:11–31). I shall translate and comment on most of this passage, breaking it into several text blocks in order to help the reader understand this complex and vexing ritual.

The biblical account begins:

> If any man's wife commits adultery and acts unfaithfully towards him, and a man has sex with her unbeknownst to her husband, and she keeps hidden that she has defiled herself, without being forced, and there is no witness against her, and a fit of jealousy comes over him and he is enraged in jealousy at his wife that she has defiled herself, or a fit of jealousy comes over him and he is enraged in jealousy at his wife that she has not defiled herself, the man shall bring his wife to the priest. (Numbers 5:12–15)

From the very beginning, we see this is about concern for women cheating on men, and *not* vice versa. Indeed, the biblical (and subsequently the rabbinic) definition of adultery is: a married woman who has sex with a man other than her husband (the punishment for which is death; see Leviticus 20:10; Deuteronomy 22:22). Therefore, a married man can only commit adultery if the woman with whom he has sex is married to another man. (It is for this reason that I always render the Hebrew word *'isha* in this biblical narrative as "wife" and not "woman," since the issue is always that she is married at the time of suspected intercourse.) The husband suspects that his wife has committed adultery, but he cannot prove it—since there are no witnesses to testify to the fact that his wife committed an act of consensual, adulterous sex. But even though this act of adultery may or may not have happened, the husband is enraged with jealousy. He cannot abide Schrödinger's cat; he simply must know.

In order to get to the bottom of this, the husband takes his wife, along with some food for an offering (Numbers 5:15), to a priest. Next:

> The priest shall bring her forward and make her stand before the Lord. The priest shall take sacral water in an earthen vessel and, taking some of the dirt that is on the ground of the Tabernacle, the priest shall put it into the water. The priest shall make the wife stand before the Lord and uncover the wife's head and place upon her hands the meal offering of remembrance, which is a meal offering of jealousy. And in the priest's hands shall be the water of bitterness (Hebrew *mey ha-marim*) that induces the spell. The priest shall make her take an oath, and say to the wife: "If a man has not had sex with you, and if you have not committed adultery in defilement while married, be immune from [the harmful effects of drinking] this

water of bitterness that induces the spell. But if indeed you did commit adultery while married and defiled yourself, if a man other than your husband had sex with you"—then the priest shall make the wife take an oath with the oath of cursing, and the priest says to the wife—"may the Lord make you a curse and an oath amongst your people, when the Lord makes your thigh sag and your belly swell. And may this water that induces the spell enter into your womb, making the belly swell and the thigh sag." And the wife shall say: "Amen! Amen!" (Numbers 5:16–22)

Since no human can "prove" beyond a reasonable doubt whether the wife has committed adultery, a ritual test must occur, in which God will provide testimony. Like drinking a radioactive liquid tracer before a medical test, the bitter waters (here called "the water of bitterness") help with the diagnosis. Before we learn about how the drink is prepared, we are told that the wife is stood before God and made to take an oath. She must swear that she did not have sex with another man. Given the seriousness of oaths in the ancient world, one would presume that someone might confess rather than violate the Third Commandment by swearing a false oath (see Exodus 20:7; Deuteronomy 5:11). The priest declares that if she is innocent, nothing will occur—she will be immune to any physical harm. But if she is lying and has sworn falsely, then there will be noticeable physical side effects. While the precise meaning of these physical effects is debated (perhaps it refers to a distended uterus and miscarriage), the results are understood to be ontological and observable. The spell enters into her womb (a word that could also be translated as "intestines," "bowels," or simply "inside of body," but the context here suggests that they are thinking of a womb) and works its magic—proving either her fidelity or infidelity. The wife consents (to the extent that we can imagine this as our modern notion of informed and willing consent) by replying "Amen! Amen!" to the priest.

And then, the priest prepares the concoction:

> The priest shall write these curses on a scroll and rub it off into the water of bitterness. And he shall make the wife drink the water of bitterness that

induces the spell, so that the water that induces the spell enters into her in order to cause bitterness.... And when he has made her drink the waters, then if she has defiled herself and acted unfaithfully towards her husband, the water that induces the spell shall enter into her in order to cause bitterness, and her belly shall swell and her thigh shall sag; and the wife shall become a curse among her people. But if the wife did not defile herself and is pure, then she is innocent and will become pregnant. (Numbers 5:23–24, 27–28)

The wife is forced to drink what sounds like a disgusting cocktail: water, mixed with dirt and ink. Based on her physical reaction, she is either declared guilty or innocent (and, in the latter case, it would seem that she also becomes pregnant).

By way of concluding this ritual, Numbers 5:29–31 notes:

This is the law of jealousy, when a wife acts unfaithfully while married and defiles herself, or when a man has a fit of jealousy and he is enraged in jealousy at his wife: the wife shall be made to stand before the Lord and the priest shall execute this entire law. The husband shall be clear of guilt, but that woman shall suffer her guilt.

This summary reminds us of the gender asymmetry that pervades this ritual: the husband fears no repercussions for making an accusation, but the wife incurs punishment if the suspicion is "proven" to be true. Therefore, a man can initiate this ritual without fear of guilt, which is not the case for a woman. And a woman could never initiate this ritual.

The Rabbis have much to say about this ritual. One text in particular has received significant scholarly attention, because it uses this ritual to raise the question of teaching Torah knowledge to a daughter (see, e.g., Alexander 2015, 200–205; Boyarin 1995, 170–80; Hauptman 1998, 22–25; Wegner 1988, 161–62). While there is the expectation that a father teaches his son Torah, whether he does the same for his daughter does not go without saying (see Alexander 2015, 184–88). Therefore, we learn:

She hardly finishes drinking before her face becomes green, her eyes bulge, and her veins swell, and they say: Take her away! Take her away! So that she does not defile the Temple Court!

> But if she has merit, it would suspend [the punishment] for her.
>
> There is merit that suspends [punishment] for one year, there is merit that suspends [punishment] for two years, [and] there is merit that suspends [punishment] for three years.
>
> Hence Ben Azzai says: A man is obligated to teach his daughter Torah, so that if she drinks [the bitter waters], she will know that the merit suspends [the punishment] for her.
>
> Rabbi Eliezer says: Anyone who teaches his daughter Torah, it is as if he taught her lasciviousness.
>
> Rabbi Yehoshua says: A woman prefers one *qav* [of material possessions] and lasciviousness rather than nine *qav* [of material possessions] and abstinence. (*m. Sotah* 3:4)

The text opens with a woman being forced (see *m. Sotah* 3:3) to drink the bitter waters and then suddenly having an extreme physical reaction: her complexion changes as her eyes and veins bulge out. Those witnessing these events take place shout that she must be removed immediately from the Temple Court (on this peanut gallery, see *m. Sotah* 1:6). Why? Because she might die and her corpse would pollute the Temple.

At this moment, the text takes an odd turn by stating that, if the woman has merit, then this merit will suspend the punishment for her. Note both that she would still be deserving of punishment and that the text presumes her guilt (see Alexander 2015, 201). However, her merit delays the onset of the punishment for up to three years (for more on merit, see *m. Sotah* 3:5). Merit thus serves like a credit in one's account, from which payments are deducted. But once the account balance is down to zero, the full payment comes due.

How is merit credited to one's account? Through Torah study. For this reason, according to Ben Azzai, "A man is obligated to teach his daughter Torah." This is a cryptic statement. Some have tried to use it as support for teaching women Torah in general, but this is problematic (see Alexander 2015, 203). Is the only reason that a daughter should learn Torah is so that if, one day, she commits adultery in a consensual but unwitnessed manner and her husband suspects that it happened and forces her to drink the bitter waters, then her punishment will be delayed for up to three years? That sounds as farfetched as the complicated sentence required to explain it. If the purpose of this passage were to convey that, in general, daughters should be taught Torah, we would expect a statement like: "A man is obligated to teach his daughter Torah so she would know this law and not commit adultery."

Sensing this problem, Rabbi Eliezer argues that anyone who teaches his daughter Torah is comparable to one who taught his daughter lasciviousness. Why? Because the Torah gives her merit and a potential three-year reprieve from punishment, which the daughter would conceivably know, so she would feel more comfortable engaging in lewd sexual behavior in general (on the term "lasciviousness" [Hebrew *tiflut*], see Boyarin 1995, 171n3). This is essentially the argument made by those in favor of "abstinence only" sex education: knowledge of contraception leads to one putting that knowledge to practical use, which is why they believe it is best not to impart that knowledge at all. Better to not teach your daughter Torah, Rabbi Eliezer says, so that she will not count on charging her sins to her merit credit card.

All of this talk about lasciviousness and women culminates in Rabbi Yehoshua's claim that, if given the choice, women prefer fewer material possessions but more sex, as opposed to the opposite. (The measurement used is a *qav*, roughly equivalent to twenty-four eggs, which is not the most useful measurement in the modern era; also, scholars debate the precise size of an egg for this purpose, so just think of this term as meaning "a measure"—as in "1 measure of stuff, 9 measures of sex.") This conforms with a larger trend in rabbinic literature that imagines women as unable to exert self-control and hence ruled by their passions, especially their sexual appetite (see Satlow 1995, 158–59; Wegner 1988, 153–62). For example, we saw this concern above in *b. Ketubbot* 65a, where a woman was allowed to drink more wine with her husband around, as she is presumed unable to control her libido without his help.

Given the context of the bitter waters, it is unsurprising that this text turns to concerns for unregulated sexuality; after all, the whole point of this ordeal is that the husband suspects, but cannot prove, that his wife has committed adultery. The centerpiece of this test is the consumption of a beverage—a disgusting cocktail of water, dirt, and ink. Drinking once again serves as a gateway into themes in rabbinic literature. In this case, discussion of this highly unusual beverage leads to a conversation about teaching women Torah and the role that plays in regulating their (presumably) unquenchable thirst for sex.

WOMEN AND WINE: WHORES, IDOLATRY, AND GENDER ASYMMETRY

In several cases, rabbinic texts explicitly address how the gender of a character affects their ruling. One such instance involves Jewish/non-Jewish men drinking wine with non-Jewish/Jewish whores:

> Rava said: [If] an idolatrous whore (Hebrew *zonah*) and a Jewish man are reclining beside each other, the wine [they are sharing] is permitted because, while the desire for [sexual] transgression would be strong in them, the desire for libated wine (Hebrew *yayn nesekh*) would not be strong in them. [However, if] a Jewish whore (Hebrew *zonah*) and idolatrous men are reclining, the wine [they are sharing] is prohibited. Why? Because she is debased and enticed by them. (*b. Avodah Zarah* 69b–70a)

I must begin my analysis by explaining why I translate the Hebrew word *zonah* as "whore." In a tradition that begins in the Hebrew Bible, "whoring" (Hebrew *zonim*) describes both real and metaphorical carnal acts that violate cultural norms and theological tenets. For example, in a famous biblical text recited daily in rabbinic prayer services, Numbers 15:37–41 discusses the obligation to place fringes (Hebrew *tzitzit*) on the corners of four-cornered garments (on the gendering of the associated rabbinic rules, see Alexander 2015, 211–34). The reason given for this prescription is that seeing them there will remind you not to "go whoring" after other gods (Numbers 15:39). Fanciful rabbinic interpretations read this injunction not only metaphorically, but quite literally (see Harvey 1986; *Sifre Numbers* 115). "Whore" and "whoring" are jarring terms, which is why many translators prefer "prostitute"/"concubine" and "lusting." This, however, conceals the disruptive intention of these terms and categories. A *zonah* is a gendered body that violates normative sexual roles; it is also a gendered body that is violated. And *zonim* is a set of sexual practices that violate not only normative sexual praxis, but that are also theologically nefarious actions. For example, in the passage from Numbers 15:39, the one who goes whoring is cheating on God. Biblical and postbiblical texts imagine God and Israel/Jews as in a monogamous relationship, so to "whore" is a serious accusation, and translating *zonah* and *zonim* as "whore" and "whoring" reveals these important (and admittedly often problematic) assumptions. We cannot conceal them; rather, as scholars and readers we must struggle with them, especially since their legacy of gendered violence and oppression continues to confront us today.

The very term "whore" would therefore trigger an entire set of assumptions about the *zonah* as a transgressive gendered body. This explains the presumptions in the text about both sexual relations (*zonah* as physically transgressive) and idolatrous practice (*zonah* as theologically transgressive). Further support for such presumptions is the dining posture described therein, as reclining was a gendered and often sexualized dining posture in the ancient Mediterranean world. Ancient Mediterranean texts describe elite men as reclining. "Proper" women usually do not recline, so when a woman is depicted as such, it often indicates that she is understood to be sexually available. These associations changed over time in the ancient Mediterranean, but the Rabbis envision reclining as the dining posture of the elite male (in general, see Roller 2006; Rosenblum 2012; Smith 2003).

Now that we understand that the women depicted in this text are understood to be transgressive bodies arranged in a transgressive posture, we are prepared to analyze the unit as a whole. This passage imagines two scenarios: in the first scenario, an idolatrous whore (*zonah*) reclines with a Jewish man and drinks wine; in the second scenario, a Jewish whore (*zonah*) reclines with idolatrous men and drinks wine. If rabbinic legislation is truly symmetrical, then the gender of the idolater or Jew should not matter and the status of the shared wine should not change. However, as we see in the text, gender is a variable that affects the status of the wine; hence, the rabbinic legislation is asymmetric in regard to gender and wine.

In this case, the wine that a male Jew shares with a non-Jewish female whore is permitted for Jewish consumption, but the wine that a male non-Jew shares with a Jewish female whore is not. (Note: the fact that the latter involves "men" in the plural does not affect the argument.) The reasons provided for this different status are quite telling. In the former case, both the non-Jewish whore and the Jewish man are deemed desirous of sex but not desirous of libating wine. In the latter case, the non-Jewish men are understood to be so driven to libate wine that they are compelled to do so, even before engaging in sexual acts. For them, libation comes before libido. Remember the rabbinic understanding of non-Jews as "compulsive libationers" discussed in chapters 3 and 5 (see Stern 2013). The Jewish whore in this case is viewed as having been debased and enticed by the non-Jewish men, and thus she submits to their desires. Hence, their shared wine is prohibited.

The fact that wine shared by a Jewish male and a non-Jewish whore is not deemed libated wine at first seems to contradict *Sifre Numbers* 131, the text discussed in chapter 3 in which a non-Jewish woman demands that a Jewish man, intoxicated with wine and lust, bow to her idol before they engage in intercourse. However, note that she does not libate the wine in that text, but rather demands that he bow to her (conveniently and provocatively concealed) idol. She is also not described as a "whore." Therefore, while *Sifre Numbers* 131 complicates sharing wine with a non-Jewish woman, the present text does not necessarily address the exact same issue. Here, the question is about priorities and inclinations. Note that the Jewish man here is interested in libido, not libations; the non-Jewish men, however, are "compulsive libationers" who cannot focus on anything else before they scratch their insatiable pagan itch.

In both scenarios, however, women are passive. They submit to male desire. Though both scenarios imagine women as passive and men as active, the submissions of non-Jewish and Jewish women are not the same. When a non-Jewish whore submits to a Jewish man, they share wine and physical intimacy. In doing so, however, she is described neither as being "debased" nor "enticed" by him, even though she submits to his will. When a Jewish whore submits to non-Jewish men, however, she is "debased and enticed by them." Here, assumptions about the Other intertwine with presumptions about gender.

Finally, neither scenario depicts a man as a "whore." While the men may engage in transgressive practices, they are not "whores"—a term gendered as female. One could not switch the roles performed by males and females in this text; they are not interchangeable because these laws are not symmetric. The gender of the one drinking the wine matters.

BLACK MAGIC WOMAN

Another gender asymmetry is encountered in the rabbinic presumption that women are more inclined to magic than men. Of course, we could offer multiple historical examples—from Medea to the Salem witch trials to Sabrina the Teenage Witch—that remind us that this is a popular assumption, both ancient and modern. This belief appears numerous times in rabbinic literature, from a statement in the Babylonian Talmud that "most women practice witchcraft" (*b. Sanhedrin* 67a), to a claim made by Hillel, a famous sage, after whom a building is named on many college campuses, that "the more wives, the more witchcraft" (*m. Avot* 2:7).

This gendered assumption leads to several fascinating, and indeed humorous, encounters between male Rabbis and witchy women. For example, *b. Sanhedrin* 67b reports the following:

> Yannai arrived at a certain inn. He said to them: "Give me a drink of water." They brought him a lentil and water porridge. Seeing the lips of the woman [who served him] moving, he poured out a little of it, [which] turned into scorpions. He said to her: "I drank of yours, now come and drink of mine!"

> He gave her a drink [and] she turned into a donkey. He rode her down to the marketplace. Her girlfriend came [and] broke the spell. [Thus,] he was seen riding upon a woman in the marketplace.

Thirsty Yannai arrives at an inn and orders a drink of water. He is served a watery porridge, but before he can drink it, he notices his waitress's lips moving. In rabbinic literature, whispering women is a code for women practicing magic, so he immediately suspects her of magical malice. His suspicion is confirmed when he pours out a little of his beverage (not as a pagan would pour out a libation, but as a rabbinic scientist would pour out some liquid in order to verify a theory) and it transforms into scorpions. While I am not a medical professional, I believe it uncontroversial to assert that drinking scorpions is bad for your health. Therefore, Yannai rightly concludes that this woman is a witch who intends to cause him harm.

Having confirmed her magical identity, note what Yannai does: he coerces her to drink his own enchanted concoction! As discussed further in chapter 5, despite the Rabbis' grave concerns about "magic," they neither deny its efficacy nor hesitate to learn it. In some cases, they even practice it, although this is often seen as self-defense against an impious attack. In what sounds like a modern game of Dungeons and Dragons, Yannai parries the witch's scorpion attack with a spell of his own, which turns the witch into a donkey.

At this point, the gendered assumption of women as witches and women as sexual temptresses intertwine. Instead of merely changing her into a donkey and walking away, Yannai rides the "donkey" down to the marketplace, the most public area in town. (On gender in the rabbinic marketplace, see Baker 2002, 77–112.) The sexual innuendo of Yannai riding this particular "donkey" in public is laid bare when the witch's girlfriend comes along and breaks Yannai's spell. As a result, "he was seen riding upon a woman in the marketplace."

Yannai takes his revenge too far. Ironically, his sexualized ride of the donkey/woman actually renders him effeminate in the rabbinic gaze. The Rabbis believe that women tempt men, and not necessarily the other way around. They spend far more time worrying about the corrupting influence that women have on men, rather than vice versa (as is the usual gendered presumption in modern Western society). For instance, *b. Sotah* 7a (cf. *b. Qiddushin* 81a) requires that, if a man must go on a long journey with a woman, he should bring along two other men as chaperones to protect him against female seduction. Should one of his male companions need to step away in order to relieve himself, the man will then still have one male chaperone present and would not be left alone with a potential temptress. Recall also the reclining whores and non-Jewish women with concealed idols discussed above (*b. Avodah Zarah* 69b–70a; *Sifre Numbers* 131). This assumption is built on the notion common throughout the ancient Mediterranean that only males are capable of "self-control"—that is, only males can regulate and discipline their minds and bodies. Females are believed to be slaves to their passions, while males are capable in theory—if not always in practice—of controlling their thoughts and actions (see Satlow 1996). Males who lacked self-control were thus deemed effeminate in most ancient Mediterranean cultures.

And this is why the ending suggests that Yannai has gone a step too far and, in doing so, forfeits his masculine identity. Up until the very end of the story, Yannai is a masculine rabbinic male. He detects a witch's magic and avoids falling prey to it. He then counters with his own spell, which proves effective. He could have stopped there. At that point, he has bested a witch and transformed her into a beast. Where he loses self-control is when he mounts the woman and rides her down to the market. Then, in the most public place in town, another witch bests him, breaking his spell and putting him in the compromising position of being "seen riding upon a woman in the marketplace." His lack of self-control leads to a woman casting her spell on him and embarrassing him in a sexually explicit manner in public. Yannai therefore goes from being viewed as a masculine rabbinic male who vanquishes a witch to being seen as an effeminate, uncontrolled, and sexually compromised male mounting a woman like a donkey in the middle of town.

Since the majority of women were presumed to be witches, encounters with women were fraught potentially with moral, theological, and especially sexual danger. In embodying the witch, women are understood as both sexually and spiritually seductive. Rabbinic men must be careful, then, in their interactions with women. And even if they uncover a tricky witchy woman, males must be careful to exhibit self-control and merely neutralize the whispering witch, rather than mount her like a donkey and ride her into town.

BEER AND BEYOND THE GENDER BINARY

Thus far, we have only discussed gender in binary terms: male and female. This is because:

> Rabbinic legal thinking ... aims first and foremost at instituting a rather pronounced gender grid, imposed on the social organization of Jewish society as the rabbis envisioned it. Most of the individual laws of rabbinic halakhah apply to either men or women. Differently put, in rabbinic legal thinking it is almost always important whether the halakhic agent is a man or a woman. (Fonrobert 2007, 271)

Gender in binary terms therefore is an important aspect of rabbinic legal thinking. But, as you might expect by now, just because the Rabbis like to think in binary terms, does not mean that they think in binary terms about their binary terms.

Whatever does that mean? While the Rabbis construct a gender grid in which men and woman are the two categories, they also devote time to various categories that are "neither-nor" or "both this and that" (Fonrobert 2007, 272–73). Therefore, the two gender categories of the Rabbis are really six. The first two are the two main gender categories into which the Rabbis wish everything to fit: male and female. Third and fourth, there are "the dual-sexed hermaphrodite" (Hebrew *'androginos* from Greek) and "his parallel, the nonsexed or not-yet sexed person [Hebrew *tumtum*]" (Fonrobert 2007, 272). Fifth and sixth, there are the *saris*, often translated as "eunuch," and the *'aylonit*, which refers to a person identified as "female" at birth but who then, at the onset of puberty, develops "male" characteristics and is infertile.

These additional four gender categories are employed by the Rabbis to analyze bodies and embodied practices that do not conform to their binary gender grid. For example, the Rabbis presume heterosexual intercourse to be normative, and raise serious concerns about homoerotic intercourse (especially in regard to male-male encounters), but may a man have sex with an *'androginos*? (See *t. Yevamot* 10:2, where the answer is: it depends upon whether "he comes upon him in the way of males" or not; see Satlow 1994, 17–18.) Further, the categories of *saris* and the *'aylonit* "have much more to do with the legal determination of an inability to reproduce than with differentiating between sexual identities" (Fonrobert 2007, 280).

Though the *saris* and the *'aylonit* are discussed most often in regard to their infertility, they are still part of the larger discourse about gender categories in rabbinic literature. An interesting example of how this works is in regard to Levirate marriage (Hebrew *yibum*). Levirate marriage occurs when a man dies without bearing any children. His brother is obligated to marry his widow and procreate, so that the deceased's children will bear his name (in general, see Deuteronomy 25:5–10). If the brother of the deceased does not wish to do so, one of the most bizarre biblical rituals occurs: the widow stands before the Elders, unties his shoe, spits in his face, and says, "Thus shall it be done unto the man who does not build up his brother's house!" (Deuteronomy 25:9).

Levirate marriage merits its own tractate of the Mishnah and Talmud: *Yevamot*, the plural of *yibum*. *Yevamot* is the first tractate in the Order of Women (Hebrew *Nashim*), an Order that considers gendered bodies and practices that depart from those of the normative rabbinic male. At one point, the Mishnah discusses the ritual refusal of Levirate marriage, known as *ḥalitzah* (from the Hebrew word used in Deuteronomy 25:9 for untying his shoe) and whether this ritual applies to a *saris* (*m. Yevamot*

8:4–5). After all, if a *saris* is man, he would be eligible for Levirate marriage; but a *saris* is also sterile, so can he really marry his deceased brother's childless widow for the purposes of procreation? Further, is an *'aylonit* subject to Levirate marriage and/or *halitzah* (m. Yevamot 8:5)?

In discussing the case of the *saris*, m. Yevamot 8:4 distinguishes between two different types: the *saris 'adam* (literally, "eunuch of man") and *saris hamah* (literally, "eunuch of sun/heat"). The *saris 'adam* is a man-made eunuch—that is, he was born with both testicles and was fertile, but was subsequently castrated. In contrast, a *saris hamah* is sterile from birth. According to one tradition, a *saris hamah* is a "eunuch of the sun," having never seen a single sunrise as a fertile male (y. Yevamot 8:5, 9d). But, as I note above, the Hebrew word *hamah* can also mean, "heat." With all of this background in mind, we turn to a text that illustrates many of these issues:

> What is the case of a *saris hamah*?
> Rav Yitzhak bar Yosef said that Rabbi Yohanan said: [This refers to] anyone who did not see one moment of *kashrut*.
> How do we know [whether he is a congenital *saris*]?
> Abaye said: Anyone who [from birth] urinates and does not form an arch [with his urine, is a congenital *saris*].
> What causes this to occur? When his mother baked [bread] at noon and drank *marqa'* beer [while pregnant with him]. (b. Yevamot 79b–80a)

Our text opens by inquiring about the term *saris hamah* that appears in m. Yevamot 8:4. A tradition is introduced that provides a definition: a *saris hamah* is a congenital *saris*. I left the term *kashrut* untranslated here because, while *kashrut* (the abstract Hebrew noun of *kasher*, or "kosher," meaning "fit/valid/permissible/suitable") is most often associated with food, the Rabbis use the term to refer to a variety of other contexts in which they assess the validity of a person/object/substance for a given category. In fact, the Hebrew Bible never refers to food as kosher. As a congenital *saris*, there is never a moment when the *saris hamah* is "kosher" in regard to procreation.

The text continues to seek further clarification. Are we sure that this refers to a congenital *saris*? Abaye offers a criterion: if he could never form an arch when he urinates, then he is a *saris* from birth. This suggests that the person has never been able to urinate from a standing position, a position gendered as male (for further gendered conversation about urination, see *b. Bekhorot* 44b). And what causes this congenital condition? Here is where the meaning of *ḥamah* as "heat" comes into play. While pregnant, the *saris ḥamah*'s mother engaged in hot activities that raised her body temperature significantly enough to cause a birth defect (on rabbinic views on embryonic development, see Kessler 2009). As anyone who has spent time in a hot kitchen in the summer can attest, baking bread in a hot oven at the hottest time of the day takes a physical toll. This raising of her bodily temperature is viewed to affect the embryonic development of her child, rendering them a "eunuch of heat." The role that *marqa'* beer plays in this process is unclear for two reasons. First, *marqa'* usually means, "diluted" and refers to beverages mixed with water to limit their potency. But why would diluted wine affect fetal development? After all, it not only lowers the alcohol content, but also is usually seen as quite healthy. To cite one relevant example: Abaye's mother suggests drinking "diluted (Aramaic *marqa'*) wine" in order to lower a fever (*b. Gittin* 67b; discussed in chapter 9). Second, did the mother bake in a hot oven on a hot day *and* drink diluted beer, or were these separate acts?

Regardless of what role beer drinking plays in this narrative, we discover much about gender in rabbinic literature from this passage. First, we needed to learn that the gender binary of the Rabbis requires discussion of categories that transcend the binary. Second, we had to discuss the heavily gendered concept of Levirate marriage. Third, we clarified the two different categories of *saris*. Fourth, we explored how gendered urination positions influence the definition of a congenital *saris*. Fifth, we are told how maternal actions affect the embodied development of her fetus.

CONCLUSION

As we have seen throughout this chapter, gender matters. In every text we read—rabbinic or otherwise—there are assumptions about gendered bodies and practices. And by unpacking them, we gain significant insight into larger cultural values.

By way of conclusion, I would point to another rabbinic (and, indeed, cross-cultural) gendered practice: using beverages as a metaphor for women and sex. Women are compared to drinks when, among other things, discussing their physical appearance (e.g., *b. Shabbat* 62b–63a, which uses the metaphor of red or white wine to discuss their skin's complexion); and their husbands' view of them (e.g., *t. Sotah* 5:9, a discussion that kicks off with the assertion: "Rabbi Meir used to say: Just as one evaluates food, so too one evaluates women"). Further, the act of intercourse itself is discussed in beverage-related terms. For example, the minimum amount of time necessary for intercourse is compared to the amount of time needed to mix a glass of wine (*t. Sotah* 1:2; and parallels noted in Satlow 1995, 127n36); and illicit sex is described as "stolen waters" (quoting Proverbs 9:17; e.g., *y. Sotah* 1:4, 16d; *b. Sanhedrin* 75a; Weingarten 2010, 363–64). Finally, we learn in the following manner that, while having sex, a man should only think of the woman with whom he is having intercourse:

> "So that you do not follow your heart [and your eyes, after which you go whoring" [Numbers 15:39, discussed above].
> From this [verse], Rabbi said: A man should not drink from one cup and set his eyes on another cup. (*b. Nedarim* 20b; see Neis 2013, 131–35)

In all of these instances, men are the normative subjects, and women are the objects. Men are the consumers, and women are the consumed; or, in a more apt metaphor, men are the drinkers, and women are that which is drunk.

Yet, to return to the observations by Elizabeth Shanks Alexander cited at the beginning of this chapter, we should not forget that whereas ancient rabbinic texts may perceive men as the drinkers and women as that which is drunk, modern readers can switch the hand that holds the cup. Women (and other people who feel marginalized and/or excluded from ancient rabbinic texts) can now participate in ritual Torah study; and, in doing so, they can become the drinkers and define what is, and is not, in their cup.

SUGGESTED READINGS

Alexander, Elizabeth Shanks. 2015 [2013]. *Gender and Timebound Commandments in Judaism.* New York: Cambridge University Press.

Balberg, Mira. 2014. *Purity, Body, and Self in Early Rabbinic Literature.* Berkeley: University of California Press.

Bentley, Amy. 2014. *Inventing Baby Food: Taste, Health, and the Industrialization of the American Diet.* Berkeley: University of California Press.

Berkowitz, Beth A. 2018. *Animals and Animality in the Babylonian Talmud.* New York: Cambridge University Press.

Biale, David. 1997. *Eros and the Jews: From Biblical Israel to Contemporary America.* Berkeley: University of California Press.

Boyarin, Daniel. 1995 [1993]. *Carnal Israel: Reading Sex in Talmudic Culture.* Berkeley: University of California Press.

Destro, Adriana. 1989. *The Law of Jealousy: Anthropology of Sotah.* Atlanta, GA: Scholars Press.

Eilberg-Schwartz, Howard. 1990. *The Savage in Judaism: An Anthropology of Israelite Religion and Ancient Judaism.* Bloomington: Indiana University Press.

Fonrobert, Charlotte Elisheva. 2000. *Menstrual Purity: Rabbinic and Christian Reconstructions of Biblical Gender.* Stanford, CA: Stanford University Press.

———. 2007. "Regulating the Human Body: Rabbinic Legal Discourse and the Making of Jewish Gender." In *The Cambridge Companion to the Talmud and Rabbinic Literature,* ed. Fonrobert and Martin S. Jaffee, 270–94. New York: Cambridge University Press.

Geller, Markham J. 2004. "Diet and Regimen in the Babylonian Talmud." In *Food and Identity in the Ancient World,* ed. Cristiano Grotanelli and Lucio Milano, 217–42. Padua, Italy: S.A.R.G.O.N.

Harvey, Warren Zev. 1986. "The Pupil, the Harlot, and the Fringe Benefits." *Prooftexts* 6: 259–71.

Hauptman, Judith. 1998. *Rereading the Rabbis: A Woman's Voice.* Boulder, CO: Westview Press.

Jung, Courtney. 2015. *Lactivism: How Feminists and Fundamentalists, Hippies and Yuppies, and Physicians and Politicians Made Breastfeeding Big Business and Bad Policy.* New York: Basic Books.

Kessler, Gwynn. 2009. *Conceiving Israel: The Fetus in Rabbinic Narratives.* Philadelphia: University of Pennsylvania Press.

Kraemer, Ross Shepard. 2011. *Unreliable Witnesses: Religion, Gender, and History in the Greco-Roman Mediterranean.* New York: Oxford University Press.

Lapin, Hayim. 2012. *Rabbis as Romans: The Rabbinic Movement in Palestine, 100–400 CE.* New York: Oxford University Press.

Neis, Rachel. 2013. *The Sense of Sight in Rabbinic Culture: Jewish Ways of Seeing in Late Antiquity.* New York: Cambridge University Press.

Peskowitz, Miriam B. 1997. *Spinning Fantasies: Rabbis, Gender, and History.* Berkeley: University of California Press.

Pomeroy, Sarah B. 1995 [1975]. *Goddesses, Whores, Wives, and Slaves: Women in Classical Antiquity.* New York: Schocken Books.

Roller, Matthew B. 2006. *Dining Posture in Ancient Rome: Bodies, Values, and Status.* Princeton, NJ: Princeton University Press.

Rosenberg, Michael. 2018. *Signs of Virginity: Testing Virgins and Making Men in Late Antiquity.* New York: Oxford University Press.

Rosenblum, Jordan D. 2012. "Inclined to Decline Reclining? Women, Corporeality, and Dining Posture in Early Rabbinic Literature." In *Meals in the Early Christian World: Social Formation, Experimentation, and Conflict at the Table,* ed. Dennis E. Smith and Hal Taussig, 261–74. New York: Palgrave Macmillan.

———. 2016. "'Blessings of the Breasts': Breastfeeding in Rabbinic Literature." *Hebrew Union College Annual* 87: 147–79.

———. 2018. "Thou Shalt Not Cook a Bird in Its Mother's Milk? Theorizing the Evolution of a Rabbinic Regulation." In *Religious Studies and Rabbinics: A Conversation,* ed. Elizabeth Shanks Alexander and Beth A. Berkowitz, 175–87. New York: Routledge.

Rosen-Zvi, Ishay. 2008. *The Rite That Was Not: Temple, Midrash and Gender in Tractate Sotah.* Jerusalem: Magnes Press. In Hebrew.

Satlow, Michael L. 1994. "'They Abused Him Like a Woman': Homoeroticism, Gender Blurring, and the Rabbis in Late Antiquity." *Journal of the History of Sexuality* 5/1: 1–25.

———. 1995. *Tasting the Dish: Rabbinic Rhetorics of Sexuality.* Atlanta, GA: Society of Biblical Literature.

———. 1996. "'Try to Be a Man': The Rabbinic Construction of Masculinity." *Harvard Theological Review* 89, no. 1: 19–40.

———. 2001. *Jewish Marriage in Antiquity*. Princeton, NJ: Princeton University Press.

———. 2002. "Fictional Women: A Study in Stereotypes." In *The Talmud Yerushalmi and Graeco-Roman Culture*, ed. Peter Schäfer, 3: 225–43. Tübingen: Mohr Siebeck.

Schofer, Jonathan Wyn. 2010. *Confronting Vulnerability: The Body and the Divine in Rabbinic Literature*. Chicago: University of Chicago Press.

Smith, Dennis E. 2003. *From Symposium to Eucharist: The Banquet in the Early Christian World*. Minneapolis: Fortress Press.

Stern, Sacha. 2013. "Compulsive Libationers: Non-Jews and Wine in Early Rabbinic Sources." *Journal of Jewish Studies* 64, no. 1: 19–44.

Tompkins, Kyla Wazana. 2012. *Racial Indigestion: Eating Bodies in the 19th Century*. New York: New York University Press.

Weingarten, Susan. 2010. "Gynaecophagia: Metaphors of Women as Food in the Talmudic Literature." In *Food and Language: Proceedings of the Oxford Symposium of Food and Cookery 2009*, ed. Richard Hosking, 360–370. Totnes, Devon, UK: Prospect Books.

Wegner, Judith Romney. 1988. *Chattel or Person? The Status of Women in the Mishnah*. New York: Oxford University Press.

FIVE

Magic, Idolatry, and Illicit Religious Practice

The Rabbis see themselves as the divinely ordained arbiters of licit and illicit practice, believing that God gave them the authority to decide what is right and wrong. Therefore, they understand themselves to be solely responsible for policing the boundaries between "proper" religious practice and "improper" deviant behavior. Of course, from a scholarly, second-order perspective, what is "proper" and "improper" often look very similar, and usually differ based on the perspective of the one making the claim. Heresy, much like beauty, is in the eye of the beholder.

Put into the broader context of the academic study of religion, improper thought or action—what I refer to throughout this chapter as "illicit religious practice"—is often a symbolic inversion, that is, a mirror image of what a given community considers to be proper thought or action—what I call "licit religious practice." There are recent studies of the concept of "heresy" (e.g., Berzon 2016), but for present purposes I focus on the fact that rabbinic discourse about illicit practice follows a broader trend in the study of religion, wherein illicit practice is viewed as an inversion (or, from an internal polemical perspective, a *perversion*) of licit religious practice.

Before turning to a discussion of relevant rabbinic beverage texts, we should take a moment to reflect on a classic work on symbolic inversion by the scholar of religion Bruce Lincoln. In his discussion of symbolic inversion in religious discourse, Lincoln cites what might seem like an odd data set: professional wrestling. In seeking to show why Sgt. Slaughter and Brutus Beefcake (both of whom, I must admit, I followed in my childhood) are worthy of consideration by "serious" scholar, he asserts:

> It is easy to describe professional wrestling as if it were a joke or a parody. Such descriptions, however, are not only condescending, but also superficial. To be sure, it is not a subtle sport, or a mode of discourse suited to refined bourgeois tastes. Its gestures are spectacular, its contents exaggerated, and its characters larger than life. This notwithstanding, the ritual and dramatic structure of professional wrestling is anything but simple, and its efficacy is anything but negligible: These need to be studied in further detail. (Lincoln 2014 [1989], 155)

This same statement applies to the subject of this book: beverages are serious business, even if—and perhaps especially because—many view them as frivolous diversions. As Bruce Lincoln contends, "serious" theory can often be informed and developed through discussion of seemingly "frivolous" topics.

In this chapter, we encounter several rabbinic texts in which the theme of illicit religious practice is explored in a discussion of beverages. Such practices are often seen as symbolic inversions of what the Rabbis believe to be licit practices regarding both drinking and that which is drinkable.

THEIR WINE: LIBATION AS SYMBOLIC INVERSION

The rabbinic paragon of illicit religious practice is idolatry, which they refer to as *'avodah zarah*, literally, "foreign worship." Fundamentally, the Rabbis understand idolatry as a practice that symbolically inverts licit religious practice, because, at its very core, idolatry presumes the authority and reverence of a deity or deities besides the singular God of the Rabbis. Further, beverage-related practices are actually an excellent window into rabbinic views of idolatry for two reasons: (1) the Rabbis understood idolatry in general as requiring action, not just belief, and unambiguously cultic action at that (see Schwartz 2001, esp. 165–66); and (2) one of the most—if not *the* most—common cultic actions they describe is idolatrous libation to a pagan deity (e.g., *m. Avodah Zarah* 5:1–11).

As we learned in chapter 3, the Rabbis imagine non-Jews to be "compulsive libationers" (Stern 2013). This is in direct opposition to the Rabbis, seen as exhibiting self-control and offering proper benedictions over wine. However, once again note that the Rabbis—who are terrified of pagans pouring wine that a Jew might drink as a libation to an idolatrous deity—neither prohibit drinking wine nor drinking wine with non-Jews. While they heavily regulate these, they do not ban them outright.

This constant concern regarding "compulsive libationers," but not total taboo of either the general product or general population of pagans, often allows wine and wine-related practices to serve as a symbolic inversion of licit rabbinic practice. Prior to drinking their wine, rabbinic Jews offer a blessing to the "Creator of the fruit of the vine" (*m. Berakhot* 6:1; see also chapter 7). Idolaters, on the other hand, are driven to libate to their (from a rabbinic perspective, false) deity/deities, taking their obsession to comical extremes (see *m. Avodah Zarah* 5:4–5, discussed in chapter 3). How They—meaning the social and religious Other—act in regard to Their wine is indicative of Their general actions: illicit, the polar opposite of Us, that is, the rabbinic Jews.

An interesting example of how the Rabbis walk the fine line between allowing wine, but avoiding Their wine (and, by association, Them) is encountered in the form of "cooked wine" (Hebrew *yayin mevushal*). According to the Rabbis, cooking wine renders it unfit for pagan ritual use, since "cooked wine is not subject to the libation [prohibition]" (*b. Avodah Zarah* 30a). However, this only covers wine that was not originally "libated wine" (Hebrew *yayin nesekh*). In the case of the latter:

> Rabbi Ila said: We learned in a *baraita'*: Cooked wine of idol worshippers that was initially [raw] wine is prohibited. (*b. Avodah Zarah* 29b)

Rabbi Ila's statement is worth unpacking. First, he cites a *baraita'*, a rabbinic tradition reputed to be of tannaitic origin that is cited in an amoraic text. Therefore, he asserts that his statement is based on an earlier precedent (which may or may not be true). Second, he points out that any wine in its raw (i.e., uncooked) state that is in possession of idolaters (Hebrew *'ovdey kokhavim*; literally, "worshippers of the stars") is prohibited. Cooking is deemed an act of fixing the status of wine. If the wine was in the status of "libated wine" wine prior to being cooked, then cooking does not transform its status. Cooking hits the pause button; it does not rewind. "Libated wine" is "libated wine," whether cooked or uncooked. However, if wine is *not* "libated wine" and then is cooked, its status is fixed as non-libated wine. It remains in its initial (permitted) state no matter what occurs subsequently. So even if a bunch of "compulsive libationers" were left alone with a jug of such wine, its status remains immutable. Why? Because the idolater would not libate cooked wine. Therefore, there is no need to fret.

Significantly, the Rabbis make the assertion that cooked wine is not suitable for pagan libation despite the fact that no external evidence supports this claim. This absence of external evidence from pagan sources is thrown into further relief when we consider that the Rabbis discuss the status of cooked wine in other contexts, as well. For example, cooked wine fulfills the ritual wine-drinking obligation for Passover (*y. Pesahim* 10:1, 37c; discussed further in chapter 6) and, in the process, gives its drinker a wicked hangover. It would seem, rather, that the Rabbis are finding a way to accommodate a social and economic reality wherein they are surrounded by non-Jews (on this accommodation in general, see Lapin 2012; Schwartz 2001; and for modern implications of this ruling, see Horowitz 2016, 130, 144–45, 153–58). Rather than withdraw completely from society—as done by some ancient Jewish groups, like the community that authored the Dead Sea Scrolls—they chose to remain in a world full of gods. In order to navigate this cultural landscape, they imagined non-Jewish actions as symbolic inversions of their own practices: whereas Jews licitly bless their wine, pagans illicitly libate their wine. However, so long as a Jew observes a non-Jew's entire interaction with wine, then this eternal vigilance allows for Jews and non-Jews to share a table, and even a nice glass of wine. And if the wine is boiled (as seems to be the meaning of "cooked" here), then the laws are relaxed a bit more, since the Rabbis understand such wine to be invalid for pagan libation. The fact that this loophole is almost certainly a creation of the Rabbis and does not represent actual non-Jewish religious opinion need not deter us. On the contrary, this very fact highlights the discursive function of the loophole: it reminds us that the symbolic inversion of Their wine practices are all about Us. These discussions are prescriptive, not descriptive; they portray the world the Rabbis wished to live in, not necessarily the one in which they actually lived.

DRINKING FROM A STATUE AND KISSING AN IDOL

Idol worship is the inversion of proper rabbinic ritual, which entails worship of the one true God. As noted above, idol worship requires an unambiguous cultic action (see Schwartz 2001, esp. 165–66, 170). Hence, one engages in idolatry:

> ... whether he worships [an idol in the manner it is normally worshipped]; or sacrifices; or burns incense; or pours a libation; or bows; or accepts it as a god, saying: "You are my god." (*m. Sanhedrin* 7:6)

These acts are unambiguous. For instance, it does not get any clearer than a person declaring: "You, O idol, are my god!" I think we can all agree that that person is an idolater. *m. Sanhedrin* 7:6 continues on to detail other actions vis-à-vis the idol that are not quite unambiguous worship, such as hugging or kissing an idol, and that thus have negative consequences (i.e., flogging), but not the full consequence for idolatry (i.e., being stoned to death; see *m. Sanhedrin* 7:4 for more on stoning). For the latter, one must actually worship an idol in the manner that an idol is worshipped. Only then, by this unambiguous act, is that person an idolater deserving of being stoned.

Careful readers of this book might suspect where we are headed: we know about unambiguous cultic action, but what about *ambiguous* cultic action? Indeed, this is the very question that the Rabbis ask. To do so, they focus on two actions prohibited in *m. Sanhedrin* 7:6: bowing and kissing.

Already in the Hebrew Bible, bowing to an idol is a clear no-no. The Second Commandment (or, in many Christian traditions of counting, the First Commandment) declares: "You shall not bow down to Them," that is, to other gods (Exodus 20:5; Deuteronomy 5:9). But what about if it only *looks* as though I am bowing down to them? This question does not escape rabbinic attention:

> A spring that flows out of a temple of idolatry—one should not bend down in front of it and drink, because it will appear as if one bows to an idol.
> But one may turn his back and drink.
> And in a place where one is not seen, it is permissible [to drink]. (*t. Avodah Zarah* 6:5)

Imagine you are a good rabbinic Jew living in an ancient Roman city. On your daily comings-and-goings, often you encounter pagan temples. Some of these temples have water flowing from them. And sometimes you are thirsty. So what do you do?

The answer is not a clear prohibition, but rather: it depends. Let us work through the variables. First of all, intentionally bowing to an idol is clearly forbidden. Second, in general, drinking water from such a source is clearly *not* forbidden. What is forbidden, then, is *appearing* to bow to an idol. Therefore, if you were to lean over to drink directly from the water source, it might *appear as if* you were bowing to an idol, which would be forbidden. But, if you were to turn your back to the idol and then lean over to drink, then it would appear that you were drinking, not bowing. And if your act of drinking is not visible to others, then you need not turn your back to the idol. The problem is one of perception. Once it is clear that your action is not an unambiguous cultic act, then it is not deemed idolatrous. Hence, you can drink.

The question of perception arises again with the age-old question: is a kiss just a kiss? Or does it mean something more? To answer this dilemma in regard to idolatry, we turn to the next *tosefta*:

> Sculptures of faces that spout water in the cities—one may not place his mouth on the mouth of a sculpture and drink, because it will appear as if one kisses an idol.
> But one may collect [water] in his hand and drink.
> Furthermore, they said: one may not place his mouth on the mouth of a pipe and drink, because of mortal danger. (*t. Avodah Zarah* 6:6)

Anyone who has taken a stroll through modern Rome knows that sculptures of faces are a common sight. And, like the famous fountain at the entrance of the Orange Garden on the Aventine Hill (see fig. 2), some of these faces do indeed spout water out of their mouths. This fact is perhaps why the text specifies "in the cities," as cities are more likely than towns or villages to feature such expensive sculpture. Also, anyone who has taken a stroll through modern Rome knows that walking around in the hot Mediterranean sun makes you thirsty.

Once again, the problem of perception arises. The issue is not in regard to drinking the water in and of itself. (This would not be the case if the sculpture spouts wine out of its mouth; that would definitely be forbidden.) Rather, the issue is that if you put your mouth up to the sculpture in order to drink, you would *appear* to be kissing the sculpture. And, as we have learned, kissing idols is forbidden. But if you were simply to cup your hands and collect water from the face-fountain, and then drink from your hands, your actions would be unambiguously nonidolatrous. You would be drinking, not kissing.

Figure 2. Fountain at the entrance to Orange Garden, Aventine Hill, Rome. Photo: Catherine E. Bonesho and Taylor Beck.

Furthermore, the text continues, you should not place your mouth up to any pipe and drink, because doing so puts your life at risk. Of course, actual idolatry also puts your life at risk, due to the mandatory stoning to death, but the text thus far has focused not on the dangers of *actual* idolatry, but on the dangers of *perceived* idolatry. Here, then, we turn from fear of the appearance of an idolatrous act, to actual mortal danger (the same phrase appears in other Toseftan texts in regard to the threat to an infant's life due to a potential lack of breast milk (see *t. Ketubbot* 5:5; *t. Niddah* 2:5; chapter 6); and in regard to "the ways of the Amorites," discussed below). But what precisely is this mortal danger? According to *b. Avodah Zarah* 12b: "What is the danger? A leech." In this case, perception is not the issue, but rather the fear is of swallowing a leech, which is apparently a critical concern. (FYI: if you have swallowed a leech, please immediately seek medical attention; and if leech ingestion occurs on the Sabbath, please turn to chapter 6 for the remedy for this condition.)

Do not drink from any pipe, lest you swallow a leech and put your life at risk. And do not actually bow to or kiss an idol, lest we need to stone you to death. But if you are thirsty and encounter a spring flowing from an idolatrous temple or from the mouth of an idol, then just make sure that it is abundantly clear that you are neither bowing, nor kissing.

DRINKING IN YOUR EX-WIFE'S TAVERN: MAGIC AS ILLICIT RELIGIOUS PRACTICE

If idolatry is the polar opposite of rabbinic Judaism, there is another illicit religious practice to which the Rabbis devote significant attention: magic. And, as the Rabbis themselves often do, it is best to explore the contours of this by examining a rabbinic text in which it figures.

On several occasions, rabbinic men are depicted as drinking with women who attempt to practice magic on them. In one instance, discussed in chapter 4, the witch ends up being tricked by the Rabbi; as a result, he transforms her into a donkey and then rides her in the marketplace, which becomes especially embarrassing when her girlfriend breaks the spell, so that now the Rabbi is seen riding the woman *like* a donkey in public (*b. Sanhedrin* 67b). Since the Rabbis presume the majority of women to be witches, they regarded encounters with women potentially fraught with moral, theological, and especially sexual danger.

Consider the following narrative:

> And thus it was said: Ten, eight, six, [and] four are not subject to pairs [the consuming of food or drink in pairs makes one susceptible to evil forces]. They said that only regarding demons, but regarding witchcraft we also fear many.
>
> As [once happened in] the case of a certain man who divorced his wife. She went and married a man who owned a tavern. Every day, [her ex-husband] would go and drink wine. She practiced witchcraft against him, but she was unable to affect him because he guarded himself against pairs. One day he drank a lot [of wine] and did not know how much he drank.

Until sixteen [cups] he was sober and protected himself. From then on, he was not sober and he did not protect himself. She put him out a pair [of wine cups]. When he went [out of the bar], he met a certain Arab. [The drunk ex-husband] said to him: "Dead man walking here!" He went [and] grabbed a date palm tree. The date palm tree dried up and [the drunk ex-husband] burst. (*b. Pesahim* 110b)

I leave aside the wisdom of drinking in a tavern owned by your ex-wife's new husband (especially when your marriage, as this text seems to imply, did not end on the friendliest of terms). Based upon his obviously bad choice in selecting a watering hole, however, this seems to be a pretty cocky ex-husband. Every day, he walks into his ex-wife's new husband's tavern and orders an odd number of cups of wine. This matters, because only if you drink an even number of cups of wine can magic affect you.

Throughout this narrative, it is important to notice what the Rabbis do *not* do. They do not reject the efficacy of magic. In fact, the Rabbis fully believe in magic. It is effective, but illicit, much as robbing a bank is an effective, but illegal, way to get rich quick. Of course, not all "magic" is bad. The Rabbis differentiate between the "magic" of illusion, as when a magician pulls a rabbit out of a hat, and the "magic" of using an incantation to gather a patch of cucumbers (see *m. Sanhedrin* 7:11), with only the latter act being illicit. And, for the same reason that Harry Potter and his classmates study "Defense against the Dark Arts" as a mandatory component of the curriculum at Hogwarts School of Witchcraft and Wizardry, Rabbis are allowed to learn magic in order to teach it and defend against it (see *b. Sanhedrin* 68a). For the Rabbis, "magic" is very real, and hence very dangerous.

It is the very reality of magic that leads to its potency as a symbol of ritual inversion. In the rabbinic imagination, the main practitioners of "religion" are men, while the main practitioners of "magic" are women. "Magic" uses ritual words and actions in order to illicitly compel divine action (known as theurgy), whereas "religion" uses ritual words and actions in order to licitly entreat divine action. "Magic" is therefore serious business. It must be confronted and negotiated, whether in the domain of an ex-wife's tavern or in another ritual context (as Cohn 2008 argues, e.g., in regard to the magical amulet origins of *tefillin*).

With this important observation in mind, we see how rabbinic themes of gender and sexuality and magic as illicit religious practice interact throughout this narrative. Of all the gin joints, in all the towns, in all the world, the ex-husband is pretty cocky to walk into the one operated by his ex-wife every day and drink there. His hubris exposes him to dire peril when, one day, he loses track of how many cups of wine he has drunk. Given that this occurred only after he imbibed sixteen cups—while remaining sober!—should serve as a cautionary tale about binge drinking. After all, to be drunk is to exist in a state in which one lacks the masculine virtue of self-control; therefore, drunkards are neither manly nor, as we discover, are they able to keep count and thus to ward off women's magic. The masculine rabbinic male is able to ward off feminine magic, but in this case, the ex-husband's actions render him effeminate.

Too drunk to notice, the ex-husband ends up drinking an even number of cups of wine. His ex-wife, the bartender, plays the common role of the tricky, magical woman: she exacts her revenge by serving him an even number of glasses of wine (suggesting that she kept count even though he could not) and then attacks him with a magical incantation. His lack of self-control leaves him susceptible to this attack, implying that a *real* man would never be bested by a woman. A *real* man, after all, would literally mind his p's and q's—as in pints and quarts—and thus be impervious to a woman's magic.

Drunk, emasculated, and under a spell, the doomed man stumbles out of his ex-wife's current husband's tavern and encounters an Arab. The identity of this stranger as an Arab is perhaps incidental to the story and might just suggest that the ex-husband encounters a random person wandering on the street. However, I think that this is another clue about magic, since other rabbinic texts describe Arabs as practitioners of magic. For example, in one text, a "certain Arab" performs a magic trick with a camel, which the text concludes was an illusion and not *real* magic. Since it was more Houdini than Harry Potter, it is not an actual concern for the Rabbis (see *b. Sanhedrin* 67b). Regardless, the literary purpose of the "certain Arab" is to cause the drunk, emasculated, and dangerously enchanted husband to realize that he is a "dead man walking." He then explodes.

This explosive conclusion is of less interest for our present purposes than all of the background knowledge that it took to get us there. In explaining the many presumptions that shape this narrative, we not only returned to our discussion of gender asymmetry in regard to rabbinic conceptions of women and magic, but also explored how the Rabbis defined "magic" as a symbolic inversion of their "religion." Furthermore, claims of "magic" serve to delegitimize one's authority, particularly that of women. Magic is illicit religious practice, but it nonetheless exists. Rabbis need to know about magic to combat it. Knowing how many drinks to consume, for example, can save you from a nasty physical and spiritual hangover.

WHEN EVENS GET ODD: THE DANGER OF DRINKING PAIRS

As we have just learned, drinking an even number of drinks makes one susceptible to attacks by evil forces. Though the passage we read focuses on "magic," the broader section within which it is contained concerns itself primarily with demons and evil spirits (see especially *b. Pesahim* 109b–112a). Much as "magic" is an illicit but effective practice, demons and other pernicious spirits are viewed as very real threats, especially in the Babylonian Talmud. However, they can be controlled by various licit practices. For example, reciting a rabbinic prayer prior to entering a privy can neutralize latrine spirits (see *y. Berakhot* 9:6, 14b; *b. Berakhot* 60b; Septimus 2015, 45–88). And the material evidence of Aramaic bowls, many of which contain spells of noticeably Jewish and even occasionally rabbinic influence, points to a wider impact of ritual practice to ward off demons and other harmful spirits (see Mokhtarian 2015, 124–43).

To better understand how rabbinic practices protect a drinker from demons and evil spirits, we examine several selections from the broader passage (Aramaic *sugya'*). As is usually advisable, we begin at the beginning:

> "And they should not give him fewer than four [cups of wine]" [*m. Pesahim* 10:1].
>
> How could our Rabbis enact something whereby one comes into danger?! For it was taught in a *baraita'*: A person should not eat pairs, nor drink pairs, nor wipe [after defecation in] pairs, nor have sex [in] pairs.
>
> Rav Nahman said: The biblical verse states: "[It was] a night of guarding [for the Lord to bring them out of the land of Egypt; that same night is the Lord's, for guarding all of the children of Israel throughout their generations"] [Exodus 12:42]. [This means that it is] a night that is guarded from then on against harmful spirits.
>
> Rava said: The cup of blessing [i.e., the third cup consumed for the recitation of the Grace after Meals] combines [with the first two cups consumed prior to the Passover meal] for good, but does not combine for evil.
>
> Ravina said: [Though] our Rabbis enacted [the requirement that we drink] four cups [of wine at the *Seder* as symbolic of] the conduct of freedom, each one is a *mitzvah* by itself. (*b. Pesahim* 109b–110a)

Our *sugya'* begins by commenting on *m. Pesahim* 10:1, which mandates the consumption of four cups of wine as a central component of the rabbinic Passover meal ritual, the *Seder*. But four is an even number! The anonymous voice of the Talmud immediately asks a vital question: "How could our Rabbis enact something whereby one comes into danger?!" The specific danger is spelled out in the *baraita'*: pairs of various actions, including drinking, are prohibited. The reason for this prohibition is presumed knowledge: namely, that doing these actions in pairs leaves one susceptible to evil forces (demons, spirits, and magic). So how could "our Rabbis"—a common phrase that denotes that these are our guys who should be looking out for *us*—require ritual action that places *our* lives in peril?

Three different interpretative justifications are offered. First, Rav Nahman cites Exodus 12:42. As is often the case in rabbinic literature, the biblical verse is cited only partially. The presumption is that that the audience has memorized the Hebrew Bible. Seeing the small section quoted in this text cues the reader to remember the verse both in its entirety and in its original context. The biblical context of this verse is the first night of Passover, during which the Lord guards over the children of Israel. Remember that the impetus for this *sugya'* was to understand why the Rabbis ordained that one should drink four cups of wine at the Passover *Seder*, so a Passover context makes sense. Rav Nahman argues that this biblical verse proves that God guards the children of Israel against harmful spirits on the night of Passover. On this night, at least, drinking in pairs does not endanger one's life.

Rava offers a second interpretative justification: the four cups of wine at the Passover *Seder* only count as three cups. How does this rabbinic math work? As we shall learn in chapter 6, two cups of wine are consumed prior to the Passover meal, and two are imbibed afterward. The third cup, commonly referred to as the "cup of blessing" (Hebrew *kos shel berakhah*; see *b. Berakhot* 51a–52a), is part of the Grace after Meals liturgy. Rava argues that the cup of blessing combines with the first two cups. For the purposes of arithmetic, therefore, the third cup is not counted. Drinking four cups on Passover is good, but drinking pairs is bad. Rava's creative accounting turns four cups into three, and, in doing so, fulfills rabbinic requirements while keeping harmful spirits at bay.

The third interpretive justification offered by Ravina can also be understood in terms of arithmetic. Though the rabbinic enactment requires drinking four cups of wine at the Passover *Seder*, each cup is a divine commandment (Hebrew *mitzvah*) in and of itself. Therefore, the harmful spirits lying in wait cannot add four cups together ($1 + 1 + 1 + 1 = 4$) to achieve a sum of pairs and then attack. Each cup is separate. They are four single drinks, which are all odd numbers and hence prevent such attacks.

This *sugya'* goes on to describe various other strategies for avoiding drinking pairs. For example, one strategy involves getting up and walking around or going to the privy between drinks (see *b. Pesahim* 110a). Each drink therefore constitutes a separate act of drinking and does not combine into pairs. Another strategy involves developing procedures for keeping track of how many drinks one consumes. Rava counts ceiling beams to keep track of his beverage consumption, but I prefer the mental image conjured by Abaye's technique:

> When Abaye would drink one cup, his mother would place two cups in his two hands. (*b. Pesahim* 110a)

Abaye's mother thus ensured that her little boy always had an odd number of drinks (for more on Abaye's mother, see chapter 9).

But what if, despite all of these strategies and techniques, one accidentally drinks pairs? Thankfully, there is a cure.

> Rav Pappa said: Yosef the Demon told me: ...
>
> And if one forgot and happened [to drink pairs] and went out, what is his remedy? Let him hold the thumb of his right hand in his left hand and the thumb of his left [hand] in his right hand, and he should say thus: "You and I add up to three." And if he hears [a voice] that says: You and I add up to four," he should say to it: "You and I add up to five." And if he hears [a voice] that says: You and I add up to six," he should say to it: "You and I add up to seven."
>
> There was a case [where this exchange occurred] until one hundred and one. And [then finally] the demon burst. (*b. Pesahim* 110a)

We begin with Rav Pappa, the wealthy brewer and rabbinic authority, relating knowledge learned from Yosef (= Joseph) the Demon. Yosef the Demon clearly loves to teach Rabbis, because earlier on this same page of the Talmud, Rav Yosef reports that he too learned about demons and pairs from Yosef the Demon. Demons might be harmful spirits, but it is allowable to learn from them how to fight them. (The same goes for a sorceress, since later on this same Talmud page, Ameimar learns how to fend off their attacks by talking to "the chief of the sorceresses.")

Once again, notice that neither the knowledge of demons/spirits/magic, nor even necessarily the practices themselves, is illicit. What matters is the practitioner—that it is a rabbinic Jew, not a demon/spirit/sorcerer. While I omit the content of the beginning of Yosef the Demon's lesson, it pertains to what demons can and cannot do to those who drink pairs. Rather than get distracted by these details, I want to focus on the remedy. Though, before proceeding, I should note that one could read the second part (beginning with "And if one forgot...") as a separate tradition, edited together by the Talmud, and not necessarily a continuation of Yosef the Demon's lesson. While I am inclined to read them as a single unit, I have placed them on separate lines in my translation, to allow flexibility in how one reads this text.

Regardless of where this knowledge is acquired from, we now know what to do if—despite the best efforts of your mother—you walk out of a tavern having accidentally drunk pairs: hold each thumb in the opposite hand at the same time and declare that "You and I add up to three." The "You" in this formula is the second person plural (Aramaic *'atun*), which might better be translated as "y'all." So the two thumbs (= y'all) plus the person to whom they are attached ("I"; Aramaic *'ana'*) add up to three. Three is an odd number; it is safe. This same thumb-holding technique appears on *b. Berakhot* 55b as a means of warding off the Evil Eye (though a different formula is recited, one that invokes another Yosef: the biblical figure of Joseph, quoting Genesis 49:22).

But holding your thumbs and reciting this formula might not be enough. What if the thumb-holder hears a voice (presumably of a harmful spirit lying in wait to attack) that undermines this remedy by reciting its own formula: "You and I add up to four." Now, the y'all ("You") refers to the two thumbs plus the thumb-holder, and the "I" is the evil spirit, which add up to four: $(2 + 1) + 1 = 4$. While three is an odd number, which prevents any demon/spirit/magic attack, four is an even number—which means that the person is back in mortal danger. The remedy is to once again recite the formula to arrive at an odd number: "You and I add up to five." The precise arithmetic of this is less important than the fact that either the person or the harmful spirit can add one to the formula in order to make an even number odd, or vice versa. Though this scenario could repeat itself infinitely, a case example is introduced wherein a person and a demon went back and forth until they reached 101—an odd number—at which point the demon burst. Why this demon exploded is unclear. Oddly, we have ample evidence for spontaneous combustion in this regard: for example, twice on *b. Pesahim* 110b (the drunk husband, discussed above, and in another story about a wine barrel in the Land of Israel) and once on *b. Pesahim* 111b (where a demon explodes while chasing after a rabbinical student who was about to relieve himself by a caper bush).

Discussion of drinking pairs continues with more fascinating scenarios and case studies than we can discuss in detail here. For example, do two cups of wine and one cup of beer combine to make three beverages? Answer: no, the two cups of wine count as a pair of beverages (but two cups of beer and one cup of wine do combine to make three; see *b. Pesahim* 110b). Related to this topic, the general concern for lurking evil spirits arises. For example, on *b. Pesahim* 112a–b, they discuss evil spirits that hover over water at certain times (e.g., Wednesday and Friday evenings) and, in general, at night, and then describe both the physical and verbal practices used to fend off these evil spirits. (In a variant passage on *b. Avodah Zarah* 12b, we learn the name of the specific demon that concerns us here: Shavrirei.) Discussion of water spirits is not uncommon, particularly in the Babylonian Talmud (e.g., *b. Hullin* 105b). What we see in all of these contexts is that the Rabbis presume that demons, spirits, and sorcerers (the latter of whom are usually gendered as female) are clear and present dangers. They do not discount their existence. Instead, they create practices to contain and neutralize these threats. Such practices, if performed by a non-rabbinic Jew or non-Jew might have been labeled illicit religious practice. But since they are performed by and on behalf of rabbinic Jews, they are licit.

THE FRAUDULENT BUTCHER

Among the numerous actions that comprise licit religious practice are many associated with food and drink. For example, pork is not kosher, but goat meat is. And further, goat is kosher only provided that it is slaughtered and prepared according to rabbinic procedure. If the goat's blood is not properly drained or the goat meat is served with cheese (made from the milk of a goat or any other kosher animal), for instance, it is not deemed kosher. Taken together, these food practices help to create and maintain a distinct rabbinic identity (in general, see Rosenblum 2010).

Given the stakes of kosher food for rabbinic identity, regular business fraud is elevated to catastrophic status when one's business is the kosher business. In modern times, such scandals are big news. For example, two kosher scandals from the 1980s are still discussed today: one involving vinegar and another involving duck (see Horowitz 2016, 109–10; Lee 2008, 89–106). In ancient times, such scandals were also big news. In one account, a drunk fraudulent butcher meets with good, old-fashioned, an-eye-for-an-eye biblical justice:

> Once upon a time, there was a certain butcher in Sepphoris who would [fraudulently] feed Jews *nevelah* and *terefah* [two categories of nonkosher meat]. One time, on the eve of Yom Kippur before nightfall, he drank a lot of wine and became intoxicated. He climbed on the roof, fell off, and died. Dogs began licking his blood.
>
> [People] came and asked Rabbi Haninah: Is it permissible to remove him from before them?
>
> He said to them: It is written: "And holy men you shall be unto Me; you shall not eat flesh torn by beasts (Hebrew *terefah*) in the field; you shall cast it to the dogs" [Exodus 22:30]. This person robbed the dogs and fed Jews *nevelah* and *terefah*. Leave them; they are eating that which is theirs. (*y. Avodah Zarah* 2:3, 41a; cf. *Leviticus Rabbah* 5:6)

Like many shocking stories, this one begins "once upon a time" (Hebrew *ma'aseh*; on this term, see Simon-Shoshan 2012, 45–49). This tale features a "certain" butcher—a way of referring to a generic person in a rabbinic story, as was also the case above in regard to a "certain" ex-husband drinking in his ex-wife's new husband's tavern (and the "certain Arab" he met before spontaneously combusting). The key fact is that this particular butcher sells Jews non-kosher meat, passing it off as kosher.

The terms used for non-kosher food are important to briefly explain, as knowledge of their meaning is necessary to understand the rest of this story. In the Hebrew Bible, *nevelah* refers to carrion (i.e., an animal that dies a natural death), and *terefah* (literally, "torn") refers to an animal killed by another animal. Neither category of animal is slaughtered by human agency. The Rabbis alter the meaning of these terms. For them, *nevelah* refers to an improperly slaughtered animal, and *terefah* refers to a properly slaughtered animal that subsequently is rendered invalid for some reason (see *m. Hullin* 2:4; Rosenblum 2010, 68–69nn121–22). In modern terms, *terefah* has taken on an even more expansive meaning, as referring to all non-kosher food, especially pork, often considered the ultimate in *treyf* (Yiddish for "non-kosher food"). In rabbinic literature, these represent two major non-kosher categories and are often deployed to discuss non-kosher food in general.

With this information in mind, we are ready to work our way through this tale. We learn of a fraudulent butcher who runs a meat shop in Sepphoris (a city known to have a large Jewish population in antiquity), at which Jews buy "kosher" meat. We are already prepared for this butcher to be less than pious, which is why we are not surprised to learn about his pre–Yom Kippur actions. Yom Kippur is the Day of Atonement, a solemn day of prayer, introspection, and fasting. It is the day on which all souls are judged. In the words of the medieval rabbinic liturgical poem *Unetaneh Toqef* ("We Give Power"; made further popular by inspiring Leonard Cohen's 1974 song, "Who by Fire"), it is the day on which God decides: "who shall live and who shall die." Getting drunk right before Yom Kippur is exactly what you do *not* want to do. And then he does what you also do not want to do when drunk: he climbs on top of a roof, falls off it, and dies. Adding insult to injury, dogs lick his blood.

Having witnessed dogs licking up the dead butcher's blood, people come and ask Rabbi Haninah a legal question: on Yom Kippur, is it permissible to remove the corpse from before the dogs ("them")? As a holiday, certain Sabbath laws apply on Yom Kippur, which might prevent the moving of a body. Concern for the integrity of a human body intersects with concerns about allowable actions on a holiday. Furthermore, rabbinic themes overlap here, given this text's interest in the normative law (Hebrew *halakhah*) of Yom Kippur.

It is unclear at which point the butcher's fraud is discovered. Perhaps it had just been exposed, leading to his pre–Yom Kippur drinking? Perhaps it became known posthumously? Either way, knowledge of his fraudulent practice underlies Rabbi Haninah's answer. Rabbi Haninah begins by citing Exodus 22:30, a biblical verse in which *terefah* meat is explicitly banned; it should be cast to dogs. When the butcher sold such meat to Jews, he was not only engaging in business fraud and causing unsuspecting Jews to violate biblical food laws, he was stealing meat that is supposed to be thrown to the dogs. Therefore it is an act of poetic justice when dogs lick his blood, since they are recovering from his own flesh what was rightfully theirs.

As readers of this text, we are supposed to view this conclusion as justice served. Even more than simply rebalancing the scales of justice, this text serves as a clear threat to anyone who wishes to defraud Jews and lead them to transgress unknowingly. Many rabbinic practices require the help of others. For example, if I cannot make my own wine, I need to be able to trust your assurances that you have adhered to rabbinic law in order to guarantee that I am not drinking "libated wine." (Similar concerns in regard to the modern, industrial food system led to the rise of kosher certification agencies; in general, see Horowitz 2016.) Cheating the individual Jew is tantamount to cheating the entire rabbinic system, which is tantamount to cheating God.

MAKING RAIN AND DRINKING WINE

Those who have even merely dipped their toe into the sea of Talmud are probably familiar with the story of Honi the Circle-Maker (*m. Ta'anit* 3:8; *b. Ta'anit* 23a; Belser 2015, 149–83). In this story, a community suffering from a drought turns to a charismatic rainmaker (in the literal sense of the word). Honi earns his nickname by drawing a circle. He then stands within that circle and requests rain from God. Honi's methods prove effective and rain (at first a little, and then a lot) falls. Such charismatic figures are fraught with tension because they walk the line between appropriate and inappropriate action (and sometimes cross it). A rabbinic figure, Shimon ben Shetah, declares: "If you were not Honi, I would decree a ban against you!" (*b. Ta'anit* 23a). As was the case with "magic" and those who practice it, rainmaking and rainmakers are practices/practitioners that, from the rabbinic perspective, may be effective, but are not necessarily licit. The Rabbis have an entire process of licit means of petitioning for rain (discussed throughout the tractate *Ta'anit*), but rainmaking and rainmakers push the boundaries of licit practice. The case of Honi is fascinating because his story is well known, and the Rabbis devote significant attention to grappling with him and even wrapping him in the garb of a rabbinic figure in order to bring him into the fold (see Belser 2015, 161–63).

With this background in mind, we turn our attention to another charismatic rainmaker, Ilfa:

> Rabbi decreed a fast, but no rain fell.
>
> Ilfa (and some say it was Rabbi Ilfai) came down to lead prayer. He said: "He causes the wind to blow," and the wind blew. He said: "He causes the rain to fall," and the rain fell.
>
> [Rabbi] said to him: What do you do?
>
> [Ilfa] said to him: I live in a poor/distant district, where there is no wine for *qiddush* and *havdalah*. I take the trouble to obtain wine for *qiddush* and *havdalah* and cause [the Jews living in the district] to fulfill their obligation. (*b. Ta'anit* 24a)

The opening line—"Rabbi decreed a fast, but no rain fell"—contains a lot of assumed, and important, information. First of all, it presumes that the reader knows the identity of "Rabbi." As you can imagine, whoever merits "Rabbi" as their sole title is an important figure in rabbinic literature. "Rabbi" is Rabbi Yehudah ha-Nasi (= Rabbi Judah the Patriarch), who served as the patriarch, that is, the official representative of the Jewish community to the Roman government. Rabbi solidified his name by, according to tradition, editing the Mishnah in the beginning of the third century C.E. So when Rabbi issues a decree, it commands legal, ritual, and cultural respect. Secondly, the purpose of decreeing a fast is to resolve a communal crisis in the form of drought (hence the title of this tractate: *Ta'anit*, which means "Fast" in Hebrew). Prior to fasting, a series of prayers and other actions occur, leaving fasting as an option of last resort. Thirdly, despite Rabbi's authority and standing, his decree is ineffective. No rain falls. That is, until Ilfa steps up to the plate.

Ilfa comes before his community, in the position where prayer leaders stand. He then utters two prayers. These prayers are also assumed knowledge, since "He causes the wind to blow and He causes the rain to fall" is the precise formula inserted into rabbinic liturgy during the rainy season in order to beseech God for sufficient rainfall. (Today, this formula is inserted into one of the main daily prayers, the *'Amidah*, between the end of Sukkot and the beginning of Passover.) Here, a small detail is actually quite important. Notice that the text records two traditions of the rainmaker's name. The best-known is Ilfa. But there are those who believe he is actually Rabbi Ilfai. The slight difference in vocalization of the proper name is less important (Ilfai replaces a final *yud* with an *aleph*, a common-enough variant). What is really interesting is that some believe he held the title of Rabbi. "The similarity between this story and other narratives in the Yerushalmi [e.g., *y. Ta'anit* 1:4, 64b] and Bavli, which certainly involve non-Rabbis, makes it likely that this account also features a non-rabbi" (Kalmin 1999, 76). This point is also driven home by Ilfa's earlier appearance in this same tractate. On *b. Ta'anit* 21a, Ilfa and Rabbi Yohanan are study partners, but Rabbi Yohanan overhears angels prophesying his future academic prowess, so he dedicates himself to study and becomes head of his study academy; Ilfa does not hear the angels, so he does not devote himself to his studies. Note that in this text, Rabbi Yohanan is a Rabbi, but Ilfa is not.

So if Ilfa is not a Rabbi, then why call him a Rabbi? The answer to this question is found in Ilfa's answer to Rabbi's question. Rabbi's simple question ("What do you do?") suggests an incredulous tone: after all, if someone of Rabbi's stature could not bring about rain by getting the entire community to fast, then how could Ilfa—who is not even a Rabbi, let alone *the* "Rabbi" par excellence—cause God to make wind and rain?! Even more shocking is that Ilfa brings this about by simply uttering the basic prayer for rain! Why is his prayer efficacious when Rabbi's fast was not?

Ilfa replies to Rabbi's incredulous question by giving a concrete example: he gained "verbal potency through virtuous action" (Belser 2015, 80). What were his virtuous actions? Ilfa lived in a district that, depending on the manuscript variant you are reading, was either "poor" or "distant" (the two words differ only by a single letter—*daled* and *resh*, respectively—which look very similar to one another; see Mokhtarian 2015, 185n80, who suggests that "distant" is probably the preferred term). Whether Ilfa's district was impoverished or isolated, it lacked access to wine over which to recite blessings at the beginning (*qiddush*) or end (*havdalah*) of the Sabbath (on these rituals, see chapter 6). Ilfa makes a significant effort to locate wine. Indeed, the verb that I render "I take the trouble" (Aramaic *taraḥna'*) is the same verb used in *b. Pesahim* 107a, which describes two brothers who "took the trouble" (Aramaic *teraḥna'*) to obtain wine for a guest who, in contrast to locale custom, refuses to recite *havdalah* over beer (for discussion, see chapter 6). This linguistic connection suggests that the one who "takes the trouble" makes a significant effort on behalf of someone else in order to locate a beverage (particularly wine) required for their fulfillment of Sabbath ritual. In doing so, Ilfa's prayer brings about the profound effect that Rabbi's fast could not.

Commenting on the Ilfa narrative and a similar one that follows in *b. Ta'anit* 24a (in the other tale, an unnamed figure tells Rav—an important rabbinic figure whose name is the Aramaic form of Rabbi—that his meritorious act is teaching rich and poor students alike), Belser concludes: "In both tales, the rabbis stand by as witnesses to watch their own inability to bring rain reflected in the effective piety of their more plebian contemporaries. Simple but significant good deeds are the currency that invests their word and prayer with the power to bring rain" (Belser 2015, 81). Ilfa is no Rabbi, let alone *the* Rabbi. However, he is a pious man. By a simple act—making an effort to locate wine for the Sabbath—"Ilfa's prayers turn into natural miracles" (Mokhtarian 2015, 55). Taking the trouble to obtain wine for Sabbath ritual on behalf of a poor/distant community has the potential to turn the layman into the superman.

Note that Ilfa merits special supplicatory powers by taking the trouble to help others fulfill rabbinic ritual. The Sabbath rituals of *qiddush* and *havdalah* are rabbinic creations. Furthermore, when Ilfa stands before the community to lead prayer, the liturgical formula that he recites is another rabbinic creation. Is it any surprise why according to some traditions he merits the title "Rabbi"? Despite being a non-rabbinic character, Ilfa's actions are decidedly rabbinic. Therefore, when he bests Rabbi, he is besting him at his own game.

HOW TO OFFER A RABBINIC TOAST

A fascinating final case study of the theme of symbolic inversion and illicit religious practice is the curious rabbinic category of "the ways of the Amorites" (Hebrew *darkhei ha-'emori*). Noted briefly in the Mishnah (see *m. Shabbat* 6:10; *m. Hullin* 4:7), a long series of such practices appears in *t. Shabbat* 6–7. To offer a few of the myriad examples found in *t. Shabbat* 6–7:

154 / *Magic, Idolatry, and Illicit Religious Practice*

(6:1) What practices constitute "the ways of the Amorites"? ...

(6:2) He who strikes the hip, claps hands, and dances before a flame, behold, these are the ways of the Amorites....

(6:7) He who says: "Eat this date [or] this lettuce, that you should remember me by it"; ... "Sit on a broom, so that you should dream"; "Do not sit on a broom, so that you should not dream"; behold, these are the ways of the Amorites....

(6:11) He who pours out water into public streets, and says, "Here it is!" behold, these are the ways of the Amorites. If he did so [to warn] those who pass by on the street, behold, this is permitted....

(6:14) She who shouts at an oven, so that the bread should not fall; and she who puts charms into the handle of a pot, so that it should not boil over, behold, these are the ways of the Amorites. But she may put chips of mulberry [wood] or glass into a pot, so that it should boil more quickly; but the sages say: She should not do so with glass [chips], because of mortal danger....

(7:5) He who says, "Healing!" [when someone sneezes], behold, these are the ways of the Amorites. Rabbi Elazar bey Rabbi Zadoq says: one does not say "Healing!" because it interrupts Torah study. The members of the household of Rabban Gamaliel would not say "Healing!" because of the ways of the Amorites.

A variety of practices, from dancing to saying "Gesundheit!" when someone sneezes, constitute "the ways of the Amorites." This text "offers a kaleidoscope of practices that lack a clear common denominator or an obvious organizing principle" (Berkowitz 2014, 96). A few points deserve mentioning. First, the verbs that appear throughout it are a mixture of masculine and feminine—meaning that they refer to both male and female agents. "The practices mentioned here are surprisingly gender-balanced, in contrast to much of the material on magic and superstition (including rabbinic) that associates them with women" (Berkowitz 2014 97n57). We should not, however, push this observation too far. For example, one of the female-gendered verbs refers to a woman putting charms into a pot handle in order to assure that its contents do not boil over (*t. Shabbat* 6:14). This serves to reinforce an association between women and magic, although male verbs refer to other magical practices.

Second, what precisely constitutes "the ways of the Amorites" is debated. To return to the previous example, while putting "charms" (Hebrew *qesamin*) into a pot handle is deemed one of "the ways of the Amorites," putting in "chips" (Hebrew *qesamim*) of mulberry wood or glass is not, although the sages sensibly nix glass chips as dangerous to throw into a boiling pot (see pp. 136–37 above on the rabbinic phrase "because of mortal danger"). Here, the text puns: "charms" and "chips" are actually the same Hebrew word, with meaning determined by context (the slight morphological difference, *qesamin/qesamim*, is a common variant ending in rabbinic Hebrew; in the present case, it helps to highlight the pun, though it is not consistent across manuscript traditions). The use of magical charms could have been banned on the grounds of magic. But this particular practice falls under a roughly comparable, but distinct category. And defining what exactly is included in and excluded from that category remains a subject of debate.

Third, in a related point, even some of these practices that are prohibited may not actually be forbidden on the grounds of being "the ways of the Amorites." Thus I must not respond "Healing!" when I hear someone sneeze, innocuous though that seems, because this is the kind of exclamation Amorites would make. According to another tradition, however, one should not say "Healing!" for another reason: "[saying] 'healing' for the sneezers necessarily interrupts the lecture of the teacher, thus causing a waste of time during the study of the Torah" (Veltri 2015, 141). To sneeze is human; to exclaim "Healing!" is Amorite.

So what exactly is meant by "the ways of the Amorites"? Scholars are not completely certain. First, we do not know why the Amorites are singled out, when they are but one of many peoples that inhabited the land of Canaan mentioned in the Hebrew Bible (see Berkowitz 2014, 98). If there is some particular significance to Amorites, then it eludes us. Second, are these actual ancient practices? Biblical or contemporaneous to the Rabbis? Common among non-Jews, Jews, or some combination thereof? (In general, see Berkowitz 2014, 98–99.) Third, is there something distinctive about "the ways of the Amorites" as compared to magic or other categories? Why are these particular practices singled out as belonging to this category and not to others?

I ask the question again: what, then, are the "the ways of the Amorites"? Beth Berkowitz offers the most compelling explanation:

> The question remaining is the criterion for locating certain practices under this rubric and not under a different one. I would propose that one reason rabbinic legislators categorized these practices in this particular way rather than as idolatry or divination or anything else is, quite simply, that it is difficult for rabbinic legislators to put their finger on exactly what is wrong with the practices described here: They admit that there is no full-proof [sic] biblical support for their condemnation. What is clear is that the authors did not approve of these practices and wanted to outlaw them. Perhaps they considered them foreign, or magical, or overly self-oriented, or insufficiently respectful of rabbinic authority, or threatening for other reasons.... "The ways of the Amorites" is a catch-all for practices that some rabbis do not like but for which they have no clear justification to prohibit. (Berkowitz 2014, 99–100)

"The ways of the Amorites" are practices of which some Rabbis disapprove, but for which they have no clear basis in which to ground a prohibition. Given that these practices "fall through the cracks of clearer categories of prohibition as defined by the Torah" (Berkowitz 2014, 99), "the ways of the Amorites" serves as a generic forbidden category that can be invoked for assorted practices that, though not explicitly illicit, are condemned.

All of that was necessary background in order to understand how to offer a rabbinic toast. Prior to drinking a glass of wine, one is required to recite a rabbinic blessing:

> Blessed are You, Lord, our God, King of the universe, Creator of the fruit of the vine. (See *m. Berakhot* 6:1, discussed in chapter 7)

But is it acceptable to utter other words while raising a glass of wine? To find out, we may consult the Bavli's analysis of "the ways of the

Amorites" traditions (in general, see *b. Shabbat* 67a–b). Amid this conversation, we learn:

> [If one makes the following toast:] "Wine and life to the mouth of the Rabbis!" this is not [prohibited] because of the ways of the Amorites.
>
> Once upon a time, Rabbi Aqiva made a drinking party for his son, and over each and every cup that he brought out he said: "Wine and life to the mouth of the Rabbis! Life and wine to the mouth of the Rabbis and the mouth of their students!" (*b. Shabbat* 67b)

"Wine and life to the mouth of the Rabbis!" seems like an excellent toast to recite while raising a glass. Why would anyone raise concern over it? Perhaps, as I noted above, because the rabbinic wine blessing functions as words spoken over the cup, so another formula struck some as potentially problematic. Remember that "the ways of the Amorites" is a catch-all for that which might fall between the cracks: that which is not explicitly prohibited, but maybe should be. Therefore, it would seem that at least some express concern over even this lovely toast.

The text states unambiguously, however, that "Wine and life to the mouth of the Rabbis!" is not subject to "the ways of the Amorites" prohibition. In fact, no less of an authority than Rabbi Aqiva uses this very formulation extensively. It is worth taking a moment to unpack this particular tradition. First, it is introduced by "Once upon a time ..." (Hebrew *ma'aseh*) the common rabbinic phrase for introducing a tale about "an event that happened in the past which has halakhic implications" (Simon-Shoshan 2012, 45–49, quoted here at 49). We are primed then both for a story and a legal lesson. Second, Rabbi Aqiva is throwing "a drinking party (Hebrew *mishteh*) for his son." Although *mishteh* is often rendered as "wedding feast," we should not lose sight of the term's literal meaning: this celebration is centered, linguistically and otherwise, around drinking (for further discussion, see chapter 7). Third, this entire passage is an edited version of an earlier tradition that appeared in *t. Shabbat* 7:7–9:

> (7:7) He who says: "Drink and leave over!" behold, these are the ways of the Amorites. "Drink and leave over!" these are not the ways of the Amorites.

(7:8) "Drink and leave over! Wine to your lives!" these are not the ways of the Amorites.

(7:9) Once upon a time, Rabbi Aqiva made a drinking party for his son, [and] over each and every jug that he opened he said: "To the life of the Rabbis! And to the life of their students!"

Note how the Bavli's version streamlines things. First, it omits the contradicting statements in *t. Shabbat* 7:7: that "Drink and leave over!" either is or is not one of the ways of the Amorites. Second, it seems to embrace the tradition in *t. Shabbat* 7:8 that "Wine to your lives!" is not prohibited. In fact, it amplifies the wording to the even more unambiguous toast of "Wine and life to the mouth of the Rabbis!" Third, it takes the amplified wording and applies that to the Rabbi Aqiva tradition.

"The ways of the Amorites" functions as a mechanism for prohibiting practices of which (at least some) Rabbis disapprove, but there is no clear basis for prohibiting. Given its status as a catch-all category, part of the conversation necessarily includes debate about what exactly constitutes "the ways of the Amorites." The subject of how to offer a rabbinic toast exemplifies this phenomenon, as we learn that—despite the fact that such words are additional to the rabbinic wine blessing—it is allowable for a Rabbi to raise their glass with the toast "Wine and life to the mouth of the Rabbis!" After all, it was good enough for Rabbi Aqiva!

CONCLUSION

Gazing into a mirror, one sees oneself, but in reverse. When the Rabbis gaze at illicit religious practices—such as magic, idolatry, and "the ways of the Amorites"—they see a similar image: their own practices, only in reverse. This symbolic inversion often involves the Rabbis, or their mirror images, holding a drink in their hands. As we have seen throughout this chapter, from kissing an idol to raising a glass for a toast, beverages serve a key role in negotiating the various implications for Rabbis looking out into a world that often is their mirror image. Along the way, we encounter fascinating tales of spontaneous human combustion, dogs licking the blood of fraudulent butchers, and rainmakers transforming before our eyes from troublemakers into pious rabbinic figures.

SUGGESTED READINGS

Baker, Cynthia M. 2002. *Rebuilding the House of Israel: Architectures of Gender in Jewish Antiquity.* Stanford, CA: Stanford University Press.

Belser, Julia Watts. 2015. *Power, Ethics, and Ecology in Jewish Late Antiquity: Rabbinic Responses to Drought and Disaster.* New York: Cambridge University Press.

Berkowitz, Beth A. 2014 [2012]. *Defining Jewish Difference: From Antiquity to the Present.* New York: Cambridge University Press.

Berzon, Todd S. 2016. *Classifying Christians: Ethnography, Heresiology, and the Limits of Knowledge in Late Antiquity.* Berkeley: University of California Press.

Cohn, Yehudah B. 2008. *Tangled Up in Text:* Tefillin *and the Ancient World.* Providence, RI: Brown Judaic Studies.

Horowitz, Roger. 2016. *Kosher USA: How Coke Became Kosher and Other Tales of Modern Food.* New York: Columbia University Press.

Janowitz, Naomi. 2001. *Magic in the Roman World: Pagans, Jews and Christians.* New York: Routledge.

Kalmin, Richard. 1999. *The Sage in Jewish Society of Late Antiquity.* New York: Routledge.

Lapin, Hayim. 2012. *Rabbis as Romans: The Rabbinic Movement in Palestine, 100–400 CE.* New York: Oxford University Press.

Lee, Jennifer 8. 2008. *The Fortune Cookie Chronicles: Adventures in the World of Chinese Food.* New York: Twelve.

Lincoln, Bruce. 2014 [1989]. *Discourse and the Construction of Society: Comparative Studies of Myth, Ritual, and Classification.* 2nd ed. New York: Oxford University Press.

Mokhtarian, Jason Sion. 2015. *Rabbis, Sorcerers, Kings, and Priests: The Culture of the Talmud in Ancient Iran.* Oakland: University of California Press.

Rosenblum, Jordan D. 2010. *Food and Identity in Early Rabbinic Judaism.* New York: Cambridge University Press.

Schwartz, Seth. 2001. *Imperialism and Jewish Society, 200 B.C.E. to 640 C.E.* Princeton, NJ: Princeton University Press.

Septimus, Yehuda. 2015. *On the Boundaries of Talmudic Prayer.* Tübingen: Mohr Siebeck.

Simon-Shoshan, Moshe. 2012. *Stories of the Law: Narrative Discourse and the Construction of Authority in the Mishnah*. New York: Oxford University Press.

Stern, Sacha. 2013. "Compulsive Libationers: Non-Jews and Wine in Early Rabbinic Sources." *Journal of Jewish Studies* 64, no. 1: 19–44.

Veltri, Giuseppe. 2015. *A Mirror of Rabbinic Hermeneutics: Studies in Religion, Magic and Language Theory in Ancient Judaism*. Berlin: De Gruyter.

Weingarten, Susan. 2010. "Gynaecophagia: Metaphors of Women as Food in the Talmudic Literature." In *Food and Language: Proceedings of the Oxford Symposium of Food and Cookery 2009*, ed. Richard Hosking, 360–70. Totnes, Devon, UK: Prospect Books.

SIX

Sabbath, Festivals, and Holidays

Not all days on the rabbinic calendar are created equal. Some are invested with more significance than others. Alongside this symbolic significance are holiday-specific rules. In this chapter, we explore what rabbinic texts about beverages teach us about the celebration of Jewish holidays.

Before proceeding, a quick note on terminology. Throughout, I distinguish between holidays and Festival Days. Holidays are days marked as particularly special. Daily liturgy changes on holidays, and other practices may—or may not—be allowed. For example (for reasons explained shortly), if you are a bartender, you cannot go to work on the Sabbath, but you may report for duty on Purim. Festival Days, on the other hand, have a series of regulations that prohibit many normal daily activities. When I mention a Festival Day, the reader should note that certain regulations apply (for example, the bartender needs to take the day off of work). In short, all Festival Days are holidays, but not all holidays are Festival Days.

"THE WINE OF THE REGION": BEER AND SABBATH LITURGY

The Rabbis believe that all acts of eating and drinking require the recitation of ritual blessings. On holidays, these blessings vary to include mention of the specific day. For example, in modern rabbinic liturgy, the Friday evening Sabbath meal begins with a blessing over wine (Hebrew *qiddush*; literally, "declare holy" or "sanctification"), which quotes a relevant biblical passage:

> The sixth day—The heaven and earth were finished, and all of their array. And on the seventh day God finished His work that He had been doing, and on the seventh day He rested (Hebrew *va-yishbot*) from all His work that He had been doing. And God blessed the seventh day and declared it holy (Hebrew *va-yiqadesh*), because on it He rested (Hebrew *shavat*) from all His work that God in creating had done. (Genesis 1:31–2:3)

The Sabbath *qiddush* therefore contains the origin story of the Sabbath itself: on the seventh day, God rested (Hebrew *shavat*; the noun is *shabbat*) and, in an act of imitation of God (Latin *imitatio dei*), Jews commemorate this event by resting every seventh day. Since the biblical account lists night and then day (e.g., Genesis 1:31: "And there was evening and there was morning, the sixth day"), the rabbinic day begins at sunset. Thus, the seventh day begins on Friday at sunset and ends at sunset on Saturday.

Though the Hebrew Bible commands observance of the Sabbath (e.g., Exodus 20:8–11; Deuteronomy 5:12–15), many of the details are not fully spelled out. The Rabbis work out these particulars, with an aim to sanctifying time rather than space (see Heschel 1997). One area of focus concerns beverages. Indeed, while the Rabbis might quibble about the procedure, they presume "that the Sabbath must be sanctified with blessings at a Friday night meal that includes wine. You will look in vain throughout the Torah of Moses [i.e., the Written Torah] for any such requirement. But it is assumed as a firm and noncontroversial fulfillment of a divine commandment to sanctify the Sabbath" (Jaffee 2006, 77). The connection between wine and the Sabbath is so strong that it is found in the background of many accounts. For example, a discussion of law concerning the Sabbath day states that, due to festive drinking, "intoxication is common on [the Sabbath]" (*b. Eruvin* 61a).

Despite rabbinic concerns for intoxication, it would seem that when there is drinking, there is sometimes too much drinking. Further, even ancient non-Jews, such as the Roman authors Persius and Plutarch, are aware that wine plays a prominent role in Sabbath celebration (see Rosenblum 2010, 174–75).

Given the strong association between the Sabbath and wine, it is not surprising to find Sabbath laws about this beverage. Sabbath and Festival laws often intersect, and the Rabbis assume that wine is used for the ritual celebration of the Sabbath. However—especially pertinent in a Babylonian context—can one perhaps substitute beer?

This query arises in a discussion about regulations concerning the blessing over wine at the beginning of Sabbath on Friday night (Hebrew *qiddush*) and the liturgy for the conclusion of the Sabbath on Saturday night (Hebrew *havdalah*; literally, "separation" or "division"). Both ceremonies feature wine.

We begin, as rabbinic conversation so often does, with an anecdote:

> Mar Yenuqa and Mar Qeshisha, the sons of Rav Hisda, said to Rav Ashi: One time, Ameimar visited our place [on a Sabbath afternoon], and we did not have wine [with which to recite *havdalah*]. We brought him beer, but he did not recite *havdalah* [using the beer], "and spent the night fasting" [Daniel 6:19]. The next day, we took the trouble and brought him wine, and he recited *havdalah* [using the wine] and ate something. The following year, he again visited our place. [Once again,] we did not have wine. We brought beer [again to him]. He said: If so, [beer] is the wine of the region. [Therefore,] he recited *havdalah* [using the beer] and ate something. (*b. Pesahim* 107a)

Since there is so much to discuss, I pause the talmudic passage (Aramaic *sugya'*) here. The story begins with a pair of sons recounting a story. The son's names are interesting, as they literally mean "Young Master" (Aramaic *Mar Yenuqa*) and "Old Master" (Aramaic *Mar Qeshisha*). Commentators speculate whether these: (1) are their actual names; (2) are nicknames for Rav Hisda's younger and elder sons; (3) are nicknames for the son born when Rav Hisda was young and the son born when he was old; (4) they both had the same name and these nicknames distinguish them; or (5) they had the same name, which is Mar ("Master"), and these nicknames distinguish them. I note this debate because it reminds us how much we can read into even such a small detail as the names of the Rabbis reporting an event. Too often, readers skim right past this detail and ignore that this too is open for discussion and potentially useful for interpretation and analysis. For example, on *b. Avodah Zarah* 17a, the narrative of one who sins and then repents is foreshadowed in his very name: Elazar ben Durdya. In Hebrew, Elazar means "God Will Help"; in Aramaic, Durdya are the lees, or sediment, that settle at the bottom of a fermented beverage. Therefore, his very name summarizes his entire tale: God will help the one who "represents the dregs of society, the bottom of the barrel" (Wasserman 2017, 61).

After learning their names, we discover that Ameimar once came to visit Rav Hisda's sons on a Sabbath afternoon. As evening approached, they prepared to recite *havdalah*, a ritual that separates, in the words of the ritual itself,

> ... between holy and profane, between light and darkness, between Israel and the nations, between the seventh day and the six days of labor. (*b. Pesahim* 103b)

At this moment, a problem arose: the brothers had no wine. Ameimar refused to recite *havdalah* using beer. In addition, he did not eat, since the conversation earlier in this section of the Talmud related to whether one may eat prior to reciting *havdalah* (see *b. Pesahim* 106b–107a). Therefore, he went to bed hungry, having been unable to recite *havdalah*. When he woke up on Sunday morning, the brothers (apparently having recited *havdalah* using their beer) scrambled and found wine so that their buddy could recite *havdalah* (and eat). The next year, perhaps forgetting his previous experience, he visits his wine-less friends and the situation repeats itself. But now Ameimar realizes that the brothers must live in a region like Wisconsin, the state in which I wrote these very words, where beer is the preferred beverage; it is "the wine of the region." In that case, he concludes that it is acceptable to recite *havdalah* using beer, which is precisely what he does.

But is Ameimar's *havdalah* practice a general Sabbath ritual principle for all to follow? After briefly discussing other related laws learned from Ameimar's actions (for example, "it is forbidden for a person to eat before reciting *havdalah*"), the text continues:

> Rav Hisda inquired of Rav Huna: What is [the law] regarding reciting *qiddush* [using] beer? He said: Now [if this is the case in regard to] beer made from figs, dates, or Dilmun dates—which I inquired of Rav [whether they are suitable for reciting *qiddush*] and Rav [inquired] of Rabbi Hiyya and Rabbi Hiyya [inquired] of Rabbi and he could not resolve [the legal problem] for him—can there even be a question [in regard to barley] beer?!
>
> It was understood from this: it is specifically *qiddush* that we cannot recite [using] beer, but we can indeed recite *havdalah* [using beer].
>
> Rav Hisda said to them: Thus said Rav: Just as one does not recite *qiddush* over it, so too one does not recite *havdalah* over it. It was also stated: Rav Tahlifa bar Avimi said that Shmuel said: Just as one does not recite *qiddush* over it, so too one does not recite *havdalah* over it. (*b. Pesahim* 107a)

I begin again by noting the name of the Rabbis initiating the conversation. First of all, Rav Hisda appeared above, as the father of Ameimar's non-wine drinking friends. Second, I have emended the text to reverse the order of the Rabbis cited in the first line, as many commentators prefer. Elsewhere we learn that Rav Hisda was the disciple of Rav Huna (and, from *b. Bava Metzi'a* 33a, that they eventually had a big falling out), and we expect questions in rabbinic literature to be asked by students to their teachers, and not vice versa. While I do not usually note instances where I slightly alter the text, I bring this to our attention to again remind us that the names of the authorities quoted should not be ignored (though we should also not presume everything attributed to a sage to be either consistent or historically reliable).

The question arises: can one recite *qiddush* using beer? The answer is no. But rather than just say that, the text needs to explain the reasoning. Several authorities investigated whether one could recite *qiddush* using beer brewed from superior ingredients (the translations of which are debated; I follow Sokoloff 2002, 891), and they could not resolve the debate in the affirmative: in short, they could not conclude that one may, indeed, use these beers for reciting *qiddush*. And if they could not do so for these higher-quality beers, a lesser-quality beer made from barley could hardly be used for this ritual purpose. So beer is off the table with regard to the recitation of *qiddush*. But the text at first concludes that "we can indeed recite *havdalah* [using beer]." Two different traditions (one cited by our old friend Rav Hisda) are introduced that state the same ruling verbatim: beer is unsuitable for the recitation of either *qiddush* or *havdalah*.

But the text does not leave things where they stand. Why? Because there is still support for using beer for *havdalah* (further support can be found in *y. Berakhot* 8:1, 11d; and *y. Pesahim* 10:2, 37c). So a series of anecdotes are related in *b. Pesahim* 107a that seek to denigrate the position of beer in regard to Sabbath ritual. One Rabbi who praises a particular beer, declaring it "fit to recite *qiddush* over it," walks back that claim after said beer causes him intestinal trouble. In another tale, Rav Huna accuses Rav of reciting *qiddush* over beer solely because Rav has begun to profit from the sale of beer (and hence, using it instead of wine for ritual purposes would be to his own financial advantage). Furthermore, two traditions are cited that claim that *qiddush* can only be recited using wine, and not beer. However, note that the traditions continue to take issue with beer used for the recitation of *qiddush* but not *havdalah*.

It would seem clear that the Sabbath must begin by reciting *qiddush* over wine, but could possibly conclude with the recitation of *havdalah* using either wine or beer. But even if wine must be used for both rituals, the fact remains that a beverage is once again at the center of rabbinic practice and debate. Like the hole at the center of the donut, the Sabbath is an absence that defines the dough/weekdays that surround it. But what do beverages teach us about the things that one may or may not do on the Sabbath itself? It is to this question that we now turn.

DRINKING, ENDANGERING LIFE, AND WORKING ON THE SABBATH

As a weekly day of rest, the Sabbath is the commonest Jewish holiday. But just because it is the most common does not mean that it is *common*. Indeed, the Sabbath is understood as holy, not mundane. Remember that: "God blessed the seventh day and declared it holy" (Genesis 2:3). And its frequency is part of this sanctity. Requiring weekly practice establishes a rhythm that regularly reorients one's routine.

These lofty theological claims aside, rabbinic conversation about the holy Sabbath often focuses on the mundane: what daily tasks may or may not be performed on the Sabbath? For example, *m. Shabbat* 2:1–7 details the rules associated with kindling lamps and candles on Friday afternoon in order to provide light on the Sabbath—a day on which no flames may be lit (see Exodus 35:3). In many modern synagogues, this chapter—referred to by its first two Hebrew words *ba-meh madliqin* ("With what may one light...")—is included in the Friday evening liturgy. For the Rabbis, discussion of the mundane signals the holiness presumed to saturate this entire day.

While the Hebrew Bible commands that the Sabbath be celebrated, it provides a bare (and sometimes contradictory) outline of what may or may not be done on this day. For example, Sabbath observance is the fourth of the Ten Commandments. According to Exodus 20:8, this commandment requires that one "Remember (Hebrew *zakhor*) the Sabbath day, to keep it holy." But in the version of the Ten Commandments that appears in Deuteronomy 5:11, the commandment is to "Observe (Hebrew *shamor*) the Sabbath day, to keep it holy." Which one is it—"remember" or "observe"? And what exactly does it mean to "remember" or "observe"?

In order to address these issues, the Rabbis embark on an ambitious exegetical journey, which involves clarifying contradictions, filling in missing data, updating rules, creating new regulations, and extending (or limiting) the scope of some existing legislation. At the center of this legal enterprise is the rabbinic creation of thirty-nine categories of labor prohibited on the Sabbath (Hebrew *mela'khot*; see *m. Shabbat* 7:2; Cohen 2007, 134–38]). For example, the activities related to hunting a deer are separated into seven different categories of prohibited labor, including regulations against: (1) hunting the deer; (2) slaughtering it; (3) flaying and (4) salting the carcass; and (5) curing, (6) scraping, and (7) slicing its hide. Each of these are primary prohibited labors, with multiple levels of related activities falling under the general rubric. Therefore, these thirty-nine categories of labor result in an almost infinite amount of sub-sets of prohibitions.

One of the most discussed Sabbath prohibitions is number thirty-nine on the list of thirty-nine categories of prohibited labor: "taking out from one domain to another" (*m. Shabbat* 7:2). In order to allow for carrying objects between domains on the Sabbath, the Rabbis develop a legal fiction known as *'eruv* ("mixture"), in which multiple domains are "mixed" into a single domain; and therefore, one is not taking an object (e.g., a bottle of wine) from one domain into another, but is understood rather to be carrying it within the domain itself, which is permitted on the Sabbath. The topic of the *'eruv* has attracted attention in both the ancient world—where it is the subject of an entire talmudic tractate, *Eruvin*—and in modernity—where it is the subject of popular novels, such as *The Yiddish Policemen's Union* by Michael Chabon (2007), and an episode of *The Daily Show* (2011).

Of the many discussions concerning moving beverages on the Sabbath, there is one that raises several fascinating related issues:

> One may move a *shofar* [on the Sabbath] in order to give drink from it to an infant. (*t. Shabbat* 13:16)

In order to feed a hungry infant on the Sabbath, one may transport a ram's horn (Hebrew *shofar*) into which breast milk has been expressed. As we shall see below, this is part of a larger concern for infants who depend on breast milk for their survival (and about endangering life in

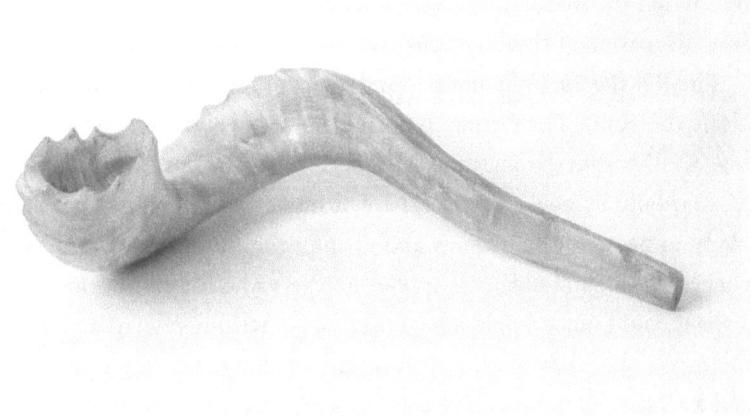

Figure 3. Shofar made in Israel in the 1960s. Photo: Ralph Grunewald.

general). Therefore, this text allows for the movement of a *shofar* on the Sabbath.

The specific vessel being moved raises additional Sabbath-related questions. Formed from a ram's horn, a *shofar* is a musical instrument, a trumpet (see fig. 3). In the world of the Rabbis, as is the case today, the *shofar* is commonly associated with the Jewish New Year (Rosh Hashanah) and the Day of Atonement (Yom Kippur). Throughout the month of *Elul* in the rabbinic calendar (usually occurring in August or September), which leads up to these holidays, and during the holidays themselves, the *shofar* is an integral part of the liturgy. The Rabbis develop a detailed ritual for blowing the *shofar*, inspired by biblical references to Rosh Hashanah as "a memorial of blowing" (Leviticus 23:24) and "a day of blowing" (Numbers 29:1). When either of these holidays falls on the Sabbath, however, the *shofar* is not blown. While the Rabbis believe that prior to the destruction of the Second Temple, the *shofar* was blown when one of these holidays coincided with the Sabbath, they assert that this is no longer the case. Thus, a *shofar* is a ritual object that should not be used on the Sabbath; and since, according to another rabbinic principle, objects that cannot be used on the Sabbath should not be carried on that day, a *shofar* should not be moved on the Sabbath. (For discussion of these various concerns, see *b. Rosh Hashanah* 29b.)

Finally, the *shofar* is not a standard drinking vessel, which is precisely the point. The normal is boring, however, and the odd is fascinating. To illustrate the matter, the Rabbis have chosen an odd example—as we should by now expect of them. A modern discussion of barware is likely to be about beer mugs and champagne flutes, not trumpets and concert flutes, and the same applies here. As a hollowed-out ram's horn, a *shofar* could indeed hold a beverage (or something else; as an interesting aside, the *shofar* pictured in figure 3 belonged to my grandfather, and a relative of mine briefly used it as a hash pipe in the 1970s). Therefore, this example offers the perfect balance between farfetched and plausible.

In addition to the drinking vessel, we should take note of the beverage in the *shofar*. As we explore in several other chapters in this book, breast milk provides a curious test case, given its vital importance to an infant's life. In the present instance, we learn about breast milk in a *shofar*, but what about the related question: may a woman actually express breast milk into a vessel on the Sabbath? For the answer, we turn to a text found earlier in this same tractate:

> A woman may not squeeze her breasts and lactate into a cup or into a dish, and then nurse her child. One may nurse neither from a non-Jewish woman nor from an impure beast. But if it was a matter of danger, absolutely nothing stands in the way of preservation of life. (*t. Shabbat* 9:22)

In general, expressing breast milk into a cup or dish—and also into a *shofar*—on the Sabbath is forbidden (on what Sabbath restrictions this violates, see *b. Shabbat* 95a; *b. Ketubbot* 60a; Hayes 2002, 208); directly nursing a child is not. And since the Rabbis are considering questions related to prohibited breastfeeding practices on the Sabbath, they then add two others: nursing from a non-Jewish woman and from an impure beast (for discussion of these two issues, see Hayes 2002, 207–12; Rosenblum 2016, 163–67).

Although *t. Shabbat* does not explain why a woman would need to express milk into a vessel prior to nursing her infant on the Sabbath, medieval rabbinic sources perhaps provide insight:

> Some medieval Jewish sources discuss a problem that occurred on Sabbath. In some cases, Jewish women suffered from a surplus of milk on Sabbath. The ruling in such a case was to allow this woman to nurse as much as possible until the pain subsided. On weekdays, these women often expressed the excess milk. But on the Sabbath, expressing milk was forbidden. The halakhic ruling was that Jewish women could nurse Christian children if such a necessity arose, in order to ease their pain. (Baumgarten 2004, 143–44)

Since medieval Jewish women's bodies did not know that it was the Sabbath, and due to pain to the one nursing and risk to the infant's life if the source of milk decreased production (note here my intentional use of utilitarian language, which should be read to reflect their concerns and not necessarily my own), medieval Rabbis relaxed a prohibition—discussed in chapter 3—against Jewish women nursing non-Jewish infants. But they did not relax the prohibition against expressing milk on the Sabbath.

This latter decision is curious because of the final sentence of *t. Shabbat* 9:22: "But if it was a matter of danger, absolutely nothing stands in the way of preservation of life"—which clearly allows for the relaxation of such Sabbath prohibitions when life is in danger. Indeed, the very phrase "preservation of life" (Hebrew *piquaḥ nefesh*) is an important rabbinic concept, wherein the preservation of life supersedes any commandment, with only three exceptions: idolatry, forbidden sexual relations, and murder. This is because humans "shall live" by performing commandments, and not die by doing so (quoting and interpreting Leviticus 18:5; see *b. Yoma* 85b; *b. Sanhedrin* 74a). Thus, to cite a relevant example, if a person experiences severe chest pains on a Friday night, and relief could be found in drinking milk directly from an animal's udder, then it would be allowed, even though this act of drinking violates rabbinic Sabbath regulations (see *b. Ketubbot* 60a). A Jew may violate any Sabbath prohibition in order to save that person's life. The only exception to this general principle is if, for example, saving a life required committing an act of idolatry. (As farfetched as that might sound, the Rabbis consider a roughly analogous case; see Schäfer 2007, 52–62.) Of course, although one not only may—but must—violate all but three Sabbath prohibitions in order to save a life, many discussions of such situations detail the optimal way to do so in order to minimize (or even eliminate) the transgression (e.g., *y. Eruvin* 10:12, 26d describes how to draw water on the Sabbath for a sick person).

The theme of danger to life and its effect on Sabbath regulations is not only encountered in rabbinic conversations about breast milk. For example, what happens if a person swallows a leech on the Sabbath and hot water is required for the remedy? In chapter 5, I promised to answer this very question. We learn:

> For Rabbi Hanina said: If one swallows a water leech, it is permitted to heat water for him on the Sabbath.
> And once upon a time there was a certain person who swallowed a water leech and Rabbi Nehemiah permitted heating water for him on the Sabbath. In the meantime, said Rav Huna son of Rav Yehoshua, let him swallow vinegar. (*b. Avodah Zarah* 12b)

Swallowing a leech was considered to be potentially life-threating. So if one swallows a leech on a Saturday morning, then Sabbath rules are relaxed in order to prepare a remedy immediately. "You shall not kindle a fire throughout your settlements on the Sabbath day," Exodus 35:3 declares, but when life is at stake, you may kindle a fire and boil water to treat a leech swallower. While the water is coming to a boil, the victim may take a swig of vinegar to temporarily relieve the symptoms. But vinegar is a palliative, not a substitute for hot water—hence the need to violate Sabbath law in the effort to save a life.

While these examples do not provide an exhaustive list of Sabbath restrictions, regulations, or the categories of prohibited labor, they offer insight into how rabbinic conversation about Sabbath law seeks to understand the limits of what actions can and cannot be performed on this weekly holiday. In particular, we learn about how concern for the preservation of life allows for the violation of almost any law (Sabbath-related or otherwise).

"WINE GLADDENS THE HEART OF MAN": DRINKING ON FESTIVAL DAYS

Sabbath occurs every week, but it is not the only event on the rabbinic calendar. Throughout the year, there are several Festival Days. These "Good Days" (Hebrew *yom tov*) are governed by many of the same rules and regulations as the Sabbath, though they also have more flexibility and allowances. They are therefore often discussed in relation to the Sabbath. One important area of difference between Sabbath- and Festival-law relates to food and drink. The Festival kitchen is allowed to be a busier place, as noted in *m. Betzah* 5:2:

> The only difference between a Festival and the Sabbath is in the preparation of food alone. (cf. *m. Megillah* 1:5)

The Rabbis developed an elaborate series of regulations governing Festival Days, but the holidays themselves, and many of their basic conceptions, originate in the Hebrew Bible. In order of their appearance in the rabbinic calendar, these Festival Days are Rosh Hashanah (New Year); Yom Kippur (Day of Atonement); Sukkot (Tabernacles, connected to harvest traditions and commemorating the Israelites' post-Exodus wandering in the desert); Passover (commemorating the Exodus from Egypt); and Shavuot (Pentecost, which is important for unclear reasons in the Hebrew Bible, though eventually understood as commemorating the giving of the Torah at Mount Sinai). Three of these Festivals—Sukkot, Passover, and Shavuot—are deemed Pilgrimage Festivals, on which pilgrimage to Jerusalem (or a suitable alternative practice) is required. I shall not discuss these holidays and their evolution in detail (for a brief overview, see Satlow 2006, 86–89, 175–79), but it is important to know that the Rabbis elaborate on the observance of and legislation governing these days.

Festivals are times to be festive. And how does one go about being festive?

> It is a commandment for a man to make his children and his dependents happy on the Festival.
>
> How does he make them happy? With wine, as it is written: "and wine gladdens the heart of man" [Psalm 104:15].
>
> Rabbi Judah says: Women with what is appropriate for them, and children with what is appropriate for them. (*t. Pisha* 10:4)

Though this text refers to one particular Festival—Passover—the sentiment applies equally to all others: one should be happy on a Festival, and wine makes one happy, so drink wine on Festivals! The need to provide wine on a Festival is understood as a commandment (Hebrew *mitzvah*). This understanding is heavily gendered, as this commandment is incumbent upon men, who must make their children and dependents (likely referring to their wives) happy. Furthermore, Rabbi Judah suggests that wine might not be appropriate for all. As later commentators note, Rabbis commonly presume that, in lieu of wine, women prefer colorful garments and children prefer treats like roasted grains and nuts (see Lieberman 2002, 196). It is for this reason that I used an antiquated translation of Psalm 104:15: "wine gladdens the heart of man"—"man" and not the more gender-inclusive "humanity," because though wine brings Festival joy, the one imagined as holding that wine cup is, more often than not, imagined as a man (e.g., *b. Berakhot* 35a, which extrapolates about the songs of male Temple officials based on Judges 9:13: "... wine, which gladdens God and men").

The gendering of wine consumption is discussed in other chapters of this book, and the presumption that men drink on Festivals is encountered in many texts. For example, in the midst of a conversation about priests getting drunk in the Temple, we learn:

> [Rav Aha] came before Rav Ashi [for help resolving a legal matter]. [Rav Ashi] said to him: Go today and come back tomorrow, for Rav did not

appoint an *'amora* by his side from [when he began to enjoy] the Festival meal until the next day, because of drunkenness. (*b. Keritot* 13b)

The precise legal matter requiring resolution is unimportant. I can make this assertion because this same tradition appears in at least two other passages. On *b. Zevahim* 18a, it arises in a similar context (priests drinking), but on *b. Betzah* 4a–b the *halakhic* (meaning "legal") issue concerns cooking on a Festival Day eggs that were laid on the Sabbath. What is important is that, when intoxicated on a Festival Day, one should not appoint an *'amora* – a speaker who, as part of rabbinic classroom instruction, would repeat the words of the instructor loud enough for all in the audience to hear (for references to this practice, see Sokoloff 2002, 139). And just to clarify why one should not teach on this day and under these conditions, *b. Betzah* 4a–b notes that, were the Rabbi to have taught then, in his state of inebriation he might have cited the wrong legal opinion!

I note these other two variant texts for another reason: the Rabbis who were drinking are not the same in each case (for example, in the case of *b. Betzah* 4a–b, it is our favorite beer baron, Rav Pappa). However, they all cite Rav's precedent of not teaching on holidays "because of drunkenness." Drinking in earnest begins at the Festival meal, which in Aramaic is *yoma' tava'* ("The Good Day"; the equivalent of the Hebrew *yom tov*)—meaning both the Festival itself and the main Festival meal. Therefore, it would seem that Rabbis festively drinking on Festival Days is fairly common. This point is reinforced in another text, in which a Rabbi makes accommodations in the order of ritual practice when the timing of a Festival and the Sabbath coincide; he allows extra time between certain ritual actions, "in order that they do not enter into the *mitzvah* [commandment] drunk" (*y. Pesahim* 5:1, 31d). *L'chaim!*

Note, however, that the Rabbis also discuss drinking other, non-intoxicating, beverages on Festival Days. Thus, we learn:

> Once upon a time, the people of Tiberias put a cold water pipe into a channel of hot water. The sages said to them: If [one wants to use such water] on

the Sabbath, it is like water heated on the Sabbath—forbidden for washing and for drinking; [if one wants to use such water] on a Festival Day, it is like water heated on a Festival Day—forbidden for washing, but permitted for drinking. (*m. Shabbat* 3:4; on this text, see Simon-Shoshan 2012, 47–48, 111–16)

Using ancient technology, the people of Tiberias (a city in the north of Palestine, along the western coast of the Sea of Galilee) embark on an ambitious civic project: they pipe cold water through natural hot springs, which heats the cold water, providing the citizens with a renewable source of hot water for washing and drinking. On your average day, this solution presents no problems, only solutions to how to heat water without modern plumbing. But on Sabbath and Festival Days, this presents a potential problem (as does drawing water from a water channel in general; see *m. Eruvin* 8:7; and *y. Eruvin* 8:8, 24d). We have already learned that kindling a fire and rabbinically related heating issues are prohibited on the Sabbath. However, regulations for Festival Days are slightly different, and certain acts of heating are allowed, such as heating water for drinking (see *m. Betzah* 2:5). Therefore, the sages inform the people of Tiberias that hot water sourced from their civic infrastructure is forbidden for use on the Sabbath, and permitted only in regard to hot water for drinking on a Festival Day.

In many rabbinic texts, the anonymous voice of "the sages" depicts their ruling as a unified and authoritative voice. As Moshe Simon-Shoshan notes:

> The water-pipe story further emphasizes this ideal of centralized rabbinic authority by not naming any individual rabbi or group of rabbis. Rather, it was simply "the sages" who issued their ruling to the people of Tiberias. Who is included in "the sages"? By deploying such a vague term, the Mishnah suggests that a ruling cited by "the sages" represents the uncontested opinion of the entire rabbinic class. It is as if "the sages" were a corporate entity speaking with one voice. (2012, 114)

When views are attributed to "the sages," therefore, we should always remember that this designation creates a centralized authority and unified viewpoint that may—or may not—reflect ancient reality. Some of these instances may indeed reflect majority opinion, but many occurrences likely reflect an attempt to present the Rabbis as communal authorities for communities that may—or may not—have embraced, agreed with, or even known about their opinions. So once again, I caution the reader against reading these texts necessarily as *descriptive* of actual, ancient events and practices, rather than as *prescriptive* of how a particular ancient Jewish group desired events and practices to unfold.

STRAINING WINE AND BREWING BEER ON INTERMEDIATE FESTIVAL DAYS

Beverages have already taught us about Sabbath and Festival regulations. But what about days sandwiched between Festival Days? These "Intermediate Festival Days" (Hebrew *ḥol ha-moʿed*; literally: "non-sacral days of the Festival") occur when Festival Days bookend non-Festival days. For example, on both Sukkot and Passover, the beginning and the end days are Festival Days, but the days in between are non-Festival days. These non-Festival days are invested with some significance, making them like Festival Days, but also, at the same time, they are like other, non-sacral days. They are semi-sacred, quasi-Festival Days. Given the hybrid status of these days, as readers of this volume should by now expect, the Rabbis devote significant attention to spelling out which Festival rules and regulations do—and do not—apply to Intermediate Festival Days. In fact, this is the subject of an entire tractate (*Moʿed Qatan*; literally: "Little Festival"), which covers a variety of topics, including practical issues such as whether it is permissible to clip fingernails and toenails on Intermediate Festival Days (indeed, it is; see *b. Moʿed Qatan* 18a).

To what extent do rules related to Festival Days also apply to the Intermediate Days of a Festival? This is especially important because if a person begins to do something on these days, they need to know whether they can continue doing it during the Festival Day that is right around the corner. One area in which this very concern arises is in regard to brewing beer on Intermediate Festival Days. But to understand this question, we first need to examine Sabbath- and Festival-related rules for the straining of wine.

According to *m. Shabbat* 20:1:

> Rabbi Eliezer says: One may suspend a strainer on a Festival Day [but not on the Sabbath], and one may put [wine] through a strainer on the Sabbath [and, thus, also on a Festival Day].
>
> But the sages say: One may neither suspend a strainer on a Festival Day nor put [wine] through a strainer on the Sabbath, but one may put [wine] through a strainer on a Festival Day.

As discussed earlier in this chapter, there are a series of elaborate Sabbath prohibitions, which the Rabbis group into thirty-nine categories of prohibited labor (see *m. Shabbat* 7:2; Cohen 2007, 134–38). Some of these extend to Festival Days, and others do not. And some of those that extend to Festival Days also extend to Intermediate Festival Days, and others do not. In *m. Shabbat* 20:1, these questions come up in regard to straining wine. In the ancient world, as today (though to a much lesser extent due to modern technology), stored wine contains sediment. One way to separate wine from sediment is to pour the wine through a strainer. Such a pre-drink routine becomes potentially problematic if doing so is classified as a category of prohibited labor. Is suspending a strainer over a drinking cup an act of "building"? Does the physical act of putting wine in a strainer—of pouring it through the sieve—constitute "selecting"? If so, both are categories of prohibited labor according to *m. Shabbat* 7:2.

Rabbi Eliezer considers these questions and concludes that both placing and using a wine strainer is allowed on a Festival Day. However, only the latter is permitted on the Sabbath. The anonymous sages, representing the plurality of rabbinic opinion, disagree: both are prohibited on the Sabbath, and only the latter is permitted on a Festival Day. It would seem that wine poured on the Sabbath and on the Festival Day will have sediment in it—that is, unless you remember to set up your strainer prior to the beginning of a Festival Day.

In its commentary on this mishnah, the Babylonian Talmud adds three interesting elements. First, it introduces the concept of subterfuge, that is, of using a permitted action as a pretext to allow for another action that would have been prohibited on its own. Second, it considers the impact on beer, as well—which makes sense, since Babylonians were beer drinkers. Third, it considers how this legislation affects drinking habits during the Intermediate Festival Days. Therefore, we discover:

> Rabbah bar Rav Huna said: One may employ a subterfuge (Hebrew *ma'arim*) with regard to [suspending] a strainer on a Festival Day [by using it] to hold pomegranates in it, and [then, once it is already set up, pour wine through it and] hold sediment in it.
>
> Rav Ashi says: Provided that he holds pomegranates in it [first]. (*b. Shabbat* 139b)

I pause the text here in order to fully appreciate Rabbah bar Rav Huna's brilliant artifice. Setting up a strainer through which to pour wine on a Festival Day is still forbidden. However, remember that *m. Shabbat* 20:1 allows the physical act of straining wine on a Festival Day; it merely prohibits setting up an apparatus to do so. This is where pomegranates prove useful. A popular fruit, pomegranates ripen around August, making them ideal for eating on Rosh Hashanah and Sukkot (which usually occur in either September or October; on pomegranates, see Marks 2010, 479–80). Therefore, if I were to set up a strainer in order to hold pomegranates—a permitted action—on a Festival Day, and then, once it was set up, were to use it to filter my wine—another permitted action—then I would have managed to achieve my intended goal without violating rabbinic law (Hebrew *halakhah*). I would have sediment-free wine and have effectively worked around the prohibited action.

This is why Rav Ashi's provision is important. For this subterfuge to be licit, one needs to actually place pomegranates in the strainer first. Failure to do so would mean that the strainer was explicitly set up for the purpose of straining wine. That would be forbidden. But if I were to set up a strainer, and then were to place pomegranates in it, I would have effectively "proven" that my explicit purpose in setting up the strainer was to hold pomegranates. And once I have proven that, if I were to remove all of the pomegranates and then use that same strainer to catch sediment from wine that I pour through it, then that would be permissible on an Intermediate Festival Day. Note however that the text explicitly acknowledges that this is all a subterfuge. (For other examples of legal subterfuges, see *t. Yom Tov* 3:2; *y. Shabbat* 2:6, 5b–c; and *b. Shabbat* 65b.) In the equivalent of an ancient wink, it admits that this pomegranate trick is just that—a trick, a subtext to work around a prohibited action in order to achieve a desired, and now permissible, goal. Where there is a will, there is a way—especially when wine is involved!

Now we turn to beer. Remember, the Babylonian Talmud was composed in a cultural context in which beer is the beverage of choice, not wine. Therefore, much as we might expect a text compiled in Italy to discuss coffee and wine, while one edited in England might focus on tea and ale, we should expect conversations about wine in the Babylonian Talmud to quickly pivot towards beer. And that is precisely what happens in the continuation of our text:

> How is this [case in regard to straining wine] different from that which is taught in a *baraita*: One may brew beer on [the Intermediate Days of] the Festival, when it is necessary [for drinking] on the Festival; but if it is not necessary [for drinking] on the Festival, [then brewing] it is forbidden. [This ruling applies to brewing] both date beer and barley beer. Even though one has old [beer available for Festival drinking], one may employ a subterfuge and drink from the new [freshly brewed beer].
>
> There, [in regard to the beer subterfuge,] the matter is not apparent; here, [in regard to the wine subterfuge,] the matter is apparent. (*b. Shabbat* 139b; cf. *b. Mo'ed Qatan* 12b)

We begin with a question: how is the case of straining wine on an Intermediate Festival Day different from a case involving brewing beer on such a day? To establish the similarities and differences between these two case studies, the Talmud cites a *baraita*, a tradition reputed to be of tannaitic origin that is cited in an amoraic text. In citing what the text claims to be an earlier tradition, a case study of beer is introduced. The *baraita'* presumes that brewing beer on a Festival day itself is prohibited. But what about brewing beer on an Intermediate Festival Day? As usual, the answer is: it depends. If the beer is being brewed specifically for celebration of the fast-approaching Festival Day, then go ahead and brew it. But, if the beer is being brewed for use on a regular day sometime after the Festival itself has concluded, then that act of brewing is prohibited. In this way, the connection between the Intermediate Festival Day and the Festival Day itself is made explicit: actions on these semi-sacred days should be weighed in relevance to the surrounding Festival Days. So beer brewed for use on a Festival is allowed, but an act of brewing that constitutes preparation for time beyond Festival time detracts from the holiness of this time and therefore is forbidden.

This ruling applies to two different kinds of beer: beer brewed from dates and beer brewed from barley. This is important because of their relevance to the two Festivals on which Intermediate Festival Days occur: Passover and Sukkot. On Passover, barley is one of the Five Species that fall under the category of "leaven" (Hebrew *ḥametz*), and thus cannot be combined with water and consumed on this Festival (see *b. Berakhot* 36b–37a). Barley beer would therefore be impermissible throughout the entirety of Passover—whether on a Festival Day or an Intermediate Festival Day (as noted in *b. Pesaḥim* 42b). But date beer would be kosher for Passover. (Fun fact: in recent years, given the obvious Jewish ritual benefits on Passover, plus the added benefit of being gluten-free, some modern craft brewers have begun producing date beer.)

On Sukkot, when leaven is not prohibited, barley beer would not be a concern. And neither would date beer. But date beer actually has an added benefit for the celebration of Sukkot: the date palm is one of the Four Species that play a key role in the ritual celebration of Sukkot (see Leviticus 23:40; *m. Sukkot* 3:8–4:7; Rubenstein 1995). The date-palm frond (Hebrew *lulav*), along with branches of the other members of the Four Species [myrtle, willow, and citron; Hebrew *hadas*, *'aravah*, and *'etrog*], is used in an elaborate performative ritual practice in the rabbinic Sukkot liturgy. This might not have been at the forefront of their minds, but drinking date beer on Sukkot certainly accords with the general spirit of this particular Festival.

Next, we return to the concept of subterfuge. In this case, even though one has old beer on hand, one may brew new beer on an Intermediate Festival Day and then imbibe that fresh beer on the Festival Day itself. So what do we learn from this new evidence? Well, if beer is an important part of my Festival celebration, and I have either none or an insufficient supply, I may brew more on the Intermediate Days of the Festival. But what if I have an ample supply of beer? According to this *baraita'*, I may still brew new beer and consume that beer on the Festival Day; and my supply of old beer then can be used for drinking on non-Festival days that follow. Therefore, regardless of actual necessity for Festival celebration, I may claim the need for beer as a legal fiction for brewing beer on an Intermediate Festival Day.

However, in the last line of this passage, the anonymous voice of the Talmud correctly asserts that the beer subterfuge is not quite the same as the previous one employed for straining wine. In the case of the beer subterfuge, brewing beer on an Intermediate Festival Day for consumption on a Festival Day is allowed. Furthermore, not only is the actual act itself permitted, but there is no way for the casual observer to know how much beer any given brewer has stored away for use on or after the Festival. In the case of the wine subterfuge, straining wine on an Intermediate Festival Day is allowed, but setting up the strainer itself is not. Therefore, if the casual observer witnessed a person suspending a strainer without putting pomegranates in it, the presumption would be that the person set up the strainer for the explicit purpose of straining wine and consequently, in doing so, violated rabbinic law. The matter would be apparent and a visible subterfuge must be employed—hence, the need for pomegranates. As such, these cases are roughly comparable, but with an important caveat: in the case of brewing beer, there is no visible action needed to make the matter of subterfuge apparent.

Like the hole in a donut, Intermediate Festival Days are an absence in the middle of a substance; and yet what might seem like blank space both defines and is defined by that which surrounds it. Beverage-related rabbinic law therefore can be used to exemplify the various issues raised by the semi-sacred Intermediate Festival Days. And it not just the Intermediate Days themselves, but the fact that they are surrounded by Festival Days, which make these days such fascinating case studies in complex *halakhah*. Along the way, we encounter the concept of subterfuge. Here we see the Rabbis at their tricky best, trying to figure out a legal loophole that allows for licit drinking without violating rabbinic law. Were these texts to be created today, they almost certainly would employ our present language of communication: namely, emoticons. The wine and beer subterfuges would therefore be accompanied by winking faces, to hint at the witty playfulness of these claims. And perhaps the text would end with the comment ROTFL—Rabbi On the Floor Laughing.

FOUR CUPS OF WINE: ALCOHOL AND THE PASSOVER SEDER

Commemorating the Exodus from Egypt recounted in the Hebrew Bible, Passover is a holiday that ties together much of what we have learned in this chapter already. In addition to being composed of both Festival and Intermediate Festival Days, Passover is the Festival Day most associated with alcohol. Why? Because the central rabbinic Passover rite is the *Seder* ("Order" in Hebrew), a meal that requires the consumption of four cups of wine, accompanied by the *Haggadah* ("Telling" in Hebrew), the ritual recitation of the Passover story.

The liturgical and culinary history of the Passover *Seder* is fascinating (see, e.g., Bokser 2002; Kulp 2005; Rosenblum 2010, 63–68, 162–70). Throughout *m. Pesahim* 10, the details of the *Seder* are explained; indeed, much of the modern *Haggadah* draws on this chapter of the Mishnah.

Using Proverbs 23:31 as a proof text, *y. Pesahim* 10:1, 37c (cf. *y. Shabbat* 8:1, 11a) states that the commandment (Hebrew *mitzvah*) specifically requires drinking four cups of red wine. The importance of drinking wine at the Passover is presumed from the very start of *m. Pesaḥim* 10:

> On the eve of Passover, close to [the time of] *minḥah*, a person should not eat until it becomes dark. And even the poorest person in Israel should not eat until he reclines. And they should not give him fewer than four cups of wine, even if [the wine comes] from the soup kitchen. (*m. Pesaḥim* 10:1)

Around the time of *minḥah*—the daily afternoon sacrifice during the time of the Temple that the Rabbis translate into a daily afternoon prayer service—consumption of food should cease. This rule applies even to the poorest Jew, for whom hunger is a daily occurrence.

But on Passover, there is a light at the end of the hungry tunnel for the poorest Jew: the *Seder*. As *m. Pesaḥim* 10:1 notes: "And even the poorest person in Israel should not eat until he reclines." One of the many ancient Mediterranean dining practices that the Rabbis incorporate into the Passover *Seder*, reclining is a dining posture reserved for the wealthy (in general, see Roller 2006). Reclining requires that the diner lie down and support his body by leaning on his left arm and eating with his right. (I use male pronouns here, because the Rabbis likely understood reclining to be a male practice; see Rosenblum 2012; contrast Hauptman 2014, 45–49.) Reclining diners must be served food. Therefore, this act of eating divides the world into those who can afford to eat like this, and those who cannot (some of the latter are involved in serving food to the former). On Passover, acting as though they were wealthy, even the poor recline.

As a commemoration of the Israelites' liberation from slavery, this reversal of fortune is of symbolic importance for this Festival; and it is for this reason that accommodations are made so that even the poorest Jew can enjoy freedom—if only for one meal, on one evening per year. This symbolism results in a special allowance: on Passover, the communal soup kitchen (Hebrew *tamḥui*; see Gardner 2015, 84–110, esp. 95–97) provides four cups of wine—much as many modern soup kitchens in the United States of America provide turkeys and fixings on Thanksgiving.

On Passover, a poor Jew not only eats while reclining, like the wealthy, but drinks wine too. And not just a little, four cups of wine. Reading through *m. Pesahim* 10, we learn that four cups of wine punctuate the *Seder:* cup one in the beginning (10:2); cup two after the consumption of symbolic foods (10:4); cup three for the recitation of the Grace after Meals (10:7; for more on this "cup of blessing," see chapter 5); and cup four for an additional post-meal liturgy (10:7). For a few hours at least, therefore, the poor are entitled to eat and drink as though they were free and wealthy at public expense.

Wine not only marks this day as special, it also can serve a role in preparing for the special day itself. Thus, we learn:

> Rava would drink wine all [throughout the day] on the eve of Passover, so that he would whet his appetite in order to eat more *matzah* in the evening. Rava said: On what basis do I say that wine whets the appetite? For it is taught: "Between these cups, if one wants to drink, he may drink; between the third [cup] and the fourth, one may not drink" [*m. Pesahim* 10:7]. If you say that wine satiates, why may one drink [additional wine between these cups]? Indeed, eating *matzah* [under such conditions would then be] gorging! Rather, learn from this [that wine] whets the appetite. (*b. Pesahim* 107b–108a)

In the hours leading up to the eve of Passover, food is not consumed. Rava would not eat, but he would drink wine. However, he did so for the same reason that one should refrain from eating: in order to be hungry to eat *matzah*—the unleavened bread that is a central food on Passover (see *m. Pesahim* 10:5; Marks 2010, 393–97).

Rava cites a portion of *m. Pesahim* 10:7 stipulating that one is allowed to drink wine "between these cups"—meaning between either the first and second, or second and third of the four cups of wine at the *Seder.* The first cup of wine is consumed at the very beginning and the second cup in the course of the meal. Both cups are consumed before or during the actual *Seder* meal. In fact, *matzah* makes its appearance in the *Seder* in between these two cups (*m. Pesahim* 10:3). The third cup, however, is consumed as part of the Grace after Meals, which means that the eating portion of the evening has concluded. Wine is not needed to whet the appetite anymore, which—Rava argues—is why wine can be consumed between either the first and second or second and third cup, but not thereafter. After that, it would just be extra drinking and might muddle the ritual role played by those two final cups of wine.

This point is accented in the Jerusalem Talmud's commentary on *m. Pesahim* 10:7:

> Why [is it prohibited to drink between the third and fourth cups?]
>   So that one does not become intoxicated.
>   [But] is not one already intoxicated?!
>   What is the difference between wine [drunk] during the meal and wine [drunk] after the meal? Wine [drunk] after the meal causes intoxication, [whereas wine drunk] during the meal does not cause intoxication. (*y. Pesahim* 10:8, 37d)

Drinking wine with food tempers its intoxicating effects. Hence, the first two cups of wine are balanced out by various ritual and festive foods. Once the meal ends, however, alcohol is the only item left on the menu. For this reason, one should only drink the required final two cups. Anything else would cause intoxication, and *y. Pesahim* 10:1, 37c (cf. *y. Shabbat* 8:1, 11a) describes some Rabbis' epic post-Passover drinking headaches.

Returning to *b. Pesahim* 107b–108a, the text then brings up a theoretical argument: "If you say that wine satiates," that is, if you believe that wine offers sustenance as food does, then how can you be allowed to drink additional wine? As is often the case in rabbinic literature, this is an instance of one text presupposing that you have read another text. On *b. Berakhot* 35b, Rava's pre-Passover drinking routine appears in the context of regulations governing food and wine blessings. In that text, the issue revolves around whether wine is sustenance enough to be counted as food for the purposes of making certain blessings. Therefore, if one believes that wine satiates like food does, then drinking extra wine would fill you up, since you would be gorging yourself on both *matzah* and wine. This view is rejected. Wine does not satiate like food; rather it whets the appetite. So drink four cups of wine on Passover. And several cups prior to Passover. And maybe even a few extra during the *Seder*—that is, at least until the third cup is poured. After that, you can only have two more cups.

While there are many more rules associated with Passover, regulations concerning the four cups of wine give us insight into important elements of the rabbinic celebration of this Festival Day. And while Passover is the Festival Day most associated with alcohol, it is not the Jewish holiday most associated with drinking. For that, we need to turn to Purim, which is a day for ritual celebration, but also, as a non-Festival holiday, is a day on which normal business and activities are allowed.

MANSLAUGHTER, MIRACLES, AND THE MEGILLAH: INTOXICATION AND THE LIMITS OF CELEBRATION

The Jewish holiday of Purim commemorates the events described in the biblical book of Esther, which recounts a supposed incident in which the wicked Haman hatches an evil plot to have all of the Jews of Susa, Persia, murdered. His plot is discovered and eventually foiled. As a result, Haman and his co-conspirators experience the violent fate that they had planned for all Persian Jews.

People today usually think of Purim more as some combination of a Jewish Halloween and a Jewish Mardi Gras. These associations spring from the way that Purim is commonly celebrated. First, marking this celebration as different from all other Jewish holidays, many Jews arrive at synagogue in outfits that range from those of characters in the biblical story (often Esther or Mordecai, her uncle) to the kinds of costumes common at any modern Halloween party (though, for adults, perhaps a little less risqué), imparting a sense of joviality and levity to the event. Second, the central liturgical practice of Purim is the recitation of the book of Esther, known as the *Megillah* (meaning "scroll"). The importance of this particular *megillah* can be found as early as the Mishnah: while there are five biblical books referred to as "scrolls" (Hebrew plural *megillot*), all of which are read as part of the liturgy of different Jewish holidays, the mishnaic tractate *Megillah* focuses almost entirely on rules associated with the *megillah* of Esther. Over time, the custom developed of a raucous reading of the *Megillah* that resembles a sporting event in which the opposing team (or, in this case, the wicked Haman) is booed every time he is mentioned, and the home team (Esther and friends) is cheered. Third, drinking to excess is common. Rabbinic literature usually mandates moderation in alcohol consumption, but Purim is the exception. On this day, intoxication—usually frowned upon—is seen as positive and even, according to some sources, obligatory!

The combination of apparel, amusement, and alcohol make Purim a popular holiday for children, for undergraduates on college campuses, and yes, even for adults. And while the central role that alcohol and intoxication plays in Purim was recognized even in antiquity, so too was the dangerous potential of this loss of control. Go to a synagogue in March (when the holiday usually falls on the modern Jewish calendar) and ask anyone celebrating the holiday about drinking on Purim and they will probably say something about the Talmudic obligation to drink until one does not know the difference between Haman and Mordecai. But ask them about the potential dangers of said drinking also detailed in the Talmud and most will stare at you blankly. Yet both the injunction to become intoxicated and the warning of potential dangers are on the same page of the Babylonian Talmud, the one immediately following the other:

> Rava said: A person is obligated to become intoxicated on Purim until he cannot distinguish between "Cursed is Haman" and "Blessed is Mordecai."
> Rabbah and Rabbi Zeira prepared a Purim meal together. They became intoxicated. Rabbah slit the throat of Rabbi Zeira. The next day, [Rabbah] prayed and revived him. The following year, [Rabbah] said to [Rabbi Zeira]: Shall Master come and we will prepare a Purim meal together? [Rabbi Zeira] said to [Rabbah]: Not every time does a miracle occur! (*b. Megillah* 7b)

Rava insists that becoming intoxicated is a Purim obligation, but this injunction does not exist in isolation. While it has been taken out of context and recited amid Purim revelry, in the Talmud it is very much in context (see Wimpfheimer 2011, 24–30). It has been placed immediately preceding an anecdote that suggests a tempering (if not a Temperance) of Rava's words. After we read Rava's view on obligatory Purim drinking, we learn of Rabbah (or, in some manuscripts, Rava) and Rabbi Zeira sharing a drunken Purim meal. In the midst of their celebration, Rabbah gets carried away and slits the throat of his friend, Rabbi Zeira. The verb for slitting the throat is that used of standard ritual animal slaughter. Therefore, he is described as slitting Rabbi Zeira's throat like an animal. However, Rabbah seems to have no knowledge of what he has done, and he passes out in a drunken stupor. When he awakes in the morning, he realizes what he has done and prays to God to revive his dead friend. Thankfully, his prayers are answered, and Rabbi Zeira returns to life. A year passes, and Rabbah once again invites his friend to party together on Purim. Though we have no sense of how their relationship has evolved since the bloody Purim incident, there might be a hint of sheepish acknowledgement of his previous act in the fact that, in his invitation this year, Rabbah addresses Rabbi Zeira with deferential respect—as "Master." Sensibly, however, Rabbi Zeira declines.

Rabbi Zeira's response suggests that we should read this entire anecdote as placed in this order by the editors of this tractate in order to serve as a caution and tempering of Rava's earlier assertion. Even at times of celebration—indeed, even at this moment when intoxication might be deemed obligatory—self-restraint should not completely go out the window. Read together, the Rabbah and Rabbi Zeira narrative serves to moderate Rava's assertion. (While Rabbah was Rava's teacher, we should not expect that he shared with his students a personal story in which he drunkenly kills his friend!) Moderation in alcohol consumption remains a rabbinic ideal. Even at this moment, when the rules are relaxed, one should not go too far. There is a fine line between drinking until you forget, and drinking until you do something you regret.

CONCLUSION

Texts concerning the consumption of beverages on Sabbath, Festivals, and holidays have taught us much about rabbinic conceptions of these sacred times. Debates about the use of beer in ritual introduced us to Sabbath liturgy and practice, and exploration of breastfeeding and liquid remedies for leech-swallowing instructed us about Sabbath work restrictions. We then learned how ancient methods of heating water and straining beer and wine explicate the complex *halakhah* of Festival Days. Finally, two case studies of excessive drinking taught us about the important Festival of Passover and the holiday of Purim.

SUGGESTED READINGS

Baumgarten, Elisheva. 2004. *Mothers and Children: Jewish Family Life in Medieval Europe*. Princeton, NJ: Princeton University Press.

Bokser, Baruch M. 2002 [1984]. *The Origins of The Seder: The Passover Rite and Early Rabbinic Judaism*. Reprint. New York: Jewish Theological Seminary.

Chabon, Michael. 2007. *The Yiddish Policemen's Union*. New York: Harper Collins.

Cohen, Shaye J. D. 2007. "The Judean Legal Tradition and the *Halakhah* of the Mishnah." In *The Cambridge Companion to the Talmud and Rabbinic Literature*, ed. Charlotte Elisheva Fonrobert and Martin S. Jaffee, 121–43. New York: Cambridge University Press.

Daily Show, The. 2011. "The Thin Jew Line." Aired March 23. www.cc.com/video-clips/1jsrl7/the-daily-show-with-jon-stewart-the-thin-jew-line (accessed June 14, 2019).

Gardner, Gregg E. 2015. *The Origins of Organized Charity in Rabbinic Judaism*. New York: Cambridge University Press.

Hauptman, Judith. 2014. "Thinking about the Ten Theses in Relation to the Passover Seder and Women's Participation." In *Meals in Early Judaism: Social Formation at the Table*, ed. Susan Marks and Hal Taussig, 43–57. New York: Palgrave Macmillan.

Hayes, Christine E. 2002. *Gentile Impurities and Jewish Identities: Intermarriage and Conversion from the Bible to the Talmud*. New York: Oxford University Press.

Heschel, Abraham Joshua. 1997 [1951]. *The Sabbath: Its Meaning for Modern Man*. New York: Noonday Press.

Horowitz, Elliott. 2006. *Reckless Rites: Purim and the Legacy of Jewish Violence.* Princeton, NJ: Princeton University Press.
Jaffee, Martin S. 2006 [1997]. *Early Judaism: Religious Worlds of the First Judaic Millennium.* 2nd ed. Bethesda: University Press of Maryland.
Kulp, Joshua. 2005. "The Origins of the Seder and Haggadah." *Currents in Biblical Research* 4: 109–34.
Lieberman, Saul, ed. 2002 [1962]. *The Order of Mo'ed.* In *The Tosefta: According to Codex Vienna, with Variants from Codex Erfurt, Genizah Mss. and Editio Princeps (Venice 1521), together with References to Parallel Passages in Talmudic Literature and a Brief Commentary.* 5 vols. New York: Jewish Theological Seminary.
Marks, Gil. 2010. *Encyclopedia of Jewish Food.* Hoboken, NJ: John Wiley & Sons.
Roller, Matthew B. 2006. *Dining Posture in Ancient Rome: Bodies, Values, and Status.* Princeton, NJ: Princeton University Press.
Rosenblum, Jordan D. 2010. *Food and Identity in Early Rabbinic Judaism.* New York: Cambridge University Press.
———. 2012. "Inclined to Decline Reclining? Women, Corporeality, and Dining Posture in Early Rabbinic Literature." In *Meals in the Early Christian World: Social Formation, Experimentation, and Conflict at the Table,* ed. Dennis E. Smith and Hal Taussig, 261–74. New York: Palgrave Macmillan.
———. 2016. "'Blessings of the Breasts': Breastfeeding in Rabbinic Literature." *Hebrew Union College Annual* 87: 147–79.
Rubenstein, Jeffrey L. 1995. *The History of Sukkot in the Second Temple and Rabbinic Periods.* Atlanta, GA: Scholars Press.
Satlow, Michael L. 2006. *Creating Judaism: History, Tradition, Practice.* New York: Columbia University Press.
Schäfer, Peter. 2007. *Jesus in the Talmud.* Princeton, NJ: Princeton University Press.
Simon-Shoshan, Moshe. 2012. *Stories of the Law: Narrative Discourse and the Construction of Authority in the Mishnah.* New York: Oxford University Press.
Sokoloff, Michael. 2002. *A Dictionary of Jewish Babylonian Aramaic.* Baltimore: Johns Hopkins University Press.
Wasserman, Mira Beth. 2017. *Jews, Gentiles, and Other Animals: The Talmud after the Humanities.* Philadelphia: University of Pennsylvania Press.
Wimpfheimer, Barry Scott. 2011. *Narrating the Law: A Poetics of Talmudic Legal Stories.* Philadelphia: University of Pennsylvania Press.

SEVEN

Prayer and Ritual

In the previous chapter, we discussed various regulations concerning holidays. But even your average ordinary day is governed by myriad rabbinic rules. To offer two examples: (a) while there is rabbinic debate about whether to put your right shoe on first and then the left one, or vice versa, no one questions that normative rabbinic law (Hebrew *halakhah*) should encompass these mundane details (*b. Shabbat* 61a); and (b) two different Rabbis explain their sneaking into the privy to observe their mentors defecate by saying: "It is Torah and I must learn it!" (*b. Berakhot* 62a; see Schofer 2010, 64–67).

In this chapter, we turn our attention to rabbinic conversation about prayer and ritual on non-holidays. From blessing drinks to praying after drinking, and from asking for someone's hand in marriage in exchange for a glass of wine to drinking at funerals, once again beverages have much to teach us about rabbinic literature.

"CREATOR OF THE FRUIT OF THE VINE": WINE AND BLESSINGS

Punctuating the day, alongside these rules for mundane practices, is a series of blessings. In fact, the very first tractate of both the Mishnah and the Talmud is named "Blessings" (Hebrew *Berakhot*). According to one tradition, these blessings throughout the day add up:

> Rabbi Meir used to say: A person is obligated to recite one hundred blessings every day. (*b. Menahot* 43b)

One particular daily domain in which blessings appear is the dining room. The act of raising a glass, and the words spoken while doing so, serve as powerful external and internal indicators that the drinker is participating in, or rejecting, a particular theology. Therefore, by examining rabbinic conversation about these blessings, especially in regard to wine, we learn how the simple act of drinking reinforces a larger system of rabbinic belief (see Kraemer 2009, 73–86).

Our exploration of rabbinic blessings begins with a summary of blessings recited over various foods:

> How does one recite a blessing over fruit?
>   For fruit of the tree, one says: "... Creator of the fruit of the tree"; except for wine, for upon wine, one says: "... Creator of the fruit of the vine."
>   And for fruit of the earth, one says: "... Creator of fruit of the earth"; except for bread, for upon bread, one says: "... Who brings forth bread from the earth."
>   And for vegetables, one says: "... Creator of fruit of the earth." (*m. Berakhot* 6:1)

While the rest of *m. Berakhot* 6 clarifies and expands these blessings, there is plenty here to digest. First, this mishnah presumes basic knowledge of rabbinic liturgy and hence only quotes the second part of each blessing. Readers are expected to know the standard introductory formula to each of these blessings: "Blessed are You, Lord, our God, King of the universe ...." As we have seen throughout this book, readers often enter a rabbinic conversation at the midway point and not at the beginning. Second, we learn that different foods have different blessings. Though the general blessing "... by Whose word everything came into being" (*m. Berakhot* 6:2) can cover all generic food, different foods merit different blessings. Third, certain foods are singled out as special within their category. For example, a grape receives one blessing ("... Creator of the fruit of the tree") while wine—a fermented grape—receives another ("... Creator of the fruit of the vine").

Why does all of this matter? Because:

> A person should not taste anything until reciting a blessing, as it is said: "The earth is the Lord's and the fullness thereof" [Psalm 24:1].
> One who derives benefit from this world without [first reciting] a blessing has stolen sacred property, until all of the commandments [relevant to blessings have been performed, which then] permit it to him. (*t. Berakhot* 4:1)

The earth and all of its contents belong to God. Taking anything from it—such as a grape—is stealing. However, the act of reciting a blessing desacralizes the food; in essence, it transfers ownership, allowing humans to partake thereof (see Kraemer 2009, 75–77). Therefore, if one does not recite a blessing, then one has stolen from God. Bad idea. But also, if one recites the wrong blessing, then the food has not transferred ownership, so this too is theft of divine property. In order to fulfill one's ritual obligation—and not steal from God—one must not only recite *a* blessing, but must recite *the correct* blessing.

Every act of eating or drinking thus requires rabbinic Jews to pause and consider how that food fits into their larger concepts and categories. First, as food, it belongs to God until a blessing is recited. Second, the item must be sorted according to its rabbinic classification in order to determine what blessing is the correct blessing. Third, in the process of this sorting, hierarchies emerge. For example, as noted above, a grape requires a generic fruit-tree blessing, but grape wine necessitates the more specific wine blessing. When consuming all "fruit of the tree," the whole product and the pressed juice or liquid receive the exact same blessing (e.g., apple/apple juice, olive/olive oil); that is, unless the pressed juice is wine, which requires a special blessing (an observation noted in *y. Berakhot* 6:1, 10a).

The fact that wine and bread, in particular, merit their own blessings points to the importance of bread and wine in the ancient diet. Note that even though meat is highly prized, it does not earn its own blessing. (Over meat, one recites the generic blessing: "... by Whose word everything came into being.") The so-called Mediterranean Triad of wine, bread, and olive oil—regarded as an accessory to bread, much like ketchup on the modern french fry—were dietary staples for Jew and non-Jew alike in the ancient Mediterranean (see Kraemer 2009, 78–79; Rosenblum 2010, 24–30). Given the prominence of these foods in their diet, the fact that they each receive their own blessing is not surprising.

The special status of wine that this indicates also leads to conversations about blessing wine being used as a vehicle to discuss other rabbinic concerns. For example, in an exposition of *m. Berakhot* 6:1, a tradition similar to the one from *t. Berakhot* 4:1 that we just learned above appears, with an interesting twist:

> Our Rabbis taught in a *baraita'*: It is forbidden for a person to derive benefit from this world without [first reciting] a blessing, and anyone who derives benefit from this world without [first reciting] a blessing has stolen sacred property. What is his remedy? He should go to a sage.
>
> He should go to a sage?! What can [a sage] do for him? Heck, he has [already] committed the forbidden action!
>
> Rather, Rava said: He should go to a sage beforehand, and [the sage] will teach him [the *halakhah*] of blessings, in order that he should not come to commit theft of sacred property. (*b. Berakhot* 35a)

This passage begins by citing a *baraita'* (Aramaic plural *baraitot*), a rabbinic tradition reputed to be of tannaitic origin that is cited in an amoraic text. In some instances, *baraitot* seem to be invented in order to backdate a later tradition, akin to how a student could invent a fact, edit a Wikipedia entry to include that invented fact, and then cite Wikipedia as a source for said invented fact. However, in this case, we have evidence from a tannaitic source, quoted above, that contains a very similar tradition. The only element missing—the quotation from Psalm 24:1—appears immediately after this passage, where it is cited in two different traditions (see *b. Berakhot* 35a–b).

At first, the substance of this tradition is familiar to us. Before tasting anything, a person must make a blessing. Otherwise, they commit theft of sacred property (Hebrew *me'ilah*), since only a priest (or God) may make use of consecrated stuff (in general, see Leviticus 5:15–26; and the tractate *Me'ilah*). But then, the passage (Aramaic *sugya'*) takes an unexpected twist. If a person eats food without blessing and then realizes their mistake, how do they remedy the situation? Unsurprisingly, the rabbinic answer is: consult a Rabbi.

After citing this tradition, the anonymous voice of the Talmud repeats the final line of the *baraita'* for emphasis: "He should go to a sage?!" Although there is no punctuation in the standard text of the Talmud, the ?! marks best reflect how this line should be read: that is, with a mixture of shock, curiosity, and incredulity. This is followed by an editorial remark: "What can [a sage] do for him? Heck, he has [already] committed the forbidden action!" Obviously, I have taken some liberties with my translation. The exclamation that I translate as "Heck" (Aramaic *ha'*) is often rendered as something more innocuous, such as "Behold!"; "Lo!"; "Why!"; or "Indeed!" (for example, see the next text below, in which I note where *ha'* appears). I chose "Heck" because I wished to idiomatically convey the shock. After all, the question being asked is an incredulous one: what can a sage do, since the horse has left the barn?! A Rabbi cannot go back in time and undo the theft that has already occurred.

Rather than view this remark as referring to an ex post facto undoing, Rava offers a new interpretation. It is not a retroactive remedy; instead, it is a preventive measure. If students attend their rabbinics classes, then they will learn proper practice, including the *halakhah* of blessings. Therefore, they will know that eating without blessing is tantamount to stealing sacred property. Notice that this elevates the role of the sage: without regular consultation of a Rabbi, one is liable to violate any number of prohibitions. Rabbinic knowledge functions as "transformative knowledge" (Jaffee 2006, 230–40). It changes the way one thinks, acts, and speaks. Remember from above that there are rabbinic ways to put on one's shoes and to relieve oneself in the privy, among many other mundane practices. *Halakhah* regulates every action and interaction, resulting in embodied changes in those who follow this path.

In addition to the ontological, psychological, and theological transformations of rabbinic knowledge, the role of proper blessings now serves to highlight—and indeed, to further authorize—the authority of the rabbinic sage. As a good friend of Rava's states in another text: "Abaye said: It is a commandment (Hebrew *mitzvah*) to heed the words of the sages" (*b. Hullin* 106a; see Rosenblum 2018, 86–87). (Fun fact: Rava and Abaye so loved to argue with one another that *b. Sukkah* 28a refers to one sage studying "the argumentative discussions of Abaye and Rava.") Sages save you from mistakes big and small. Thus, a tradition that was initially about the importance of blessing morphs into a tradition about the importance of learning—and heeding—the words of a sage about the importance of blessing.

The authority of the sages continues to be relevant to conversation about wine blessings when, on the other side of this same Talmud page, our friend Rava makes another appearance:

> But does wine satiate? Indeed (Aramaic *ha'*), Rava would drink wine all [throughout the day] on the eve of Passover, so that he would whet his appetite in order to eat more *matzah* [in the evening].
>
> A large amount [of wine] whets the appetite, a small amount satiates.
>
> But does [wine] satiate at all? Is it not written: "and wine gladdens the heart of man ... and bread satiates the heart of man, etc." [Psalm 104:15]—[thus implying that] it is bread that satiates, [whereas] wine does not satiate? [No, this is not what the verse implies.] Rather, [this verse teaches that] wine does both: it satiates and gladdens; bread, [on the other hand,] certainly satiates, but it does not actually gladden.
>
> If so, we should recite three blessings over [wine, as is required for bread]?!
>
> People do not make [wine] the basis of their meal.
>
> Rav Nahman bar Yitzhak said to Rava: What if one did make [wine] the basis of his meal?

[Rava] said to him: When Elijah comes, he will tell us whether [wine] can serve as the basis [of a meal]. Currently, at any rate, this opinion is universally rejected. (*b. Berakhot* 35b)

We enter this text in the middle of a discussion (which is why it begins "But ..."). The conversation revolves around why wine merits its own blessing in *m. Berakhot* 6:1, but olive oil does not. We have just learned that this is because "wine satiates, but olive oil does not satiate" (*b. Berakhot* 35b), which prompts the inquiry into whether wine does, indeed, satiate. To answer this question, a tradition about Rava is cited: throughout the day leading up to Passover, Rava would drink wine in order to whet his appetite for *matzah* (cf. *b. Pesahim* 107b–108a, discussed in chapter 6, which includes this same tradition attributed to Rava). Rava's penchant for pre-Passover wine-drinking indicates that drinking wine whets one's appetite. But it does not prove that wine "satiates." Thus, the anonymous voice of the Talmud asserts that drinking a lot of wine, as Rava does every year, whets the appetite; whereas drinking a small amount of wine, satiates.

But the question remains: does wine *really* satiate? After all, Rava's tradition of "pre-gaming" (to use a contemporary undergraduate parlance) before Passover is only proof that drinking wine makes you really hungry. It does not prove that wine satiates. To get to the bottom of this, the Rabbis turn to a biblical verse that we have encountered before, Psalm 104:15, the first half of which ("and wine gladdens the heart of man ...") was discussed in chapter 6. This *sugya'* investigates whether the latter part of this verse ("... and bread satiates the heart of man") provides new and relevant information. Does the fact that only bread is mentioned as satiating in Psalm 104:15 mean that wine gladdens, but is excluded from satiating?

This assertion is implicitly rejected. To make this rejection more explicit and to clarify the transition here, I have added to my translation: "[No, this is not what the verse implies.]" Instead, what does this *sugya'* argue that Psalm 104:15 teaches? Wine is versatile—it both gladdens and satiates. Bread, on the other hand, is a one-trick pony—it only satiates. How precisely this is to be inferred from the verse, and why this is the preferred interpretation of Psalm 104:15, is left tacit.

Having argued that Psalm 104:15 "proves" that wine satiates, the text raises a related issue. The terse wording "If so" is used to inquire that, if it is indeed the case that wine satiates, then why does wine not require the longer version of Grace after Meals after its consumption? I leave aside the various differences between postconsumption blessings, since the reader simply needs to know that wine requires a shorter version of Grace after Meals, and not the longer version that bread necessitates. Yet again, the text presumes detailed knowledge that it does not provide. However, so long as we understand that bread requires a longer version of Grace after Meals than wine, we can follow the argument: if wine really satiated, why then does it not require the longer version of Grace after Meals mandated for bread—the gold standard of satiation? In short, it is because people establish a meal on the basis of bread, but "People do not make [wine] the basis of their meal."

As the centerpiece of the meal, bread not only satiates, but also deserves a special, extended postconsumption liturgy. Wine gladdens and likely even satiates, but wine does not make a meal. Of course, there is always the "what if" question, so loved by the Rabbis: but "What if one did make [wine] the basis of his meal?" Having been asked this very question, Rava replies: "When Elijah comes, he will tell us whether [wine] can serve as the basis [of a meal]. Currently, at any rate, this opinion is universally rejected." Elijah is a biblical prophet who, according to the Rabbis, will be a harbinger of the coming of the Messiah. Therefore, certain unresolved earthly problems must await Elijah's arrival to be sorted out (for other examples, see *m. Bava Metzi'a* 1:8; *b. Menahot* 45a). But until then, popular rabbinic opinion is determinative: everyone agrees that wine does not make a meal. Hence, wine may satiate, but it requires only the shorter version of Grace after Meals postconsumption.

BLESSING WITH YOUR MOUTH FULL

We continue exploring rabbinic blessings by turning to a text in which two themes prominent throughout this chapter appear: first, the human tendency to forget; and second, how to resolve such unintended ritual errors. Thus, we learn:

> Rav Huna said: Consider the case of one who put [food] in his mouth, and forgot and did not bless: if it was liquid, he spits it out; if it was solid food, he tucks it in to the sides [of his mouth].
> Rabbi Yitzhaq bar Mari, in the presence of Rabbi Yosi the son of Rabbi Abun, [said] in the name of Rabbi Yohanan: Even [in regard to] solid food, he spits it out; for it is written: "My mouth shall be filled with Your praise, [and with] Your glory, all the day" [Psalm 71:8]. (*y. Berakhot* 6:1, 10b)

According to Rav Huna, liquids should be spat out, but solid food can be pushed to the side of the mouth so that the appropriate blessing can be recited. In an alternate rabbinic tradition both liquids and solid food must be spat out, for how can I praise God with food in my mouth if it "shall be filled with Your praise" (Psalm 71:8)? Modern parental advice not to talk with one's mouth full is also ancient liturgical advice: do not bless with your mouth full.

In many ways, this advice is in line with that offered in the previous section: to avoid blessing mistakes, consult a sage, who will teach you both how to avoid and how to correct a ritual error. A further example of this is encountered in the Babylonian Talmud's parallel version of this tradition (see *b. Berakhot* 50b–51a). After citing a variant text (with different Rabbis cited and different wording), another relevant tradition appears:

> They inquired of Rav Hisda: One who ate and drank, and did not recite a blessing, should he return and recite a blessing?
> He said to them: Should one who ate garlic and his breath smells, return and eat garlic again, so that his breath should continue smelling?! (*b. Berakhot* 51a)

Again, a ritual error has occurred: one has eaten and forgotten to recite the appropriate blessing but realized the mistake. Should one go back and recite the blessing retroactively? How long one has to remedy this situation is discussed in *m. Berakhot* 8:7 and *y. Berakhot* 8:8, 12c. Rav Hisda's reply about garlic eating is a rabbinic twist on the cliché that "two wrongs do not make a right."

BLESSING THE WRONG BEVERAGE

Taking a drink without first offering a blessing is—as we have learned above—considered theft of sacred property, but offering a blessing transfers ownership of it from God to the consumer. As noted above, one must not only recite *a* blessing, but *the correct* blessing.

The Rabbis take this issue seriously and ask an interesting question: what if I start to bless one drink, and, midway through my recitation, I realize that the liquid in my cup is actually another beverage, so I switch and complete the blessing for the actual drink in my hand—have I completed my obligation and transferred ownership of said beverage from God to myself?

> "Where they said: to lengthen [(the blessing), one is not permitted to shorten (it); to shorten, one is not permitted to lengthen (it); to seal (the blessing with a concluding formula), one must seal (it); to not seal it, one is not permitted to seal (it)" (*m. Berakhot* 1:4)].
>
> It is obvious [that in a case] where one is holding a cup of wine in his hand and he thinks that it is beer, and he begins reciting a blessing with the intention of [reciting the blessing over] beer, but [then, realizing that he is holding wine,] he concludes with [the blessing over] wine, he has fulfilled his obligation. Even if he had said "... by Whose word everything came into being," [which, as the blessing over beer, was his original intention] he would have fulfilled his obligation, for it is taught [in *m. Berakhot* 6:2]: "For all [foods], if one says '... by Whose word everything came into being,' he fulfills his obligation."
>
> But [in a case] where one is holding a cup of beer in his hand and he thinks that it is wine, and he begins reciting a blessing with the intention of [reciting the blessing over] wine, but [then, realizing that he is holding beer,] he concludes with [the blessing over] beer, what [is the *halakhah*]? Do we follow the main part of the blessing or do we follow the seal? ...
>
> The general rule of the matter: Everything follows the seal. (*b. Berakhot* 12a)

So what if one begins reciting the blessing for one beverage and then realizes that the cup contains a different one and switches in mid-recitation? In this mishnah, we learn that one must recite a blessing the way that the Rabbis ordained; one cannot deviate and lengthen or shorten it. As is often the case, the text omits an important part of the mishnah, it being presumed that readers will remember it and connect the dots. I supply the relevant information: namely, that one must include or omit the seal of the blessing—that is, the concluding formula—as directed by the sages (e.g., the seal of the blessing over wine is "... Creator of the fruit of the vine").

Rabbinic literature often asks such curious questions. For example, elsewhere there is an investigation into what happens if a Jew starts to slaughter an animal and then allows a non-Jew to finish the act of slaughter, or vice versa (see *t. Hullin* 1:2; Freidenreich 2011, 50–51; Rosenblum 2010, 80–81). Such questions raise more complex variables. They usually require complex "it depends" kinds of answers, rather than simple, binary "yes/no" solutions.

In the first scenario here, the text claims that "It is obvious" (Aramaic *peshita'*) that switching mid-blessing would not be a problem. Why? Because, despite at first intending to bless wine, one would have concluded with the seal of a wine blessing ("... Creator of the fruit of the vine"). And, even if one had used the blessing over beer and blessed wine, this would not be a problem. Why? Because the seal of the blessing over beer is the general blessing ("... by Whose word everything came into being") and *m. Berakhot* 6:2, quoted in our text, declares: "For all [foods], if one says '... by Whose word everything came into being,' he fulfills his obligation." Further, since the opening formula is the same for all foodstuffs, and the seal works for both beverages, the person would have actually recited a correct blessing from start to finish! Therefore, this one-size-fits-all blessing would have fulfilled any obligation to bless, even wine.

But does the incorrect intentionality of the first half of a blessing invalidate the correct recitation of the second half of a blessing? This is what the second scenario asks. If I begin to bless what I believe to be a cup of wine and then realize it is beer and switch to the beer blessing, which matters more: (1) that I incorrectly intended to bless wine in "the main part of the blessing" (i.e., in the "Blessed are You, Lord, our Lord, King of the universe ...." formula); or (2) that I concluded the blessing with the proper seal for blessing beer? If the former matters more, then I have not fulfilled my obligation to bless the beverage; but if the latter matters more, then I have fulfilled my obligation. So which is it?

The answer turns out to be rather straightforward. After offering a similar scenario in regard to confusing blessings in another liturgical context (of which I omit discussion for the sake of brevity and because it does not add anything new), a general rule is supplied. In sum: "Everything follows the seal." Therefore, so long as you catch your error in time to recite the proper seal, then you have fulfilled your obligation. If not, then you need to redo the blessing. This is why the reference to the seal in *m. Berakhot* 1:4, which began this entire passage, was so important to include: in the end, it is all about the end—that is, the seal of the blessing.

Left unanswered is why the person confused the beverages in the first place. Was it an honest error? Or, given the fact that the cup contained either beer or wine, was the drinker perhaps intoxicated? This raises an issue that we explore in the next three sections of this chapter: the *halakhah* of praying under the influence.

PUI: PRAYING UNDER THE INFLUENCE

As we have seen in several other chapters, intention is important to the Rabbis. For example, did I intend to swim or did my drunk friend accidentally push me in the water? (See *m. Makhshirin* 5:1; discussed in chapter 8.) And we have also seen that the Rabbis prefer one to be self-controlled and sober. So we should not be surprised that they question the status of a prayer offered by a drunk person.

> Rabbah bar Rav Huna said: One who drank [alcohol] should not pray; but if he did pray, his prayer is [valid] prayer. One who is drunk should not pray; and if he did pray, his prayer is an abomination. (*b. Eruvin* 64a)

Whether a person has had one glass of wine or the whole bottle, Rabbah bar Rav Huna claims that they should not drink and pray. However, the prayer of the former is still a valid prayer, while that of the latter is an abomination. To pun on a common adage about the proper sequencing of alcohol consumption: prayer before beer, you're in the clear; beer before prayer, and God will glare.

It would seem that any alcohol affects intentionality, so it should be avoided prior to prayer. (Elsewhere, there is a report that one Rabbi would not even pray in a house where beer was present; see *b. Eruvin* 65a.) But if one is still relatively sober, their prayer is valid prayer. In contrast, drunk people are not in control, and hence their prayer is an abominable act. (On various other legal ramifications of, and culpabilities for, actions committed by a drunk person, see *b. Eruvin* 65a.) Yet, as in any legal system, definitions are important. So what is the level of alcohol consumption that renders one guilty of PUI—of Praying under the Influence?

> What is the definition of "one who drank [alcohol]" and what is the definition of "one who is drunk"?
> "One who drank [alcohol]" is anyone who is able to speak before the king.
> "One who is drunk" is anyone who is not able to speak before the king. (*b. Eruvin* 64a)

I have omitted several interesting, but irrelevant, sections of this *sugya'*, since the definition of PUI is contained in a tradition that cites extraneous information. I note this fact, however, because it informs us about another feature of rabbinic literature: earlier sources are often cited for one piece of information, but the entire source material is included, even if it is irrelevant to the topic at hand. Rabbinic traditions were often memorized together for various reasons (e.g., to aid in memorization; due to historical associations; because they are attributed to the same authority), and so they are often quoted in full, even when only part is necessary for the matter at hand.

What this tradition teaches us is that there is a practical test to see whether one performs valid prayer: if they are too drunk to speak to the king (a reference to God), then their prayer is abominable; but if they could manage to carry on an appropriate conversation with the king, then they are sober enough to offer a valid prayer. "The king" here likely stands for any important person, so this same litmus test could be applied to others, such as a professor or a boss. Note that neither a drinker nor a drunk *should* pray (or attend class!) in such a state. But if they do, this test establishes the result.

There is much more to this *sugya'*, to which we shall return in chapter 9. But now we turn to a related question: what about praying in a mental state akin to that achieved through drinking?

"DRUNK, BUT NOT FROM WINE": PUNCH-DRUNK PRAYER

We have established that "a drunk person is forbidden to pray" (*y. Berakhot* 4:1, 7a; *b. Berakhot* 31a), as doing so renders the prayer "an abomination" (*b. Eruvin* 64a). According to another tradition, "a drunk person who prays is like one who worships idols" (*b. Berakhot* 31b). So, clearly, praying under the influence is prohibited. But what about praying while punch-drunk?

This questions serves as an excellent example of the rabbinic enterprise. We know that x is forbidden, but is y—which is very similar to x, but not exactly x—also forbidden? To wit: We know that praying while drunk is forbidden, but what about praying while punch-drunk? Punch-drunk is a term that refers to the disorientation that comes from either a physical punch (like that experienced by a boxer, hence the name) or an emotional punch (like that experienced by a teenager rejected by the person with whom they wanted to go to the prom). Both result in a state of being dazed and confused with a literal and/or metaphorical concussion. This experience is equated with being drunk, though no alcohol is involved.

So are drunk and punch-drunk equivalent? As it turns out, indeed they are:

> "One should only stand to pray [in a serious state of mind" (*m. Berakhot* 5:1)].
> Rabbi Yirmiyah [said] in the name of Rabbi Abba: One who returns from a journey is forbidden to pray. And what is the reason [for this ruling]? "Therefore, listen to this, afflicted one, and drunk, but not from wine" [Isaiah 51:21].
> Rabbi Zeriqan [said that] Rabbi Yohanan [said] in the name of Rabbi Elazar the son of Rabbi Yosi the Galilean: One who is distressed is forbidden to pray. It is only reasonable [to derive this ruling] from exegetical interpretation of this verse: "Therefore, listen to this, afflicted one, and drunk, but not from wine" [Isaiah 51:21]. (*y. Berakhot* 5:1, 8d)

This *sugya'* begins by citing *m. Berakhot* 5:1, the mishnah upon which it comments, which examines issues related to concentration during prayer. For example, what if a king greets you while you are praying? Or a snake winds around your heel? Should you interrupt your prayer? (The answer, by the way, is no.) The mishnah has in mind one prayer in particular: the *'Amidah*, a central component of the daily rabbinic prayer service, which the Rabbis refer to as "The Prayer" (in general, see Hoffman 1998). This important prayer (and others as well) should only be recited while "in a serious state of mind" (Hebrew *koved ro'sh*; literally, "heaviness of head").

This assertion leads to the ruling that "One who returns from a journey is forbidden to pray." Coming home from a long road trip, one is exhausted and in neither the physical nor mental condition to pray with complete concentration. They are not in the "serious state of mind" that rabbinic prayer demands. This ruling is said to be derived from a verse in Isaiah, in which an "afflicted one" (Hebrew *'aniyah*; which can also be translated as "weary/tired/weak one") is also described as punch-drunk: that is, "drunk, but not from wine." The rabbinic logic is clear: one who is drunk is forbidden to pray; one who returns from a journey is like one who is drunk; therefore, one who returns from a journey is forbidden to pray. As some commentators point out, this association might further reflect an interpretation of Psalm 102:24, which states: "He weakened my strength on the way." The Hebrew verb for "weakened" (*'inah*) shares the same root as "afflicted one" (*'aniyah*); and "on the way" (*ba-derekh*) is the same word that I render as "journey" (*ba-derekh*) above. If this suggestion is correct, then the connection between "weakened" and "on the way" helped link the initial ruling with the verse from Isaiah 51:21.

Continuing the association between punch-drunk and drunk via Isaiah 51:21, another ruling is stated: "One who is distressed is forbidden to pray." Anyone who has ever been distressed knows that, at that moment, they are not "in a serious state of mind." Rather, their thoughts are a million miles away, worrying about their problems. Here, it seems that the "afflicted one" is weary from stress. Therefore, it is reasonable to offer Isaiah 51:21 as scriptural support for this ruling. (Note that the word play present in the previous ruling allowed for a connection with Psalm 102:24, which is not the case here.)

Whether drunk from wine or drunk, but not from wine—that is, drunk or punch-drunk—prayer is forbidden. Having resolved those concerns, we turn to a somewhat related question: what do you do when you miss prayers due to drinking?

OOPS! WE FORGOT TO PRAY: PRAYERS MISSED DUE TO DRINKING

Missing prayers due to drinking might seem like a topic buried deep in rabbinic literature, if indeed it is treated at all. But, as we have seen so many times throughout this book, the Rabbis are interested in abnormal scenarios more than the average, everyday mundane experience. In fact, this very topic arises in the first thirty words of the first chapter of the first book in the first Order of the Mishnah:

> Once upon a time, [Rabban Gamaliel's] sons came [home late] from a drinking party. They said to him: We have not recited the evening *Shemaʻ*. He said to them: If the dawn has not yet come, you are [still] obligated to recite [the evening *Shemaʻ*]. (*m. Berakhot* 1:1)

This anecdote begins with a common Hebrew word used for introducing rabbinic stories: *maʻaseh*, referring to something in the past that has "halakhic implications" (Simon-Shoshan 2012, 45–49, at 49) and often translated as "It once happened..." or "It once occurred that..." or even simply "Once..." To highlight the blend of fact and fiction in these stories, I prefer "Once upon a time." The veracity of these events is less relevant than the legal lesson imparted, much as it does not matter whether there actually was a historical boy who cried "wolf." What matters is what that story teaches us.

The tale of Rabban Gamaliel's sons appears in the middle of a conversation about when one may recite the evening *Shemaʻ*. The text does not define this liturgy, presuming that everyone already knows that it is a central rabbinic prayer composed of three scriptural passages (Deuteronomy 6:4–9 and 11:13–21; Numbers 15:37–41). Based on the biblical phrase "When you lie down and rise up" (Deuteronomy 6:7; 11:19), the Rabbis hold that this prayer should be recited twice daily: once in the morning and once in the evening. But until what time is the evening *Shemaʻ* recited? That is the subject of a debate. And it is after Rabban Gamaliel offers his own opinion of until when the evening *Shemaʻ* may be recited (unsurprisingly, the text states: "Rabban Gamaliel says: Until the dawn comes") that this story appears.

As noted in other chapters, a common Hebrew phrase for a rabbinic wedding feast is *beyt ha-mishteh*, which literally means "the house of drinking" (elsewhere, they use the Hebrew term *mishteh*, which simply means "drinking [party]," which also appears in at least one ancient synagogue inscription; see Satlow 2001, 179). Rendering this simply as "wedding feast" misses the fact that weddings are understood to be times of celebration and, as the very words themselves attest, drinking. It would seem that weddings often featured an open bar in antiquity, as they do today. This is also important because it gives us some context for the scene that unfolds in Rabban Gamaliel's house when his sons return home late at night reeking of alcohol.

Though fictionalized, the summary of this text by Simon-Shoshan reveals how many read this text:

> I have loved this tale ever since I first read it as a child. I pictured R. Gamliel's sons stumbling through the backdoor of their house in the wee hours of the morning, hoping not to disturb their sleeping family. To their surprise, they find their father at the kitchen table in his dressing gown, deep in study. The sight of their father reminds them that the festivities have distracted them from their obligation to accept the yoke of heaven through the recitation of the Shema. Their father looks up from his book with a mixture of concern and rebuke. He informs them that it is still possible to rectify their lax behavior, provided the night has not yet ended. (Simon-Shoshan 2012, 1)

I must confess to a less pious reading of this passage. I always imagine the sons sneaking back into the house and being caught by their father. In order to avoid a lecture (and being grounded), they wisely ask their father a legal question: "Oops! We forgot to pray! Is it still permissible for us to recite the evening *Shemaʿ*?" Knowing that their father is a scholar who cannot resist the urge to expound on matters of *halakhah*, they ask him for a legal ruling, which he offers. In doing so, he forgets that his sons have arrived home after curfew and drunk. (He also does not alert them to the fact that, as we have just learned, they should not pray after drinking!)

But is this accent on alcohol a modern reading into the text? In addition to internal evidence in the text itself, there is evidence from the Babylonian Talmud that suggests that even ancient interpreters took the drinking context of this passage seriously. In its commentary in *m. Berakhot* 1:1, the following story appears:

> For there was a certain pair of Rabbis who got drunk at the wedding feast for the son of Rabbi Yehoshua ben Levi. They came before Rabbi Yehoshua ben Levi. He said [to them]: Rabbi Shimon is worthy enough to be relied upon in an emergency. (*b. Berakhot* 9a)

This section of the Talmud is discussing Rabban Gamaliel's opinion that the evening *Shema*ʿ can be recited "Until the dawn comes" (*m. Berakhot* 1:1). Earlier in this *sugya*ʾ, an opinion is offered by Rabbi Shimon ben Yohai that:

> sometimes a person may recite the *Shema*ʿ twice in the day: once before the dawn comes and once after the dawn comes, and fulfills through these his obligation both for day and for evening [recitations of the *Shema*ʿ]. (*b. Berakhot* 8b)

In examining this proposition, the story of two intoxicated Rabbis is told. In this case, the context is clear: while the event is referred to by a more neutral name ("wedding feast"; Aramaic *hilulaʾ*), the Rabbis are explicitly described as drunk. So drunk, in fact, that they either forgot or were unable to recite the evening *Shema*ʿ; or, in line with what we learned in the previous section, did not do so, since praying while drunk is an abomination. In the morning, they have both physical and spiritual hangovers, and so they inquire of Rabbi Yehoshua ben Levi, a respected authority and, as father of the groom, the host of the party at which they overindulged. In response, he says: Rabbi Shimon is worthy enough of an authority to follow his opinion here, so you can recite the *Shema*ʿ twice (once right before dawn and once after dawn) and fulfill your obligation.

In these instances, stories about drinking and missing prayers are integral components of larger discussions about proper prayer times and what to do when—whether for reasons in or out of our own control—prayer does not occur within those given times.

WINE AND BETROTHAL:
WITH THIS WINE I THEE WED?

We looked into attending the wedding of an idolater's son in chapter 3, and chapter 4 discusses the marriage contract (Hebrew *ketubbah*). Here, we turn our attention to the role that wine plays in conversation about betrothal.

Rabbinic marriage consists of two distinct rituals: betrothal (Hebrew *qiddushin*; literally: "sanctification") and the marriage ceremony itself (often referred to in Hebrew as *huppah*, meaning "wedding canopy"; see, e.g., *t. Ketubbot* 1:4). Modern rabbinic tradition combines both and performs them on the same day, but in antiquity these were distinct rituals separated by an often lengthy period of time (see Kanarek 2014, 67–105; and, in general, Satlow 2001). Because betrothal represents the beginning of a legal relationship, the Rabbis devote an entire tractate (aptly titled *Qiddushin*) to determining what constitute valid acts of betrothal. As we should expect by now, many of these conversations consider the extraordinary rather than the ordinary. High school sweethearts fall in love and both consent to engagement? Boring. Not the Rabbis' cup of tea. More representative of rabbinic examination of betrothal is the following:

> A certain man was drinking wine in a tavern; a certain woman came [and] said to him: "Give me one cup."
>
> He replied to her: "If I give you [a cup of wine], will you become betrothed to me?"
>
> She said to him: "Pour me a drink!"
>
> Said Rav Hama: Every [response such as] "Pour me a drink!" means nothing. (*b. Qiddushin* 9a)

To summarize: a woman walks into a tavern and asks a man for a glass of wine. He inquires, "If I give you a glass of wine, will you marry me?" To which the woman replies: "Just give me my wine!" Are they engaged? Rav Hama says no.

This passage is part of a much larger *sugya'* that considers various conditional betrothals (i.e., we are betrothed if *x* occurs). Surrounding our own passage, for example, are similar cases in which a woman asks a man for beads or dates (see *b. Qiddushin* 8b–9a). In each instance, the man offers them on condition that they become betrothed, and she requests that he give her the beads/wine/dates. Does her answer—which does not actually reply to his marriage proposal—constitute an act of betrothal? Rav Hama (and, in another instance, Rav Zevid) immediately says no, but there is a brief debate about whether, in fact, they might be betrothed. However, the anonymous voice of the Babylonian Talmud settles the matter, declaring: "And the law is that she is not betrothed" (*b. Qiddushin* 9a).

Betrothal initiates a complex series of legal relationships, so it matters whether a couple are actually engaged. This example does not map completely the enormous territory that rabbinic conversation on this topic covers, but it exemplifies how rabbinic literature goes about asking whether two people are betrothed. In this case, the woman is understood to ask for wine, not a wedding.

DRINKING IN THE HOUSE OF A MOURNER: A FUNERAL IS NOT A DANCE PARTY

A wedding is a time of rejoicing; a funeral is obviously a time of mourning. Biblical and rabbinic texts describe both the distress felt by the mourner and the ritual regulations that govern the mourning process (see Olyan 2004; Kanarek 2014, 106–38; Valler 2011). And just as there are wedding feasts, so too there are mourning feasts.

At such mourning feasts, friends and colleagues are expected to comfort the mourner. They should treat the occasion with the seriousness that it demands. That does not mean that they cannot drink. But, as we are about to learn, they must not drink too much:

> Rabbi Yitzhaq bar Rabbi Hava the Scribe suffered a tragic loss. Rabbi Mana and Rabbi Yudan visited him. There was good wine, and they drank a lot and laughed.
>
> The next day, they wanted to visit him [again]. He said to them: "Rabbis, is that what a person does to his friend? The only thing missing for us yesterday was that we would get up and dance!" (*y. Berakhot* 3:1, 6a)

One should not to confuse drinking in a rabbinic house of mourning with the beverage-induced levity of a traditional Irish wake. It is unsurprising that the text asks next, how much drinking is too much?

It is taught [in a *baraita'*]: Ten cups one drinks in the house of a mourner: two [cups] before the meal; five during the meal; and three after the meal.

These are the three after the meal: one for Grace after Meals; one for acts of kindness (Hebrew *gemilut ḥasadim*); and one for those who console mourners.

And when Rabban Shimon ben Gamaliel died, they added three more: one for the sexton of the community (Hebrew *ḥazan ha-keneset*); one for the head of the community; and one for Rabban Gamaliel.

But when the rabbinic court (Hebrew *beyt din*) saw that they were regularly becoming intoxicated, they decreed and returned [the *halakhah*] to its original state. (*y. Berakhot* 3:1, 6a; cf. *b. Ketubbot* 8b)

When visiting the house of a mourner, then, guests should drink ten cups of wine. Since Passover ritual only requires four cups (see chapters 2 and 6) and "the sages set four [cups of wine] as a limit for intoxication" (*Numbers Rabbah* 10:8; discussed in chapter 9), ten cups seems like an awful lot of wine. The order in which these drinks should be consumed is also spelled out: two before the meal, five during, and three after. In a parallel text, the ordering is slightly different:

Three before eating in order to loosen the bowels; three while eating in order to digest the food in the bowels; and four after eating. (*b. Ketubbot* 8b)

In this version, the first six cups aid in digestion, and, as the text goes on to note, the final four correspond to the first four benedictions of the Grace after Meals (on these, see *b. Berakhot* 48b).

If ten cups of wine is a lot, following the death of an important rabbinic authority, the number increases still further: two more for communal leaders, plus one more for the sage (in the parallel on *b. Berakhot* 48b, the number increases to four, with an additional cup for the Temple). But thirteen or fourteen cups regularly leads to intoxication, as we learned from the case of Rabbis Mana and Yudan. So the sages decree that the law should revert to the original ruling: ten cups of wine per mourning meal. Notably, they do not ban drinking; they merely cap the amount drunk—which still is at a level that qualifies as binge drinking!

Mourning is a moment of personal loss that triggers a series of individual and communal rabbinic rituals of consolation. These rituals acknowledge that "many have drunk [from the cup of sorrow], and many will drink" (*b. Ketubbot* 8b). At this time, drinking is appropriate. But not too much. After all, as the old joke goes, it could lead to dancing!

CONCLUSION

In the previous chapter, beverages taught us about sacred time. In the present chapter, drinks and drinking have taught us that even the everyday is governed by a series of rules that turn mundane moments of imbibing into ritualized acts. We need to know whether it is grape juice or grape wine in a goblet, whether penitents may be drunk (or punch-drunk) before they pray, and whether ordering a drink is a marriage proposal. In all of these instances, important questions about rabbinic prayer and ritual are explored through the lens of the drinking glass. Whether drinking at an ordinary meal, or drinking with a friend in mourning, once again rabbinic conversation about beverages illuminates key aspects of important rabbinic themes.

SUGGESTED READINGS

Alexander, Elizabeth Shanks. 2015 [2013]. *Gender and Timebound Commandments in Judaism*. New York: Cambridge University Press.

Freidenreich, David M. 2011. *Foreigners and Their Food: Constructing Otherness in Jewish, Christian, and Islamic Law*. Berkeley: University of California Press.

Hayes, Christine Elizabeth. 1997. *Between the Babylonian and Palestinian Talmuds: Accounting for Halakhic Difference in Selected Sugyot from Tractate Avodah Zarah*. New York: Oxford University Press.

Hoffman, Lawrence A., ed. 1998. *The Amidah*. Woodstock, VT: Jewish Lights Publishing.

Jaffee, Martin S. 2006 [1997]. *Early Judaism: Religious Worlds of the First Judaic Millennium*. 2nd ed. Bethesda: University Press of Maryland.

Kanarek, Jane L. 2014. *Biblical Narrative and the Formation of Rabbinic Law*. New York: Cambridge University Press.

Kraemer, David C. 2009 [2007]. *Jewish Eating and Identity Through the Ages.* New York: Routledge.

Marks, Susan. 2013. *First Came Marriage: The Rabbinic Appropriation of Early Jewish Wedding Ritual.* Piscataway, NJ: Gorgias Press.

Olyan, Saul M. 2004. *Biblical Mourning: Ritual and Social Dimensions.* New York: Oxford University Press.

Rosenblum, Jordan D. 2010. *Food and Identity in Early Rabbinic Judaism.* New York: Cambridge University Press.

Satlow, Michael L. 2001. *Jewish Marriage in Antiquity.* Princeton, NJ: Princeton University Press.

Schofer, Jonathan Wyn. 2010. *Confronting Vulnerability: The Body and the Divine in Rabbinic Literature.* Chicago: University of Chicago Press.

Simon-Shoshan, Moshe. 2012. *Stories of the Law: Narrative Discourse and the Construction of Authority in the Mishnah.* New York: Oxford University Press.

Valler, Shulamit. 2011. *Sorrow and Distress in the Talmud.* Translated by Sharon Blass. Boston: Academic Studies Press.

Zahavy, Tzvee. 2007 [1987]. *The Mishnaic Law of Blessings and Prayers: Tractate Berakhot.* Atlanta, GA: Scholars Press.

EIGHT

Ritual Purity

Purity is a status. In the Hebrew Bible, purity generally refers to the relationship of a person, object, or substance to the Temple and Temple-based ritual. That which is pure is suitable for admission and/or inclusion. The binary opposite status is impurity, and that which is impure is excluded both ritually and socially (see Olyan 2000, 38–62). Unlike the common translation of this binary as "clean/unclean," pure/impure highlights the fact that these are statuses—they refer to relationships, not cleanliness. My office may thus be dirty, but pure; or clean, but impure.

Purity discussions tend to be quite technical, and the stakes are quite high: the Temple must be kept in a status of purity, so the transmission of impurity is a matter of deep theological concern. Students interested in recent studies of this system have many excellent resources from which to choose (e.g., Balberg 2014; Harrington 1993; Hayes 2002; Klawans 2000). For present purposes, however, I summarize many technical details.

WASHING WITH WINE

Liquids, which play a key role in ritual washing, are more problematic from a rabbinic purity perspective than solids. Ablutions can ritually cleanse the entire body, as is the case with ritual baths (Hebrew *miqva'ot*; Christian baptism practices derive from these), or only a part of it, such as washing a hand or foot (see Magness 2011, 16–31). The latter ablution was especially associated with priests in Temple practice. Living in a world without a Temple, however, the Rabbis often take Temple practices and translate them into a Temple-less reality, citing Temple rituals to legitimize their own authority and practices (see Cohn 2013). Such is the case with handwashing.

We should not confuse ritual handwashing with hygiene or public health. The Rabbis do not speak of washing hands in terms of modern germ theory. Rather, they discuss it either in terms of ritual purification; as simply removing food remnants from hands; as marking a separation between distinct meals; or as constituting a distinct rabbinic practice (see on the latter two Kraemer 2009, 41–43; Rosenblum 2018). The connection between handwashing and purity also leads to discussion of ritual formulae—that is, the blessing to be recited during this ritual practice.

Wine and handwashing first appear together in the Mishnah:

> These are the matters in which the House of Shammai and the House of Hillel differ in regard to meals: ... The House of Shammai say: They wash the hands and then mix the cup [of wine]. But the House of Hillel say: They mix the cup [of wine] and then they wash the hands. (*m. Berakhot* 8:1–2)

The Houses of Hillel and Shammai are often pitted against each other, as the opening line of this mishnah indicates. In general, the opinions of the House of Shammai are stricter (for six exceptions that prove the rule, see *m. Hullin* 8:1; cf. *m. Eduyyot* 5:2), but the opinions of the House of Hillel are preferred (there are eighteen exceptions, discussed further below). College campuses thus often have a Hillel building but not a Shammai building.

So we should not be surprised that the Houses of Hillel and Shammai disagree on matters in general. Furthermore, as food practices are important topics of rabbinic conversation (Rosenblum 2010a), we should not be surprised that they debate rabbinic meal rituals. And given their penchant for translating ancient priestly Temple-based rituals into contemporary rabbinic practices, their interest in ritual handwashing should not be surprising either (see Magness 2011, 18–20).

This text in the Mishnah also reflects a rabbinic interest in meal order that suggests an interaction with elite Greek and Roman dining, where wine was the preferred beverage and was served mixed (i.e., diluted with water), echoing a larger conversation about proper table decorum and culinary and commensal practices (Rosenblum 2010a; Smith 2003). This text can therefore be read as the Rabbis negotiating inherited traditions from Jewish and non-Jewish worlds in order to create distinctively rabbinic meal practices.

All of this background prepares us to understand a rabbinic text on the question of whether one may wash one's hands with wine:

> Undiluted wine: they recite over it the blessing "... Creator of the fruit of the tree," and they may wash their hands with it.
>
> But if they have diluted it with water, they recite over it the blessing "... Creator of the fruit of the vine," and they may not wash their hands with it, the words of Rabbi Eliezer.
>
> And the sages say: In either case, they recite over it the blessing "... Creator of the fruit of the vine," and they may not wash their hands over it. (*t. Berakhot* 4:3)

As in most ancient Mediterranean societies, the Rabbis regularly drank wine and believed that wine should be diluted with water to temper its potency. Based on the more formal Greek symposium and Roman convivium, or banquet, diluted wine had higher cultural status. "In R. Eliezer's opinion, the special quality of wine is expressed only in a formal setting, and in such a setting wine will be mixed. In effect, outside of the more formal context, wine is not *wine*—it is merely the fermented juice of the 'fruit of the tree'—and hence it should attract no special notice in the blessing ritual" (Kraemer 2009, 81). The sages disagree and believe that wine is always *wine*—it is always a culturally significant beverage.

The blessing over wine and the views of Rabbi Eliezer and the sages are discussed in *m. Berakhot* 6:1 and 7:5, earlier in the Mishnah; *t. Berakhot* 4:3 raises the issue of the use of wine to wash one's hands (on washing with wine in other contexts, see *t. Shabbat* 12:13; *y. Shabbat* 14:3, 14c). Rabbi Eliezer seems to suggest that when wine is not *wine*—but is merely fermented grape juice—it is accorded a lower cultural status and can thus function in the purity context as a liquid for meal-based ritual handwashing. Much as water in this context is not a beverage but a liquid for ablution, so is undiluted wine. Once wine is diluted, however, it is *wine*, and therefore it is a "beverage" and thus is not a suitable liquid for ablution. This interpretation is further supported by the fact that undiluted wine, according to Rabbi Eliezer, does not receive the special wine blessing. The sages disagree. For them, regardless of dilution, wine is always *wine*—and hence one recites the special wine blessing over it and cannot use it for ritual handwashing.

This passage in *t. Berakhot* 4:3 therefore shows us how rabbinic conversations about ritual blessings and ritual washing intersect in order to convey meaning through beverages: "the one who must bless is called upon to consider the culinary landscape and make fine distinctions. This is not, if he does the job, a flat landscape. The earth that brings forth food is rich and varied, producing high and low, better and worse. The blessings that 'notice' these differences create and reinforce them in the experience of the performer of the ritual at the very same time" (Kraemer 2009, 82). Other ritual actions also index these same categories of differentiation. One such action, as I argue in this section, is inquiring whether wine can be used for ritual handwashing prior to eating and drinking a meal. The answer, as we have seen so often throughout this book, is, it depends.

DRINKING BEER AT NIGHT: BUGS IN BEER AND WATER

Chances are that someone reading these words right now is doing so while sipping bottled water. I base this assumption on the fact that, for example, Americans open about 1,500 bottles of water per second, every day; and in California alone a billion or so plastic bottles end up in the trash each year (Salzman 2012, 176, 186). Our relationship with water in the developed world today is a far cry from that of ancient Rabbis, however, and we need to keep this in mind here.

Concern for clean water leads to concerns about both physical and spiritual health. In the next chapter, we address medical concerns (e.g., regarding demons) related to water. Here we look at issues of ritual impurity, such as that of non-kosher—and hence, as is usually the case, impure—animals in regular drinking water (and other beverages), and then at that of drunk friends in rivers. Taken together, they help to explore key aspects of rabbinic ritual purity legislation.

Ancient sources presume that water is chock full of creatures (on the modern theological issues that such bugs raise, see Kraemer 2009, 147–72), and the Hebrew Bible prohibits consumption of most of these. Only sea creatures with fins and scales may be eaten (Leviticus 11; cf. Deuteronomy 14); and all creepy-crawlies are taboo. Does that mean that water cannot be consumed? The answer—as we should expect by now—is: it depends.

A discussion of straining beer provides a good look at this rabbinic concern. Beer, like water, often contains within it potentially non-kosher creatures. Therefore, in the midst of a conversation about such wildlife in water, it is not surprising that the text turns to beer. It is also not surprising that the following text is from the Babylonian Talmud, since the Babylonian Rabbis' love of beer is well-attested:

> Rav Huna said: One may not pour out beer [through a strainer composed of] fibers at night, lest [a creepy-crawly] will come out [of the beer and creep] onto the fibers [of the strainer], and then fall into the cup. [Unaware, the beer-drinker would drink] and [in doing so] would transgress [the biblical prohibition against consuming] "[All] creepy-crawlies that creep upon the earth ..." [Leviticus 11:41]. (*b. Hullin* 67a)

The text opens with Rav Huna making a ruling regarding pouring beer through a strainer. In chapter 6, we encountered rabbinic legislation in regard to straining alcohol (specifically wine), which centered around rules related to Sabbath, Festival, and holiday laws. In this case, ritual time is not the concern; rather, the concern is the ingestion of impure creatures along with one's beer. Both Torah and taste endorsed straining ancient beer, and Rav Huna's concern is that this be done during the day. At night, without adequate light, a drinker could not be certain that one of the creepy-crawlies strained out did not subsequently jump back into the beverage. Hence, you might drink a bug with your brew. And doing so was a big deal because such creatures are biblically forbidden food. In the words of the full verse of Leviticus 11:41: "All creepy-crawlies that creep upon the earth are an abomination; they shall not be eaten."

This biblical verse is important for a technical reason. Earlier in this section of the Talmud, it is asserted that creepy-crawlies found inside liquids in a vessel are allowed. But once they creep on the earth, then they are prohibited. Remember, the biblical verse explicitly forbids "[All] creepy-crawlies *that creep upon the earth*." If they never actually creep upon the earth, then (according to the Rabbis) they are not forbidden. However, were a creepy-crawly to be strained out, creep upon the fibers of the strainer, and *then* fall back into the beer, it would be a biblically forbidden creepy-crawly, as technically it would have crept "upon the earth." (For the purposes of this text, the fibers of the strainer are deemed earth-like enough to count as creeping "upon the earth.") But given the fact that it is dark at night (no concern is raised for the fact that one is drinking beer, which might also affect one's judgment and/or vision!), beer drinkers might not notice this happen; and hence, if they saw the creepy-crawly, they might conclude that it had always been in the liquid. As a result, the beer drinker would think that it would be fine to swallow said bug, even though doing so would, in actuality, be a violation of biblical law. To prevent this confusion, Rav Huna issues his ruling.

With this knowledge, let us continue reading this talmudic passage (Aramaic *sugya'*):

If so, then even [when there is unstrained beer] in the vessel [drinking would be prohibited], lest [a creepy-crawly] emerge [from the beer and creep] onto the side of the vessel, and then fall into the vessel?!

There, this is [the creepy-crawly's] natural place. (*b. Hullin* 67a)

The anonymous interlocutor of the Talmud asks: if the concern is that once the tiny creatures in beer creep on solid ground, they are not bugs that one can ignore and drink, but biblically forbidden creepy-crawlies, should we not always presume that such creatures might have crept onto the side of the vessel and fallen back in, and hence, all beer would be prohibited? Thankfully, the answer is an immediate "no." This ruling is based on the grounds that, in the case of unstrained beer in general (what the text refers to in shorthand as "there"), it is the natural order of things for bugs to spend time in and out of the beer. The fact that they might previously have crawled out of the liquid and onto the side of the drinking-vessel need not concern the drinker, since this is normal; it does not constitute an act of "creeping." By extension, then, the straining is a deviation from the natural order of things, and when a bug creeps onto the strainer, it is classified as a creepy-crawly, to which the biblical prohibition applies.

Having introduced the distinction between the interior surface of a drinking vessel and the surface of an external object, the text continues to explore this distinction in regard to ritual purity:

And from where would you state [this distinction]?

For it was taught in a *baraita*: From where [is it learned] to include [bugs found in water in] wells, ditches, and caves, such that one may bend down and drink from them, and need not restrain oneself [from doing so]?

[Therefore, Scripture] teaches, saying: "[These] you may eat from all that are in water..." [Leviticus 11:9].

Let us take into consideration that perhaps [a creepy-crawly] will come out [of the water and creep] onto the side [of a well, ditch, or cave], and then fall [into the water]?!

Rather, this is its natural place. Here, too, this is its natural place.

Rav Hisda said to Rav Huna: There is a *baraita* that supports your [ruling]: "All creepy-crawlies that creep upon the earth..." [Leviticus 11:41], [the "all" is stated] to include insects that are filtered out [of wine by a strainer].

> The reason [that such insects are prohibited according to the *baraita'*] is that they are filtered out, but had they not been filtered out, [both the wine and the insects] would have been permitted. (*b. Hullin* 67a)

The opening phrase ("from where would you state"; Aramaic *mina' teymra'*) is technical language asking for a source for a legal ruling. Much like modern professors, ancient Rabbis demanded that their students prove their arguments and cite their sources. In this case, the supporting evidence comes from a *baraita'*, a rabbinic tradition reputed to be of tannaitic origin that is cited in an amoraic text. In good rabbinic fashion, a question is answered with a question. So what is the source for this legal ruling? A *baraita'* that opens with a question: what is the support for allowing imbibing bugs along with water directly from wells, ditches, and caves? It should be noted that the phrasing "to include" is also technical language, as Rabbis are often parsing out legal rulings to determine what they "include" and what they "exclude." So what tells us that such bugs should be included in such water and, hence, be ritually pure for ingestion? The "what" is Leviticus (which, of course, makes the "who" God—a pretty reliable rabbinic source). This is deduced from the wording of Leviticus 11:9.

Here a curious feature of rabbinic literature is apparent. In order to fully understand the logic of the text, you need to know the full biblical verse. But the text only quotes part of the verse. The expectation is that the reader has memorized the entire Hebrew Bible. Seeing the first words of the verse should therefore cue the reader to complete the rest of the verse, which is required to understand the logic of the text. It is for this reason that I did not supply the full verse above, so readers would see the knowledge presumed. Fortunately for my readers, I do not have the same expectation as the ancient Rabbis. Therefore, I now quote the full verse:

> These you may eat from all that are in water: all that have fins and scales in the water, whether in the seas or the rivers, these you may eat. (Leviticus 11:9)

I have rendered this verse in the manner that the Talmud is reading it, which is to break it into two sections. In doing so, the Rabbis argue that the first section—which is the part that they quote in the text above—

seems unnecessary. The second section ("all that have fins and scales in the water, whether in the seas or the rivers, these you may eat") teaches sufficiently what aquatic creatures can and cannot be eaten. Why then does the biblical verse begin with "These you may eat from all that are in water," which the Rabbis deem superfluous language? The Rabbis believe that God is the author of Leviticus (and the rest of the Torah), and that God never makes a mistake. Any apparent typo or repetition is attributed, not to poor editing, but to an intentional divine action. It is meant to teach the careful reader. In this case, the Rabbis believe that the second part of the verse limits the prohibition to aquatic creatures in seas and rivers.

But bugs in wells, ditches, or caves are allowed—provided that nature takes its usual course. This is why the text considers whether a bug that creeps onto the side of a well, ditch, or cave, and then falls back into said water source, is deemed a biblically forbidden creepy-crawly. It is not, the text asserts, because this is the usual daily routine of such bugs. And since this is their natural place *and* they are in a non-sea or non-river water source, then one can drink those bugs along with that water and not violate biblical law. As was the case with unstrained beer above ("there"), in the present case ("here"), the sides of the drinking vessel/well/ditch/cave are not considered "earth" and hence bugs can move to and fro. But all of this changes once an unnatural element is introduced: whether it be a strainer in the former case, or a drinking vessel in the latter. This point is interesting, because bugs in well/ditch/cave water—unlike unstrained beer—are deemed creepy-crawlies once they enter a drinking vessel. Thus, you can drink bugs in unstrained beer from a cup but can only drink unstrained well/ditch/cave water directly from the well/ditch/cave. Otherwise, you will swallow impure creepy-crawlies.

All of this information provides background for understanding the final part of the above text. It begins with Rav Hisda making a statement to Rav Huna, his friend (and sometime enemy; see *b. Bava Metzi'a* 33a). Remember that this whole *sugya* opened with Rav Huna's prohibition against pouring beer through a strainer at night. Rav Hisda now offers a *baraita'* in support of Rav Huna's opinion. According to this tradition, the "all" in Leviticus 11:41—the same biblical verse used as part of Rav Huna's ruling above—is included by God specifically in order to prohibit the ingestion of insects filtered out of wine. (Though the text does not supply the specific beverage being filtered for bugs, the verb for "filter" is used in regard to filtering wine on the Sabbath in *m. Shabbat* 20:2, so this seems a likely candidate; however, for our present purposes, it is the bugs and not the beverage that are of concern, so this identification is not crucial to my argument.) The logic of this *baraita'* is that filtered insects are biblically forbidden creepy-crawlies; however, had the insects not been filtered and had they been left in the wine, then they would simply be bugs and would be permitted for ingestion.

Bugs are not necessarily impure, but creepy-crawlies certainly are. The Rabbis therefore need to parse at what point an insect in water, beer, or wine transfers from the category of permitted to that of prohibited. Such conversations focus on the status of the bug itself. In other texts, however, the concern is about the impact on a beverage by the presence of a creature. In this latter case, the animal itself—for example, a mouse—is forbidden. But what about the beverage into which it falls? It is to this question that we now turn.

WHAT TO DO WHEN A MOUSE FALLS INTO YOUR BEER

The Rabbis focus on abstract legal principles, often to the detriment of actual lived reality. They are far more interested in the anomalous than the mundane. In short, when they hear hoof beats, they think zebras not horses.

One area where their theoretical concerns intersect with practical considerations is in regard to cooking mistakes. Anyone who has cooked food knows that things routinely go wrong in the kitchen. (Or at least they do when I am in the kitchen!) And even if you have not cooked food, then you know that things can go wrong while eating food, hence the (in)famous "five-second rule" in regard to food dropped on the floor. Such food failures raise interesting legal questions for the Rabbis. For example, what if I am cooking a kosher soup and you walk by and accidentally drop some bacon into my soup pot? Or what if you are sipping a glass of kosher wine and an idolater spills some libated wine into your glass? These are scenarios that appeal to the scholastic rabbinic mind, but also are necessary for creating a systematic legal code applicable to the messy realities of the human kitchen and table.

People are often surprised to learn that prohibited food that falls into permitted food does not necessarily render the latter ritually impure for consumption (in general, see Kraemer 2009, 55–72, and the many modern examples in Horowitz 2016). The answer, yet again, is: it depends. If the forbidden substance is no more than one-sixtieth of the permitted substance, then a general rabbinic principle is that the substance is too minute to "count" as forbidden. For example, if the piece of bacon that you drop in my soup is small enough, then I could still enjoy my soup. Of course, as precise as this measurement sounds, in actuality it is quite difficult for me to know with absolute certainty that your bit of bacon is one-sixtieth of my soup. One needs to estimate the ratio and err on the side of caution.

Alongside the one-sixtieth principle is another rabbinic cooking mixture rule: the taste principle. According to the taste principle, a forbidden substance mixed into a permitted substance renders the latter forbidden when it imparts a discernible taste to the mixture. There are some obvious issues with this concept. For example, taste buds vary, so your palate might be more refined than mine and, as a result, you will detect flavors that I cannot. And, even more important, I cannot know if something is impure unless I taste it. Thus, if I taste my soup and realize that it has a distinct bacon flavor, I have now eaten non-kosher food; and if I taste my soup and taste no bacon, then I have eaten kosher food. (I leave aside the issue of how someone who presumably never tasted a prohibited substance, for example, pork, would know what it tastes like.) The proof is literally in the pudding.

There are other issues that the taste principle raises. For example:

> Libated wine is prohibited, and it renders prohibited [any substance in which it is mixed] in any quantity whatsoever. [Libated] wine [mixed] in [non-libated] wine, and [libated] water mixed in [non-libated] water [renders prohibited the non-libated liquid] in any quantity whatsoever. [But libated] wine [mixed] in [non-libated] water or [libated] water [mixed] in [non-libated] wine [renders prohibited the non-libated liquid only] when it imparts taste.
>
> This is the general rule: [if a libated] substance [is mixed] with [a non-libated] substance of the same kind, [then it renders prohibited the substance in which it is mixed] in any quantity whatsoever; but [if a libated substance is mixed] with a [non-libated] substance of a different kind, [then it renders prohibited the substance in which it is mixed only] when it imparts taste. (*m. Avodah Zarah* 5:8)

We have already learned in several other chapters about the various issues concerning "libated wine" (Hebrew *yayn nesekh*). Given that this is a beverage category of great concern, you would expect the first ruling: namely, that libated wine is prohibited and the presence of *any* libated wine in a beverage renders the entire liquid impure. And this is what the text seems to argue at first, which is why I supply the words "[any substance in which it is mixed]" in my translation. But then the text continues, muddying the waters. At this point we encounter the taste principle. Libated wine mixed in non-libated water only renders the water prohibited when the water tastes like "wine-water" and not just regular water. In actual practice, this would require a heavily diluted liquid.

To clarify matters, a general principle is introduced. (Unfortunately, general principles—in which complex cases are summarized with a broad, basic concept applicable to most variables—are rare in rabbinic literature.) If like is mixed with like—meaning wine with wine, or water with water—then the entire mixture is prohibited. But if like is mixed with unlike—meaning wine with water or water with wine—then the entire mixture is prohibited *only* if the prohibited substance imparts flavor to the permitted substance. Therefore, if I mix libated wine with non-libated wine, the resulting mixture will *always* be prohibited; but if I mix libated wine with water, I *might* be able to drink the resulting beverage, provided that the libated wine does not impart flavor to the water. Of course, the only way to tell whether the latter is pure for consumption is to drink it, so that problem remains.

Having introduced the taste principle, we are ready to turn our attention to the mouse in our beer. To begin with, the mouse is explicitly prohibited in the Hebrew Bible (Leviticus 11:29). So the question of eating (or rather, *not* eating) a mouse is already resolved. But what if a mouse—an impure creature—falls into my pure beer?

> Once there was a mouse that fell into a barrel of beer. Rav prohibited that beer. The Rabbis stated this in the presence of Rav Sheshet, [and then commented]: Let us say [that Rav] is of the opinion [that if a prohibited substance] imparts taste to make [a permitted substance] taste worse, [then] it is prohibited [to consume the resulting mixture]. [But] Rav Sheshet said to them: In general, Rav is of the opinion [that if a prohibited substance] imparts taste to make [a permitted substance] taste worse, [then] it is permitted [to consume the resulting mixture]. But here [in regard to the mouse], it is a unique case, since [a mouse] is, in fact, quite repulsive, and people distance themselves from it; and even so, the Merciful One prohibited it. Therefore, [despite the fact that the mouse] imparts taste to make [the beer] taste worse, nevertheless it is prohibited. (*b. Avodah Zarah* 68b)

The text begins anecdotally: once a mouse fell into a barrel of beer. The rabbinic game is afoot, as the status of the beer and what legal principles apply are now up for debate. We immediately learn that Rav prohibited this beer. But his reason for doing so is not reported. Much like a math teacher, the Rabbis dislike an answer that fails to show its work—that is, to offer the logic behind a ruling. Hence, an inquiry into Rav's reasoning ensues.

An anonymous group of Rabbis report to Rav Sheshet the curious incident of the mouse in the beer and Rav's ruling thereon. In doing so, they offer their opinion: it would seem that Rav considers that, when a prohibited substance imparts taste to a permitted substance, the resulting mixture is prohibited, regardless of whether the flavor is yummy or yucky. We leave aside the practical matter of how long a mouse actually needs to be in a beer before it imparts flavor (a quick dunk might not transfer any "mouse-flavor," but several days—whether alive or dead—in the barrel is probably a different story). I leave aside the question of how a rabbinic Jew would know what flavor a mouse would impart to beer, being that: (a) one would presume that they never ate mouse, let alone drank mouse beer; and (b) even today with modern technology, it is difficult to brew beer with a consistent flavor profile (on the science behind this, see Rogers 2014). Instead, I focus on the fact that the Rabbis' suggested logic for Rav's ruling does not seem to accord with an earlier tradition:

> This is the general rule: any [permitted substance] that derives benefit by [libated wine] imparting taste, is forbidden; [but] any [permitted substance] that does not derive benefit by [libated wine] imparting taste, is permitted. (*m. Avodah Zarah* 5:2)

This rule applies to libated wine, usually the most strictly treated of all beverages, so one would imagine that it would apply similarly in other cases.

Rav Sheshet's reply perhaps subtly addresses this issue. First off, it should be noted that Rav Sheshet has not always had the nicest things to say about Rav (for example, his suggestion that some of Rav's rulings were issued when Rav was too tired to think clearly is cited seven times in the Talmud; e.g., *b. Yevamot* 24b and parallels). Either despite this history or out of deference to the anonymous Rabbis with whom he is in dialogue, Rav Sheshet first claims that, in general, Rav's opinion concurs with the general rule proposed in *m. Avodah Zarah* 5:2: a forbidden substance must not only impart taste, but must impart a *good* taste in order to render forbidden a permitted substance with which it has mixed. If it imparts no taste, or a *bad* taste, then the mixture is permitted. Instead, according to Rav Sheshet, Rav's logic was that the mouse in the beer is actually a unique case (Hebrew *ḥiddush*). As such, the general rule does not apply. In this unique case, however, a mouse is deemed so repulsive that people would flee from the mouse (and the mouse-flavored beer), so no biblical prohibition would have been needed to prevent its consumption. Even so, God ("the Merciful One") saw fit to prohibit the mouse, a creature from whom humans flee (in addition to Leviticus 11:29, see Isaiah 66:17). This seems unnecessary. But remember, none of God's words are "unnecessary"; they are *all* instructive. So why did God prohibit the mouse? To teach a law in regard to this unique case: unlike with other prohibited substances—even those as taboo as libated wine—a mouse renders beer prohibited even when the taste it imparts lessens your drinking experience. Mouse-flavored beer is a special case pertinent to ritual impurity.

The *sugya* continues by introducing a technical discussion that I will summarize, as the conclusion is the most important part for our present purposes. First, a question is raised that involves comparing mouse-beer to semen. The details of this comparison need not concern us (it relates to the transmission of ritual impurity), but it is worth noting that the Rabbis often turn to semen in regard to ritual impurity. While semen (and menstrual blood, a bodily fluid similarly popular with them as an example) might not be reoccurring subject matter in many college classrooms, in the rabbinic study academy, such topics often arise. Next, a question is raised regarding mice: are they really so repulsive? After all, "are they not served on the table of kings?!" (*b. Avodah Zarah* 68b). This is immediately answered with a clarification: kings eat the field mouse, whereas Rav Sheshet's "repulsive" mouse is a city mouse. I leave aside whether this distinction is actually true, or even whether it is a difference of semantics, much as modern fancy restaurants serve "squab" but not "pigeon."

Continuing on, the text returns to an issue noted above:

> Rava said: The *halakhah* is: [if a prohibited substance] imparts taste to make [a permitted substance] taste worse, [then] it is permitted [to consume the resulting mixture]. (*b. Avodah Zarah* 68b)

Although Rav Sheshet's ruling does not accord with normative rabbinic law (Hebrew *halakhah*), the Talmud does not discard it, but attempts to understand and assimilate it into its larger legal system. In order to do so, an analogous case is introduced, in which a mouse falls into vinegar (*b. Avodah Zarah* 68b–69a). However, we quickly learn that that specific case is not quite analogous, because: (a) vinegar has a sharper flavor than beer, making it harder to distinguish the mouse taste; and (b) the mouse that fell in vinegar disintegrated, whereas the mouse in beer presumably remained whole. After a little more discussion, the *sugya'* concludes by stating:

> And the *halakhah* is: both in this [case of a mouse in vinegar] and this [case of a mouse in beer], in sixty [parts permitted substance to one part mouse, the mixture is permitted], and the same principle applies to all prohibited substances in the Torah. (*b. Avodah Zarah* 69a)

Therefore, the text concludes that a different principle applies. Though we began above by discussing the taste principle, the applicable procedure is to apply the one-sixtieth principle. It was not about the mouse taste, but the mouse quantity.

While both principles establish whether a mixture of permitted and prohibited substances is allowed, it is not always clear which principle applies. This is an important lesson that the mouse in our beer teaches. A forbidden thing is not necessarily forbidden. It depends. One can only parse the intricacies of "it depends" by referring to the proper principle. And an important part of the rabbinic legal system—and indeed any legal system—is in determining which legal principle applies to the case at hand. So the next time a mouse falls in your beer—or any biblically forbidden substance falls into any permitted substance, for that matter—you now know to calculate its ratio, not to sample its flavor.

WHAT TO DO WHEN YOUR DRUNK FRIEND PUSHES YOU INTO A RIVER

Imagine two friends, walking along a river. While following the switchbacks of the riverbank, they reminisce about old times. And, because this story appears in this book, of course they do so while drinking alcohol. Eventually, one friend—now very drunk—turns to the other and pushes him into a river. What are the implications for the rabbinic ritual purity system?

> [If] one immersed himself in a river, and there was before him another river and he crossed through it, the second [river's water] purifies the first [river's water].
>
> [If] his drunk friend pushed him [into a river post-immersion], and likewise his animal, the second [river's water] purifies the first [river's water].
>
> But if [the drunk friend pushed the person/animal] while horsing around, [then] behold, this is "But if water is put upon ..." [Leviticus 11:38] (*m. Makhshirin* 5:1)

This short mishnah requires a lengthy explanation. To begin, one must understand the concept of *makhshirin*, which is also the name of this tractate of the Mishnah. From the same Hebrew root as the word "kosher" (*k-sh-r*), which generally means "fit/proper/appropriate," *makhshirin* in this context refers to a status in which an object (often food) is susceptible to (often referred to as "prepared for") ritual impurity if it comes into contact with (most, but not all) liquids. More specifically, it refers to the liquids themselves that transmit this ritual impurity.

To understand this concept, imagine a regular wall. As I write these words, I am staring at one, made of drywall and painted some institutional shade of "off-white." Were I to take a magnet and hold it to that nonmetallic wall, as soon as I let go of the magnet it would fall to the floor. However, were I to paint that wall with magnetic paint and then to repeat my experiment, the magnet would stick to the wall. This is what the concept of *makhshirin* gets at. If a substance is not "prepared for" ritual impurity, then like a magnet on a nonmetallic wall, liquid does not transfer ritual impurity; impurity does not "stick." However, if the substance becomes "prepared for" ritual impurity, it is now susceptible to the transmission of ritual impurity, much as the wall attracts a magnet after being painted with magnetic paint. The tractate *Makhshirin* in general explores the contours of how, like a magnet, impurity either sticks (transfers from an impure to a pure object) or does not stick when it comes into contact with certain liquids. If you are having trouble grasping this concept, know that you are not alone; the laws related to *makhshirin* are quite complex, as one student discovered: according to *y. Shabbat* 7:2, 9c, Yehudah bar Rabbi spent six months studying the tractate *Makhshirin* and then promptly flunked a test on the subject!

Here we need to understand the difference between water from the first river and water from the second river. (This is different from the rabbinic concept of "first waters" and "second waters," which has to do with ritual handwashing before and after a meal; see Rosenblum 2018). In the first instance, a person intentionally enters a river in order to bathe. Intentionality is key, since it is only because this person *intended* to get wet in it that the liquid "prepares for" ritual impurity (on intentionality in this respect, see Balberg 2014, 90–95; Eilberg-Schwartz 1986, 28–31, 44–45). Subsequently, that person crosses another river. In doing so, the person wades through it, but does not get wet *intentionally*, but simply in the process. The water is a side effect, not a desired goal. Unlike the first water, which was intentionally "put upon" in order to bathe, this second water is unintentional and does not "prepare for" ritual impurity. Therefore it washes away the first; and hence, it "purifies the first [river's water]."

This background helps us understand the second case, in which a drunk friend pushes either a person or an animal into a second river. While we do not learn whether the person pushed (or the animal, for that matter) is drunk, this is not important here; rather, what matters is that the person doing the pushing is not sober. It is the intentionality of the one doing the pushing that matters. Therefore, because the person/animal pushed into the second river does not enter the river via an intentional act, the case is deemed as above and the second river's water purifies the first river's water. But if the drunk pusher did so while horsing around, the second river's water is in the same status as the first, so it cannot purify the first. The reasoning behind this latter case should be familiar to anyone who has seen a group of children (or, for that matter, drunk adults) playing near a pool: inevitably, one child—or a drunk adult acting like a child—will playfully try to throw another into the pool. This is an *intentional* act. The intentionality defines the action and, as a result, the water "put upon" the one thrown into the water "prepares for" ritual impurity.

In this text, then, water is neutral, as on the pH scale. Only with the introduction of an intentional act does water move from neutral to a status in which it can impart impurity. And that takes us to the final issue: the biblical verse. The point of the last line of this text, citing Leviticus 11:38 ("But if water is put upon..."), is that if the drunk person pushed in their friend/friend's animal in jest, that constitutes an intentional act, and the water on the friend/animal transmits ritual impurity. Once again, the text presumes its audience knows Leviticus. Leviticus 11:34–38 discusses various laws related to carcass and liquid impurity in verses that form the basis for all of the rabbinic legislation regarding liquids "preparing for" the transmission of ritual impurity. The key part of Leviticus 11:38 is: "But if water is put upon the seed... it is impure for you." The Rabbis believe that water has to intentionally come into contact with the person (numerous such examples appear throughout *m. Makhshirin*). And further, they believe that the liquids need to be potable in order to "count." Their logic for this criterion is Leviticus 11:34, which states: "and any liquid that may be drunk ... shall be impure." For the Rabbis, God is once again the intentional teacher, and so the modifying clause "that may be drunk" is instructive: only drinkable liquids "count":

> There are seven liquids [that "prepare for" ritual impurity]: dew, water, wine, oil, blood, milk, and bee's honey. (*m. Makhshirin* 6:4; further, see *m. Makhshirin* 6:5; *t. Shabbat* 8:24–28)

An additional clarification appears elsewhere:

> But rather [the sages] said: seven liquids ["prepare for"] ritual impurity, and all other liquids ["prepare for"] ritual purity. (*m. Terumot* 11:2)

Only those seven named above "count"; no other beverage does, and other beverages thus cannot transmit ritual impurity in regard to the biblical category of "But if water is put upon ..." from Leviticus 11:38.

While this short mishnah has required a long explanation, the concepts learned along the way will serve us well as we consider two interesting case studies in regard to four of the seven liquids mentioned above, milk/blood and wine/oil.

ON DRINKING BODILY FLUIDS: "MENSTRUAL BLOOD TRANSFORMS AND BECOMES BREAST MILK"

Blood is the most tabooed liquid in the Hebrew Bible. And menstrual blood is the most tabooed form of blood (in general, see Fonrobert 2000). So drinking blood—and menstrual blood in particular—would obviously be a rabbinic (and, indeed biblical) prohibition. After all, blood is tabooed and various ritual impurity implications attach to it (e.g., as we have just seen, it "prepares for" ritual impurity). Given this unambiguous prohibition, breast milk presents a potentially ambiguous, and hence for the Rabbis fascinating, test case.

The connection between breast milk and menstrual blood might not seem obvious. That is, unless you are well read on ancient medicine, a scholar of medical humanities, or went to medical school before the nineteenth century, in which case you would have learned the then common belief that when a woman becomes pregnant, her menstrual blood transforms into breast milk (see Schiebinger 2004, 55–56; Yalom 1997, 70, 93, 207, 211–12). The Rabbis subscribe to this notion too. In the words of *b. Niddah* 9a: "menstrual blood transforms and becomes breast milk."

As transformed menstrual blood, breast milk raises many fascinating questions regarding ritual purity. For our present purposes, two particular issues warrant further discussion (in general, see Rosenblum

2016, 153–59): what happens after breast milk "transforms" back into the status of menstrual blood, and what happens if breast milk comes into contact with any surface other than the interior of an infant's mouth?

We have already learned that the Rabbis believe that when a woman becomes pregnant, her "menstrual blood transforms and becomes breast milk" (*b. Niddah* 9a). But how does the process reverse itself and what are the purity implications thereof? For this, we turn to *t. Niddah* 2:3, which states:

> An infant continues to suckle for twenty-four months. From that point forward, [the infant] is like one who suckles an abomination, the words of Rabbi Eliezer.
>
> But Rabbi Yehoshua says: An infant continues to suckle even for five years. [However, if the infant] weans and returns [subsequently to breastfeed] after twenty-four months, [then] behold, this is like one who suckles an abomination.

Rabbinic texts presume twenty-four months to be the standard postpartum nursing period. Therefore, this text opens by asserting that, for twenty-four months, an infant suckling breast milk presents no purity concern for the infant. But once that period elapses, the breast milk "transforms" back into the status of menstrual blood. That means that the infant is drinking breast milk, but that breast milk now has the status of menstrual blood. Hence, the infant suckles an abomination (cf. Hayes 2002, 210). Rabbi Yehoshua offers a practical work-around. Is twenty-five-month-old breast milk an abomination? It depends. If the infant has continuously suckled, then the purity status of the breast milk does not transform, even after sixty months! If, however, the infant has been weaned (literally in Hebrew, "separates [from the nipple]") and then returns to suckle at twenty-five months, the breast milk is indeed an abomination. In this latter case, infants do not need breast milk to survive—they can eat solid food—so the purity status of the post-twenty-four-month breast milk has transformed. In the former case, however, rabbinic purity legislation is lenient, because the infant has not been weaned and needs the breast milk to survive.

The previous example presumes that the infant suckles directly from a woman's nipple. However, the Rabbis display concern for the purity implications of breast milk, should it come into contact with any surface other than the interior of an infant's mouth. This concern is because:

> ... a woman's milk—which is designated only for children—renders impurity whether [the lactation occurred] intentionally or unintentionally ... (*m. Makhshirin* 6:8)

Regardless of intentionality, a woman's breast milk is "prepared for" ritual impurity, so the Rabbis worry that it could leak at any moment and transmit impurity. This conception is heavily gendered, because the Rabbis are concerned generally that women have leaky, uncontrolled bodies (see Balberg 2014, 173). In fact, the Rabbis imagine a scenario in which men lactate, and presume that their breast milk would not have the same purity implications (*m. Makhshirin* 6:7). This is for two reasons: (1) men do not menstruate, so their breast milk is not deemed to be transformed menstrual blood; and (2) were men to lactate, they would be presumed to be able to control their bodies and thus only to do so with intentionality (Rosenblum 2016, 154–55).

Lactation compounds the presumed leaky body of a woman, since the Rabbis worry that a liquid with the status of menstrual blood—the most tabooed of bodily fluids—could leak in novel ways. For example:

> [If, unintentionally,] milk drips from the breasts of a woman [in the state of ritual impurity], and drops into the air-space of an oven, [the oven becomes] impure, since [an impure] liquid renders impurity whether [it is dropped] intentionally or unintentionally. (*m. Kelim* 8:11; cf. *b. Shabbat* 143b–144a; *b. Keritot* 13a–b)

Breast milk raises significant and complex purity concerns for the Rabbis.

LIBATED WINE AND RITUAL IMPURITY

If blood is the most tabooed bodily liquid, wine is the most tabooed beverage. The primary concern about wine, as noted above and in previous chapters, is that it might have been poured as a libation to an idol, and hence would be classified as "libated wine." This leads to an almost paranoid fear in which non-Jews are imagined as "compulsive libationers," lying in wait to libate any and all wine to their idols (see Stern 2013).

This fear also has implications for the rabbinic purity system. According to *t. Zavim* 5:8:

> Wine that [a Jew] saw a Gentile libate, if it is in the amount of an olive's bulk, [then] it imparts a stringent impurity. But if not [in the amount of an olive's bulk, then] it only imparts the impurity of liquid.
>
> And the remainder of the Gentile's wine, even though it is prohibited on account of libated wine (Hebrew *yayn nesekh*), only imparts the impurity of liquid alone.

If a Jew witnesses a Gentile actually pouring out wine to an idolater, then the wine is clearly libated wine. And since there is no doubt about its status, such wine imparts a stringent impurity, which "most likely indicates an impurity like corpse impurity, defiling by contact, carriage, and overhang" (Hayes 2002, 220)—meaning that it transmits ritual impurity either by coming into physical contact with, being carried from one place to another (even if not physically touched), or hanging over a person/object/substance. This severe level of impurity, however, only applies if the wine is of a sufficient volume. The minimum amount necessary to upgrade its impurity status is an olive's bulk, which is a standard minimum measure for the Rabbis. Things often need to constitute at least an olive's bulk in order to "count" for a given law, or as in the present case, to move from one status to another. If the volume is less than an olive's bulk, then the wine that a Jew witnessed a Gentile libate is still impure, but to a lesser degree: it only imparts "the impurity of liquid"—meaning that it only imparts impurity to liquids.

The remainder of the Gentile's wine, which the Jew did not directly observe being libated, has the same purity status as the less-than-an-olive's-bulk-of-witnessed-libation wine. This is where the rabbinic paranoia about Gentile libation enters the conversation. No one witnessed this wine being libated, but Gentile wine still imparts impurity to liquids simply because it is Gentile wine and, by virtue of being Gentile wine, "it is prohibited on account of libated wine (Hebrew *yayn nesekh*)." Gentile wine "is treated as if it had been offered in libation, irrespective of the likelihood of such activity or the intentions of the gentiles who made it" (Freidenreich 2011, 70). Actual practice and/or intentionality are irrelevant here. Gentile wine is libated wine, and libated wine imparts the impurity of liquid. Unless, of course, a Jew actually witnessed an act of libation, which kicks it up a notch: it now imparts a stringent impurity.

The concern for wine is not just for the wine itself, but for the various social, theological, and purity implications of "Their wine." Wine is viewed as the gateway drug. In fact, in one text, wine serves this role (alongside oil, another liquid noted above) in a rather straightforward manner:

> For Rav Aha bar Adda said in the name of Rabbi Yitzhak: They decreed against Their bread on account of Their oil; and against Their oil on account of Their wine.
>
> "Against Their bread on account of Their oil"—why is oil more deserving [of a prohibition] than bread? Rather, [the statement should have been]: They decreed against Their bread and Their oil on account of Their wine.
>
> And [they decreed] against Their wine on account of Their daughters; and against Their daughters on account of something else; and against something else on account of something else.
>
> What is "something else"? Rav Nahman bar Yitzhak said: They decreed against a Gentile child that he imparts impurity like one in the status of a *zav*, so that a Jewish child should not become accustomed to hanging out with him for the purpose of homoerotic intercourse. (*b. Shabbat* 17b; cf. *b. Avodah Zarah* 36b)

This text opens by referencing a few of the Eighteen Decrees, which are eighteen decrees of the School of Shammai that one day, due to a lack of attendance by members of the School of Hillel, the School of Shammai was able to pass (see Freidenreich 2011, 60–63). Since the Mishnah (*m.*

Shabbat 1:4) does not spell out these decrees, later sources seek to fill in the gap. We begin with a statement by Rav Aha bar Adda, in the name of Rabbi Yitzhak, that Gentile (= "Their") bread was prohibited by the School of Shammai on account of "Their" oil; and that "Their" oil was prohibited on account of "Their" wine. The anonymous voice of the Talmud interrupts at this point to seek a clarification. Why prefer bread to oil? Would it not make more sense to say that *both* "Their" bread and oil are prohibited on account of "Their" wine? After all, we know that "Their" wine is deemed libated wine and hence heavily tabooed. In a sense, both are right. The anonymous correction points out that "Their" wine is the bigger concern. However, in the ancient Mediterranean diet, bread was a staple food, but so was olive oil, into which bread is dipped. Here I am reminded of a friend who drowns his french fries in ketchup, declaring that the purpose of the french fry is to deliver ketchup into his mouth. In the ancient world (and even today in many parts of the Mediterranean), bread is secondary to olive oil, much as the french fry is secondary to the ketchup for my friend. Either way, all agree that wine is the bigger issue, and so "Their" bread and oil were prohibited in order to erect barriers at the table, preventing social intercourse. After all, if you eat together, you might end up sharing wine.

While we know that "Their" wine is prohibited on account of the fear of libation, we now learn an additional reason: as we saw also in chapter 3, there is a fear that social intercourse will lead to sexual intercourse. There is a direct line drawn from "Their" bread to "Their" bed (Rosenblum 2010b). And once a Jew engages in sexual intercourse with "Their daughters," it is a slippery slope that leads down the path to idolatry. This is what is meant by the first "something else," since it is a term often deemed too feared and abhorrent to mention, much like cancer or Voldemort.

But what about the second "something else"? The Talmud asks that very question: "What is 'something else'?" Until now, social and theological concerns have clearly been the primary driving force. It is here that impurity enters the conversation. The second "something else," according to Rav Nahman bar Yitzhak, refers to a decree against Gentile children. The logic behind this decree requires some explanation. First, we learn that a Gentile child "imparts impurity like one in the status of a *zav*." A *zav* (Hebrew plural *zavim*) is a person with certain genital discharges. A person in this status is understood to transmit ritual impurity, which then results in concomitant social stigmas against them (e.g., Leviticus 15:11; Olyan 2008, 54–56; Rosenblum 2010a, 132–35). Therefore, any association with a Gentile child raises potential red flags in regard to purity. Second, it is worth noting that the gender of this sentence is in the masculine: a male child is like a male *zav*. The Rabbis almost always default to the masculine grammatical gender and, in general, presume a male audience, but in this case, the grammatical gender is quite important: the text focuses on a concern regarding Jewish *boys* associating with non-Jewish *boys*. For if this were to be a regular occurrence, then it might lead to Jewish boys becoming accustomed to hanging out with non-Jewish boys, which would then lead to homoerotic intercourse. As Michael Satlow has noted, this conclusion is both unexpected and striking (1995, 211). Given our prior knowledge, we would have expected a heteronormative interpretation, which is what I have provided up until this final section. After all, "[they decreed] against Their wine on account of Their *daughters*." Here, however, the text turns its attention not to concerns between males and females, but between males and males. As Satlow observes:

> The force of this twist might have been to warn those Jews who thought that a Gentile's statutory impurity does not prevent association, and maybe even intercourse, between Jewish and Gentile adolescent boys (or men) that they were mistaken. Purity is used as the weapon to keep Jewish and non-Jewish adolescent boys apart, due to the fear that a Jew who becomes acquainted with and accustomed to a non-Jew will succumb to the temptation of homoerotic intercourse. (1995, 211)

Purity creates social, theological, and sexual boundaries. In this instance, purity functions as a mechanism of separation in order to prevent social intercourse that might lead to homoerotic intercourse—a category of intercourse that raises numerous concerns for the Rabbis (see Satlow 1995, 185–222). It is a reminder that purity can be a weapon in the battle against temptation.

CONCLUSION

Liquids are more problematic than solids in the rabbinic purity system, and exploring beverages allows us to uncover fascinating texts that consider some of the complex variables that liquids present. Along the way, we learn several rabbinic concepts, such as how bugs and mice in beer teach the one-sixtieth and taste principles (and when to apply each principle); and how a drunk friend pushing you in a river is instructive of being "prepared for" ritual impurity, as well as the importance of intentionality and how that affects purity status. Case studies related to bodily fluids (breast milk and blood) and staple ingredients (wine and olive oil) further reveal the gendered and embodied implications of purity regulations. And, as we have seen throughout, "it depends" is often the best answer to any rabbinic question.

SUGGESTED READINGS

Balberg, Mira. 2014. *Purity, Body, and Self in Early Rabbinic Literature*. Berkeley: University of California Press.

Cohn, Naftali S. 2013. *The Memory of the Temple and the Making of the Rabbis*. Philadelphia: University of Pennsylvania Press.

Eilberg-Schwartz, Howard. 1986. *The Human Will in Judaism: The Mishnah's Philosophy of Intention*. Atlanta, GA: Scholars Press.

Fonrobert, Charlotte Elisheva. 2000. *Menstrual Purity: Rabbinic and Christian Reconstructions of Biblical Gender*. Stanford, CA: Stanford University Press.

Freidenreich, David M. 2011. *Foreigners and Their Food: Constructing Otherness in Jewish, Christian, and Islamic Law*. Berkeley: University of California Press.

Harrington, Hannah K. 1993. *The Impurity Systems of the Qumran and the Rabbis: Biblical Foundations*. Atlanta: Scholars Press.

Hayes, Christine E. 2002. *Gentile Impurities and Jewish Identities: Intermarriage and Conversion from the Bible to the Talmud*. New York: Oxford University Press.

Horowitz, Roger. 2016. *Kosher USA: How Coke Became Kosher and Other Tales of Modern Food.* New York: Columbia University Press.
Klawans, Jonathan. 2000. *Impurity and Sin in Ancient Judaism.* New York: Oxford University Press.
Kraemer, David C. 2009 [2007]. *Jewish Eating and Identity through the Ages.* New York: Routledge.
Magness, Jodi. 2011. *Stone and Dung, Oil and Spit: Jewish Daily Life in the Time of Jesus.* Grand Rapids, MI: William B. Eerdmans.
Olyan, Saul M. 2000. *Rites and Rank: Hierarchy in Biblical Representations of Cult.* Princeton, NJ: Princeton University Press.
———. 2008. *Disability in the Hebrew Bible: Interpreting Mental and Physical Differences.* New York: Cambridge University Press.
Rogers, Adam. 2014. *Proof: The Science of Booze.* Boston: Houghton Mifflin Harcourt.
Rosenblum, Jordan D. 2010a. *Food and Identity in Early Rabbinic Judaism.* New York: Cambridge University Press.
———. 2010b. "From Their Bread to Their Bed: Commensality, Intermarriage, and Idolatry in Tannaitic Literature." *Journal of Jewish Studies* 61, no. 1: 18–29.
———. 2016. "'Blessings of the Breasts': Breastfeeding in Rabbinic Literature." *Hebrew Union College Annual* 87: 147–79.
———. 2018. "The Unwashed Masses: Handwashing as a Ritual of Social Distinction in Rabbinic Judaism." *Historia Religionum* 10: 79–90.
Salzman, James. 2012. *Drinking Water: A History.* New York: Overlook Duckworth.
Satlow, Michael L. 1995. *Tasting the Dish: Rabbinic Rhetorics of Sexuality.* Atlanta, GA: Society of Biblical Literature.
Schiebinger, Londa. 2004 [1993]. *Nature's Body: Gender in the Making of Modern Science.* 2nd ed. New Brunswick, NJ: Rutgers University Press.
Smith, Dennis E. 2003. *From Symposium to Eucharist: The Banquet in the Early Christian World.* Minneapolis: Fortress Press.
Stern, Sacha. 2013. "Compulsive Libationers: Non-Jews and Wine in Early Rabbinic Sources." *Journal of Jewish Studies* 64, no. 1: 19–44.
Yalom, Marilyn. 1997. *A History of the Breast.* New York: Ballantine Books.

NINE

Health and Hygiene

Unlike modern Western culture, the Rabbis do not deem medicine and religion to be separate domains. Therefore, rabbinic literature considers both applied medicine and the STEM fields—science, technology, engineering, and math—for their impacts on and by other legal issues. For example, do life-threatening maladies warrant the treatment of Jews by a healer who invokes the name of Jesus (see *t. Hullin* 2:22; Schäfer 2007, 52–62)? The efficacy of the cure is not the issue; the concern is "Should I?" and *not* "Could I?" In this way, medicine (and, indeed, all STEM-related subjects) in rabbinic literature often falls more into the domain of what we might call "ethics," in that the concerns are about values rather than mere descriptions of medical procedures.

In this chapter, we explore how rabbinic texts about beverages help us to understand the ways in which the Rabbis conceive health and hygiene. Over and again, we shall find that when the Rabbis discuss the role of beverages in proper diet and regimen, they are discussing how drinks and drinking affects and is affected by normative rabbinic law (Hebrew *halakhah*). For the Rabbis, Torah is embodied knowledge and practice—what Martin Jaffee refers to as "transformative knowledge" (2006, 230–59)—so God's will extends beyond the synagogue and the study academy and into domains that today are occupied by medical professionals (physicians, nurses, psychologists, nutritionists, etc.), personal trainers, and health gurus.

DRINKING TO HEALTH: L'CHAIM!

Raising a glass and exclaiming "*L'chaim!*"—literally "To life!"—is a well-known practice. The toast appears in modern song lyrics from very disparate genres: from the 1964 Broadway show *The Fiddler on the Roof* ("To life, to life, *l'chaim!* / *l'chaim, l'chaim*, to life!") to the 2009 song "I Gotta Feeling" by the pop band The Black Eyed Peas ("Fill up your cup—drink! / *Mazal tov!*—*l'chaim!*"), reminding everyone that they are, quite literally, drinking to their health. And the Rabbis agree.

In the many texts discussed in this chapter, the connection between beverages and health becomes apparent. We begin by exploring how the Rabbis understood the regular consumption of beverages to be a key component of a healthy dietary regimen. For example, we learn:

> And Rava bar Shmuel said in the name of Rabbi Hiyya: After everything you eat, eat salt; and after everything you drink, drink water; and [by following these dietary practices], you will not be harmed....
>
> And another *baraita'* taught: [If] one ate any food and did not eat salt, [or if] one drank any beverage and did not drink water—during the day, one worries about bad breath; and during the night, one worries about '*askerah*.
>
> Our Rabbis taught in a *baraita'*: One who makes his food float in water will not suffer intestinal ailments.
>
> And how much [water should one drink with food]? Rav Hisda says: One cup per loaf of bread. (*b. Berakhot* 40a)

The recommendation that one drink lots of water is sound from both ancient and modern medical perspectives: keeping hydrated is a good idea. This advice appears three times in this text; the second instance, repeating the statement attributed to Rabbi Hiyya almost verbatim, is omitted here, and the third, advocating a cup of water to each loaf of bread, is a *baraita'*, a tradition reputed to be of tannaitic origin that is cited in an amoraic text.

This *baraita'* provides new information regarding what specific harm is of concern: day drinking may cause bad breath, and night drinking may cause *'askerah*. As is also the case today, bad breath is an issue in the ancient world (see Preuss 2004, 170–71). For example, "Shall one who ate garlic and his breath smells, return and eat garlic again, so that his breath should continue smelling?" (*b. Berakhot* 51a) is a rabbinic idiom for "two wrongs do not make a right." This idiom presumes that garlic makes one's breath smell, and that smelly breath is less than desirable. This is an issue during the day because that is when halitosis is most likely to have social repercussions—as you interact with more people, and hence expose them to your bad breath. The nocturnal concern of *'askerah* probably refers to a condition like croup, which involves swelling of the airways, resulting in difficult breathing and a barking cough. Perhaps *'askerah*, which appears often in rabbinic literature (see Preuss 2004, 157–60), is an issue particularly at night because it would disrupt sleep. Ingesting water after drinking another beverage is understood to prevent both maladies.

The importance of drinking water continues in the immediately following *baraita'*, where we learn that "one who makes his food float in water will not suffer intestinal ailments." Making food float in water refers to drinking a significant amount of water with food—that is, enough to make it float (which, according to Rav Hisda, is in a ratio of one cup of water per loaf of bread). Doing so prevents intestinal ailments, likely referring to dysentery, a common medical concern in rabbinic literature (see Preuss 2004, 180–82). Today, many readers might not think of this malady as a major concern, given the availability of cheap and fast-acting remedies. However, such intestinal ailments are common in many parts of the modern world, where people regularly suffer from them, sometimes fatally. People often only think of this as affecting travelers, where—from the standpoint of our text—ironically the issue is often contaminated drinking water (see Salzman 2012,

72–112). But this was clearly a concern for the Rabbis, who ordain that upon leaving the privy, one recite the following blessing:

> Blessed [are You, Lord, our God, King of the universe] who formed the human being with wisdom, and created in it many orifices and cavities. It is revealed and known before the throne of Your glory that if one of them opened or if one of them became stopped up, it would be impossible to stand before You. (*b. Berakhot* 60b)

As this blessing conveys, the Rabbis were well aware of human vulnerability as creatures of flesh and blood (see Boyarin 1995, 34; Schofer 2010, 53–76, esp. 67). The connection they draw between regular consumption of liquids and digestive health is not limited to this text. For example, elsewhere we learn:

> And if you want, I can say [that children should not be taught new biblical lessons on the Sabbath] because on the Sabbath they eat and drink [more than on weekdays] and they feel sluggish.
> As Shmuel said: A change of diet is the beginning of intestinal ailments. (*b. Nedarim* 37b)

As the first line indicates, this tradition appears in a discussion of why children should not be taught new lessons about the Hebrew Bible on the Sabbath (see *b. Nedarim* 37a–b). The reason? On the Sabbath, everyone—adults and children alike—eats and drinks more than usual (on Sabbath drinking, see chapter 6). As a result, they are both physically and mentally too sluggish to assimilate new information (literally, "the world is heavy on them"; Aramaic *ve-yaqir 'aleyhon 'alma'*).

This leads to Shmuel's statement that changing one's diet is the root cause of intestinal ailments. Shmuel's medical advice was apparently quite popular, since it is cited in several other texts (e.g., *b. Ketubbot* 110b; *b. Bava Batra* 146a; *b. Sanhedrin* 101a). But Shmuel was not the only rabbinic authority to associate health with diet—and particularly with consumption of alcohol. And sometimes the authority cited is not a Rabbi, but his mother.

DELIRIUM TREMENS AND ABAYE'S MOTHER'S MEDICAL ADVICE

Commenting on *m. Gittin* 7:1, a text that discusses the case of a man "seized with delirium" who then demands a divorce from his wife, the Babylonian Talmud states:

> What is "delirium"? Shmuel said: One whom new wine of the winepress has harmed.
> Then why does it not state: "One harmed by new wine"?!
> The wording [of *m. Gittin* 7:1] teaches that the spirit that causes this illness is called "Delirium."
> So what is the difference? [This knowledge is necessary] for [the preparation of] a magical amulet.
> What is its remedy? Red meat broiled on coals and diluted wine.
> Abaye said: My mother told me that for a one-day fever, [the remedy is to drink] a pitcher of water; for a two-day fever, let blood; for a three-day fever, [feed the patient] red meat broiled on coals and diluted wine.…
> (*b. Gittin* 67b)

Note that this text starts by defining "seized with delirium." The generative goal therefore is to understand the medical condition that prompts a *halakhic* ruling. In this case, the Babylonian Talmud wants to understand what "seized with delirium" means, because one afflicted with this malady may threaten to divorce his wife, but his words have no legal effect, since he is not deemed to be sufficiently lucid. In his current (though not necessarily permanent) state, he is incapable of informed consent, thus he cannot divorce his wife.

In the midst of answering this *halakhic* question, a discussion about medical definitions and remedies ensues. "Delirium" (Hebrew *qordiaqos*) here refers to delirium tremens, colloquially called "the DT's," a serious symptom of withdrawal from alcohol (on this condition in rabbinic literature, see Preuss 2004, 320–21). If this is, indeed, the medical condition, then why does the Mishnah use the term "delirium" rather than simply state that this is "One harmed by new wine"? This is an important legal question, as the Talmud uses technical terminology (the Aramaic phrase here is *ma'y nafqa' minah?*—literally: "What goes out from it?" but idiomatically: "What is the practical *halakhic* difference?") in order to indicate that it is asking if there is any legal lesson to be derived from this language. As we might expect by now, the answer to this question is, "Yes, of course there is!" Thanks to the Mishnah using this wording, we learn that "delirium" is caused by a spirit, whose name happens to be *Qordiaqos* – a.k.a., Delirium. Temperance advocates in the United States in the 1840s began to refer to rum as "Demon Rum" (see Smith 2013, 35–37). They saw this "demon" as literal, not metaphorical; for them, there was a real Spirit in these spirits. Likewise with the Rabbis, and knowledge of the demon's specific name is necessary in order to prepare an efficacious amulet to ward him off. (Recall that "magic" is not considered to be ineffective; it just requires rabbinic regulation.) However, the Rabbis do not dwell on this issue here. Rather, they propose a dietary cure.

So what is the rabbinic remedy prescribed to patients presenting with "delirium"? They should eat red meat broiled on coals and drink diluted wine. From a modern perspective, we might reasonably question offering wine to one suffering from delirium tremens, but the Rabbis believe that wine possessed important healing properties. Elsewhere we learn:

> The best of all remedies am I, wine; in a place where there is no wine, there medicines are needed. (*b. Bava Batra* 58b)

But it is important to note what kind of wine is offered: diluted wine and not new wine. While the former is watered down and hence lower in alcohol by volume, the latter is wine in its full, unadulterated potency. The former is the drink of the self-controlled and temperate; the latter is the beverage of the uncontrolled boor. (Incidentally, new wine has other carnal effects, including increasing excrement; see discussion below; *Avot d'Rabbi Natan* B:48; and on excrement in rabbinic literature, see Schofer 2010, 53–76.) Therefore, this remedy suggests eating nourishing protein and a low-alcohol beverage (which, given the bacteria likely present in most available water sources, is probably a more healthy and hygienic option).

The talmudic passage (Aramaic *sugya'*) then records a series of remedies that Abaye learned from his mother. The fact that some of her medical advice for treating fever matches verbatim the previous remedy generates the inclusion of this material here (on fever in rabbinic literature, see Preuss 2004, 160–64). Given the gender of the one dispensing this medical advice, we should not be surprised that her prescriptions are viewed by both the ancient text and many modern scholars as "folk remedies" as opposed to the "serious" medical wisdom of the anonymous *male* Rabbis (e.g., Preuss 2004, 161; and for important criticism of this approach, see Fonrobert 2000, 151–59). Yet, all of the medical advice that Abaye's mother offers reads as both legitimate and normal medical knowledge from the perspective of the ancient (if not necessarily the modern) world. First day, drink plenty of fluids. Second day, let blood (on bloodletting, see the next section below). And third day, eat coal-broiled red meat and drink diluted wine.

In addition to learning that Abaye's mother did not agree with the adage "Feed a cold, starve a fever," and that the gender of the one dispensing medical advice affects how it is viewed, we also learn that beverages commonly figure in rabbinic texts discussing health and hygiene. In this instance, the entire conversation about the role that beverages play in healing and nutrition results from inquiries into the *halakhah* of rabbinic divorce. But, as we are about to learn, this is not the only legal domain in which beverages appear.

LETTING BLOOD AND STEALING WINE

Common in ancient, medieval, and even modern medicine, the practice of bloodletting as a medical procedure is known—and even endorsed—by the Rabbis (see Preuss 2004, 248–57; Brain 2009). In fact, we have just encountered evidence that supports this claim: "Abaye said: My mother told me ... for a two-day fever, let blood" (though

Sokoloff [2002, 806] prefers the reading of this text as prescribing the ingestion of fennel [Aramaic *simra'*] rather than bloodletting [Aramaic *sakoray*]). Drinking—especially drinking wine—features prominently in rabbinic discussions of bloodletting. And, once again, we see that it is out of a concern for the contours of *halakhah* that such discussions arise.

An extended discussion of bloodletting is encountered on *b. Shabbat* 129a–b. As its title suggests, this tractate is predominantly about *halakhah* related to the Sabbath (Hebrew *shabbat*). This discussion is generated out of commentary on *m. Shabbat* 18:3 (cited *b. Shabbat* 128b), which primarily considers the *halakhah* of delivering a baby on the Sabbath. Out of concern for the woman in labor (and her child), several leniencies are granted. For example, one may light a lamp despite explicit biblical prohibitions against doing so on the Sabbath (*b. Shabbat* 128b; and for the biblical prohibition, see Exodus 35:3). The Mishnah's own words are quite telling: out of concern for her life, "one may profane the Sabbath on her account" (*m. Shabbat* 18:3).

The commentary in the Babylonian Talmud shifts to bloodletting when a woman who has given birth is compared to a sick person. Much as in current United States law, in which pregnancy and birth are considered an illness (and hence covered under the Family and Medical Leave Act, popularly known by its acronym FMLA), the Rabbis conclude:

> There is no difference between a woman who gave birth and a sick person. (*b. Shabbat* 129a)

Bloodletting then becomes the medical procedure that the Talmud uses in order to spell out the implications of this claim. At first, the text discusses the importance of replacing nutrients after bloodletting:

> Rav Yehudah said [in the name of] Rav: One should always sell [even] the beams of his house and buy shoes for his feet. [Yet] if one let blood and has nothing to eat [immediately after the procedure], he should sell [even] the shoes that are on his feet and provide from these the requirements of a meal.

> What are "the requirements of a meal"?
> Rav says: Meat. And Shmuel says: Wine.
> Rav says "meat" [because] "life" replaces "life." And Shmuel says "wine" [because] "red" replaces "red." (*b. Shabbat* 129a)

One must sell anything necessary in order to procure a post-bloodletting meal (cf. *Leviticus Rabbah* 12:1, in which an alcoholic old man sells the beams of his house, not for food, but for more wine; see Zellentin 2011, 51–94). But what constitutes such a "meal"? As we should expect by now, the answer is debated. According to Rav, a "meal" requires meat, whereas Shmuel argues that a "meal" requires wine. Each sage has a justification for his assertion. For Rav, meat and blood are both "life," so one is needed to replace the loss of the other. (Rav's argument draws on biblical notions that blood is "life"; see Genesis 9:4; Rosenblum 2016b, 19–20.) For Shmuel, wine and blood are both "red," so one is needed to replace the loss of the other.

The text continues on to report the post-bloodletting "meal" of several sages:

> On the day that Shmuel was bled, they made for him a cooked dish of spleen. Rabbi Yochanan would drink [wine] until the aroma came out of his ears. And Rav Nahman would drink [wine] until his spleen floated in it. Rav Yosef would drink [wine] until [the aroma] came out of the incision of the scalpel. Rava would seek three-year-old wine. (*b. Shabbat* 129a)

As an organ whose primary purpose is to filter blood, the association between spleen and "red" makes sense. But how does the patient know when one has "replaced" the "red" lost via bloodletting? In most cases, it would seem, once there is enough wine in the system to have a noticeable—and likely intoxicating—effect.

The text then turns to a fascinating legal discussion: namely, can one engage in deception in order to obtain a post-bloodletting meal?

> Rav Nahman bar Yitzhak said to his rabbinic disciples: I beg of you, on the day that [you] let blood, tell your wives "Nahman is visiting us." And all deception is forbidden, except for this deception, which is permitted. One

who was bled and cannot afford [to buy wine] should take a worn-out *zuz* and go to seven taverns [to use the old coin in order to taste wine] until he has tasted a quarter *log* [of wine]. (*b. Shabbat* 129a)

Rav Nahman tells his students that, after bloodletting, they may lie to their wives and tell them that he—their venerable teacher—is coming to dinner. The presumption here is that their wives would prepare a magnificent feast in anticipation of feeding their husbands' teacher, which their husbands could then consume post-bloodletting. I leave aside two seemingly obvious (from the gendered perspective of ancient Mediterranean culture) marital issues: (1) why would a wife not prepare a nice meal for her husband after such a medical procedure?; and (2) what kind of discussion will ensue when the husband shows up without his teacher and, while eating the magnificent feast that she prepared for Rav Nahman, informs his wife of his subterfuge?

Instead, the *halakhic* issue of interest here is that of deception. Remember that this text began above by stating that eating after letting blood is more important than even wearing shoes. So this is an extraordinary case. Does that mean that can one take extraordinary measures? In general, deception is forbidden. (Though this claim here likely refers to "deception" with regard to bloodletting, deception is generally frowned upon in rabbinic literature; however, see the famous case of lying to a less-than-beautiful bride on her wedding day, discussed on *b. Ketubbot* 16b–17a.) In this case, however, deception is necessary in order to prevent risk to life. Therefore, not only can a man lie to his wife, but he can engage in the ancient equivalent of passing bad checks. How this worked was that the poor blood letter would go to a tavern and sample wine, pretending to have sufficient funds to purchase it. He would then try and pay for the wine with a worn-out coin (a *zuz*, discussed below in the next section). Since such a coin would not be accepted as currency, he would leave without any additional wine, but having drunk some wine samples. After going to seven taverns, he would have imbibed about a quarter *log*, a small liquid measure often used as a minimum amount in rabbinic literature, and would be medically safe. Doing so is tantamount to stealing, but the Rabbis allow it in such a case. Why? Because "if one let blood, drinking [should occur] immediately" (*b. Shabbat* 129b).

RAV BIBI DRINKS BEER: MEDICAL SIDE EFFECTS OF BOOZING

Concern for life is not confined to discussion of bloodletting. Sometimes it is the beverage in your cup that can place your life in danger. As is the case with modern medicine, this potential threat is not always the intended result, but is rather a side effect. Side effects—which are really just effects, though not necessarily desired or anticipated ones—can be fatal, benign, or even advantageous (e.g., in the case of Viagra, originally intended to treat hypertension).

Rav Bibi's drinking habits figure in a discussion of the quantity of certain substances that, if carried from one domain to another on the Sabbath, would constitute a violation of Sabbath law (*m. Shabbat* 8:2–7). According to *m. Shabbat* 8:4, the amount of lime that violates Sabbath transportation law is "enough to smear lime [on] the littlest of girls." While lime was used in ancient construction (for example, to plaster walls; see *m. Shabbat* 8:5), the present context suggests its other use: as a depilatory, that is, a beauty aid for hair-removal. With this in mind, we are prepared to interpret the following claims made in regard to Rav Bibi, his daughter, and his drinking habits:

> Rav Bibi had a daughter. He smeared her with lime limb by limb, and he took 400 *zuz* [as a bride-price] for her.
> There was a certain Gentile in his neighborhood. He [also] had a daughter. He smeared her [entire body] with lime all at once, and she died.
> He said: Rav Bibi killed my daughter!
> Rav Nahman said: Rav Bibi, who drinks beer, his daughter requires lime treatments; [but] we who do not drink beer, our daughters do not require lime treatments. (*b. Shabbat* 80b; cf. *b. Mo'ed Qatan* 9b)

After smearing his unnamed daughter limb by limb with lime to make her conform to societal notions of female beauty, Rav Bibi successfully marries her off (on the marriage situation that this implies, see Satlow 2001, 314n128), extracting a significant bride-price: 400 *zuz* ("the denomination found most frequently in rabbinic texts.... [whose editors] frequently use the figure 200 *zuz*... to indicate a minimum amount that an individual needs to support himself and his household for a full year" [Gardner 2015, 115]).

Rav Bibi's Gentile neighbor observes this series of events and then turns his attention to his own unnamed daughter. He likely perceives her as having too much body hair and, having seen the transformation in Rav Bibi's daughter, has an idea. He subjects his daughter to lime treatments. However, unlike Rav Bibi, who "smeared her with lime limb by limb," the Gentile neighbor "smeared her [entire body] with lime all at once." Perhaps for this reason, or for another that we are about to learn, the daughter dies. Understandably upset, he proclaims: "Rav Bibi killed my daughter!"

But did Rav Bibi *really* kill his daughter? No. First of all, Rav Bibi neither told him to perform, nor himself applied, this beauty treatment. Second, Rav Bibi smeared the lime on his own daughter limb by limb, rather than covering her entire body with it all at once. Rav Nahman introduces a third important caveat: Rav Bibi drank beer while his neighbor apparently did not. Implied in Rav Nahman's statement is that not only did Rav Bibi drink beer, but so too did his daughter. Here, the commentary by the medieval commentator and reputed wine-maker Rashi seems on point: "Beer darkens and increases [body] hair" (Rashi on *b. Shabbat* 80b). Beer is understood to make her hairy—and, thus, less marriageable. As a beer-drinker, Rav Bibi's daughter has darker and more abundant body hair; hence, the need for depilatory lime treatments. As a non-beer-drinker, the Gentile's daughter has acceptable body hair; hence, lime treatments are not required and tragically proved fatal.

Elsewhere in the Babylonian Talmud, beer is deemed as having positive effects on one's health, and even on one's complexion (e.g., *b. Ketubbot* 77b; *b. Shabbat* 110b; Geller 2004, 237–40). But the perception that beer has negative side effects also can be detected, especially in texts that betray Palestinian influence. For example, though preserved in the Babylonian Talmud, the Talmud of a beer-drinking region, the following Palestinian (and hence pro-wine-drinking) tradition appears:

> Our Rabbis taught in a *baraita'*: Three things increase excrement, bend the stature, and take away a five-hundredth of a person's eyesight. These are: [1] coarse black bread; [2] new beer; and [3] raw vegetables.
>
> Our Rabbis taught in a *baraita'*: Three things decrease excrement, straighten the stature, and illuminate the eyes. These are: [1] refined white bread; [2] fatty meat; and [3] old wine ....
>
> Everything that is beneficial for this, is harmful for that; and [everything] that is harmful for this, is beneficial for that; except for moist ginger, long pepper, unrefined white bread, fatty meats, and old wine, which are beneficial for one's entire body. (*b. Pesahim* 42a–b; cf. *b. Eruvin* 55b–56a)

Note that this text features two *baraitot* (the Aramaic plural of *baraita'*), which are traditions cited in an amoraic text that are reputed to be of tannaitic origin. The Tannaim wrote from the location and perspective of Palestine; the Amoraim composed their texts both in Palestine and Babylonia. In this instance, these traditions offer "both positive and negative observations about the effects of certain foodstuffs on digestion and health, clearly from the perspective of Palestine looking eastwards [towards Babylonia]" (see Geller 2004, 224–27, here 226). So we expect a pro-wine bias to this medical advice.

In the first *baraita'*, we learn that three foods increase the production of excrement, bend one's back, and diminish eyesight—clearly negative side effects of their consumption. (Foods are not the only cause of these ailments; e.g., according to *b. Ketubbot* 111a, sitting too much is bad for bowel health and walking too much is bad for vision.) These foods have various social connotations in a Roman context, and Palestine is a Roman province. For example, while all Romans (and Roman subjects) eat bread, in a way that "reflects social divisions: it could be consumed conspicuously or in the most humble way and form" (Garnsey 2002 121). Today we might think of so-called "peasant bread" as a healthy and expensive bread product and white bread as unhealthy and cheap, but for much of human history, the opposite was true. In a Roman context, coarse black bread (Hebrew *pat qibar*; from the Latin *panis cibarius*) was seen as cheap, low-status food. Eating this type of bread signals that one is of lower socioeconomic standing, which probably contributes to poorer health in general for the same varied reasons that it does in the modern world. Beer, as we have noted throughout this book, is viewed in Palestinian sources as an inferior beverage from the perspective of culture, socioeconomic status, and health. For example, though modern medicine asserts that beer (due to brewer's yeast) can actually be beneficial for the production of breast milk, one Palestinian rabbinic source claims that a nursing's wife's wine allowance should be increased, because "wine increases the [production of] breast milk" (*y. Ketubbot* 5:13, 30b; see Rosenblum 2016a, 157–63; and on women drinking wine, see chapter 4). The reference to "new beer," in this context, perhaps implies that beer in the ancient world could only be kept for about two weeks before it spoiled, whereas wine—as we shall see—could not only be stored for longer times, but also improves with age. Finally, and in a distinct contrast from today, raw vegetables were considered unhealthy (though cooked vegetables are beneficial; see Geller 2004, 225n27; Preuss 2004, 565–66). For example, in a *baraita'* in *b. Berakhot* 44b, we also learn that "all raw vegetables make one pale." Subsequent commentary adds that they should not be consumed immediately after a bloodletting and that those on a raw vegetable diet emit a foul odor (and they should especially be avoided prior to breakfast, when you are hungry and their smell might upset your empty stomach).

In the next *baraita'*, we learn that three foods decrease the production of excrement, straighten one's back, and improve eyesight—clearly positive side effects of their consumption. Though the order does not completely match the previous tradition, these three foodstuffs are seen as the physical and cultural opposites of the previous three: refined white bread versus coarse black bread; fatty meat versus raw vegetables; and old wine versus new beer. From a Roman perspective, these foodstuffs build a better physical and cultural body.

After these *baraitot* appear, the Talmud begins to frame them. I omit the first part of this process (the ellipses) because it seeks to clarify a few terms and does not add much for our purposes (e.g., "'Old wine': [this refers to] really old wine"). The next narrative framing is what really interests me, because it reflects a Babylonian perspective that nuances Palestinian traditions. First, it states a general principle: "Everything that is beneficial for this, is harmful for that; and [everything] that is harmful for this, is beneficial for that"—that is, the basic premise of a side effect. Now we see that a food might help one part of the body, but harm the other, or vice versa. So maybe beer is not all bad. Second, we learn that there are exemptions from this general principle, since certain foods "are beneficial for one's entire body." Yet, even these beneficial foods have their limits. For example, a *baraita'* in *b. Berakhot* 57b states that recently ill or currently sick people should avoid fatty meat—so fatty meat does not always do a body good. And even wine can have its limits, as the renowned ancient Greek physician Galen himself notes: "It is clear, however, that the use of wine must be avoided at a time of inflammation; otherwise there is nothing to prevent us giving it" (Johnston and Horsley 2011, 1: 453, *Method of Medicine*, IV.7). But Galen stipulates that "otherwise there is nothing to prevent us giving it"—meaning that wine is generally advisable. The preference for wine, fatty meat, and refined white bread remains, but the framing softens the Palestinian perspective. The Babylonian viewpoint allows for a second medical opinion, in which beer (among other things) is not always bad for one's health.

However, both beer and wine are sometimes bad for one's health. Specifically, the foam on top of beer and wine is best avoided. As we learn:

> And Abaye said: Formerly, I used to say [that] the reason one does not drink foam [on the top of beverages] is because of repulsiveness, [but] Master told me: Because it causes pleurisy.
>
> Drinking [foam] causes pleurisy; blowing into [foam] causes headaches; [and] pushing [foam] away causes poverty.

What is its remedy? Let [the foam] sink [into the beverage].

For pleurisy [caused by drinking the foam] of wine, [one should drink] beer; [caused by drinking the foam] of beer, [one should drink] water; [caused by drinking the foam] of water, there is no remedy.

And this is what people say: Poverty follows the poor. (*b. Hullin* 105b)

Foam on top of such beverages comes from carbon dioxide produced during the fermentation process (in champagne, the resulting bubbles define the drink). "In research, people assume beer with a thick head and substantial lacing (the tracery of bubbles left on the inside of a glass) is going to taste better than beer without it" (Rogers 2014, 73–78, here at 76; Bamforth 2011).

Abaye originally thought that drinking foam was to be avoided because it is repulsive, but then he receives advice from someone other than his mother: Master tells him that drinking foam causes pleurisy, inflammation of the tissue around the lungs that causes chest pain, especially when breathing (the symptoms gave rise to the Aramaic term for pleurisy, *barsam*, deriving from New Persian for "breast" [*bar*] and "swelling" [*sām*] [Sokoloff 2002, 247]; on this in rabbinic literature, see Preuss 2004, 173–74). Furthermore, we are told that blowing foam causes headaches (on which, see Preuss 2004, 304–5) and pushing foam away causes poverty. Put simply: foam causes chest, head, and financial pain.

Despite these concerns, people still desire to drink wine and beer. So what is the remedy that allows for the removal of harmful foam in order to imbibe the beverage? One should let the foam sink into the beverage, at which point the harmful foam is deemed to dissipate. It would seem that the concern is drinking the foam straight.

But what happens if one actually drinks the harmful foam? The text lays out an order of beverages that help: if wine foam is ingested, then drink foamless beer; if beer foam is ingested, then drink foamless water; but there is no cure for ingesting water foam. The beverages are presented in descending order of cost: wine cost more than beer (there is only one grape season annually, while beer can be made year-round from stored grain); and water is freely available. Leaving aside the question of what water foam might be, the end result is that if all you have to drink is water, and you drink water foam, then there is no remedy for the malady that befalls you. This explains the proverb—introduced by a standard rabbinic formula for a popular saying ("And this is what people say")—that poverty always follows after the poor person (for references in rabbinic literature, see Sokoloff 2002, 872). Those who can only afford to drink that which is free, are left with no recourse if they drink foam. Only those that have the means to drink beer or wine have a remedy.

DRINKING, MODERATION, AND SELF-RESTRAINT: "WINE ENTERS, INTELLIGENCE DEPARTS"

In the ancient Mediterranean, moderation and self-restraint were lauded virtues. As implied in the very term "virtue"—from the Latin root *vir*, meaning "man"—virtues commonly are understood to be characteristics of bodies and minds gendered as male (see Foucault 1990). Moreover, virtue was regarded as including moderation in alcohol consumption, with similar gendered assumptions (see Beer 2010, 84–100; Pomeroy 1995, 153–54). The Rabbis agree with their broader society on this, although believing that Torah study is the unique path to self-restraint and moderation (see Satlow 1996). Therefore, when they discuss the cultivation of virtue, they do so from the perspective of the impact of temperance on Torah, and Torah on temperance.

One extended example of this theme is encountered in discussion of the *nazir*, a layperson who takes a vow to abstain from certain practices, one of which is drinking any intoxicant, especially wine. Commenting on Numbers 6:3 ("from wine and [any] intoxicant he shall abstain..."), several other wine-related biblical passages are explored, which leads to the following:

> What is [the meaning of] "to mingle intoxicants" [Isaiah 5:22]? For they would mix strong wine with weak wine in order to become intoxicated thereby.

Once upon a time, there was a certain group of dissolute men who would sit around and drink wine until midnight, but could not become intoxicated. [Additional] wine was brought to them [and] they decided to mix wine with wine. They kept on doing so until the wine got them drunk, [whereupon] they stood and beat each other in their intoxication. The uproar spread throughout the city and the guard came and arrested them and handed them over to the government and they all perished. Who brought this on them? The wine that they drank. And concerning them [and their ilk], it is said: "who come to inspect mixed wine" [Proverbs 23:30]. "Mixed wine" only [refers to] wine [mixed] with wine. Thus, [this is the meaning of]: "and men of strength to mingle intoxicants" [Isaiah 5:22].

And as a result of this, they cause the Torah to be forgotten and pervert justice, as it is written afterwards: "that justify the wicked for a reward" [Isaiah 5:23]. And [also] it says: "Lest he drink and forget the statute" [Proverbs 31:5], [which means: lest] they forget the Torah, which was given by the hand of the lawgiver, namely Moses. (*Numbers Rabbah* 10:8)

Wine often figures in the Hebrew Bible (see MacDonald 2008, 22–23), allowing the Rabbis to link multiple passages together to make the point that wine causes Torah to be forgotten. In a Greek and Roman context, wine is mixed with water in order to dilute it. As noted above, drinking undiluted wine is considered an act of excessive drinking. Therefore, when the members of this certain group of men mix wine with wine, they live up to their moniker of "dissolute men" (Hebrew *zalin*). Just in case this was not obvious, the text explicitly informs us that these dissolute men mixed wine with wine because they had been drinking wine all day (and most of the night) and were still not drunk. Finally, this wine-with-wine mixture does the trick and then the dissolute men do what drunk dissolute men do: they start a bar brawl. This fight spreads across the city, leading to their arrest. They are handed over to the government (likely implying the Roman government, which is the generic evil government in the background—and sometimes the foreground—of much of rabbinic literature), which promptly executes them.

These dissolute men and their ilk are identified with those spoken of in Proverbs 23:30. Commenting on "the facetious tone" of this verse in its original context, Michael Fox notes: "The sots come to 'inspect' or 'investigate' wine, as it were. We can picture them hunched over their cup, staring dully at the object of their 'study'" (2009, 741). They study wine instead of Torah. Thus, "they cause the Torah to be forgotten" and "pervert justice." This also explains why Isaiah 5:23 follows Isaiah 5:22: when strong men mingle intoxicants, they pervert justice and offer the wicked a reward, while the righteous suffer. Drinking wine, they forget the legal and ethical lessons taught by the divine statutes (Hebrew *ḥuqaq*), which were delivered to Israel by the hand of the Moses, the lawgiver (Hebrew *ḥoqeq*; a similar word-play appears in *Numbers Rabbah* 10:4).

Skipping a few lines of wine-related exegesis, the theme of drinking and forgetting continues:

> Wine enters, intelligence departs. Wherever there is wine, there is no intelligence.
>
> Wine enters, secrecy departs. "Wine"—its numerical value is seventy; and "secrecy"—its numerical value is seventy.
>
> Intelligence is distributed into four parts [of the body]: two [parts are distributed] into the two kidneys, one part into the mouth, and one part into the heart....
>
> The intellect was placed in these four receptacles, and corresponding to them the sages set four as a limit for intoxication: a quarter [*log*] of undiluted wine, which is [equivalent to] four cups of [diluted wine]. [If] a man drinks one cup [of diluted wine], which is a quarter, one-quarter of his intelligence departs; [if] he drinks two cups, two-quarters of his intelligence depart; [if] he drinks three cups, three-quarters of his intelligence depart, and his heart becomes disturbed, and immediately he begins to speak inappropriately; [if] he drinks a fourth cup, all of his intelligence departs, the kidneys are entirely dulled, his heart is disturbed, and the tongue ceases to work—he wants to speak, but he is not able to, but rather his tongue is tied.
>
> Therefore, they say [that] a priest who drank a quarter [*log*] of [undiluted] wine is invalid for Temple service, [and] an Israelite who drank a quarter [*log*] of [undiluted] wine is invalid for serving as a judge. [Taken

together, this is] to teach you that no good comes from wine; thus it is written: "from wine and [any] intoxicant he shall abstain ..." [Numbers 6:3]. (*Numbers Rabbah* 10:8)

Studying Torah takes a lot of brainpower, and drinking too much wine reduces one's ability to think. It makes one not only dumber but less likely to be a good keeper of secrets. The connection between these two side effects of wine ingestion is derived via *gematriya'*, an interpretive activity in which each letter of a word is converted into a number and then the numbers are analyzed (see Lieberman 1994, 69, 72–73). For example, the number 18 is considered an important and fortuitous number because the Hebrew word for "life" (*ḥai*) is composed of two letters: *ḥet* = 8 and *yud* = 10, which add up to 18. This same practice, which is also used in rudimentary cipher codes for encrypting information, briefly made headlines worldwide through debates about "the Bible Code"—which claimed to uncover number patterns in the biblical text that predicted world events (see Ellenberg 2014, 89–101). In this case, both "wine" (Hebrew *yayin*; composed of the letters *yud* + *yud* + *nun* = 10 + 10 + 50) and "secrecy" (Hebrew *sod*; composed of the letters: *samekh* + *vav* + *daled* = 60 + 6 + 4) add up to 70, which is viewed as hermeneutically meaningful, divinely authorized, and intentional. (The numerical equivalency of "wine" and "secrecy" also appears in *b. Sanhedrin* 38a, where it is deployed by Rabbi Hiyya to defend his drunken sons!)

Next, we learn that intelligence is divided into quarters and distributed into four parts of the body (I omit the discussion of biblical proof texts that justify this division). Each kidney receives one quarter of intelligence, which makes sense because the Rabbis considered the kidneys to be the seat of deliberation. The mouth, from which wise or foolish words are uttered, receives one quarter. And the heart, viewed as the seat of reason (as we today refer to the mind), receives the other quarter (on drinking affecting the heart, and reasoning, also see *b. Bava Batra* 12b). This also explains why four cups of wine have such a profound effect: after one cup, one kidney still works, but a smart person is just a little duller; after two, perhaps the person either has one kidney still working or the heart can compensate; after three cups, the person's mouth might still work, but deliberation and reason have departed; and finally, after four cups, all intelligence has departed and kidneys, heart, and mouth can no longer offer any guidance. Sensibly, the sages prohibited both Temple priests (Hebrew *kohanim*) and lay Israelite judges from conducting regular business after drinking four cups of wine.

The number four is not incidental, since it is the common number for drinking to excess. For example, four cups of wine are consumed at the Passover *Seder*, a performative ritual meal designed to commemorate a time—if only fleeting for some, such as enslaved Jews—of independence and freedom from oppression. A quarter *log* of undiluted wine—which equals four cups of diluted wine—becomes a common measure of binge drinking (on the terms undiluted/diluted, see *Sifre Numbers* 23; and on the fact that Italian wine is considered stronger and thus to intoxicate in a smaller measure, see *b. Eruvin* 64b). The fourth cup is the straw that breaks the camel's back in terms of self-restraint. In chapter 4, we learned, for example:

> It is taught in a *baraita*: One cup [of wine] is beneficial for a woman; two [cups] is a disgrace; three [cups lead to her] making explicit sexual propositions; four [cups leads to her] making sexual propositions even to a donkey in the marketplace, [since she is so drunk that] she does not care [with whom she has sex]. (*b. Ketubbot* 65a)

The theme of not working as either a priest or a judge while drunk appears elsewhere in rabbinic literature (e.g., *b. Eruvin* 64a; *b. Ketubbot* 10b). Connected with this theme is the idea that excessive drinking reduces one's ability to judge and keep secrets. But drinking itself is not disparaged, just excessive drinking:

> Rabbi Hanina said: Anyone who can be appeased while [drinking] his wine, possesses an attribute of his Creator, as it is said: "And the Lord smelled the pleasing aroma, etc." [Genesis 8:21].
> Rabbi Hiyya said: Anyone who remains clear-headed while [drinking] his wine, possesses the attributes of seventy elders. The numerical value of

"wine" is seventy; and the numerical value of "secrecy" is seventy. Wine enters, secrecy departs.

    Rabbi Hanin says: Wine was created only to comfort mourners and to grant a reward to the wicked, as it is said: "Give beer to the one who is perishing[, and wine to the bitter of soul]" [Proverbs 31:6].

    Rabbi Hanin bar Pappa said: Anyone in whose home wine is not poured like water has not attained a state of blessedness, as it is said: "and He will bless your bread and your water" [Exodus 23:25]. Just as bread may be bought with Second Tithe funds, so too "water" may be bought with Second Tithe funds. And what is it [the "water" that God blessed in Exodus 23:35]? Wine. But [the biblical verse] calls it "water" [to teach that] if in his home [wine] is poured like water, there is [a state of] blessedness, but if not, [then there is] not.

    Rabbi Ilai says: By three things may a person's [character] be discerned: by his cup, by his wallet, and by his anger. And [others] say: also by his laughter. (*b. Eruvin* 65a–b)

This *sugya'* contains many of the same concepts encountered above, but in a much more nuanced manner. (Once again note that the part of the biblical verse that is crucial for interpreting the passage is omitted, as the Rabbis expect their readers to remember the entire text—yet another reason not to drink excessively, since it leads to memory loss.) It begins by stating that anyone who becomes appeased while drinking possesses a divine attribute. This is especially born out by the biblical verse cited. In the Flood narrative in Genesis 8:21, God smells the aroma of a sacrifice made by Noah, finds the aroma pleasing, and decides to never doom the earth and its inhabitants again. God's smelling is equated with human drinking, so drinking in tranquility becomes *imitatio dei*—an act of divine imitation.

Likewise, anyone who remains clear-headed while drinking possesses the attributes of seventy wise elders. Not coincidentally, seventy is the number of judges who sit on the Sanhedrin, the ancient rabbinic equivalent of the U.S. Supreme Court (on the Sanhedrin, see Berkowitz 2006, 12–17). A judge must be deliberate and discreet, a point driven home by the use of *gematriya'* already familiar to us. In short: a clear-headed drinker is a sober thinker.

Next, a tradition appears that points to one of the problems of alcohol: while wine comforts those mourning (who are "bitter of soul," although beer relieves the pain of the deathbed), it also gives a reward to the wicked. Of course, the reward to the wicked is fleeting, as they will be judged harshly in the future. But for now, wine is their reward. Similarly, the relief wine offers the mourners is fleeting, since they will sober up to the harsh reality of their loss. This is borne out by the verse from Proverbs 31:6, which is understood to refer to the mourner and to the wicked, both of whom are "the bitter of soul," though for different reasons. Wine's "main power is causing forgetfulness, for better *and* worse" (Fox 2009, 887). Yet, as we shall see, the negative aspects of wine can be moderated by temperate drinking.

This last point brings us to the tradition that pouring out wine like water in one's home indicates that one has attained a state of blessedness. Wine was expensive, so being able to drink it as freely as water certainly indicated one's wealth. To prove that the owner of such a home has achieved blessedness, a biblical verse is introduced. Only, there is a problem. In Exodus 23:25, the beverage is "water." And "water" is not "wine." Except when it is. This is one such a case. How do we get there? The text introduces the concept of the class of tithes called Second Tithes (see Deuteronomy 14:22–26; and the entire Mishnah tractate *Ma'aser Sheni*). Without getting too technical, one could convert certain crops into money by selling them, and then use that money to purchase and consume certain foods in Jerusalem; in doing so, the requirements to offer Second Tithes would be met. However, earlier in this tractate, it was taught that one may not purchase water with Second Tithe funds (see *m. Eruvin* 3:1; *b. Eruvin* 26b–27b). In contrast, Deuteronomy 14:26 specifically allows one to purchase wine and beer using Second Tithe funds. So when God said "water" in Exodus 23:25, God meant "wine." According to a general rabbinic principle, discussed in chapter 2, God is the author the Torah and designed every word intentionally. There are no mistakes, only opportunities to learn. So why did God say "water" instead of "wine"? In order to teach that this "wine" should be poured out like "water" in a home where there is a state of blessedness.

Lest the reader thinks that pouring out wine like water is unambiguously positive, a final lesson appears, which returns to concepts discussed in the beginning of this passage. Wine becomes a litmus test. You can judge a person based on how they hold their liquor (and also by how they spend their money and by their general temperament, and possibly by their sense of humor). This statement allows for viewing one who engages in moderate drinking—and even one who drinks a bit more than that but is a clear-headed and jovial drinker—in a positive light. But not so for one who drinks immoderately—or is a mean drunk. To pun on a famous phrase from Shakespeare: for wine is neither good nor bad, but drinking makes it so.

SKELETAL REMAINS: A GRAVEDIGGER REPORTS ON WINE AND BONES

Many of the themes discussed throughout this chapter appear when we stand at the ancient graveside and gaze down at skeletal remains. From this visual autopsy, we learn:

> It was taught in a *baraita*: Abba Shaul says: I used to be a gravedigger and I would gaze at the bones of the dead. [Based on my research, I learned:]
> One who drinks undiluted wine, his bones are burned;
> [one who drinks excessively] mixed [wine], his bones are dry;
> [and one who drinks wine mixed] properly, his bones are lubricated.
> And anyone whose drinking exceeds his eating, his bones are burned;
> [whose] eating exceeds his drinking, his bones are dry;
> [but whose eating and drinking are balanced] properly his bones are lubricated. (*b. Niddah* 24b)

Our *sugya* begins with a *baraita*, which cues us to presume not only that this is an earlier source, but that it is a tradition that originates in Palestine. (While this attribution may be factual or otherwise, it is worth noting that Abba Shaul [Hebrew for "Daddy Saul"] was indeed a

Tanna.) Therefore, as we have noted above, we expect a pro-wine-drinking ideology, rather than the pro-beer-drinking ideology of Babylonian traditions.

After informing us that his resume includes a stint as a gravedigger, Abba Shaul tells us what that job experience taught him about skeletal remains (on ancient Jewish burial practices, see Fine 2010). The lifetime excesses or temperance of individuals become embodied, literally inscribed on their bones. Those who habitually drink undiluted wine leave behind a pile of burned bones; those who drink excessively mixed wine become a pile of dry bones. In the case of the former, they drank overly alcoholic wine; in the case of the latter, they drank overly watered-down wine. Too much burns, too little dehydrates. But those who drink properly mixed wine leave behind lubricated bones.

Reading the bones, we learn a rabbinic version of the Goldilocks Principle. Too much wine harms the body. But so too does too little wine. Just the right amount of wine, however, ensures that one's bones are properly lubricated (Hebrew *mishuḥin*; literally "oiled"). To drive this home further, this point is reiterated, via a statement about the ratio of alcohol to food in one's diet: too much alcohol burns the bones; too little alcohol (and, concomitantly, too much food) dries the bones; but a properly balanced diet results in lubricated bones.

Proper dietary regimen requires one to neither drink too much, nor too little, but just the right amount. And the proof of one's lifetime practice is burned (sometimes literally) into one's bones. This latter point indicates another manner in which this text connects to themes discussed throughout this chapter. This *baraita'* appears as part of a commentary on *m. Niddah* 3:3–4, which discusses the rabbinic laws of purity in regard to certain kinds of miscarriages. In the midst of exploring these issues, Abaye inquires about the amount of undiluted wine required for a pregnant woman to drink in order to result in a certain type of miscarriage. It is this *halakhic* inquiry that inspires the Talmudic editors to include this *baraita'* (and then, cued by this association, they include also two other *baraitot* about Abba Shaul's experiences as a gravedigger, where, among other things, we learn that "Abba Shaul was the tallest [man] in his generation" [*b. Niddah* 24b]).

CONCLUSION

It should be no surprise that beverages figure widely in rabbinic texts on health and hygiene, since humans deprived of liquid die much more quickly than if starved of food but allowed water. The Rabbis are aware of the importance of proper hydration. Without water, there is no life, hence:

> Water is called life, as it is said: "In that day, water of life shall go forth from Jerusalem..." [Zechariah 14:8]. (*Avot d'Rabbi Natan* A:34; cf. B:43)

From Abaye's mother's medical advice to the lessons imparted by the former gravedigger Abba Shaul, and from drunken brawls to passing bad checks in order to buy wine, we have learned how rabbinic conversations about proper diet intersect with various areas of *halakhah*.

SUGGESTED READINGS

Bamforth, Charles W. 2011. "Foam." In *The Oxford Companion to Beer*, ed. Garrett Oliver, 366–67. New York: Oxford University Press.

Beer, Michael. 2010. *Taste or Taboo: Dietary Choices in Antiquity*. Totnes, Devon, UK: Prospect Books.

Berkowitz, Beth A. 2006. *Execution and Invention: Death Penalty Discourse in Early Rabbinic and Christian Cultures*. New York: Oxford University Press.

Boyarin, Daniel. 1995 [1993]. *Carnal Israel: Reading Sex in Talmudic Culture*. Berkeley: University of California Press.

Brain, Peter. 2009 [1986]. *Galen on Bloodletting: A Study of the Origins, Development and Validity of his Opinions, with a Translation of the Three Works*. New York: Cambridge University Press.

Brumberg-Kraus, Jonathan, and Betsey Dexter Dyer. 2011. "Cultures and Cultures: Fermented Foods as Culinary 'Shibboleths.'" In *Cured, Fermented and Smoked Foods: Proceedings from the Oxford Symposium on Food and Cookery 2010*, ed. Helen Saberi, 56–65. Totnes, Devon, UK: Prospect Books.

Ellenberg, Jordan. 2014. *How Not to Be Wrong: The Power of Mathematical Thinking*. New York: Penguin Press.

Fine, Steven. 2010. "Death, Burial, and Afterlife." In *The Oxford Handbook of Jewish Daily Life in Roman Palestine*, ed. Catherine Hezser, 440–62. New York: Oxford University Press.

Fonrobert, Charlotte Elisheva. 2000. *Menstrual Purity: Rabbinic and Christian Reconstructions of Biblical Gender*. Stanford, CA: Stanford University Press.

Foucault, Michel. 1990 [1985]. *The Use of Pleasure: Volume 2 of The History of Sexuality*. Translated by Robert Hurley. New York. Vintage Books.

Fox, Michael V. 2009. *Proverbs 10–31: A New Translation with Introduction and Commentary*. New Haven, CT: Yale University Press.

Gardner, Gregg E. 2015. *The Origins of Organized Charity in Rabbinic Judaism*. New York: Cambridge University Press.

Garnsey, Peter. 2002 [1999]. *Food and Society in Classical Antiquity*. New York: Cambridge University Press.

Geller, Markham J. 2004. "Diet and Regimen in the Babylonian Talmud." In *Food and Identity in the Ancient World*, ed. Cristiano Grotanelli and Lucio Milano, 217–42. Padua, Italy: S.A.R.G.O.N.

Jaffee, Martin S. 2006 [1997]. *Early Judaism: Religious Worlds of the First Judaic Millennium*. 2nd ed. Bethesda: University Press of Maryland.

Johnston, Ian, and G. H. R. Horsley, eds. and trans. 2011. *Galen: Method of Medicine*. 3 vols. Cambridge, MA: Harvard University Press.

Lieberman, Saul. 1994 [1950]. *Hellenism in Jewish Palestine*. 2nd ed. Reprint. New York: Jewish Theological Seminary of America.

MacDonald, Nathan. 2008. *What Did the Ancient Israelites Eat? Diet in Biblical Times*. Grand Rapids, MI: William B. Eerdmans.

Pomeroy, Sarah B. 1995 [1975]. *Goddesses, Whores, Wives, and Slaves: Women in Classical Antiquity*. New York: Schocken Books.

Preuss, Julius. 2004 [1978]. *Biblical and Talmudic Medicine*. Translated and edited by Fred Rosner. New York: Rowman & Littlefield.

Rogers, Adam. 2014. *Proof: The Science of Booze*. Boston: Houghton Mifflin Harcourt.

Rosenblum, Jordan D. 2016a. "'Blessings of the Breasts': Breastfeeding in Rabbinic Literature." *Hebrew Union College Annual* 87: 147–79.

———. 2016b. *The Jewish Dietary Laws in the Ancient World*. New York: Cambridge University Press.

Salzman, James. 2012. *Drinking Water: A History*. New York: Overlook Duckworth.

Satlow, Michael L. 1996. "'Try to be a Man': The Rabbinic Construction of Masculinity." *Harvard Theological Review* 89, no. 1: 19–40.

———. 2001. *Jewish Marriage in Antiquity*. Princeton, NJ: Princeton University Press.

Schäfer, Peter. 2007. *Jesus in the Talmud*. Princeton, NJ: Princeton University Press.

Schofer, Jonathan Wyn. 2010. *Confronting Vulnerability: The Body and the Divine in Rabbinic Literature*. Chicago: University of Chicago Press.

Smith, Andrew F. 2013. *Drinking History: Fifteen Turning Points in the Making of American Beverages*. New York: Columbia University Press.

Sokoloff, Michael. 2002. *A Dictionary of Jewish Babylonian Aramaic*. Baltimore: Johns Hopkins University Press.

Zellentin, Holger Michael. 2011. *Rabbinic Parodies of Jewish and Christian Literature*. Tübingen: Mohr Siebeck.

Conclusion

In a famous passage, the fifth-century B.C.E. Greek historian Herodotus says of the Persians:

> ... it is their custom to deliberate about the gravest matters when they are drunk; and what they approve in their counsels is proposed to them the next day by the master of the house where they deliberate, when they are now sober and if being sober they still approve it, they act thereon, but if not, they cast it aside. And when they have taken counsel about a matter when sober, they decide upon it when they are drunk. (Godley 1999, 173–75, *Persian Wars* 1.133)

While the Rabbis would disapprove of deliberating weighty matters while intoxicated (as discussed in chapters 2, 6, and 9), they would agree that drinking plays a central role in one's individual, communal, and theological life.

Throughout this book, I have argued that exploration of rabbinic texts about drinks and drinking can serve to introduce key themes in rabbinic literature. Beverages appear everywhere from biblical interpretation to medical opinions. Glasses are raised at weddings, at funerals, at Sabbath feasts, and at everyday meals. Rabbis visit taverns and the homes of colleagues, where ordinary and extraordinary events unfold. Tales are told and people explode. Wine and beer most often fill the rabbinic cup, though other beverages, such as water and milk (from both human and non-human animals), appear as well. I have neither investigated every rabbinic theme nor every aspect of every theme and/or beverage explored herein. My goal has not only been to introduce rabbinic themes, but also to demonstrate the joy encountered in the mental workout of swimming in the sea of Talmud. In short, I aim not only to wet your whistle but also to whet your appetite. As with drinking wine before Passover (see chapter 6), I hope that you are hungry to consume more.

In light of this hope, and in addition to the resources noted in chapter 1 and in the "Suggested Readings" at the end of each chapter, I want to take a moment to recommend that readers who are thirsty for more rabbinic literature should begin by imbibing more rabbinic texts. Knowledge of Hebrew and Aramaic is useful, needless to say, but there are numerous accessible English translations, including the Artscroll, Koren, Soncino, and Steinsaltz editions of the Babylonian Talmud and other rabbinic texts. As a teacher, I often require affordable source books such as Schiffman 1998, Rubenstein 2002, and Solomon 2009. For those who wish to read online, I highly recommend www.sefaria.org, which provides not only English translations and the original Hebrew and/or Aramaic texts of classical rabbinic documents, but a growing collection of source sheets prepared by educators, thus allowing readers to learn a variety of texts, topics, and themes.

At the conclusion of every Babylonian Talmud tractate in the modern standard printed edition, the following formula appears:

> We shall return to you [Name of the Last Chapter]; and Tractate [Name] is concluded.

After completing the study of a tractate, there is a tradition of reciting a ritual liturgy (Aramaic *hadran*; meaning: "We shall return") and then offering a festive meal (known in Hebrew as a *siyum*; meaning: "completion"). As we might expect, after "drink[ing] their words with thirst" (*m. Avot* 1:4), students not only eat, but drink, on these festive occasions.

So I invite my readers to partake of this tradition. Pour yourself a drink and celebrate. But then sober up and return to read once again.

SUGGESTED READINGS

Godley, A. D. 1999 [1920]. *Herodotus: The Persian Wars: Books I–II*. Reprint. Cambridge, MA: Harvard University Press.

Rubenstein, Jeffrey L. 2002. *Rabbinic Stories*. New York: Paulist Press.

Schiffman, Lawrence H. 1998. *Texts and Traditions: A Source Reader for the Study of Second Temple and Rabbinic Judaism*. Hoboken, NJ: Ktav Publishing House.

Solomon, Norman. 2009. *The Talmud: A Selection*. New York: Penguin Books.

GLOSSARY

AGGADAH from the Hebrew verb "to tell." A category of rabbinic texts defined by its interest in narrative. A variety of topics are labeled *aggadah*, from parables to folklore, though they are all assumed to contrast with the legal category of *halakhah*.

'AMIDAH a central component of the daily rabbinic prayer service, this liturgy also is referred to as "The Prayer" (Hebrew *ha-tefillah*).

AMORA/AMORAIM/AMORAIC "Speakers" or "Explainers" in Aramaic. The Amoraim (singular Amora) are the second major group of rabbinic figures, active in both Palestine and Babylonia from the mid-third until roughly the early sixth centuries C.E.

'ANDROGINOS a dual-sexed hermaphrodite. Hebrew, from Greek.

'ARAVAH "willow" in Hebrew; one of the four species used in Sukkot ritual.

'AVODAH ZARAH "foreign worship" in Hebrew, i.e., idolatry.

'AYLONIT Hebrew term for a person identified as "female" at birth who at the onset of puberty develops "male" characteristics and is infertile.

BAR "son" in Aramaic.

BARAITA' "outside" in Aramaic (plural *baraitot*). Refers to a rabbinic tradition reputed to be of tannaitic origin that is cited in an amoraic text. This attribution of earlier authorship may or may not be accurate.

BEYT HA-MIQDASH Hebrew term referring to the Temple. Literally, "The House of Holiness/Sanctification."

BEYT HA-MIDRASH Hebrew term referring to the rabbinic study-house. Literally "The House of Study."

BEN "son" in Hebrew.
BEY "son" in Hebrew.
DARKHEI HA-'EMORI "the ways of the Amorites" in Hebrew. A collection of practices of which some Rabbis disapprove, but for which they have no clear basis in which to ground a prohibition.
'ERUV "mixture" in Hebrew. A rabbinic legal fiction in which multiple domains are "mixed" into a single domain. Since carrying objects from one domain into another is prohibited on the Sabbath, this allows for transporting objects farther on the Sabbath than would otherwise be allowable.
'ETROG "citron" in Hebrew; one of the four species used in Sukkot ritual.
GEMARA' the amoraic commentary on Mishnah; from an Aramaic root meaning both "to complete" and "to learn."
GEMATRIYA' An interpretive activity in which each letter of a word is converted to a number and then the numbers are analyzed for their interpretive value. Based on the rabbinic presumption of divine authorship, *gematriya'* assumes God intended these numbers to be added and interpreted. Hebrew, from Greek.
GER "resident outsider," in Hebrew. The Hebrew Bible devotes significant attention to regulations governing this category.
GEZERAH SHAVAH Hebrew term for analogy, one of the basic rabbinic hermeneutic principles, which allows for the comparison of multiple biblical passages based on shared language, such as word repetition.
HADAS "myrtle" in Hebrew; one of the four species used in Sukkot ritual.
HAGGADAH "Telling" in Hebrew. The *Haggadah* is the ritual recitation of the Passover story, which functions as the central liturgical script for the rabbinic Passover *Seder*.
HALAKHAH normative rabbinic law, from the Hebrew meaning "path" or "way." Also refers to a category of rabbinic texts defined by its attention to legal matters. The adjective is *halakhic*.
ḤALITZAH from the Hebrew word used in Deuteronomy 25:9 for untying a shoe, this refers to the ritual refusal of a woman to partake in Levirate marriage (Hebrew *yibum*) and marry a brother of her deceased husband, with whom she had no children.
ḤAMETZ "leaven" in Hebrew. This category of food can neither be consumed, owned, nor derived benefit from on Passover.
HAVDALAH "separation" or "division" in Hebrew. A rabbinic ritual that serves to distinguish the sacred time of *Shabbat* or a holiday from the secular day that follows.

ḤIDDUSH Hebrew term referring to a unique legal case or legal innovation.

ḤUPPAH "bridal canopy" in Hebrew. Often refers to the rabbinic wedding ceremony.

KASHRUT abstract Hebrew noun of *kasher* ("kosher"), meaning "fit/valid/permissible/suitable," often associated with food. The Rabbis use the term to refer to a variety of contexts in which they assess the validity of a person/object/substance for a given category.

KETIV Aramaic for "that which is written," a rabbinic practice wherein a potentially problematic biblical word or phrase is preserved as written (*ketiv*), but pronounced in a corrected form when read aloud liturgically (*qere*).

KETUBBAH Hebrew term referring to a boilerplate rabbinic marriage contract, which stipulates economic arrangements and other responsibilities of both parties.

KUTI/KUTIM Samaritan/Samaritans in Hebrew. Though Samaritans claimed a shared history with ancient Israelites, they branched off and forged a similar, but distinct, path. For this reason, the Rabbis consider them to be an intermediate group, sometimes included in Us, and other times in Them.

LOG Hebrew for a common rabbinic small measure of liquid volume. A quarter of a *log* of undiluted wine is often deemed equivalent to four cups of diluted wine.

LULAV "date-palm frond" in Hebrew; one of the four species used in Sukkot ritual.

MA'ASEH Hebrew term best translated as "Once upon a time ...," referring to an (often fictional) event in the past that has pedagogical and/or legal implications.

MAKHSHIRIN often translated as "prepared for ritual impurity," this Hebrew term refers to an object that is susceptible to ritual impurity if it comes into contact with a liquid that transmits ritual impurity. More specifically, it refers to the liquids themselves that transmit this ritual impurity.

MAMZER Hebrew term (plural *mamzerim*) for a child conceived as a result of incest or adultery.

MASEKHET "web" in Hebrew (plural *masekhtot*), a tractate of Mishnah or Talmud.

MATZAH "unleavened bread" in Hebrew. The central food consumed on Passover.

MAYIM HA-MARIM "the bitter waters" in Hebrew. The biblical ritual in which a suspected adulteress must submit to an elaborate ritual ordeal, which is understood to "prove" her guilt or innocence.

ME'ILAH Hebrew for theft of sacred property.

MELA'KHOT Hebrew for thirty-nine categories of labor prohibited on the Sabbath.

MIDRASH from a Hebrew root meaning "to investigate," a rabbinic interpretative practice governed by certain rules as to this investigation can occur. *Midrash* can refer to the actual interpretive activity and to collections of these interpretations, so both to the process and the product (i.e., a text).

MINḤAH Hebrew term for the daily afternoon sacrifice during the time of the Temple, which the Rabbis translate into a daily afternoon prayer service.

MIQVEH "ritual bath" in Hebrew (plural *miqva'ot*). Immersion in a *miqveh* is part of the ritual purification process. Especially associated with *niddah* purification ritual and conversion.

MISHTEH "drinking party" in Hebrew. Usually refers to a wedding feast.

MITZVAH "commandment" in Hebrew.

NAZIR Hebrew term for laypersons who vow to abstain from wine (and various associated foodstuffs), refrain from cutting their hair, and not become ritually impure through contact with corpses.

NEVELAH "carrion" in Hebrew. In the Hebrew Bible, an animal that dies a natural death. The Rabbis change the meaning of the term to refer to an improperly slaughtered animal.

NIDDAH "menstruant" in Hebrew, the status of a woman who is menstruating, which has ritual impurity implications.

'OLAM HA-BA' "the world to come" in Hebrew. A future time when the scales of justice will be rebalanced, the wicked will receive their punishment, and the righteous their reward. Unlike *'olam ha-zeh*, the world to come will endure forever.

'OLAM HA-ZEH "this world" in Hebrew. The present reality, ephemeral in contrast to *'olam ha-ba'*.

'ONAH Hebrew term referring to the conjugal rights that a husband owes his wife.

'OVDEY KOKHAVIM "worshippers of the stars" in Hebrew. A common rabbinic term for idolaters.

PARSHAH section of the Hebrew Bible in Hebrew.

PASSOVER one of the three Pilgrimage Festivals, Passover (Hebrew *Pesaḥ*) commemorates the Israelites' Exodus from Egypt.

PIQUAḤ NEFESH "preservation of life" in Hebrew. According to the Rabbis, the preservation of life supersedes any commandment, with only three exceptions: idolatry, forbidden sexual relations, and murder.

QERE "that which is read" in Aramaic. A rabbinic practice in which a potentially problematic biblical word or phrase is preserved as written (*ketiv*), but pronounced in a corrected form when read aloud liturgically (*qere*).

QIDDUSH "declare holy" or "sanctification" in Hebrew. Refers to the blessing over wine before the Friday evening Sabbath meal (and other holidays).

ROSH HASHANAH "head of the year" in Hebrew. The Jewish New Year.

SARIS "eunuch" in Hebrew.

SEDER "Order" in Hebrew. Central rabbinic Passover ritual, which includes recitation of the *Haggadah* and consumption of *matzah* and four cups of wine.

SHABBAT "Sabbath" in Hebrew. The day of rest, lasting from sundown on Friday night until sundown on Saturday night. Work is prohibited and a variety of liturgical and eating and drinking practices are mandated on *Shabbat*.

SHAVUOT "Weeks" in Hebrew. One of the three Pilgrimage Festivals, important for reasons unclear in the Hebrew Bible. Eventually, the Rabbis associated Shavuot with the commemoration of the giving of Torah at Mount Sinai.

SHEMA' "Hear!" in Hebrew, a central rabbinic prayer, recited twice daily. Composed of three scriptural passages (Deuteronomy 6:4–9 and 11:13–21; Numbers 15:37–41).

SHOFAR ram's horn in Hebrew, a trumpet blown in the month leading up to Rosh Hashanah and Yom Kippur, on which holidays the *shofar* is an integral part of the liturgy.

SOTAH "suspected adulteress" in Hebrew. A woman suspected of committing adultery, but with no substantiating proof, can be forced by her husband to undergo the bitter waters test (Hebrew *mayim ha-marim*).

SUGYA' Aramaic term referring to a textual unit in the Talmud (plural *sugyot*).

SUKKOT "Booths" in Hebrew. One of the three Pilgrimage Festivals, Sukkot commemorates the conclusion of the yearly harvest season.

TAMḤUI communal soup kitchen in Hebrew.

TANNA/TANNAIM/TANNAITIC "Repeaters" or "Teachers" in Aramaic. The Tannaim (singular Tanna) were the first major group of Rabbis active from ca. 70 C.E. until the middle of the third century C.E.

TEFILLIN Hebrew term often translated as "phylacteries." *Tefillin* are leather boxes containing certain biblical verses that are worn on the head and arm by men (and, in modernity, by women in some communities) during morning prayer services (though not on *Shabbat*). In the early rabbinic period, *tefillin* were worn by some Rabbis throughout the day.

TEREFAH "torn" in Hebrew. Refers in the Hebrew Bible to an animal killed by another animal. The Rabbis change the meaning of the term to refer to a properly slaughtered animal that is then rendered invalid for consumption for another reason.

TORAH SH-BE'AL PEH "Oral Torah" in Hebrew. Part of the Rabbis' dual conception of Torah, Oral Torah encompasses the rabbinic traditions that are perceived to be part of the ongoing process of divine revelation.

TORAH SH-BIKHTAV "Written Torah" in Hebrew. Part of the Rabbis' dual conception of Torah, Written Torah refers to the Hebrew Bible and the foundational role it plays in justifying rabbinic tradition of commentary, interpretation, and expansion.

TUMTUM refers in Hebrew to a person not yet assigned a binary sex status.

YAYIN MEVUSHAL "cooked wine" in Hebrew. Libated wine (Hebrew *yayn nesekh*) is forbidden, but rabbinic tradition holds that, once cooked, wine cannot be used by pagans for the purposes of libation. Hence, this category of wine is permissible for use by rabbinic Jews.

YAYN NESEKH "libated wine" in Hebrew. Wine is the only beverage suitable for pouring out in libation to a deity/deities, so the Rabbis express extensive concern that they not imbibe or interact with "libated wine."

YIBUM "Levirate marriage" in Hebrew (plural *yevamot*). According to the Hebrew Bible, a man is obligated to marry the widow of his deceased brother's childless widow.

YOM KIPPUR "The Day of Atonement" in Hebrew. A day of introspection, repentance, and fasting.

ZAV in Hebrew, a person afflicted with genital discharge (plural *zavim*). According to the Hebrew Bible, a person in this status both has and transmits ritual impurity.

ZONAH "whore," in Hebrew. Gendered as female, this term refers to a body that is physically transgressive of rabbinic sexual norms, and/or, in a metaphorical manner, to bodies that are transgressive of rabbinic theological norms. Starting in the Hebrew Bible, it also refers to Israel, gendered as female, violating its theologically monogamous relationship with God.

SUBJECT INDEX

Abaye: avoidance of pairs, 144; on beverage foam, 258–59; mother's medical advice, 125, 250, 269; on rabbinic authority, 197; Rava's arguments with, 197
Abbahu, Rabbi, 59, 60; bright face of, 63
Abraham (patriarch): smashing of idols, 60; weaning party of, 57–58
Adam, Eve's seduction of, 47
adultery: association with wine, 43–47, 55, 106; bitter waters ritual for, 110, 111–16; fools' insults concerning, 50; husbands', 111; oaths on, 112; polluting of Temple, 113, 114; punishment for, 114–15; rabbinic definition of, 111; wives', 105, 110–16. See also *sotah* (suspected adulteress)
agriculture, tractates on, 30
Aha bar Adda, Rav: on Gentile bread, 239, 240
Ahai, Rav: on non-Jewish beer, 75
alcohol: abstention from, 43–46, 260; effect on intentionality, 204; gendered assumptions concerning, 66; mixtures of, 260–62; Passover *Seder* and, 183–87; in rabbinic literature, 66–67; role in social boundaries, 66–93. *See also* beer; drinking; drunkenness; wine
Alexander, Elizabeth Shanks, 98, 126
Alexander the Great, 15
Ameimar: blessing with beer, 163, 164–65; conversation with sorceress, 144
Ami, Rabbi: on drinking, 52
'Amidah (daily prayer): conditions for reciting, 206; for rain, 151
'amora (Rabbi's aide), 175
Amoraim (Speakers), 21; *baraitot* of, 92; on beer drinking, 256
Amorites (Canaanites), 155
Amorites, ways of, 137; *Bavli* on, 156–57; charms in, 155; as forbidden category, 156; gender-balanced, 154; illicit religious practice in, 155; magic in, 155, 156; practices constituting, 154; symbolic inversion in, 153–58; toasts in, 156–59; use in prohibiting practices, 158
amulets, protection against delirium tremens, 248, 249
animal slaughter, non-Temple, 30
Aqiva, Rabbi: on fowl, 83–84; toast of, 157

Arabs, as practitioners of magic, 140–41
Aramaic language: gendered words of, 6–7; in Hebrew Bible, 10
'arayot (forbidden sexual relations), 51, 52; qere and ketiv of, 55
Ashi, Rav, 174–75
'askerah, caused by night drinking, 246
Assi, Rabbi: on drinking, 52
Ava, Rav, 174–75
Avodah Zarah (tractate): cultural influences on, 30; on idolaters' weddings, 73; social surveillance in, 69–70; wine in, 68–70. See also idolatry
'aylonit (gender category), 123; Levirate marriage and, 124

Ba'al Pe'or, 72; Israelites' worship of, 71
Babylonia: beer drinking in, 72, 73, 74, 99, 180, 268; rabbinic learning center in, 20. See also Bavli (Babylonian Talmud)
baptism, Christian, 217
baraitot (tannaitic traditions), 92; on bad breath, 245, 246; on blessing, 195, 196; on bones, 267–68; on brewing beer, 180–81, 182; on cooked wine, 133; on creatures in water, 222–23, 225; on excrement, 256; on fatty meat, 258; on food health effects, 256–58; on mourning, 213; on pairs of actions, 142; on vegetables, 257; on water drinking, 245–46; on wine, 105–6; on women's wine drinking, 264
Bar Kokhba revolt, rabbinic movement and, 19
Bavli (Babylonian Talmud): age of, 30; on betrothal, 211; commentaries on, 30–31; comparison with Yerushalmi, 30; cultural environment of, 31; on delirium tremens, 248; demons in, 141; English language editions of, 274; on idolaters' weddings, 73–74;

kosher milk in, 77; legal argumentation in, 31; micro/macro levels of, 31; on omission of prayer, 209; on Purim drinking, 188; on ritual error, 200; on straining beer, 220; structure of, 31; on subterfuge, 179; sugyot from, 31; water spirits in, 146; on ways of the Amorites, 156–57; wine drinking in, 61–62. See also Talmud
beauty, gendered concept of, 100
beer: in Babylonia, 72, 73, 74, 99, 180, 268; Babylonian Rabbis' love of, 72, 220; blessing of, 72; brewed from barley, 181; brewed from dates, 181; brewing on Intermediate Festival Days, 180–81, 182; bugs in, 220–22, 225, 242; causing body hair, 255; cost of, 259; diluted, 125; drinking with non-Jews, 73–75; in embryonic development, 124, 125; flavor profiles of, 229; foam on top of, 258–59; gendered assumptions about, 98; impure creatures in, 220–22, 228–31, 242; incorrect blessing for, 201, 203; leading to intermarriage, 74, 75; libation prohibition and, 74–75; mice falling in, 228–31, 242; non-Jews', 75, 93; qiddush using, 165–66; recitation of havdalah using, 163–65, 166; relief for the dying, 266; Sabbath liturgy and, 161–66; side effects of, 255; socioeconomic status of, 72–75, 257; spoilage of, 257; strained, 220–22
Belser, Julia Watts, 153; on Bavli, 31
Ben Azzai, on teaching Torah to daughters, 114
Ben Bag Bag, 37
Berakhot (Seder), 22, 27
Berekiah, Rabbi, 59
Berkowitz, Beth: on Amorites, 156
bestiality, non-Jews', 77, 106
betrothal (qiddushin): conditional, 211; rabbinic examination of, 211–12

beverages, 3; aid to social digestion, 93; in daily life, 192; dangers of, 75–76, 254; in dietary regimes, 244–69; on Festival Days, 173, 175–76; incorrect blessings for, 201–3; as internal/external Other boundary, 93; licit/illicit practices concerning, 131, 158–59; meaning conveyed through, 219; as metaphor for women/sex, 126; *midrash* concerning, 37; rabbinic exegesis of, 37; on Sabbath, 162; uncovered, 75–76; use in put-downs, 93. *See also* beer; drinking; water; wine
Bibi, Rav, 76; drinking habits of, 254, 255; use of lime, 254–55
Bible. *See* Hebrew Bible; Torah
Bible, King James, 79
Bible code (numerology), 263
bitter waters *(mayim ha-marim)*, 98; preparation of, 112–13; result of drinking, 112, 113, 114
bitter waters ritual, 110, 111–16; gender asymmetry in, 113; wives' oaths in, 112
The Black Eyed Peas, "I Gotta Feeling," 245
blessings: alterations to, 202; "Amen" response to, 91–93; of beer, 72; of bread, 194; of breasts, 56; desacralization of food, 194, 196; everyday, 192–93; familiarity with, 193; *halakhah* of, 196; incorrect, 201–3; of meat, 195; non-Jews' response to, 91–93; over food, 193–95; over wine, 90–91, 194–95, 198, 218, 219; rabbinic authority through, 197; retroactive, 200; using beer, 163–66. See also *havdalah*; *qiddush*
blood, ritual purity concerning, 235. *See also* menstrual blood
bloodletting, 250–54; during childbirth, 251; deception following, 252–54; for fever, 250; meals following, 252–53; replacing nutrients following, 251–52; Talmud on, 251; wine following, 250–53
bodies, Israelite: absorption of Torah, 40
body, distribution of intelligence in, 262, 263–64
body, female: sexual transgressions of, 45, 117, 120–22; uncontrolled, 110, 237
bones: *baraita'* on, 267–68; effect of wine on, 267–68
Bourdieu, Pierre: on misrecognition, 70
bowls, Aramaic: spells on, 141–42
boys, Jewish: associating with Gentile boys, 241
bread: black versus white, 256–57; blessing of, 194; eaten with water, 245–46; Gentile, 239–40; health effects of, 256–57; in Mediterranean Triad, 68, 195; Roman consumption of, 256–57; Samaritan, 90; sustenance through, 197, 198–99
breastfeeding: compulsory, 108–9; as contract labor, 108; as divine miracle, 56–60; duration of, 236; embodiment of motherhood, 58; following divorce, 107–9; husbands' support for, 4; male, 58–60; modern conceptions of, 107; by non-Jewish women, 170; obligations concerning, 107–10; rabbinic texts on, 107–10; restrictions on, 77; Sabbath practice of, 170–71, 190; Sarah's, 57–58
breast milk: expressed into *shofar*, 168–69, 170; gendered assumptions about, 98, 104, 107; lack of, 137; male, 58–60, 109–10; production of, 257; release of, 110; ritual purity concerns of, 77, 110, 235–37, 242; as social boundary, 76–78; transformation from menstrual blood, 109, 235, 236–37
breasts, blessings of, 56
brides, lying to, 253

bugs: in beer, 220–22, 225, 242; creeping upon the earth, 220, 221, 223; pure and impure, 220–25; in water, 222, 223

calendar, rabbinic: symbolic significance in, 161
carrion *(nevelah)*, 147, 148; in Hebrew Bible, 84; prohibitions on, 84–85; rabbinic law on, 83
Chabon, Michael: *The Yiddish Policemen's Union*, 168
charms, in ways of the Amorites, 155
cheese: abstention from, 80; consumption of, 80–81; eaten with fowl, 82–83, 86–87, 88
childbirth: *halakhah* on, 251; as illness, 251
childrearing, restrictions on Jewish women, 78
children, Festival treats for, 174
children, Gentile: impurity of, 239, 241
Chronicles, history of Israel in, 14
Cohen, Leonard: "Who by Fire," 148
commandments, negative, 79, 80, 82; on fowl, 84
consolation, rituals of, 214
convivia, wine at, 67
cooking: mistakes, 226; pure and impure mixtures in, 226
corpses, ritual impurity of, 238
Cyrus, King, 14

daily life, *halakhah* on, 192, 197
The Daily Show (2011), *Eruvin* on, 168
dark arts, defense against, 139–41
date palms, in Sukkot liturgy, 181–82
Dead Sea Scrolls, Second Temple in, 15
decorum: gendered advice about, 98; performative, 98–99
dehydration, death from, 269
delirium tremens: in alcohol withdrawal, 248; remedies for, 248, 249

demons: in *Bavli*, 141; exploding, 146; knowledge from, 144; licit knowledge of, 145; rabbinic protection from, 142; Rabbis' belief in, 146; techniques for combatting, 145–46. *See also* spirits
Deuteronomy: on adultery, 111; beverage prohibitions in, 79, 83; on carrion, 83, 84; on food, 99, 220; on idols, 135; on oaths, 112; on pork, 62; rain in, 40; on Sabbath observation, 162, 167; on tithes, 266; on widows, 123
diarrhea, women's avoidance of, 101
dining: classical, 218; sexualized postures for, 117. *See also* eating; meals
disorientation, prayer during, 205–7
divorce, breastfeeding obligations following, 107–9
drinking: of bodily fluids, 235–37; categorization of, 80; in communal life, 273; cultural assumptions concerning, 66; danger of pairs in, 141–46; at Festival meals, 175; following study of tractate, 274; as *imitatio dei*, 265; incorrect blessing for, 201–3; during Intermediate Festival Days, 179, 180; licit/illicit practices concerning, 131; medical side effects of, 254–60; mixed, 260–62; moderation in, 189, 266; mourning and, 212–14; before Passover, 185–86, 197, 198, 274; pauses in, 144; Persians' habits in, 273; from pipes, 137–38; prayer missed due to, 207–10; regulation of, 4; reinforcement of rabbinic belief, 193; ritual blessings for, 161–62; ritual celebration of, 4; seasonal, 66; self-restraint in, 260–67; in theological life, 273; thumb-holding technique for, 145; of unblessed beverages, 201; at wedding feasts, 208–10; with witches, 138; before

Yom Kippur, 147–49. *See also* alcohol; beer; water; wine drinking
drinking vessels, interior versus exterior of, 222
drunkenness: actions committed during, 204; amount of wine for, 263–64; definition of, 204–5; folly of, 51–52; loss of self-control in, 140; memory loss in, 265, 266; midrashic puns concerning, 52; multiple interpretations of, 51–53; Persian, 273; prayer during, 203–5, 214; Proverbs on, 14; at Purim, 187–89; pushing people in rivers during, 231–35; rabbinic attitudes to, 2; reasons for, 66; on the Sabbath, 162–63, of wives, 106. *See also* alcohol

eating: categorization of, 80; following study of tractate, 274; gendered advice on, 101; prior to *havdalah*, 164, 165; rabbinic practices of, 218; ritual blessings for, 161–62; while reclining, 184, 185. *See also* food; meals
Ecclesiastes: canonical status of, 48; reading of, 14
Elazar ben Durdya, 164
Elazar bey Rabbi Zadoq, Rabbi, 154
Eliezer, Rabbi: on breastfeeding, 236; on diluted wine, 218, 219; on Sabbath wine, 178; on teaching daughters Torah, 114, 115; on wine for wives, 104–6
Elijah, coming of, 199
elimination, bodily: gendered advice on, 101–2
embryonic development, in rabbinic literature, 125
'eruv ("mixture"), in Sabbath prohibitions, 168. *See also* mixtures
Eruvin (tractate), 168
Esther, book of: in Purim celebration, 187

Eve: gaze of, 46; mixing of Adam's wine, 45–47; seduction of Adam, 47
Evil Eye, warding off, 145
excrement: *baraita'* on, 256; in rabbinic literature, 249
Exodus: cultic offerings in, 12; laws of, 12; Moses narrative of, 12–13; need for water in, 39; promised land in, 12–13; Tannaitic Midrashim on, 28

Family and Medical Leave Act (FMLA), 251
feet, washing of, 217
fennel, for fever, 251
Festival Days: beverages on, 173, 175–76; commandments on, 5; drinking at meals, 175; food on, 173; *halakhah* concerning, 179–83, 190; versus holidays, 161; Pilgrimage, 173; Rabbis' drinking on, 175; rules for, 25, 161, 173; versus Sabbath, 173; strained wine on, 178–80; subterfuge on, 179–80, 182; wine on, 68, 174
Festival Days, Intermediate, 177–83; beer brewing on, 180–81, 182; drinking during, 179, 180; *halakhah* on, 179–83; rules for, 177; straining wine on, 182
fever: Abaye's mother on, 250; bloodletting for, 250; treatments for, 250–51
Five Scrolls *(megillot)*, 14, 29
flatulence, women's avoidance of, 101
foam (on beverages): dissipation of, 259; health effects of, 258–60
food: blessings over, 193–95; desacralization of, 194, 196; on Festival Days, 173; health effects of, 256–58; licit practices for, 147–49; in rabbinic identity, 147; ratio of wine to, 268; ritual impurity of, 226–27, 242; wine drinking with, 186, 268. *See also* bread; eating; fowl; meals

food, impure: one-sixtieth principle of, 226, 231, 242; taste principle of, 226–27
fools, on Torah, 49
fools, non-Torah-talking, 49–51; spontaneous combustion of, 50–51
fowl: eaten with cheese, 82–83, 86–87, 88; eaten with dairy, 82–85; negative commandments on, 84; rabbinic disagreements about, 83, 85–86; social fractures and, 82–86; taxonomic classification of, 82–83
fowl's head *(resha')*, cooked in milk, 85
Fox, Michael, 262
friends *(ḥaverim)*, at meals, 89
fringes *(tzitzit)*, on garments, 116

Gamaliel, Rabban (patriarch): genealogical line of, 17, 19; on missed prayer, 208, 209; sons' drinking party, 2, 28, 208, 209
Garden of Eden, wine in, 45–47
gaze, rabbinic, 46
gemara' (amoraic commentary), 29
gematriya' (numerology), 263–64; concerning judges, 265
gender, 4; in Aramaic, 6–7; in assumptions about breast milk, 98, 104, 107; in assumptions about virtue, 260; binary, 122–23, 125; and breastfeeding obligations, 107–10; in covenantal community, 98; cultural constructions of, 96, 126; decorum in, 98; in organization of Jewish society, 122; presumptions concerning Other, 119; rabbinic attitudes on, 2, 6–7, 96–127; rabbinic categories of, 122–25; in ritual purity, 237, 242; social dichotomy in, 86; in Torah study, 97
gender asymmetry, 2, 100; in bitter waters ritual, 113; concerning breast milk, 107; in magic, 119–22, 141; in marriage, 103–4; in wine drinking, 116–19, 174

Genesis: canonical status of, 48; family dramas in, 11–12
Genesis Rabbah, 29
God: authorship of Leviticus, 224; authorship of Torah, 36, 37, 41–43, 46, 48, 63, 266; blessings bestowed by, 56; editorship of Torah, 41–47, 48, 63; justice of, 19; as source of life, 56; transmission of wisdom, 36. *See also* intentionality, divine
Grace after Meals, 142; following bread consumption, 199; following wine consumption, 199; during mourning, 213; at Passover *Seder*, 186
grammatical errors, divine intentionality of, 54–55
Great Assembly, transmission of wisdom to, 36
Greek language, in Hebrew Bible, 10
guests *('akhsena'in)*, at meals, 89

Haggadah, at Passover *Seder*, 183
halakhah (rabbinic law): *aggadah* and, 22–23; applicable principles in, 231; of blessings, 196; on bodily functions, 102; on childbirth, 251; concerning Festival Days, 179–83, 190; concerns Festival Day cooking, 175; on daily life, 192, 197, 214; on delirium tremens, 248–49; expansive nature of, 25; on fowl and cheese, 83; gender categories of, 122–25; implication for rabbinic stories, 208; on Intermediate Festival Days, 179–83; on male breast milk, 109–10; medical definitions in, 248; on menstruating women, 86–87; *midrash* and, 60; misrecognition of non-Jewish practice, 70; narratives of, 23; on prayer during disorientation, 205–7; on prohibited substances, 230; related to *makhshirin*, 233; on the Sabbath, 173, 251; Sabbath versus Festival, 173; specific and general, 2;

on straining alcohol, 220–21; subterfuge in following, 179–80, 182–83, 253; tort law, 25; unique cases (*ḥiddush*) in, 229–30. *See also* rabbinic literature
Hama, Rav: on betrothal, 211–12
Haman (book of Esther), 187
handwashing: purity and, 217; wine and, 217–18, 219
Hanin, Rabbi, on benefits of wine, 265
Hanina, Rabbi, 7; on drawing water, 172; on licit food practice, 147; on wine drinking, 264
Hanin bar Ammi, Rav, 87, 89
Hanin bar Pappa, Rabbi: on blessedness of wine, 265
Hanukkah, 15; *halakhic* discussion of, 24
Ha-Shem (title for God): non-Jews' use of, 91–93; Samaritans' invoking of, 92–93
Hasmonean dynasty, appeal to Rome, 15
havdalah (Sabbath blessing), 150, 152; eating prior to, 164, 165; rabbinic creation of, 153; using beer, 163–65, 166; using wine, 164. *See also* blessings
health: divine will in, 244–45; drinking to, 245–47; in rabbinic literature, 244–69. *See also* medicine
Hebrew Bible: Aramaic passages in, 10; carrion in, 84; on consumption of sea creatures, 220, 223; Creation stories of, 11; divine editorship of, 41–47, 48, 63; family dramas in, 11–12; Greek passages of, 10; historical problems of, 11; interpretations of, 11, 36–63; languages of, 10; Latin passages of, 10; memorization of, 59, 143, 223; misspelling in, 37; multiple interpretations of, 51–53; mythic history of, 11–12; negative commandments of, 79, 80, 82, 84; *niddah*-related prohibitions in, 87–88; nomenclature of, 10; noncanonical books of, 48; normative/authoritative edition of, 48; number patterns in, 263; opportunities for interpretation, 11; rabbinic authors' perception of, 11; on Sabbath, 162, 167; sacrifice in, 9; as scholarly designation, 11; structural elements of, 9; thematic elements of, 9. *See also* Torah, Written
Hebrew language: gendered words of, 6–7; singular/plural interpretations of, 57
Hellenism, in Jewish communities, 15
hermaphrodites: in rabbinic literature, 122; sex with, 123
Herodotus, on Persian drinking, 273
Hidary, Richard, 85–86
Hillel, on witchcraft, 119
Hillel, House of, 239; on fowl and cheese, 82–83, 87; on handwashing, 217
Hisda, Rav: advice to daughters, 98–103; on bread and water, 245, 246; on creatures in liquids, 222, 224; on garlic eating, 200–201; on *qiddush*, 165; sons of, 163–64; on straining of water, 225
Hiyya, Rabbi, 50, 51; use of *gematriya'*, 263, 265; on wine drinking, 264–65
holidays: commandments on, 5; versus Festival Days, 161; midrashic sermons for, 29; rules for, 161
Homiletic Midrashim, 29
Honi the Circle-Maker (rainmaker), 150
Hosea, on unfaithful wives, 105
Hullin (tractate), 30
human combustion: as divine retribution, 51; following wine drinking, 47–51
Huna, Rav: on *qiddush* over beer, 166; on ritual errors, 200; on straining beer, 220–21, 224–25

husbands, Jewish: adultery by, 111; living apart from wives, 104–5; obligations towards wives, 103–6
hydration, importance of, 269

idolaters, restrictions on midwives for, 78. *See also* non-Jews; Others, external
idolatry *('avodah zarah)*, 4; inversion of rabbinic ritual, 134; perceived, 135–38; as requiring action, 133; stoning for, 135, 137, 138; as symbolic inversion, 131–32; water from temples of, 135–38
idols: ambiguous actions involving, 134–38; bowing to, 135–36; kissing, 134, 135, 136
Ila, Rabbi: on cooked wine, 133
Ilai, Rabbi: on character judgment, 265
Ilfa (rainmaker), 150; prayers of, 151; and Rabbi Yohanan, 152; virtuous actions of, 152
Ilfai, Rabbi, 151
Immi, Rabbi, 76
infants: obligation to feed, 107–10; recognition of mothers, 108
intelligence: distribution in body, 262, 263–64; effect of wine drinking on, 260–67; for Torah study, 263
intentionality, divine: concerning misspellings, 54–55; effect of alcohol on, 204; of grammatical errors, 54–55; recovery through *midrash*, 43; of Torah, 36, 43, 47, 53–54, 57, 224, 266
intentionality, in ritual impurity, 233–35, 242
intoxication. *See* alcohol; drunkenness
inversion, symbolic, 130; idolatry as, 131–32; magic as, 139–40; non-Jewish action as, 134; of Others' wine, 134; in ways of the Amorites, 153–58
Isaiah: on disorientation, 206; Greek/Hebrew differences in, 10

Israel: fall to Assyrians, 13; following destruction of Temple, 17; ritual failings of, 13; Roman rule over, 15; unfaithful wives metaphor for, 105
Israelites: liberation from slavery, 184; as opposite of non-Jews, 79; wandering in desert, 39–40; whoring with Moabites, 71; worship of Ba'al Pe'or, 71

Jaffee, Martin, 244
jealousy, law of, 113
Jerusalem, laments for, 13
jewelry, wives' desire for, 104, 105
Jews: drinking with non-Jews, 69–71; eating with non-Jews, 134; in idolatrous society, 133–34; at non-Jewish weddings, 73–74; sexual intercourse with Gentiles, 240. *See also* husbands, Jewish; men, Jewish; wives, Jewish; women, Jewish
Jews, non-rabbinic: combatting of demons, 146; eating with rabbinic Jews, 82; as Internal Others, 79; meat-milk interactions of, 81–82
Jews, pre-rabbinic: understanding of meat-milk prohibition, 81
Job (patriarch), nurturing of orphans, 58, 59
Joseph (patriarch), nurturing of family, 58, 59
Joshua, transmission of wisdom to, 36
journeys, prayer following, 206–7
Judah, fall to Babylon, 13
Judah, Rabbi: on wine consumption, 174
Judaism, ancient: history of, 9–16
judges: *gematriya'* concerning, 265; on Sanhedrin, 265; wine permitted for, 262, 264
justice, divine: for destruction of Temple, 19; in This World, 19

Kahana, Rav, 97
ketiv (that which is written), 54–56

ketubbot (marriage contracts), 103–4, 210
Ketuvim (Writings), 11; genres of, 13–14
kidneys, intelligence in, 263–64
knowledge: from demons, 144; limits of, 46; of magic, 145; manna symbolizing, 39; transformative, 196, 244
kohanim (Temple priests), wine permitted for, 264
kosher: certification of industrial food, 149; fraud concerning, 147–49
Kraemer, David, 81; on venomous other, 75–76

Lamentations, reading of, 14
Latin language, in Hebrew Bible, 10
Latin literature, gendered assumptions in, 106
law. *See halakhah* (rabbinic law)
"L'Chaim!" (toast), 245
leeches, swallowing of, 137, 138, 172, 190
legal pluralism, 51; multiple normative views of, 86
Leviticus: on adultery, 111; divine authorship of, 224; on drunkenness, 234; on food, 220, 221, 222, 223, 228; on impure creatures, 221, 223; on intoxication, 54; on locusts, 80; Midrash on, 28; on *niddah*, 88; on pork, 62; on Rosh Hashanah, 169; on sexual intercourse, 45; on Sukkot, 181; on usury, 62
libations: idolatrous, 72, 73; at Jerusalem Temple, 68; by non-Jews, 69; to pagan deities, 132; as symbolic inversions, 131–34. *See also* wine, libated
lime: as cosmetic, 254–55; death from, 255
Lincoln, Bruce: on symbolic inversion, 131
liquids: ritual purity of, 220, 242; in ritual washing, 216–17; sustaining, 40; tranmission of ritual impurity, 232, 238. *See also* drinking; water

locusts, cooked in milk, 80

Ma'aser Sheni (tractate), on Second Tithes, 266
Maccabees, revolt of, 15
magic, 4; amulets, 248, 249; Arabs as practitioners of, 140–41; effectiveness of, 141; gender asymmetry in, 119–22, 141; gendered assumptions about, 98; as illicit religious practice, 138–41; of illusion, 139, 141; licit control of, 141; licit knowledge of, 145; Rabbis' defense against, 139, 141; versus religion, 139; spells, 141–42; susceptibility of pairs to, 141–46; as symbolic inversion, 139–40; techniques for combatting, 145–46; in ways of the Amorites, 155, 156; women and, 154–55
makhshirin (susceptibility to impurity), 232; laws related to, 233
Makhshirin (tractate), 232–33, 234
mamzerim (bastards), marital restrictions on, 50
Mana, Rabbi, 212
manna, symbolizing of knowledge, 39
marriage, Levirate: gendered concept of, 125; ritual refusal of, 123–24
marriage, rabbinic: rituals of, 211
Masada, 15
matzah, at Passover *Seder*, 185, 198
McHugh, Susan: *Dog*, 3
meals: food/wine ratio in, 268; grace after, 91; guests and friends at, 89; learning following, 247; post-bloodletting, 252–53; wine required for, 253. *See also* eating; food
meat: blessing of, 195; categorization of, 81; cooking with milk, 79–85; fatty, 258
medicine: *halakhah* on, 248; rabbinic ethics of, 244; rabbinic wisdom on, 250. *See also* health

Mediterranean diet: staples of, 240; Triad (wine, bread, olive oil), 68, 195
Megillah, recitation of, 187–88
Megillah (tractate), 188
Me'ilah (tractate), 196
Meir, Rabbi: on women/food association, 126
Mekhilta d'Rabbi Ishmael, 28
Mekhilta d'Rabbi Shimon bar Yoshai, 28
memorization: of Hebrew Bible, 59, 143, 223; of rabbinic literature, 204–5
men, Jewish: as consumers, 126–27; controllable bodies of, 110; effeminate, 120–21, 140; ritual purity status of, 87; social dichotomy from women, 86
menstrual blood, transformation into breast milk, 109, 235, 236–37
menstruation: cheese/milk prohibitions and, 86–90; marital separation during, 86–90; *miqva'ot* following, 88; taboos of, 87; two minds in, 87, 88–89. See also *niddah*
mice: falling into beer, 228–31, 242; falling into vinegar, 231; field versus city, 230; impurity of, 228, 230; taste of, 229–31
midrash (interpretive practice), 23–24; alternative interpretations in, 43–44; analysis of God's commandments, 60; concerning beverages, 37; puns in, 52; recovery of divine intention, 43; on Sarah, 56–57
midwives, non-Jewish, 77–78
milk: abstention from, 80; categorization of, 81; cooking meat with, 79–85; cooking with, 79–82; fowl and, 83–86; kosher status of, 76–77; preparation of, 76; regulations concerning, 79–82. See also breast milk
milk, goats': cooking kids in, 79, 82, 83, 84
milking, by non-Jews, 77

minhah (afternoon sacrifice/prayer service), food consumption following, 184
miqva'ot (ritual baths), 217; following menstruation, 88
miscarriages, laws of purity concerning, 268
Mishnah: citation of biblical texts, 80; on fowl and cheese, 83; Levirate marriage in, 123; on missed prayers, 207–8; Orders of, 26–27; rabbinic authority in, 176–77; relationship to Tosefta, 27–28; Yehudah ha-Nasi's redaction of, 20, 26
mishteh gadol (drinking party), 157; Abraham's, 57–58
misspellings, divine intentionality concerning, 54–55
mixtures: of alcohol, 260–62; libated and non-libated, 227–28, 229; like with unlike, 227–28; prohibited, 86, 88, 90, 226–27; taste in, 226–30
moderation: in drinking, 189, 266; in Mediterranean culture, 260
modesty, rabbinic advice on, 100–101
Mo'ed Qatan (tractate), 177
monogamy, as metaphor for monotheism, 71
Mordecai, midrash on breastfeeding, 58–60
Moses: discourse of rain, 40–41; Exodus narrative of, 12–13; Israelites' rebellion against, 39; as rabbinic figure, 23; revelation of Torah to, 21, 22, 25, 36, 41–42, 173
mourning: drinking and, 212–14; Grace after Meals during, 213; rituals governing, 212; wine as comfort for, 265, 266

Nahman, Rav: on Passover, 142, 143
Nahman bar Yitzhak, Rav, 197; on bloodletting, 252–53; on Gentile children, 239, 240

nazir, abstention from wine, 43–45, 260
Nelson, Willie, 66
Nevi'im (Prophets), 11; narratives of, 13
niddah (menstruating woman): knowledge of husband, 87; rabbinic law on, 86–87; ritual purity rules for, 87–88, 109; temporary status of, 88. *See also* menstruation
Noah (patriarch), nurturing of ark, 58, 59
non-Jews: around cooked wine, 70; beer drinking with, 73–75; beer of, 93; bestiality of, 77, 106; as compulsive libationers, 69, 118, 132, 238; drinking with Jews, 69–71; eating with Jews, 134; libations by, 69; milking by, 77; as opposites of Israelites, 79; response to blessings, 91–93; sexual intercourse with Jews, 240; snake metaphor for, 75–76; wine drinking with, 67, 132; wine regulations concerning, 68–72, 75. *See also* idolaters; Others, external
Numbers: on adultery, 110–13; on intimacy with Moabites, 71; wine/adultery connection in, 43–45
Numbers Rabbah, 32; on abstention from wine, 45–46

oaths, violation of, 112
olive oil: Gentile, 239, 240; in Mediterranean diet, 240
Orange Garden fountain (Aventine Hill, Rome), 136, 137 *fig.*
Orders (*Sedarim*, of Mishnah), 26–27; names of, 27; tractates *(masekhtot)* of, 27
Others: beverages as boundary for, 93; illicit wine practices of, 132; presumptions about gender in, 119; in regulation of wine, 68–72; Self and, 66; separation from, 4; venomous, 75–76
Others, external, 78–79; gender in, 86. *See also* idolaters; non-Jews
Others, internal, 67; Jew-*ish*, 90–93; Samaritans, 90–93; social boundaries with, 78–82

pairs, susceptibility to magic, 141–46
Palestine, Roman: bread consumption in, 256–57; social environment of, 67
Palestine, Syrian: rabbinic learning center in, 20
Pappa, Rav, 175; on beer drinking, 75, 98; on drinking in pairs, 144; on drinking with idolaters, 74
Passover, 173; barley on, 181; date beer during, 181; drinking after, 186; drinking before, 185–86, 197, 198, 274; food consumption during, 184; guarding of Israelites during, 143; non-Festival days of, 177; reversal of fortune in, 184
Passover *Seder*: alcohol and, 183–87; culinary history of, 183; food at, 185; Grace after Meals at, 186; *Haggadah* at, 183; liturgy of, 183; *matzah* at, 185, 198; performative ritual of, 264; post-meal liturgy, 185; reclining during, 184, 185
Passover wine, 61, 68, 142–43, 183–87; from communal soup kitchen, 184; cooked, 133; drinking between cups, 185–87; four cups of, 183, 184–85, 187, 213, 264; preparation of, 185
Patriarch, office of, 17
patriarchate, in Yavneh Legend, 19
Persians, drinking habits of, 273
Persius, on Sabbath wine, 163
Pesiqta d'Rav Kahana (*midrashic* sermon), 29
Pesiqta Rabbati (*midrashic* sermon), 29
Pharisees, rabbinic movement and, 18

Philo of Alexandria, on cooking with milk, 79, 81
Pilgrimage Festivals, 173
pipes, danger of drinking from, 137–38
pleurisy, cause of, 259
Plutarch, on Sabbath wine, 163
pomegranates, use as subterfuge, 179–80, 182
pork, forbidding of, 62
poverty, cause of, 258–59
prayer: commandments on, 5; concentration during, 206; daily, 206; during disorientation, 205–7; during drunkenness, 203–5, 214; following journeys, 206–7; missed due to drinking, 207–10; neutralizing evil spirits, 141; for rain, 151, 152, 153; in weakened state, 207; while disoriented, 205–7
Promised Land: conquest of, 13; return to, 14
Proverbs: canonical status of, 48–49; on intoxication, 14; on limits of knowledge, 46; mixed wine in, 261–62; *qere* and *ketiv*, 54–55
Psalms, wine drinking in, 67
puns, *midrashic* practice of, 52
Purim: intoxication at, 187–89; liturgical practice of, 187–88; as non-Festival holiday, 187; popularity of, 188; work on, 161

qere (that which is read), 54–56
Qeshisha, Mar, 163–64
qiddush (blessing), 150, 152; over wine, 162, 166; rabbinic creation of, 153; using beer, 165–66. *See also* blessings
Qiddushin (tractate), 211
qordiaqos (delirium tremens), 248–49
Qordiaqos (spirit), 249

Rabbah: drinking at Purim, 188–89; teaching of Rava, 189
"rabbi" (title), 18

rabbinic knowledge, as transformative, 196
rabbinic literature: background knowledge for, 3–4; biblical texts in, 80, 223; breastfeeding in, 107–10; categories and categorization of, 24–26; categorization of drinking, 80; contingency in, 25; contradictions in, 47–51; creative interpretations in, 60; descriptive, 177; embryonic development in, 125; English translations of, 274; excrement in, 249; feminist Jewish readers of, 97–98; gender categories of, 122–25; gendered assumptions concerning, 2, 96–127; gendered words in, 6–7; health and hygiene in, 244–69; hypothetical scenarios in, 24; intestinal ailments in, 246; intoxicants in, 66–67; magic in, 119–22; major documents of, 26–32; male heteronormative, 96–98; masculine grammatical gender in, 241; medicine/religion connection in, 244; memorization of, 204–5; partial quotations of, 59; proscriptive, 177; rabbinic prehistory in, 18–19; repetition in, 47; ritual errors in, 202; Self and Other in, 66; sexuality in, 96–127; source material in, 204–5, 223; STEM-related subjects in, 244; textual units of, 26–32; themes of, 4–5; translations of, 5–8; women's witchcraft in, 119–22. *See also halakhah* (rabbinic law)
rabbinic movement, 16–21; Bar Kohkba revolt and, 19; centers of learning for, 20; concepts of, 21–24; disciple circles of, 18; dominant cultures affecting, 20; history of, 4; patronage of, 19; Pharisees and, 18; prehistory of, 18–19; in Yavneh Legend, 18–19
rabbinic sages, in Yavneh Legend, 16–17

rabbinic study academies, 3–4, 23, 24; Babylonian, 21; feminist participation in, 98. *See also* Torah study

Rabbis: on abnormal scenarios, 207; alternative interpretations of, 44; as arbiters of religious practice, 130; authority of, 23, 41, 48, 176–77, 197, 217; belief in magic, 139; as communal authorities, 177; on cooking mistakes, 226; defense against magic, 139, 141; dietary practices of, 81–82; drinking on Festival Days, 175; embrace of wine drinking, 67, 218; encounters with witches, 119–20; following fall of Second Temple, 16; fools' insults to, 50; hermeneutical principles of, 41, 46; interpretive activity of, 60; intoxicated, 209–10; medical wisdom of, 250; on Moses' discourse of rain, 40–41; post-Temple authority of, 23; scholarship on, 3; social advice from, 98–103; transmission of wisdom to, 36; water metaphors of, 39

Rabbis, Babylonian: beer and, 72, 220

rain: fasting for, 150–51; Moses' discourse of, 40–41; prayers for, 151, 152, 153

rainmaking: licit practices concerning, 150–53; by non-Rabbis, 151, 159; through piety, 153

Rashi, Rabbi, 55; on beer side effects, 255; commentary on *Bavli*, 31; on drunkenness, 53; on overeating, 101

Rav (rabbinic figure), 153; on bloodletting, 251–52; on mice in beer, 228

Rava: arguments with Abaye, 197; on drinking in pairs, 144; on drinking with whores, 116; on Passover wine, 143, 185–86; pre-Passover drinking, 197; on Purim drinking, 189; on unblessed food, 196; on wine, 106; on wine as sustenance, 198, 199

Rav Huna, Rabbah bar: on prayer, 204; on subterfuge, 179

Ravina, on Passover wine, 142, 143

religious practice, illicit, 5; as inversion of proper practice, 130–31, 158; justifications for, 156; magic as, 138–41; rabbinic discourse on, 130; in ways of the Amorites, 153–58, 155. *See also* ritual impurity

religious practice, licit: concerning food and drink, 147; Rabbis as arbiters of, 130; for rainmaking, 150–53; for winemaking, 149. *See also* ritual purity

Revelation at Mount Sinai, 22, 25, 41–42, 173; in rabbinic theology, 12; tradition of, 36; unfolding in Torah, 21

ritual: affecting differentiation, 219; commandments on, 5; errors in, 200–205; of Sabbath wine, 152, 153, 162–63; Temple-based, 218

ritual impurity: of beer, 220; of corpses, 238; exclusion in, 216; of food, 226–27, 242; of Gentile children, 239, 241; of homoerotic intercourse, 241–42; intentionality in, 233–35, 242; libated wine and, 237–42; of mice, 228, 230; of non-Jewish wine, 239, 240; quantities needed for, 238; in semen, 230; social concerns of, 240; substances prepared for, 232–33, 242; susceptibility to, 232; taste in, 226–30, 242; theological concerns of, 240; through physical contact, 238; transmission of, 216, 232–33, 238; of *zavim*, 241. *See also* religious practice, illicit

ritual purity: of aquatic creatures, 220, 223–24; boundaries of, 241–42; concerning blood, 235; concerning breast milk, 235–37, 242; gendered conceptions of, 237, 242; of Jewish men, 87; of liquids, 220, 242; of meals, 218; miscarriage and, 268;

ritual purity *(continued)*
rules for menstruating woman, 87–88, 109; of Temple, 216; in washing, 216–19; as weapon against temptation, 242. *See also* religious practice, licit
river water, pure and impure, 232, 233–34
Rome: fountain sculptures of, 136, 137 *fig.*; rule over Israel, 15
Rosh Hashanah (New Year), 173; *shofar* on, 169

Sabbath: as absence defining week, 166; breastfeeding during, 170; categorization of, 25; childbirth on, 251; commandments on, 5; endangerment on, 167–73; expressing breast milk on, 170–71; versus Festival Days, 173; *halakhah* on, 173, 251; Hebrew Bible on, 162; intoxication on, 162–63; light for, 167; observance of, 167–68; preservation of life on, 171–73; prohibited labor on, 178; rabbinic exegesis on, 167–68, 172–73; remembrance of, 167–68; sanctity of, 167; sluggishness after eating on, 247; transportation on, 254; water use on, 172, 176; work during, 161, 167–73; work prohibited on, 168. See also *havdalah* (Sabbath blessing)
Sabbath liturgy: beer and, 161–66; at conclusion of Sabbath, 163
Sabbath wine: classical authors on, 163; *havdalah* with, 164; rituals of, 152, 153, 162–63; strained, 178, 225
sacrifice, in Hebrew Bible, 9
Samaritans: bread baked by, 90; invoking *of Ha-Shem*, 92–93; as Jew-*ish*, 90–93; wine of, 90
Samson, as *nazir*, 43
Sanhedrin, judges of, 265
Sarah (matriarch): breastfeeding by, 57–58; *midrash* on, 56–57

saris (eunuch): congenital, 124, 125; infertility of, 123, 124; man-made, 124; refusal of Levirate marriage, 123–24
Satlow, Michael: on female virginity, 100; on Yavneh Legend, 17–18
sea creatures: consumption of, 220, 223–24; ritual purity of, 223–24
Seleucids, Maccabean revolt against, 15
self-control: in defense against magic, 140; in drinking, 260–67; loss in drunkenness, 140; masculine, 140; in Mediterranean culture, 260; men's lack of, 121; in wine drinking, 264; women's, 115
semen, ritual impurity in, 230
sexual intercourse: beverage-related terms for, 126; forbidden, 51, 52; with hermaphrodites, 123; heterosexual normative, 123; homoerotic, 241–42; listening idiom for, 72; rabbinic advice on, 102–3
sexuality, 4; cultural constructions of, 96; drunkenness and, 106; euphemisms of, 102; "proper" practices of, 96; rabbinic attitudes to, 96–127; unregulated, 115–16
Shabbat (tractate), Hanukkah in, 24
Shammai, House of: Eighteen Decrees of, 239; on fowl and cheese, 82–83, 86; on Gentile bread, 240; on handwashing, 217
Shaul, Abba: height of, 269; on wine and bones, 267–68
Shavrirei (demon), 146
Shavuot ("Weeks" festival), 173; Torah knowledge and, 61
Shema' (rabbinic prayer): conditions for reciting, 208, 209, 210; recitation following drinking, 2; scriptural passages in, 208, 209
Sheshet, Rav: on prohibited substances, 228–29, 230
Shimon, Rabbi: authority of, 10, 209

Shimon ben Gamaliel, Rabban: mourning for, 213; on separate minds, 87; on wine, 69
Shimon ben Kosiba (Bar Kokhba), 19
Shimon ben Shetah, on rainmaking, 150
shofar (ram's horn), 168–70, 169 *fig.*; breast milk expressed into, 168–69, 170; liturgical use of, 169; moving on Sabbath, 170; ritual blowing of, 169
Sifre Deuteronomy, 28
Sifre Numbers, 28
Simon-Shoshan, Moshe, 176; on Rabbi Gamaliel, 209
sitting, negative heath effects of, 256
skeletal remains, effect of wine on, 267–68
Smith, Andrew, 38
Snoop Dogg, 66
social boundaries: beer as, 72–75; breast milk as, 76–78; concerning fowl, 82; with internal Others, 78–82; role of intoxicants in, 66–93; wine as, 67–72
Song of Songs, reading of, 14
sorceresses, defense against, 144
sotah (suspected adulteress), 43; ritual test for, 110, 111–16; separation from other women, 44. *See also* adultery
spells, on Aramaic bowls, 141–42
spirits: latrine, 141; licit knowledge of, 145; rabbinic protection from, 142; Rabbis' belief in, 146; techniques for combatting, 145–46; water, 146. *See also* demons
spontaneous combustion, demon's, 146
spontaneous combustion, human, 141, 148; divine retribution in, 50–51
springs, common ownership of, 38
subterfuge: Babylonian Talmud on, 179; in Festival Day law, 179–80, 182–83; following bloodletting, 252–53; in following *halakhah*, 179–80, 182–83, 253
sugyot (rabbinic passages), 7, 26; from *Bavli*, 31

Sukkot (Tabernacles), 173; date palms on, 181–82; non-Festival days of, 177
symposia, wine at, 67

Ta'anit (tractate), on drought, 151
Talmud: on beer subterfuge, 182; on bloodletting, 251; creation of, 21; Levirate marriage in, 123; on Purim drinking, 188, 189; on wine as sustenance, 198. *See also Bavli*; *Yerushalmi*
Tanakh (acronym), 10
Tanhuma (Homiletic Midrash collection), 29
Tannaim (Repeaters): on beer drinking, 256; origin of, 20–21
Tannaitic Midrashim: *aggada* in, 28; *halakhah* in, 28; redaction of, 28
taste, in ritual impurity, 226–30
tefillin, magical origins of, 140
temperance, impact on Torah, 260–61. *See also* self-control
temperance movement, U.S., 249
Temple, First: destruction of, 9; rebuilding of, 14
Temple, Second: debates over, 14–15; destruction of, 14, 15–16, 169; purity of, 216; wine libation at, 68
Ten Commandments, "count" of, 10
terefah ("torn" meat), 147, 148; banning of, 149
theurgy (divine action), illicit compelling of, 139
This World (*'olam ha-zeh*): divine justice in, 19; water in, 38
Tiberias (Palestine), hot water for, 175–76
Tithes, Second, 265, 266; forbidden purchases with, 266
toasts, rabbinic: blessings in, 156–59
Torah, 10–11; all-encompassing nature of, 36–37; brightening of face, 60–63; contradictions in, 42; divine authorship of, 36, 37, 46, 48, 63, 266; divine editorship of, 41–47, 48, 63;

Torah *(continued)*
divine intentionality of, 36, 43, 47, 53–54, 57, 224, 266; divine source of, 41; dual Revelation of, 21, 23; embodied knowledge of, 244; eternal good of, 25–26; euphemisms in, 55; forgetting through wine drinking, 261–63; giving women merit, 114; grammatical errors in, 53–56; impact of temperance on, 260–61; imperfect perfection of, 63; joy of learning, 60–63; misspellings in, 42, 53–56; normative rabbinic scrolls of, 42, 42 *fig.;* nourishing liquid metaphors, 40; *qere* and *ketiv*, 54–56; *Rabbah* for, 29; rain metaphors for, 40–41; revelation to Moses, 21, 22, 25, 36, 41–42, 173; spiritual survival through, 38–39, 40; teaching to daughters, 113–16; water symbolization for, 38–41. *See also* Hebrew Bible

Torah, Oral *(torah sh-be'al peh)*, 21, 36; cloud metaphor for, 22, 36–37; diverse forms of, 41; explication of written Torah, 37; legal system of, 22; updating process of, 22

Torah, Written *(torah sh-bikhtav)*, 21–22, 36; hard copy metaphor for, 36; organization of, 37; updating of, 36. *See also* Hebrew Bible

Torah study: gendered, 97; intelligence for, 263; ritual liturgy following, 274; women's, 98, 127. *See also* rabbinic study academies

Tosefta: Orders of, 28; redaction of, 27; relationship to Mishnah, 27–28

tradition, rabbinic: concerning cooked wine, 70, 76; from non-Jewish worlds, 218; of revelation at Mount Sinai, 36

Unetaneh Toqef ("We Give Power"), 148
urination, gendered positions for, 124, 125

usury, condemnation of, 62

vegetables, *baraita'* on, 257
Vespasian (emperor of Rome), in Yavneh legend, 16
Viagra, original purpose of, 254
violence, gendered, 117
virgin birth, linguistic evidence for, 10
virginity, female: testing for, 100
virtue, gendered assumptions about, 260
visitors, women's greeting of, 102

washing: of feet, 217; hygiene and, 217; ritual, 216–19
wastefulness, rabbinic advice on, 98
water: access to, 38; acts of intentionality concerning, 233–35; bottled, 220; bugs in, 222, 223; contaminated, 246–47; in dietary regimen, 245–46; embodiment of knowledge, 39–40; in Exodus, 39; foam on, 260; heating of, 172, 176, 190; medical concerns about, 220; non-libated, 227; rabbinic authority as, 41; symbolization of Torah, 38–41; from temples of idolatry, 135–38; unstrained, 224–25; use on Sabbath, 172, 176; vital function of, 38. *See also* beverages; drinking
water drinking: intestinal ailments and, 245–47; proportion of bread for, 245, 246
wedding feasts *(beyt ha-mishteh)*: drinking at, 208–10; non-Jewish, 73–74; wine at, 68
whores: drinking wine with, 116–19; violation of normative roles, 117
whores, idolatrous: dining while reclining, 117; submitting to Jewish men, 119; use of idols, 118
whores, Jewish: debasement by non-Jewish men, 119; drinking with non-Jewish men, 117

whoring: gendering of, 44; as metaphorical theological act, 71
wickedness, separation from, 44
widows, Jewish: Levirate marriage for, 123
wine: abstention from, 45–46; aging, 257; aid to digestion, 213; allowances for wives, 104–6; amount needed for drunkenness, 263–64; assocation with adultery, 43–47, 55, 106; in *Avodah Zarah*, 68–70; *baraita'* on, 105–6; beneficial, 106; betrothal and, 210–12, 214; blessings over, 90–91, 152, 194–95, 198, 218, 219; as cause of miscarriage, 268; in classical dining, 218; comforting of mourners, 265, 266; cost of, 259, 266; effect on bones, 267–68; effect on inflamation, 258; at Festival Days, 68, 174; foam on top of, 258–59; four cups of, 183, 263–64; in Garden of Eden, 45–47; gendered assumptions about, 98, 104; gladdening the heart, 173–77, 198; handwashing and, 217–18, 219; *havdalah* using, 164; in household budgets, 108; incorrect blessing for, 201, 203; invalidation of judges' service, 262, 264; leading to transgression, 43; licit assistance in making, 149; as litmus test, 267; mourning and, 212–14; *nazir's* abstention from, 43–45, 260; new, 249; versus not-wine, 218–19; numerical value of, 263, 265; old, 258; prohibited mixtures of, 227–28; proper amount for women, 105–6; *qiddush* over, 162, 166; rabbinic blessing for, 68; ratio of food to, 268; regulation concerning non-Jews, 68–72, 75; as reward for the wicked, 265, 266; role in social intimacy, 70–72; for Sabbath ritual, 152, 153, 162–63; Samaritan, 90; as social boundary, 67–72; stealing of, 253–54, 269; straining of, 178–80, 182, 190, 225; as sustenance, 186–87, 197–99, 198, 199; undiluted, 219; unmixed *(akratos)*, 67; in witchcraft, 138–41. *See also* Passover wine; Sabbath wine

wine, cooked, 132; *baraita'* on, 133; fixed status of, 133; as invalid for pagan libation, 70, 132, 134; non-Jews around, 70; at Passover, 133; rabbinic traditions concerning, 70, 76

wine, diluted, 125, 218–19; in classical antiquty, 261; for delirium tremens, 249

wine, kosher: modern industry of, 70

wine, libated *(yayn nesekh)*, 69, 132; drinking with whores, 116; of idolaters, 72, 117, 133; impurity of liquid in, 239; mixed with non-libated liquids, 227–28, 229; prior to being cooked, 133; prohibition of, 80, 227; ritual impurity and, 237–42

wine, non-Jewish: ritual impurity of, 239, 240

wine drinking: in *Bavli*, 61–62; binge, 264; bright face in, 60–63; effect on intelligence, 260–67; in even numbers, 139, 141, 142; following bloodletting, 250–53; with food, 186, 268; forgetting of Torah through, 261–63; gender asymmetry in, 117–19, 174; human combustion following, 47–51; with non-Jews, 67, 132; during Passover, 61; by pregnant women, 268; in Psalms, 67–68; rabbis' embrace of, 67, 218; Self and Other in, 67; self-control in, 264; side effects of, 263; temperate, 266; with whores, 116–19

wisdom, divine: transmission to, 36; water metaphor for, 38–41

witchcraft, women's, 119–22, 138; use of wine in, 138–41; whispering in, 120

witches, 121–22; drinking with, 138

wives, Jewish: adulterous, 105, 110–16; breastfeeding obligations, 107–10; conjugal rights of, 104; desire for jewelry, 104, 105; divorced, 107–9; drunken, 106; household budgets for, 10; husbands' obligations towards, 103–6; living apart from husbands, 104–5; lying to, 252–53; wine allowances for, 104–6

women: and magic, 154–55; passivity of, 118–19; sexual danger from, 120–22, 138; wine-drinking, 264, 268

women, Jewish: advice on eating for, 101; breastfeeding restrictions on, 77; childrearing restrictions on, 78; as consumed, 126–27; corruption of men, 121; dining posture for, 117; Festival treats for, 174; greeting of visitors, 102; midwives, 78; proper amount of wine for, 105–6; in rabbinic literature, 97; self-control of, 115; social dicotomy from men, 86; social propriety for, 99; transgressive bodies of, 45, 117, 120–22; uncontrolled bodies of, 110, 237; undisciplined, 121. See also *niddah* (menstruating woman); whores, Jewish; wives, Jewish

women, Moabite: Israelites' whoring with, 71

women, non-Jewish: breastfeeding by, 170; Jewish men's drinking with, 71–72

women, pregnant: wine drinking by, 268

World to Come (*'olam ha-ba'*): divine justice in, 19; spiritual survival in, 38

wrestling, professional, ritual/dramatic structure of, 131

Yael, murder of Sisera, 13
Yavneh (Israel), rabbinic study center of, 17

Yavneh Legend, 16–19; patriarchate in, 19; rabbinic movement in, 18–19

Yehoshua, Rabbi: on breast milk, 236; on women's lasciviousness, 114, 115–16

Yehoshua ben Levi, Rabbi: authority of, 209

Yehuda, Rav: on bloodletting, 251–52

Yehuda bar Rabbi, study of *Makhshirin*, 233

Yehudah ha-Nassi, Rabbi (patriarch), 19; editing of Mishnah, 86; fasting decree by, 151; redaction of Mishnah, 20, 26; Tannaim group of, 20

Yenuqa, Mar, 163–64

Yerushalmi (Jerusalem Talmud): citations of, 30; comparison with *Bavli*, 30; *gemara'* of, 29–30; on *halakhah*, 29; redaction of, 30; scholarship on, 30; structure of, 29. See also Talmud

Yevamot (tractate), 123

Yirmiya, Rabbi: on prayer, 206

Yitzhak, Rabbi: on drinking with idolaters, 74

Yitzhak bar Yosef, Rav: on congenital *saris*, 124

Yitzhaq bar Rabbi Hava, Rabbi, 212

Yohanan, Rabbi: and Ilfa the rainmaker, 152

Yohanan ben Zakkai, Rabban, 16–17

Yom Kippur (Day of Atonement), 173; drinking before, 147–49; Sabbath laws on, 149; *shofar* on, 169

Yosef, Rav: on fowl and cheese, 86; on menstrual prohibition, 88

Yosef the Demon, teaching of Rabbis, 144–45

Yosi the Galilean, Rabbi: prohibition on fowl, 83–86

Yudah bey Rabbi Ilai, Rabbi: among Tannaim, 61; bright face of, 60–63

Yudan, Rabbi, 60, 212; on Mordecai, 58–59

Zadoq, Rabbi, 17, 97
zalin (dissolute men), 261
zavim (persons with genital discharges), ritual impurity of, 241
Zeira, Rabbi: drinking at Purim, 188–89

Zera'im (Seder), on agriculture, 27
Zeriqan, Rabbi: on prayer, 206
Zevid, Rav: on betrothal, 211–12
zuz (coin), 253; in bride-price, 255

CITATION INDEX

Avot d'Rabbi Natan		84b			41
A4:40–77	16	87a			57
A:34	269	*b. Bava Qamma*			
B:43	269	35a			99
B:48	249	*b. Bekhorot*			
		44b			125
b. Avodah Zarah		*b. Berakhot*			
3b	38	8b			210
8a–b	73, 74	9a			209
12b	137, 146, 172	12a			201
17a	164	23a–b			22
22b	106	31a			205
26a	78	31b			205
29b	70, 133	35a–b			195
30a	70, 76, 132	35a			174
31b	74, 76	35b			186, 198
36b	75, 239	36b–37a			181
68b	228, 230	40a			245
68b–69a	231	44b			257
69b–70a	116, 121	48b			213
b. Bava Batra		50b–51a			200
58b	249	51a			246
146a	247	51a–52a			143
b. Bava Metzi'a		55b			145
33a	165, 224	57b			258
65a	75, 99	60a–b			22
83b	93	60b			141, 247

62a	97, 192	25b	55		
b. Betzah		b. Menahot			
4a–b	175	29b	42		
b. Eruvin		43b	193		
13b	51	45a	199		
26b–27b	266	b. Mo'ed Qatan			
53b	102	9b	254		
55b–56a	256	12b	180		
61a	162	18a	177		
64a	204, 205, 264	b. Nedarim			
64b	264	20b	126		
65a	204	37a–b	247		
65a–b	265	49b	61		
b. Gittin		b. Niddah			
6b	51	9a	235, 236		
45a	102	24b	267, 269		
56a	17	b. Pesahim			
56a–b	16	42a–b	256		
59b	52	42b	181		
67b	125, 248	68b	61		
b. Hullin		103b	164		
67a	220, 222, 223	106b–107a	164		
105b	146, 259	107a	32, 72, 152, 163, 165, 166		
106a	197				
116a	85	107b–108a	185, 186, 198		
b. Keritot		109b–110a	142		
13a–b	237	109b–112a	141		
13b	175	110a	144		
b. Ketubbot		110b	139, 146		
4b	87	111b	146		
8b	213, 214	112a–b	146		
10b	100, 264	113a	75, 99		
16b–17a	253	b. Qiddushin			
60a	170, 171	8b–9a	211–12		
61a	87	45a	74		
64b–65a	104	81a	121		
65a	106, 115, 264	b. Rosh Hashanah			
65b	108	29b	170		
77b	255	b. Sanhedrin			
110b	247	17b	52		
111a	256	38a	263		
b. Makkot		67a	119		
23b–24a	79	67b	119–20, 138, 141		
b. Megillah		68a	139		
7b	188	74a	171		

75a	126	Daniel			
101a	247	6:19	163		
b. Shabbat		Deuteronomy			
13a	87, 89, 101	5:4–21	10		
17b	239	5:9	135		
21a–24b	24	5:11	112, 167		
30b	48, 50	5:12–15	162		
31a	21	6:4–9	208		
61a	22, 192	11:13–21	208		
62b–63a	126	14	220		
65b	180	14:8	62		
67a–b	157	14:21	79, 83, 84		
80b	254, 255	14:22–26	266		
86b	61	20:19	99		
95a	170	22:22	111		
110b	255–56	25:5–10	123		
128b	251	31–34	13		
129a	252, 253	32:2	40		
129a–b	251				
129b	254	Ecclesiastes			
130a	85	8:1	61, 63		
139b	179, 180	Esther			
140b	99, 100, 102	2:5	58		
143b–144a	237	2:7	58		
b. Shevu'ot		Exodus			
22b–23b	80	1:15–16	12		
b. Sotah		1:22–2:10	12		
7a	121	2:11–12	12		
b. Sukkah		3–4	12		
28a	197	5:1	12		
49b	68	7–12	12		
b. Ta'anit		12:42	142, 143		
7a	7, 40	14:26–29	12		
21a	152	15:22–26	39		
23a	150	19	36		
24a	150, 153	19–31	12		
b. Yevamot		20:1–13	13		
24b	229	20:5	135		
79b–80a	124	20:7	112		
b. Yoma		20:8	167		
74b–75a	51, 52, 55	20:8–11	162		
75a	53	21:1–17	10		
85b	171	22:25	62		
b. Zevahim		22:30	147, 149		
18a	175	23:19	79		

23:25	265, 266	Job	
34:15	73	31:17	58
34:15–16	71	Joshua	
34:26	79	24:31	36
35:3	21, 167, 172, 251	Judges	
Genesis		4:18–21	13
1:1–2:4a	11	9:13	174
1:31–2:3	162	13–16	43
2:3	167	Leviticus	
2:4b–25	11	5:15–26	196
3:6	45, 46, 48	11	220
6:21	58	11:7	62
8:21	264	11:9	222, 223
9:4	253	11:21–22	80
9:20–22	11	11:29	228, 230
12:1–3	11	11:34–38	234
17:1–22	11, 56	11:38	232, 235
20	56	11:41	220, 221, 222, 225
21:7	56, 58	15:11	241
21:8	56	18:5	171
26	56	18:18	45
32:23–33	12	18:19	88
37	12	20:10	111
40	12	20:18	88
44:1–17	12	23:24	169
47:7	58	23:40	181
49:22	145	25:36	62
49:25	56	Leviticus Rabbah	
Genesis Rabbah		5:6	147
19:5	16	12:1	54, 252
30:8	58, 59		
38:13	60	Mark	
		9.5	18
Herodotus		11.21	18
Persian Wars 1:133	273	14:45	18
Hosea		m. *Avodah Zarah*	
2:7	104, 105	2:1	77
		2:4	68
Isaiah		2:6	77
5:22	260, 261	4:8–5:11	68
5:23	261, 262	5:1–11	132
7:14	10	5:2	229
51:21	206, 207	5:4–5	69, 132
66:17	230	5:8	227

m. Avot		m. Ketubbot	
1:1	36	5:5	107
1:4	18, 274	5:8	104
1:5	102	5:9	108
2:7	119	m. Makhshirin	
5:22	37	5:1	203, 232
m. Bava Metzi'a		6:4	234
1:8	199	6:5	234
m. Bava Qamma		6:7	59, 109, 237
7:7	62	6:7–8	60
9:2	25	6:8	237
m. Berakhot		m. Megillah	
1:1	2, 23, 28, 68, 208, 209, 210	1:5	173
1:4	201, 203	m. Menahot	
5:1	206	8:6	70
6:1	68, 132, 156, 193, 195, 198, 219	m. Niddah	
		3:3–4	268
6:2	193, 201, 202	m. Pesahim	
8:1–2	217	10	68, 183, 184
8:7	200	10:1	142, 184
8:8	91	10:3	185
m. Betzah		10:5	185
2:5	176	10:7	185, 186
5:2	173	m. Sanhedrin	
m. Eduyyot		7:4	135
5:2	217	7:6	134, 135
Mekhilta d'Rabbi Ishmael		7:11	139
Beshalah Vayehi		m. Shabbat	
1	39	1:4	239–40
m. Eruvin		2:1–7	167
3:1	266	3:4	176
8:7	176	6:10	153
m. Gittin		7:2	168, 178
7:1	248	8:2–7	254
m. Hullin		18:3	251
2:4	148	20:1	179
4:7	153	20:2	225
8:1	80, 82, 87, 88, 217	m. Sotah	
8:2	87, 89	1:6	114
8:3	83	3:3–5	114
8:4	83, 85	9:9	110
m. Kelim		m. Sukkot	
8:11	237	3:8–4:7	181
		m. Ta'anit	

3:8	150	Psalms	
m. Terumot		24:1	194, 195
8:4–5	75	1:8	200
11:2	234	102:24	207
m. Yevamot		104:15	14, 67–68, 174, 197, 198–99
8:4–5	123–24	137	13–14
Numbers		Sifre Deuteronomy	
5:11–31	110	306	40
5:12–15	111	Sifre Numbers	
5:16–22	112	23	264
5:23–24	113	115	116
5:27–28	113	131	71–72, 118, 121
5:29–31	113		
6:2	44, 45	t. Avodah Zarah	
6:3	260, 263	3:1–3	77
15:37–41	116, 208	4:6	73
15:39	116, 117, 126	6:5	135
25:1–3	71	6:6	136
28:1–8	9	t. Bava Metzi'a	
28:7	68	6:17	62
29:1	169	t. Bava Qamma	
Numbers Rabbah		6:15	38
10:1–4	43	t. Berakhot	
10:2–4	44, 54	1:1	28
10:3	45	4:1	194, 195
10:4	46, 262	4:3	218, 219
10:8	213, 261	5:21	92
		t. Hullin	
Philo of Alexandria		1:2	202
On the Virtues 142–44	79	2:22	244
Proverbs		t. Ketubbot	
9:17	126	1:4	211
23:21	46	5:5	108, 137
23:30	261–62	t. Niddah	
23:31	45, 49, 51–52, 54, 183	2:3	236
		2:5	137
26:4	48, 50	t. Pisha	
26:4–5	49	10:4	67, 174
26:5	48	t. Shabbat	
30:2	45	6–7	153
30:3	45, 46, 47	6:14	154
31:5	261	7:7–9	157–58
31:6	265, 266	8:24–28	234

9:22	170, 171	*y. Hagigah*	
12:13	219	1:1, 75d	41
13:16	168	*y. Ketubbot*	
t. Sotah		5:13, 30b	108, 257
1:2	126	*y. Nedarim*	
5:9	126	2:4b, 37b	80
t. Yevamot		6:6, 39c	80
10:2	123	*y. Pesahim*	
t. Yom Tov		5:1, 31d	175
3:2	180	10:1, 37c	61, 133, 183–84, 186
t. Zavim		10:2, 37c	166
5:8	238	*y. Shabbat*	
		1:7, 3d	77
y. Avodah Zarah		2:6, 5b–c	180
2:3, 41a	30, 76, 147	7:2, 9c	233
5:4, 44d	90	8:1, 11a	61, 183, 186
y. Berakhot		14:3, 14c	219
3:1, 6a	212, 213	*y. Sheqalim*	
4:1, 7a	205	3:2, 47c	61
5:1, 8d	206	*y. Sotah*	
6:1, 10a	194	1:4, 16d	126
6:1, 10b	200	3:4, 18d	41
8:1, 11d	166	*y. Ta'anit*	
8:8, 12c	200	1:4, 64b	151
8:9, 12c	91, 92	*y. Yevamot*	
9:4, 14b	22	1:6, 3b	51
9:6, 14b	141	8:5, 9d	124
y. Eruvin			
8:8, 24d	176	Zechariah	
10:12, 26d	172	14:8	269

Founded in 1893,
UNIVERSITY OF CALIFORNIA PRESS
publishes bold, progressive books and journals
on topics in the arts, humanities, social sciences,
and natural sciences—with a focus on social
justice issues—that inspire thought and action
among readers worldwide.

The UC PRESS FOUNDATION
raises funds to uphold the press's vital role
as an independent, nonprofit publisher, and
receives philanthropic support from a wide
range of individuals and institutions—and from
committed readers like you. To learn more, visit
ucpress.edu/supportus.

www.ingramcontent.com/pod-product-compliance
Lightning Source LLC
Chambersburg PA
CBHW030522230426
43665CB00010B/732